The
JEWISH
CONDITION

The
JEWISH
CONDITION

ESSAYS ON CONTEMPORARY

JUDAISM HONORING

Rabbi Alexander M. Schindler

EDITED BY

Aron Hirt-Manheimer

UAHC PRESS   ◆   NEW YORK

Publication of this volume
has been made possible
through the generosity of the
Esther S. and Hyman J. Bylan
Memorial Fund

✦   ✦   ✦

Library of Congress Cataloging-in-Publication Data
The Jewish condition : essays on contemporary Judaism honoring
Rabbi Alexander M. Schindler / edited by Aron Hirt-Manheimer.
      p.   cm.
Includes bibliographical references.
ISBN 0-8074-0535-3. — ISBN 0-8074-0540-X (pbk.)
1. Reform Judaism—United States.   2. Judaism—Relations—
Christianity.   3. Christianity and other religions—Judaism.
4. Judaism and social problems.   I. Schindler, Alexander M.
      II. Hirt-Manheimer, Aron, 1948–
      BM197.J48   1995
      296.8'346—dc20   95-31542
                                        CIP

CONTENTS

ACKNOWLEDGMENTS   viii
A TRIBUTE   ix
Henry A. Kissinger

INTRODUCTION
Albert Vorspan
Ohev Yisrael, Alexander M. Schindler: A Profile   1

I · If I Am Only for Myself, What Am I?
Dialogue, Pluralism, and Tolerance

William Cardinal Keeler
Catholic-Jewish Relations in the Twentieth Century   16

Joan Brown Campbell and *Jay T. Rock*
Christian-Jewish Relations in America   40

Julius Lester
Blacks, Jews, and Farrakhan   52

Leonard Fein
American Pluralism and Jewish Interests   63

S. Zalman Abramov
The Nature of Religious Pluralism in Israel   78

II · In the Image of God
Healing, Ethics, and Tikkun Olam

Eugene Mihaly
Let Us Make Man   92

Harold M. Schulweis
Does God Have a Conscience?   105

Jack Stern
Jewish Ethics in the Daily Life of the Jew   118

Bernard Lown
On Being a Jewish Doctor   135

Carl Sagan
Religous Leadership and Environmental Integrity   147

III · Swords into Ploughshares
War and Peace

Yehuda Bauer
Is the Holocaust Comparable to Other Genocides?
The Holocaust—Fifty Years Later   155

Albert H. Friedlander
Germany, the Jewish Community, and Reconciliation   167

Norman J. Cohen
Isaac and Ishmael, Abraham's Progeny (Genesis 21)
A Midrashic Paradigm for Modern Jews   178

Shimon Peres
Vision of a New Middle East   190

IV · Am Yisrael Chai
Talmud Torah, Identity, and Continuity

Alan D. Bennett
Talmud Torah and the Jewish Future   198

Jerome K. Davidson
NFTY and Jewish Identity   212

Rachel Adler
Women and Tradition: Talking Our Way In   230

Egon Mayer
The Outreach Movement
Making Judaism an Inclusive Religion   249

Bernard M. Zlotowitz
Patrilineal Descent   260

Arthur Hertzberg
Israel and the Diaspora: A Relationship Reexamined   269

V · Cheshbon Hanefesh
Reform: A Critical Self-Examination

Jane Evans
Intertwining Yesterday, Today, and Tomorrow
The Union of American Hebrew Congregations   290

Michael A. Meyer
From Cincinnati to New York: A Symbolic Move   302

Roland B. Gittelsohn
The Evolving Role of the Reform Rabbi   315

Margaret Moers Wenig
Truly Welcoming Lesbian and Gay Jews   327

W. Gunther Plaut
Reform as an Adjective: What Are the Limits?   350

Eugene B. Borowitz
Reform: Modern Movement in a Postmodern Era?   363

Lawrence A. Hoffman
Ritual and the Recovery of Hope
Making Reform Judaism Matter Again   379

POSTSCRIPT   400
ABOUT THE CONTRIBUTORS   402

ACKNOWLEDGMENTS

How can I begin to thank all the many dear, wonderful, and creative friends who have worked tirelessly to create this book—a tribute not only to an inspiring leader but to my soulmate. Alex once gave me a pillow embroidered with the words "Happiness is being married to your best friend." Need I say more?

Now to the heartfelt acknowledgments: To Aron Hirt-Manheimer, an editor par excellence, and to Al Vorspan, who with Aron helped to transform this project from an idea into reality. We were a unique threesome. No words can thank them for their time, effort, and love.

To all the contributors who couldn't say no—because I wouldn't give them the chance to say no. These are treasured essays, insightful, intelligent, and most relevant to us all as we approach the twenty-first century.

To the Esther S. and Hyman J. Bylan Memorial Fund for its generosity in backing our project. Hy and Esther were cherished friends and their love and dedication to the Union will always be remembered with deep appreciation.

To Stuart Benick for production, and to Annette Abramson and Kathy Parnass for their diligence in copyediting.

With love and appreciation to our UAHC family: the staff, board members, and members-at-large, who gave me the opportunity to share these wonderful years with them. What an enrichment it was for the Schindler family! We will cherish the friendships we have developed during these many years.

This book means so very much to Alex, and we hope it will be a meaningful addition to your lives as well.

Rhea Schindler

A TRIBUTE

Henry A. Kissinger

You know the old saying that if you get one hundred Jews together to resolve some problem, you will get one hundred different opinions as to how to proceed. But I venture to guess that one would find unanimous agreement that Rabbi Alexander Schindler has long been a preeminent figure of conscience and leadership, not only within the American Jewish community, but for all concerned with human issues around the globe.

Alex Schindler has been a good friend of mine for many years. He is someone for whom I have enormous respect and affection, for he is a man of profound wisdom, integrity, and loyalty. I have always enjoyed our discussions and benefited from his insights. His contributions to the dialogue on Jewish issues, human rights, and the problems of ethnic, racial, and religious conflicts—whether at home or abroad—have been far-reaching and invaluable. But, above all, he has devoted himself to the preservation of America's strength and leadership in the world community.

As Alex retires from the Union of American Hebrew Congregations, which he has guided with exceptional distinction for thirty-four years (the last twenty-two of them as its president), I would like to join in saluting an outstanding American. I am certain that he will continue to be an outspoken and perceptive voice on issues of principle and an advocate for humanitarian ideals. And I hope we shall still have a chance to get together from time to time as two old friends to share views on the direction of American policy and what is going on around the world.

INTRODUCTION
OHEV YISRAEL,
ALEXANDER M. SCHINDLER
A PROFILE

ALBERT VORSPAN

Building on the immense contributions of his predecessor, Rabbi Maurice N. Eisendrath, Alexander M. Schindler, president of the UAHC since 1973, has done more to shape the character of postwar Reform Judaism than any other leader. But, unlike Eisendrath, Alex Schindler somehow has transcended his position as the leader of merely one branch of American Judaism and has gradually emerged as a leading—perhaps *the* leading—spokesman for American Jewry, particularly in safeguarding Israel in the American political sphere.

Schindler had served for fifteen years on the UAHC staff as a regional director, then as the director of the Department of Education, and briefly as vice president when Rabbi Eisendrath died suddenly on the opening day of the UAHC Biennial Assembly in New York City in 1973. The young German-born rabbi had already been designated as Rabbi Eisendrath's successor, but he was swept into office early by the tragic death of the seventy-three-year-old incumbent only hours before Eisendrath was slated to deliver his always controversial State of the Union address.

Conferring with his stunned top staff colleagues, Rabbi Schindler was decisive: The convention would convene as scheduled, and Rabbi Eisendrath's long address would be delivered word for word by Rabbi Schindler. Eisendrath's speech was a fire and brimstone denunciation of President Richard Nixon for his Watergate malevolence. The speech was studded with barn-burning rhetoric, stopping just short of a call for impeachment of the president of the United States. Eisendrath had built a reputation for outspoken State of the Union challenges. Several staff members urged Alex not to read the most incendiary paragraphs. Why not preserve the essence of Eisendrath's case without inflaming emotions already raw from the personal tragedy of his fatal heart attack? Schindler refused to alter the speech. "I will read it as he prepared it, every single word, no editing. We owe him that." And so Schindler did.

During his own presidency, Rabbi Schindler maintained unremitting support for the social action program of the UAHC, which, under Eisendrath, had reached its climax with the establishment of the Religious Action Center in Washington. Schindler threw his full support behind the work of the Social Action Commission, and he identified himself with the liberal agenda of the day, including women's rights (especially the ordination of women), Soviet Jewry, civil rights, world peace, opposition to the death penalty, nuclear disarmament, a Marshall Plan for the poor, and gay rights. On some issues he took stands that provoked as much controversy as Eisendrath's positions had touched off. This was especially true when he railed against the moral disaster of Reaganomics at a time when the new president was riding high in the saddle of popularity. Likewise, Schindler's undisguised support for gay rights—including gay rabbis—stirred heavy opposition within and without Reform ranks.

However, while Eisendrath's positions frequently led to angry division in the leadership of the Union and even withdrawal of some congregations in protest, Schindler somehow managed to address similarly charged issues without appearing to be righteous or polarizing. Where Maurice was admired and respected but also feared and resented, Alex was respected and also loved. His leadership was characterized by immense personal warmth and self-deprecating humor. While many congregants disagreed with his views, almost to a person they liked and cherished him. Where Maurice's oratory was stern and prophetic, Alex's was poetic, often anecdotal, reflecting on his relations with his wife, Rhea, and their five children; a poignant Yiddish poem; or a tender chasidic tale. Rhea's irreverent charm added to the Schindlers' almost universal popularity.

Above all, Alex is a *mentsh*. This quality in his personal chemistry affected his relations with other Reform leaders. Where Eisendrath and Nelson Glueck, president of the Hebrew Union College-Jewish Institute of Religion, were legendary rivals—two scorpions in a bottle—Schindler and Alfred Gottschalk (both refugees from Hitlerism) were the joint architects of a more united Reform Jewish movement.

While Schindler continued Eisendrath's commitment to a strong social justice role for Reform Judaism, he broke new ground in many other major program areas. As the director of the Department of Education, he had fought for higher standards, including the establishment of day schools. The idea of day schools had been anathema to Eisendrath, who felt that day schools would compromise public education, damage separation of church and state, and ghettoize American Jewry. As president, Schindler embraced Jewish day schools and persuaded the UAHC leadership to support a modest pilot effort, which has already led to the establishment of a small but growing network of full-time Reform Jewish day schools across North America.

Similarly, Schindler pushed for a stronger emphasis on Israel, culminating in the creation of ARZA and ARZA CANADA, the Reform Zionist associations in the United States and Canada, devoted to strengthening Reform institutions in Israel. Alex greatly enlarged the movement's youth programs through the North American Federation of Temple Youth (NFTY), which sponsors more trips to Israel than does any other organization. He also presided over the development of a college program to serve Jewish youngsters on campus.

Among Schindler's greatest and proudest achievements was his conception of a Torah commentary from a Reform perspective. Published in 1981, *The Torah: A Modern Commentary*, edited by W. Gunther Plaut, was the fulfillment of that vision. This volume, the first such work in Reform Jewish history, has sold more than 200,000 copies to date.

Convinced that the Union's fundamental task is strengthening the individual synagogue, Alex pushed for a greatly expanded regional structure and a synagogue management staff to help temples everywhere. During the years of Schindler's service, the UAHC roster grew from 400 congregations in 1973 to nearly 900 in 1995. Reform became the largest and fastest growing branch of Judaism with about one million members. Indeed, Reform is the *only* liberal religious group in America that has gained in membership in the last quarter of the twentieth century.

But Alex was also a prescient pioneer, anticipating tomorrow's crises today. His leadership was marked by a keen intuition, a capacity to foresee needs and design programmatic priorities to meet those needs, resulting in the creation of the Outreach program, which challenged Jews to become "champions of Judaism" and reversed the 500-year-old tradition that discouraged converts. Seizing upon an idea that had numerous antecedents within liberal Judaism, in December 1978, at a meeting of the Union's Executive Committee in Houston, Schindler called on the Reform movement to reach out to the non-Jewish spouses of interfaith marriages and to the "unchurched" in general and welcome them as converts to Judaism.

Outreach was a brilliant and innovative program, characteristic of Schindler's propensity to see the big issue just beyond the horizon. By the 1970s, American Jewry was experiencing a rapidly increasing intermarriage rate. But the chief responses seemed to be *gevalt*ism (*Oy, gevalt!* "How terrible!") or finger pointing (it is not *us*, it is *them* causing the hemorrhage). Schindler saw that intermarriage was no longer a disaster that happened to somebody else. It was happening in most families and, for the most part, Jewish parents were no longer willing to lose their children and future grandchildren by banishing the offending married child and covering themselves with ashes and sackcloth. This profound cultural change, irreversible in an open society like America, called for a fresh and human response, a Jewishly compassionate response.

To Schindler, outreach is *not* acquiescence to interfaith marriage; it is an affirmation of Judaism. Outreach is a means by which we can reach out to the non-Jewish spouse, welcoming him or her into a warm and inviting Jewish environment, demonstrating that Judaism is a universal faith that is available to anyone who sincerely wishes to join the community and assume its obligations, including study. In his initial proposal to the UAHC Board of Trustees, Schindler did not restrict his outreach focus to interfaith couples; he projected his scope to encompass the millions of "religiously unpreferenced" Americans in search of a spiritual anchor. He was convinced that thousands of spiritual seekers, adrift from their religious moorings, would turn to Judaism if given the opportunity, and the infusion would revitalize Jewish life. Although the UAHC board saw this "plank" of the 1978 outreach proposal as excessively ambitious and put it on the back burner, the basic Outreach program as outlined by President Schindler was adopted. (At the 1993 UAHC Biennial Convention, Alex renewed his call for a Reform "missionary" program.)

Indeed, the Outreach program has revolutionized Jewish life. It has brought tens of thousands of Jews-by-choice into our midst. Outreach has banished the stigma of the convert. Jews-by-choice now represent almost half the membership in some synagogues. Introduction to Judaism programs are now offered in many cities, and outreach coordinators have been added to the staff of each of the Union's nine regional offices. The best measure of the efficacy of the Outreach program is that other denominations in Judaism, after having first dismissed the program either as an opportunistic device to repopulate our declining ranks or as a left-handed endorsement of intermarriage itself, ended up emulating outreach in their own programs. If imitation is the highest form of flattery, Reform is invariably the maligned trailblazer—and never more so than under the leadership of Rabbi Schindler.

Even as Schindler promoted outreach, he just as tenaciously urged the movement to fortify the inner life of every Jew. In pushing for "inreach," spiritual self-actualization, he has said, "What purpose is outreach, pray tell, if there is nothing within?" Schindler has repeatedly called upon Reform Jews to make Judaism a meaningful enterprise in their lives.

The same pattern of trailblazing marked Schindler's leadership in the adoption of patrilineal descent as an authentic basis for Jewish identity. Rabbi Schindler felt that gender equality meant that it was wrong for the Jewish identity of a child born into an interfaith family to be derived from only the maternal line. His studies also persuaded him that matrilineal descent had not always prevailed in Jewish history. It had emerged historically in response to given circumstances. Reform, as an evolving faith geared to adaptation and change, therefore, could and should assert gender equality. His practical sense also made him well aware of the many injustices that slavish adherence to matrilineal descent was causing children of a Jewish father and non-Jewish mother. He, therefore, advocated equality between patrilineal and matrilineal descent in determining the religious identity of such children as long as they are raised as Jews.

As in most basic innovations taken by Reform, the response by the other movements, especially the Orthodox, was apocalyptic and hyperbolic. The sundering of Jewish unity, the withdrawal of Reform into a separate sect, the destruction of Reform Judaism in Israel—these and other catastrophic consequences were predicted if Reform did not back down on this issue. Many of these hyperventilations also came from some Reform rabbis, particularly those in Israel, some of whom urged postponement of any formal action, pleading instead for consultations with the leaders of all branches before taking such a historic and irreversible step.

Rabbi Schindler replied that the same dire warnings had been sounded every time Reform adopted a bold new initiative—Friday evening Shabbat services, sermons in the vernacular, one-day Jewish festival observances, confirmation, Sunday school, the Union prayer book, a modern Torah commentary, social action, women rabbis, gay rabbis—and that most of these initiatives had ended up emulated, at least by Conservative and Reconstructionist Judaism. To Schindler, Reform spells change and modernity. Reform betrays itself if it shrinks from moral decisions and needed innovations out of fear of controversy and empty threats of division.

Alex Schindler reached the summit of American Jewish leadership when he was elected chairman of the Conference of Presidents of Major Jewish Organizations. The conference, established in 1954 by Nahum Goldmann and Philip Klutznick, was gaining respect as the authoritative address for American Jewry in all matters relating to United States policy toward Israel. Schindler's tenure (1976–1978) occurred during one of the most tumultuous and problematic moments in Israel's history: the election of Menachem Begin as prime minister. After a full generation of Labor party primacy, resulting in warm affinity between American Jews and Labor, Begin's Likud party triumphed in 1978. Most American Jews reacted with shock and indignation. Begin, the former terrorist? The hard-line right-winger? How could American Jewry possibly accept such a regime? How would Washington be able to relate to a Begin-led Israel?

Schindler, a lifelong liberal and dove, dispatched telegrams to the leaders of every Jewish organization in the Conference of Presidents, reminding them that Israel is a democracy and the Israeli people have made their choice. It is the obligation of American Jewry to sustain Israeli democracy and not seek to undermine or delegitimize it. Through strong personal leadership, Schindler aborted an incipient revolt. He and the late Yehuda Hellman, then director of the conference, flew to Israel and met with Begin. Schindler promised the prime minister that American Jews would give his government a chance and not discredit it. Schindler's powerful leadership prevailed.

Begin never forgot Schindler's role in rallying American Jewry behind the duly elected government of Israel. Indeed, an intense personal friendship developed between the American rabbi and the Israeli prime minister. Begin consulted with Schindler on the eve of the historic Camp David conference and honored Alex at a lavish state dinner in Jerusalem, at which he hailed him for "his courageous and outstanding leadership" and as "one who has written his name into the pages of the Jewish people's story of freedom, dignity, and strength." Although Begin and Schindler sometimes disagreed sharply on policy issues, their mutual affection never waned. They remained close friends until Begin's death.

Schindler was sometimes accused of having been preempted by Israeli right-wingers. But he never checked his conscience at the border. He blasted the war in Lebanon, calling publicly for the firing of Israeli Defense Minister Ariel Sharon. In a powerful protest that made headlines worldwide, Schindler publicly condemned Rabin's threat to put down the *intifada* by "breaking the bones, beatings, and force." He repudiated Shamir's concept of a Greater Israel and the obsessive proliferation of settlements. Above all, as president of the UAHC, he has repeatedly raised his voice, both publicly and privately, to demand full religious rights in Israel for non-Orthodox branches of Judaism, warning we will no longer be "beggars at the gates of Jerusalem," objects of disrespect in a Jewish state.

Under Schindler's leadership, the Reform movement established its Israel Religious Action Center in Jerusalem to mobilize Israeli public opinion behind the values of pluralism and tolerance. Within Israel, the views of Rabbi Schindler are taken with utmost seriousness and respect; he remains a household name—although many who welcome his views do not know he is a Reform rabbi.

What makes Alex run? What kind of childhood prepared him for a life of Jewish service? Alex was born in Munich, Germany, in 1925 to Sali and Eliezer Schindler. His father, Eliezer, was a Yiddish poet of some repute. His mother—strong and feisty—was a successful businesswoman. The Schindler family's fortunes changed with the advent of Nazism. To escape the Gestapo, Eliezer Schindler fled to Switzerland in 1933. For the next five years Sali Schindler supported Alex and his sister, Eva, with profits from her mail-order business. She secretly channeled funds into anti-Nazi activities while setting profits aside for the time when she and the children could escape and rejoin her husband in exile.

The wait turned out to be harrowing. In the end Sali had to entrust her two children to a German noblewoman, who later spirited them across the border to Switzerland. After Sali left Munich, she was smuggled into Poland and, with the help of the Belzer Rebbe, traveled to Hungary for an ecumenical conference, disguised as a Carmelite nun. She arrived in Budapest alone and penniless. Desperate to reach her husband in Switzerland, she tried to make a collect call from a public phone booth. At that time, however, there was no international telephone connection between Switzerland and Hungary. A man who happened to overhear her appeal approached her and asked, "Did I hear you say Schindler? Eliezer Schindler? I just left him in Switzerland. In fact, he gave me some money to attend my niece's wedding." The man insisted on giving Sali the money for her fare to Switzerland. Thus was the Schindler family reunited, safe from the Nazi death machine that had destroyed so many of their relatives.

Alex was twelve when he arrived in America with his family. He knew barely a word of English. Shy, withdrawn, and traumatized by the Nazi terror, he gave few indications of the warm and charismatic personality that would come to characterize him in adulthood. At sixteen he enrolled at CCNY, both learning the language and mastering his studies. Later his family moved from the West Side of Manhattan to Lakewood, New Jersey, where they became chicken farmers, a not uncommon occupation for Jews arriving in an America gripped by the Great Depression.

At age eighteen, Alex enlisted in the United States Army, becoming a ski trooper. He served in three campaigns in Italy, earning the Purple Heart for wounds received in battle, and won a Bronze Star

Medal for bravery in action in Europe. His military experience helped him overcome his shyness and compelled him to examine what he wanted to do with his life. He decided to pursue a career in the rabbinate, inspired by his father's lifelong example as an *ohev Yisrael*, a "lover of Israel," and his mother's fierce determination that he aspire grandly and fulfill his clear potential.

His first full-time rabbinic post was as assistant rabbi at Temple Emanuel in Worcester, Massachusetts. His warm relationship with the senior rabbi, Joseph Klein, and with the congregation resulted in a mutual love affair for six years. Even after moving from Worcester to join the UAHC staff (serving as a regional director, then as director of the Department of Education, and assuming the presidency in 1973), Alex has continued to look upon Worcester as his spiritual home base.

Schindler's early childhood experiences may have much to do with his unusual capacity to identify with people in pain. For example, his passionate championship of gay rights stems not only from a generally liberal political orientation but also from his acute awareness that gays suffered humiliation and terror at the hands of the Nazis.

What is remarkable about Alex is his capacity to support and comfort individuals in trouble. In fact, Alex's reputation in the Reform Jewish community is that of a "bleeding heart," especially when a rabbinic colleague is experiencing personal anguish or mistreatment by a congregation or by the community on account of an unpopular position. To reach out to such a person, Schindler has been willing to risk antagonizing his lay leaders and even courting personal embarrassment and ridicule. He has, on several occasions, defended and saved the reputations of individual colleagues who had been falsely charged with improprieties or smeared because of unpopular positions. A few of the most effective rabbis on the staff of the UAHC and in congregations owe their careers to Alex Schindler's intervention at moments of personal or professional crisis in their lives.

What shaped Alex Schindler, the extraordinary leader, the exceptional human being? The apple does not fall far from the tree. Here are Alex's own words in memory of his late father:

From the Tenth Anniversary of the Outreach Speech

My father, of blessed memory, was a Yiddish poet of note; his songs are still sung wherever that language is spoken and taught. He loved the Jewish people with an abounding love. And he was so proud of our spiritual legacy that he was determined to share it with non-Jews.

When I was still a child, he entranced me with stories of his escape from a Siberian prison, how he made his way by foot across the Russian steppes back to his family.

En route, he found refuge in a village in which all the residents had embraced Judaism, although they had never seen a Jew. These *gerim* ("converts") were called Subbotnikis because they observed the Sabbath zealously; they abstained from work on that day, attended worship services, read from the Torah, and eschewed discussion of worldly affairs.

For some months, my father remained in the village and became the Hebrew teacher of these Subbotnikis. During his stay, these Russian Jews-by-choice heard that a pogrom was planned against the Jews of the region's capital. They took their farm implements in hand, marched to Saratof, and successfully defended their co-religionists.

The thread of a missionary Judaism thereafter became dominant in the tapestry of my father's thoughts and actions. Indeed, in the 1930s, he co-edited a weekly journal distributed widely in central Europe and published primarily to actualize this missionary concept. *Der Ruf* ("The Summons") called upon Jews to be more assertive in their Jewishness, to make themselves known, to make our faith known to the world.

All my life, my father reminded me that people who have no mission are suspect of having no message, of possessing nothing that is sufficiently worthy to share with others. He was also the first to tell me what Albert Einstein had said: "I am sorry that I was *born* a Jew, for it kept me from *choosing* to be a Jew."

✦ ✦ ✦

Alex has been described by *Time* magazine as "the most prominent spokesman for America's disparate Jewish groups." The first Reform rabbi to be elected chair of the Conference of Presidents of Major

Jewish Organizations, he established excellent working relations with Orthodox rabbis and lay leaders. To Alex, *K'lal Yisrael* is not just a slogan. He believes passionately in the solidarity and unity of the Jewish people. Warm, humorous, generous, fun-loving, Schindler succeeded in knitting together all the diverse segments of Jewish life behind a common goal: Israel's well-being.

Alex is a fervent music lover, especially opera, and he is a fierce competitor, whether on the tennis court, at the chess board, or in politic hardball. For example, when he felt some members of the Carter administration were out to "break" the power of the so-called Jewish lobby, he led a powerful and effective counterattack.

For his service to the Jewish people, Rabbi Schindler was awarded the coveted Bublik Prize of the Hebrew University in 1978, an honor bestowed earlier on Prime Minister David Ben-Gurion and President Harry S. Truman, among others. He is a vice president of the World Jewish Congress, a member of the Governing Body of the Jewish Agency, secretary of the Joint Distribution Committee, and a vice president of the Memorial Foundation for Jewish Culture. He has received honorary doctorates from several American colleges and universities, including most recently the University of South Carolina and Lafayette, Hamilton, and Holy Cross colleges. In Israel, 500,000 trees have been planted by the Jewish National Fund in the Schindler Forest to honor, in perpetuity, one of the Jewish people's most devoted servants—*ohev Yisrael* par excellence.

· I ·

IF I AM ONLY FOR MYSELF, WHAT AM I?

Dialogue, Pluralism, and Tolerance

More progress has been made in Catholic-Jewish relations over the past two decades than in the preceding two millennia. It has been an altogether remarkable transformation. No longer do we fear the Church, as we did for so long, as our everlasting, deadly enemy, the primary source of worldwide anti-Semitism. Its sword and the rack have been shelved and replaced by the moral power of faith and the healing power of prayer.

No one in all the world was more effective in enunciating the restoration of the Church's spiritual dignity than was Pope John XXIII. Indeed, he symbolized this transformation. He was an altogether remarkable spiritual leader who reached out and touched the souls of countless millions within the Church and without, Jews not in the least among them.

We will never forget how Pope John XXIII welcomed a group of Jews who had come to demonstrate their affection for him. He greeted them with the biblical passage: "I am Joseph your brother." With these words he embraced the whole Jewish people and softened many a bitter memory. His farsighted vision paved the way for immeasurably improved Catholic-Jewish relations.

It was exactly twenty years ago this October that the Roman Catholic bishops of the Second Vatican Council repudiated the deicide charge against the Jews and denounced anti-Semitism. Their landmark statement *Nostra Aetate* marvelously, luminously transformed the way Catholics and Jews look at one another. Pope John XXIII did what President Reagan failed to do when he visited Bitburg: He recognized the past for what it was and instead of absolving the Church, he determined to transform it.

Rabbi Alexander M. Schindler
"Whither Catholic-Jewish Relations?"
Lecture at Marist College
October 1985

CATHOLIC-JEWISH RELATIONS IN THE TWENTIETH CENTURY

HIS EMINENCE, WILLIAM CARDINAL KEELER
ARCHBISHOP OF BALTIMORE

I have in my home a picture taken of a group of us, Jews and Catholics from the United States, who met with Pope John Paul II at his summer residence, Castel Gandolfo, just outside Rome in the late morning of September 1, 1987. The purpose was to seek reconciliation and understanding, after a summer of controversy and confrontation between our communities centering around the Holocaust, in preparation for the Holy Father's trip to the United States that month.[1] We had already had an intense day and a half of dialogue and had made much progress, but there remained a great deal at stake in the short time we would have with the Pope.

The encounter went well and became in itself a significant event in twentieth-century Catholic-Jewish relations. I well remember Rabbi Alexander Schindler's statement on that day, urging us to look beyond the present difficulties to see what the communities of our two ancient faiths could do together to address the urgent social and economic issues facing all of humanity. It was a statement evoking both healing of past wounds and challenges for the future. It is in that generous spirit of hope and encouragement exemplified so well by Rabbi Schindler that I take up this topic.

I must indicate at the outset that I am not a professional academic historian, and this essay, therefore, is not intended to be a distillation of the topic as one might find in an encyclopedia. Rather it represents my own reflections, informed to be sure by a sense of history but pointed more toward the practical realities our two communities have faced and still have to face within the larger American mosaic. Several historical points, however, do need to be made if the readership of this volume, which I take to be primarily Jewish, is to understand Catholic perspectives on what has happened and is happening in this century between American Jews and Catholics.

We need first to realize that we are both essentially "immigrant" communities in the United States. Indeed, our patterns of immigration are startlingly parallel, not only with regard to periods, but with regard to where we ended up in the "New" (to Europeans) World. Together Jews and Catholics formed the large part of the ethnic "working" neighborhoods of America's urban ghettos in the first half of this century. Together we have been discriminated against in terms of housing, education, and job opportunities. For example, history shows that the American labor movement has been largely a Catholic-Jewish enterprise over the decades. One thinks immediately of the Irish Catholic "Molly Maguires" in the coal fields of Pennsylvania in the 1870s, the Knights of Labor in the 1880s, and the early strikes in New York's garment industry. I remember one photo I saw some time ago of one of those strikes. The signs and placards being carried were in two languages, Yiddish and Italian, but not English.

In what follows, I shall presume the readers' knowledge of Jewish history and its internal and external struggles in this country, and I will concentrate on the Catholic experience, although I believe you will find here an echo of your own family histories as well. I will attempt to reprise briefly something of our experiences as immigrants on these shores, both in response to anti-Catholicism and to the larger social issues of the post-World War I era. It is within that broader context of American Catholic history and social teaching that I will try to place the rather remarkable story of American Catholic attitudes toward Jews and Judaism in this century.

Anti-Catholicism in American History

"To the Catholics of the City and County of Philadelphia:
"In the critical circumstances in which you are placed, I feel my duty to suspend the exercises of public worship in the Catholic churches, which still remain, until it can be resumed with safety, and we can enjoy our constitutional rights to worship God according to the dictates of our conscience."

With these words on May 12, 1844, Bishop Francis Kenrick of Philadelphia announced that he had been forced to suspend all Catholic religious services in the diocese, an act virtually without parallel in the history of the United States. For almost a week, Protestant mobs had rioted through the streets, burning scores of Catholic homes and churches while fire fighters stood by, not daring to toss a drop of water to quench the fires. It would be some days more before the belatedly summoned militia would be able to restore order to the "City of Brotherly Love."

Thus, in many less dramatic, but no less effective, ways, have Irish, Italian, Polish, Hispanic, Asian, and other Catholics been welcomed to these shores. Ironically, many Catholics came to this country fleeing religious persecution only to find it, in the words of one Irish Catholic, "translated to this side of the Atlantic," despite the glowing words of the Constitution.

Maryland, for example, was established essentially as a refuge for Catholics fleeing persecution. But Maryland, as a Catholic refuge, made the mistake in colonial times of allowing religious freedom at least for other Christians (it was only later to be one of the first states of the fledgling republic to allow full civil rights for Jews and others). Some Protestants, taking advantage of Catholic liberality, soon assumed control—and immediately disenfranchised Catholics until after the Revolutionary War. As late as the 1830s, when charges of "Catholic plots against democracy" were highly popular, Massachusetts still had an established church that was Protestant.

In 1833 the first monthly issue of *Protestant* magazine defined its goals: "We have entered upon this work, resolved...to defend the great truths of the gospel opposed by popery, and to exhibit those doctrines and practices of Roman Catholics that are contrary to the interest of mankind," charges echoed by Paul Blanshard in the 1940s and 1950s and by the Reverend Jimmy Swaggert and the Alamos in the 1980s.

Perhaps no other American religious group has been the object, over so many years, of attacks from so many organizations that have seen as their chief mission the denunciation of Catholicism. These range from the Native Americans of the 1840s through the Know-Nothing party and the American Protective Association to Protestants and Other Americans United for the Separation of Church and State, not to mention the Ku Klux Klan and other groups whose hatred encompassed Jews and blacks as well as Catholics. Catholics have been pilloried, not only with crude ethnic stereotypes ("drunken Irish," "greasy Italians," "dumb Poles," "lazy Hispanics," etc.), but consistently, and as a whole, for their religious beliefs.

Nor has anti-Catholicism been the sole provenance of a fringe element of religious bigots. It has been a mainline and even "liberal" infestation as well. The *Christian Century* on October 28, 1928, for example, editorialized in this way concerning the presidential campaign of Al Smith: "Protestants cannot look with unconcern upon the seating of a representative of an alien culture, of a medieval Latin mentality, of an undemocratic hierarchy, and of a foreign potentate in the great office of the president of the United States." *The New Republic,* which did support Smith's candidacy, still had this to say in 1927:

> It is the feeling that Catholics are subservient to an organization and a system of authority of foreign origin and with foreign interests that, in the minds of Americans, tends to disqualify a Catholic for presidency.... The Catholic church will remain an alien guest in the American body politic as long as it tries to form the minds of American Catholics by educational methods different from those used to form the minds of other American citizens.[2]

No matter whether Catholic schools were better or worse educationally or more (as was often the case) ethnically diverse than their "public" counterparts, the offense was that they were different. They were Catholic.

Similarities with the Jewish Experience

With only a few changes of names, the history of anti-Semitism in the United States could be that of American anti-Catholicism as well. The negative image of Catholics in popular culture, and especially of the clergy, is remarkably similar to that of Jews. To check this, simply look up the definitions of the terms *pharisaical* and *Jesuitical* in most dictionaries—even relatively recent ones.

One might, for example, substitute the image of a drunken wife-beater like Stanley Kowalski in *A Streetcar Named Desire* or the godfather for the Shylock or "pawnbroker" images of Jews in English literature. The sensationalism and eroticism of "Maria Monk" and "Sister Mary Ignatius Explains It All for You" hits virtually the same level of nativist fantasy as do their anti-Semitic counterparts. So, too, do the grotesque caricatures of bishops with miters turned into the mouths of alligators so popular in nineteenth-century American political cartoons.

Catholics, then as now (Hispanics, Haitians, Vietnamese, etc.), were and are seen as an economic threat to "native" American workers (as were Jews) and as antidemocratic conspirators. And, like Jews, Catholics were deeply involved in the labor movement and seen as symbols of the social dislocations of industrialization that their labor in large part made possible and as radicals to be feared for their "alien" notions of social responsibility and reform.

Curiously, then, Catholicism has been used as symbolic of almost all the evils feared by American society, whether "medievalism," totalitarianism, or modern socialism. Paul Blanshard opined in his classic anti-Catholic tome *American Freedom and Catholic Power* (he saw the two concepts as antithetical, of course) that "on the international level the most questionable moral feature of the Vatican's political record, aside from its collaboration with fascism, has been the 'neutral' maneuvering with dictators and aggressors."[3] As John J. Kane has pinpointed, Blanshard's fulminations represented a continuity with views articulated over a hundred years earlier in similar anti-Catholic sermons that "attempted to show that Catholicism and despotism were definitely allied and equally opposed to American principles of republicanism."[4] One would hope that, after the works of John Courtney Murray, S.J.; the Second Vatican Council; the election of a Catholic president; and the survival of the Republic despite it all, the type of vicious stereotyping represented by Blanshard is finally being put to rest.

Social and Economic Discrimination

The point of this exercise in recalling instances of religious and ethnic prejudice against Catholics and Jews has not been simply to allow us to tell our tales of woe to each other, though that can be useful in itself in dialogue. Rather, the point has been to give some indication of the economic and social costs of religious bigotry to the affected groups and to American society as a whole. Jews no less than Catholics may see some of their own untested beliefs about the other mirrored in the above citations and, thereby, be given pause to reflect more deeply on the necessity of intergroup collaboration in social policy questions today.

Just as was the case for Jews, Catholics until very recently have been excluded from the "better" neighborhoods of American cities, from social clubs vital to business and professional advancement, from elite private schools, and, except for small quotas, from graduate schools leading to professional and academic higher degrees.

All of these restrictions, of course, had the effect of keeping the establishment established. They also had the effect of depriving society as a whole of the energy and skills that millions of Catholics, Jews, African Americans, and other "alien" types could contribute to the economic and social welfare of the country.

Given this history, it is no wonder that the Catholic church came to be known (derisively, to those outside the Catholic community) as the "working man's church" and that its bishops have tended to be as socially reformist as they were—of necessity in a situation of religious and cultural siege—theologically conservative. Some of the most significant contributions of the Catholic community to American life have been in its involvement in the labor movement, in social action, and in civil rights causes; and in its massive commitment to health care, refugee, and migration work, to Catholic charities, and to inner-city schools, which serve the needs of the society as a whole.

Education

One of the major avenues of opportunity for upward mobility for immigrants and their children in American society has been through educational attainment. This was a difficult path for many Catholics in nineteenth-century America. Teachers in public schools were almost invariably Protestant and, with well-intentioned if misguided motivations, may have seen it as their task to "rescue" the children of the immigrants from the doctrinal and moral foibles of "papist" tradition.

Nineteenth-century public school textbooks did not hesitate to point out these evils. Parley's *Common School History* was typical:

> The popes rapidly acquired power.... Their pride was equal to their power, and neither seemed to have any bounds.... No other tyranny had ever been like theirs for they tyrannized over the souls of men.... Abbeys and monasteries became seats of voluptuousness.[5]

And social commentary: "They (the Irish)...set apart one day in the year for going to church, drinking whiskey, and breaking each other's heads with clubs."[6]

Catholic children in public schools were forced to recite Protestant prayers and sing Protestant hymns, and occasionally they suffered whippings for refusal to read from the Protestant translation of the Bible. The *Philadelphia Catholic Herald* in the 1840s reported numerous instances of proselytism in Protestant-run but publicly funded schools and orphanages throughout the city. Yet public indignation waxed high and eloquent when Bishop John Hughes of New York attempted to secure even modest funding for the fledgling Catholic school system. *The American Protestant Vindicator* in 1840 raised the cry of alarm:

> They the Catholics demand of republicans to give them funds to train their children to worship a ghostly monarchy of vicars, bishops, archbishops, cardinals, and popes! They demand of us to take away our children's funds and bestow them on the subjects of Rome, the creatures of a foreign hierarchy.[7]

Given the exclusiveness of private schools and the systematic intolerance of public schools, Catholics had little recourse but to attempt to erect their own educational system—from elementary to graduate schools. And given the fact that the community was almost entirely an immigrant one, woefully poor and lacking virtually any of the assistance offered by the larger society to other groups, Catholic achievements in educational attainment over the decades have been little short of phenomenal. They stand even today as a striking example of how American pluralism can be made to work—even despite itself at times.

Catholic Social Teaching in the Twentieth Century

I do not intend to argue for an exclusively "lachrymose" view of American Catholic history. Like Jews, many Catholics have by and large done rather well in this country and are grateful for the constitutional framework that protects our freedoms, even as we may continue to argue over some of the ways we would interpret that framework. Rather, for the particular audience of the present volume, the brief treatment of anti-Catholicism was designed to illustrate something of what Jews and Catholics have faced in common on these shores, a set of shared experiences that truly sets us apart from all previous generations of Jews and Catholics in history. This base of shared experience and sociocultural values, I believe, has enabled to emerge in this country a form of shared understanding that while remaining profoundly "Jewish" and profoundly "Catholic," respectively, is also distinctively American and, for Catholics, perhaps best understood within the context of American Catholic social teaching.

In the nineteenth century, the American bishops as a group rarely addressed themselves to the public social issues of the time, although individual bishops did speak out on suitable occasions, sometimes forcefully.[8] Historian David J. O'Brien notes that "the seven provincial and three plenary councils of Baltimore" between 1829 and 1884 issued general "pastoral exhortations" that in the main sought to encourage "church attendance, sound morality, education of children, and support for religious vocations."[9] In short, the immigrant Church naturally looked inward to its own spiritual and social needs."[10]

It was only in 1918, responding to the national-level needs of World War I, that the National Catholic War Council was formed. This body was later to become the National Catholic Welfare Conference (NCWC) and, after the Second Vatican Council (1962–1965), the present National Conference of Catholic Bishops/U.S. Catholic Conference. In 1919, Monsignor John A. Ryan, a moral theologian teaching at the Catholic University of America, was appointed the first director of the NCWC's Social Action department, a post he held until his death in 1945. Monsignor Ryan was already well known for his 1906 book *A Living Wage*, which argued that workers had a right to an income sufficient to sustain life. In 1919 the Administrative Committee of the NCWC issued what O'Brien calls "a program of proposals for social reconstruction," which urged support for organized labor, collective bargaining, federal assistance for employment and health insurance, "producers' and consumers' cooperatives," and stock and profit-sharing plans. Needless to say, the Social Action department under Ryan gave, according to O'Brien, "strong backing to most New Deal reforms" in the 1930s.[11] This period of active intervention in the major public issues of the times, O'Brien notes, "climaxed" with the bishops' statement on "The Church and the Social Order" in 1940.

It is important also to note how carefully the American bishops have tried to craft their considerations to reflect and provide practical "local" application of the universal social teachings of the Church, especially as articulated in such papal encyclicals as Leo XIII's *Rerum Novarum* (1891); Pius XI's *Quadragesimo Anno* (1931); John XXIII's *Mater et Magistra* (1961) and *Pacem in Terris* (1963); and Paul VI's *Populorum Progressio* (1967) and *Octagesima Adveniens* (1971).[12] Similarly reflecting the teachings of the current pope, John Paul II, the American bishops have within the past decade issued two major social documents, *The Challenge of Peace* (1983) and *Economic Justice for All: Catholic Social Teaching and the Economic Order* (1986).

The method of development of these recent United States Conference documents reflects the influence of the Second Vatican Council on the one hand and the experience of American Catholics on the other. Both statements were preceded by extensive consultations, not only with Catholic laity and experts in the fields to be discussed, but equally importantly with representatives of other religious communities, including, of course, the Union of American Hebrew Congregations. Both statements profited immensely from these consultations. In the case of *The Challenge of Peace*, there has been also significant follow-up with the Jewish and Protestant communities, the former embodied in the volume *The Challenge of Shalom for Catholics and Jews*, co-edited by the UAHC's Annette Daum, of blessed memory, and Eugene Fisher of the National Conference of Catholic Bishops (NCCB) Secretariat for Ecumenical and Interreligious Affairs.[13]

Throughout this century there has been a remarkable congruence of social policy views between American Catholics and Jews with regard to domestic issues, if not always on international issues.[14] While there was, frankly, very little by way of religious dialogue as we would understand it today, Jews and Catholics often found themselves on the same side of such social issues as labor and civil rights. This resulted in a *modus vivendi* that transcended mere toleration of each other to achieve active cooperation in many areas of American life. Protestants, Catholics, and Jews, for example, cooperated in founding the National Conference of Christians and Jews in direct response to the anti-Catholic bigotry that erupted to scuttle the presidential bid of then Governor Al Smith of New York.

This cooperation found many avenues in which to express itself in different communities around the country. In the late 1930s in Chicago, for example, Bishop Bernard Sheil and other clergy assisted Saul Alinsky's efforts to organize the neighborhood around the stockyards. By the early 1940s in Detroit, chapters of the Knights of Columbus and B'nai B'rith were working together on community affairs and even holding joint banquets. And the civil rights movement of the 1960s saw an intensity of interreligious cooperative activity perhaps never before achieved. The American experience of religious pluralism that would give so much to the Second Vatican Council was worked out in practice long before John Courtney Murray was able to give it a clear philosophical and theological voice. In fact, bishops of the United States brought this experience to the service of the larger Catholic community during the deliberations of the Second Vatican Council (1962–1965).

The "Century of the Shoah"

I do not need to review for readers of this book the traumatic and startling events of the twentieth century, which Pope John Paul II has called the "Century of the *Shoah*"[15] and which is also the century of the rebirth of a Jewish state in the land of Israel in fulfillment of nearly two millennia of Jewish longing.[16] Now, a peace agreement between the State of Israel and its neighbor the Palestine Liberation Organization has been signed, as well as one between Israel and Jordan. I join my fellow bishops in applauding "the courage, the imagination, and the spirit of compromise that has been shown in negotiating this major advance toward peace in the Holy Land"[17] and in praying for its successful implementation despite the difficulties it will face. It is to be hoped as well that the historic accord between Israel and the Holy See will help to facilitate the dialogue of peace in the Middle East.

I wish here only to make a few points that may help Jewish readers understand a bit better the perspectives with which Catholics tend to view these momentous events. For we must, in dialogue, bring our memories and interpretations together, as was begun, for example, in the meeting of the International Catholic-Jewish Liaison Committee (ILC) in Prague in September 1990. I was privileged to be present when representatives of the international Jewish Committee for Interreligious Consultations met with representatives of the Holy See's Commission for Religious Relations with the Jews. In four intense days of listening to overviews of the history of anti-Semitism and of the *Shoah*, of hearing witnesses, both Catholic and Jewish, describe days of unspeakable horror, devilish betrayal, and undreamed-of heroism, the delegates moved toward new understandings of one another and of what efforts needed to be made together for the sake of the future. Representatives of the Holy See received the observations of selected qualified Jewish scholars as they began their own process of reflection on anti-Semitism and the *Shoah*.

This process of exchange on the *Shoah* was continued and intensified when the ILC met in Baltimore in May 1992 for its fourteenth meeting since the Second Vatican Council, but only its first in the Western Hemisphere.[18] On that occasion a suggestion made by Cardinal Joseph Bernardin of Chicago received particular attention. He proposed that the Vatican archives for the period of World War II and the Holocaust and its immediate aftermath be made available to serious scholars, in exception to the Holy See's normal procedure for such archival materials.[19] This most helpful suggestion, if implemented, would offer new and useful insights into a critical moment of recent history.

The caution I would give to all sides of this discussion is to remember its extraordinary complexity. The world was truly at war and no single generality or set of generalities is likely to be adequate to the ambiguities of so many human beings, whether clergy or lay, acting often enough under extreme pressure. Seemingly, every day, from different sources, new evidence and material are emerging.

One can support the ongoing and objective reassessment of the evidence while urging restraint in reaching conclusions. Certainly, the ILC meeting in Jerusalem in May 1994 has moved forward this very delicate dialogue on the *Shoah*.

With regard to just American Catholics, who in large numbers fought the war against Nazi Germany, there is much to be said. When the well-known Father Charles Coughlin of radio fame slid into public anti-Semitism, for example, he was denounced by officials of the Bishops' Conference such as the above-mentioned Father John Ryan, as well as by such influential Catholic journals as *Commonweal*, which already in the early 1930s had published a devastating series of articles attacking Nazism.[20]

In March 1937, Pope Piux XI issued the encyclical *Mit Brennender Sorge* ("With Burning Concern"), condemning the false and heretical teaching of Nazism, especially its "racialism." The encyclical, written in German and smuggled into Germany, unfortunately had little effect on the subsequent history of Nazi policies. But it did have a galvanizing effect on the American Catholic community.

The American bishops, meeting in Washington in November 1938 just after Kristallnacht, utilized the entire period of a national radio broadcast they had organized to issue a series of denunciations of what one called a "shameless orgy of ruthless oppression, even extinction, willed by the mad lust for power...upon a helpless, already shackled people."[21] Gershon Greenberg, assessing the role of "American Catholics during the Holocaust," cites a number of public and private interventions of members of the Catholic hierarchy, such as the cardinal archbishops of Chicago, Philadelphia, and New York, to denounce Hitler and "to safeguard the rights of Jewish victims." Greenberg also details the numerous interventions with the United States and other governments made by the apostolic delegate of the Holy See to the United States, Archbishop Amleto Giovanni Cicognani. Archbishop Cicognani, for example, was instrumental in aiding the rescue of 15,000 Yugoslavian Jews. He also worked to make it possible to validate South American visas for Polish Jews interned in Germany, to help rabbinical students in Shanghai, and to facilitate communication on the plight of Jews throughout Europe.[22]

It may not be incidental to the work of Archbishop Cicognani or to the history of the famous Riegner memorandum of 1942 to note that the American bishops' one major joint statement during the war was issued on November 14, 1942, and contained the following strong appeal with regard to the Jewish plight:

> Since the murderous assault on Poland, utterly devoid of every semblance of humanity, there has been a premeditated and systematic extermination of the people of the nation. The same satanic technique is being applied to many other peoples. We feel a deep sense of revulsion against the cruel indignities heaped upon the Jews in conquered countries and upon defenseless peoples not of our faith. We join with our brother bishops in subjugated France: "Deeply moved by the mass arrests and maltreatment of Jews, we cannot stifle the cry of our conscience. In the name of humanity and Christian principles our voice is raised in favor of imprescriptible rights of human nature." We raise our voice in protest against despotic tyrants who have lost all sense of humanity by condemning thousands of innocent persons to death in subjugated countries as acts of reprisal, by placing other thousands of innocent victims in concentration camps, and by permitting unnumbered persons to die of starvation.[23]

Given all of this, American Catholics who lost relatives who fought the war against Hitler might be forgiven for being a little nonplussed when they read generalizations in the papers about Catholic "apathy" during World War II or about papal "silence." The 1942 and 1943 Christmas messages of Pope Pius XII as reported by, among other papers, *The New York Times* were understood at the time clearly to condemn Nazi attacks against Jews, just as Pius XI and the American bishops had done. American Catholics read with some concern that Nazi propaganda had selected Pope Pius XII as a chief target, as exemplified in the following report carried by the American press in 1943:

> A United Press report, quoting the BBC, says a German propagandist in France, identified as Dr. Friedrich, declared over the Nazi-controlled Paris radio: "Pope Pius XII has condemned the principles of the totalitarian state, has rejected racism, and has forbidden Catholics to participate in anti-Jewish campaigns. Enormous indeed is the responsibility of Pius XII for this war....

The Church (has) rejected the hand offered to her. May she bear the responsibility for this in the annals of history.[24]

Holocaust survivor Leon Wells, without seeking to adjudicate the historical issue, pushes us toward a deeper level of consideration that might also become part of our common dialogue on the meaning of the *Shoah* for Catholics and Jews by noting, with reference to the controversy over Rolf Hochhuth's polemical play *The Deputy*, that the underlying issue may for both Catholics and Jews touch on what Wells calls "the crisis of religious faith posed by the Holocaust":

> Philip Friedman describes in detail how priests and churches helped Jews in Italy, how the pope (Pius XII) was involved with helping Italian Jews, and how he even contributed a large sum of money to the Jewish synagogue in Rome.[25] I must admit that the role of the pope during those years remains a riddle to me, but I suspect that much of the condemnation of the pope derives from the old religious quarrel between faith and unbelief. Anti-Catholics may be exploiting the pope's silence to question the pope's religious and moral infallibility. On the other hand, the faithful might be tempted to blame the "deputy" of God for his failure in order to turn the question away from what God was doing during the Holocaust.[26]

If Wells is at all correct that there is a deeper level of challenge involved in the controversy over Pius XII than simply a historical assessment of an individual papacy, as I believe he may be, then we need on both sides to turn away from debate with each other over the issue and toward each other in a profoundly theological dialogue. Our memories, Catholic and Jewish, need to be "tested" against each other constantly, in honest and frank discussion, so that we can begin to forge a common memorial of the events and their significance. There is no question that many Christians and their leaders failed, nor is there a question that others acted heroically. It is clear that the policies of the Holy See contributed to the rescue of many, and it is clear that ancient negative presumptions of Christians concerning Jews and Judaism, as the Second Vatican Council insisted, must today be challenged and reformed. It is to that future-oriented Christian task that I will devote the final section of this essay.

Toward a Common Vision

In an oft-cited paper delivered at a Catholic-Jewish symposium organized by Fordham University in 1991 to celebrate its sesquicentennial, Dr. Eugene Fisher of our Conference staff commented that in his travels he has found a surprising "ignorance in much (not all) of the Jewish community concerning the official statements and practical changes effected since the Second Vatican Council in the actual teaching of the Christian churches concerning Jews and Judaism."[27] Fisher, who has long been involved in promoting among Catholics the fruits of the dialogue,[28] acknowledges:

> It takes one aback to realize that for many Jews all the careful theological and educational work among Christians of more than a generation seemingly has not happened. There exists among Jews a widespread and erroneous belief that, despite our official statements to the contrary, we Christians are "really" still teaching the same old contempt toward Jews in our classrooms. Not so! This misperception by Jews of Christian intent, as we witnessed in the Auschwitz Carmel incident among others, can breed unnecesary distrust of Christian motivations.[29]

Fisher rightly notes that a certain residual Jewish distrust of Christians is both inevitable and justifiable, given the tragedies of history.[30] I believe he is also correct to urge that we turn our attention to a better future. Certainly, the events of the past few years from the destruction of the Berlin Wall to the historic accord between Israel and the Holy See give reason to hope.

While the readers of this volume may be more familiar than most with the educational improvements that have taken place in Catholic religion courses, something of the liturgical efforts of the Church might also be noted here, especially since yet further work needs to be done in this most sensitive area of the Church's life.

Readers will appreciate the complexity and sensitivity necessary to approach matter that is at once biblical and liturgical in its range.

Yet, the mandate of the Church is clear in the Council document *Nostra Aetate* and in subsequent statements. A key text can be found in the 1974 "Guidelines" of the Holy See, which, in addition to a thorough review of Catholic education on all levels, suggested a two-fold strategy with respect to New Testament readings that pose special difficulties:

> With respect to liturgical readings, care will be taken to see that homilies based on them will not distort their meaning, especially when it is a question of passages that seem to show the Jewish people as such in an unfavorable light. Efforts will be made so to instruct the Christian people that they will understand the true interpretation of all the texts and their meaning for the contemporary believer.
>
> Commissions entrusted with the task of liturgical translation will pay particular attention to the way in which they express those phrases and passages that Christians, if not well informed, might misunderstand because of prejudice. Obviously, with a version destined for liturgical use, there should be an overriding preoccupation to bring out explicitly the meaning of a text while taking scriptural studies into account. ("Guidelines," no. 3)

Since 1974, even more work has been done to draw out the implications of this mandate, especially with reference to the Passion Narratives in the Gospels. The 1985 document of the Holy See "Notes on the Correct Way to Present the Jews and Judaism in the Preaching and Catechesis of the Roman Catholic Church" is admirably explicit in providing authoritative and helpful interpretations of problematic passages from the New Testament.

In this country, working with the Bishops' Committee for Ecumenical and Interreligious Affairs, the Bishops' Committee on the Liturgy has undertaken two very significant initiatives. First, it included in its guidelines for all liturgical translations of the Scriptures the important principle cited above, to suggest replacing "the Jews" with "religious authorities," for example, in many places, such as St. John's Gospel, where this would be appropriate to the sense of the passage. Newer translations of the New Testament for liturgical use, while not yet ready for publication, may well resolve many difficulties.

Second, the Liturgy Committee in 1988 issued a statement, *God's Mercy Endures Forever: Guidelines on the Presentation of Jews and Judaism in Catholic Preaching,* which includes specific sections on the readings of Advent, Lent, Holy Week, and the Easter season. With regard to the latter, the bishops state:

> The readings of the Easter season, especially those from the book of Acts, which is used extensively throughout this liturgical period, require particular attention from the Christians. Some of the readings from Acts (e.g., for the third and fourth Sundays of Easter) can leave an impression of collective Jewish responsibility for the crucifixion.... In such cases, the homilist should put before the assembly the teachings of *Nostra Aetate*...so that not unwarranted conclusion of collective guilt is drawn by the hearers. The Acts may be dealing with a reflection of the Jewish-Christian relationship as it existed toward the end of the first century (when Acts was composed) rather than the actual attitudes of the post-Easter Jerusalem Church.... Statements about Jewish responsibility have to be kept in context. This is part of the reconciliation between Jews and Christians to which we are all called.[31]

These are examples of the types of official materials that are available in this country. Additionally, Catholic religion textbooks, as evaluations made in 1976 and 1991 have shown, have improved dramatically in presenting a more positive portrait of Jews and Judaism. Such corrective catechesis will influence how our people "hear" the New Testament readings on Sunday.

Within the rather broad framework of this essay, please allow me to raise a few concerns from the Catholic side of the dialogue that we might fruitfully explore.[32] First, I wish to raise consideration of our joint statement with the Synagogue Council of America: "A Lesson Value: A Joint Statement on Moral Education in the Public Schools." This statement, which is very supportive of public education, noted with some irony that "in recent years there has been a growing reluctance to teach values in our public education system out of a fear that children might be indoctrinated with a specific religious belief." Yet, the document continued, "values like honesty, compassion, integrity, tolerance, loyalty, and belief in human worth and dignity are embedded in our respective religious traditions and in the civic fabric of our society.... We are convinced that, even apart from the context of specific faith, it is possible to teach these shared values."

Given the nature of American public education, a vision such as that which we were able to articulate jointly with representatives of the Synagogue Council of America can only be effectively implemented through local school boards across the country. This is a challenge that, while nationally formulated, can perhaps best be met on the congregational, parish-to-synagogue level.

Second, linked to the understanding that there are some commonly held values necessary for the preservation of a civilized society that can be articulated and asserted in the most pluralistic of settings, is a consideration of the question of pornography. Obviously, there are some First Amendment issues involved that must be carefully considered. But even after the most scrupulous attendance to these issues, there remain, I believe, some rather large areas of shared concern on which we can speak together. Child pornography, of course, comes immediately to mind, as does the related issue of the exploitation, indeed the virtual enslavement, of some women involved in the process of producing pornography. More investigation and joint reflection, I urge, is necessary to combat such evil practices. There is proof enough that pornography undermines family life and can be a step along the way to violent, even murderous, action.

A third area for further dialogue and possible joint action lies in the possibility of rethinking the issue of aid to nonpublic school students and parents. Of course, this aid or relief would have to be constitutionally approvable as several existing approaches are, or could be worked out to be, since the focus is on aid to the needy, not to specific institutions, whether religious or secular. There are a number of arguments from the common good that can be considered in such a rethinking.[33] These range from an acknowledgment of the primacy of parental responsibility for their children's education and the consequent necessity of respecting and supporting their freedom of choice to the affirmation of pluralism as opposed to governmental monopoly of education that lies at the heart of the issue.

In addition to these understandings of pluralism and personal autonomy of choice, a special note with regard to Catholic-Jewish understandings can be added. Surveys have shown that today's graduates of Catholic high schools are not only more positive toward Jews and Judaism than earlier generations of Catholics but also far more positive than the general population, which is to say graduates of public schools.

If one is serious about the full implementation of *Nostra Aetate* and other Church documents on Catholic-Jewish relations in this country, one has to acknowledge the key role that must be played by our schools in the process. Thus a reconsideration of this issue has the potential for greatly enhancing the common good of the nation, the education of children, and all of our efforts at interreligious amity as well.

The fourth area of reflection relates to a topic that I understand is also of ongoing interest in the discussions of the UAHC's own bioethics committee. Because I do not want to give any appearance of attempting to influence an internal Jewish discussion, I shall limit myself to an affirmation of the importance for our society of one such topic and as a mutual concern of the dialogue. This is the issue of euthanasia, which is quite distinct from the issue of termination of medical treatment. Here one is dealing with the active intervention by a medical professional, through lethal injection or other means, for the purpose of ending a human life. Laws as have been considered in various states raise these issues for Jews and Catholics, who have a traditional commitment to and involvement in healing professions and in hospitals and nursing homes.

Finally, I would raise, from our point of view as American Catholics, our quite natural concerns for the Christian minority in Israel and in the Territories. I do not do this from the perspective of making charges against the Israeli government, whose courage and commitment to peace, as I have said, I greatly admire. Rather, mine is a plea for greater understanding, empathy, and support for what is, for several reasons, a dwindling community witnessing to Christian faith in what we as Christians have for many centuries venerated as the Holy Land. The Palestinian Christian community is a minority within a minority and hence doubly vulnerable. This community does things and has sensitivities that the vastly larger communities surrounding it may find difficult to understand but which are quite coherent from its distinct and distinctly vulnerable point of view.

One such situation is the issue of the St. John's Hospice, now in the courts but still apparently unresolved. Because this situation directly involves religious symbols (e.g., the Orthodox Christian symbol covered over by the Jewish "settlers" in such conscious and deliberate fashion during Holy Week itself), it became and has remained a symbol of numerous perceived difficulties and interreligious sensitivities felt by the Christian minority. The statements of the UAHC and its leaders at the time of the takeover were commendable and are remembered by our bishops with gratitude.

This, I may say, emboldens me to ask for even more (perhaps a little bit of the celebrated *chutzpah* has begun to rub off on me through all these years of dialogue). That is, it would seem permissible within our dialogical relationship to continue asking our American Jewish colleagues to press further their Israeli Jewish colleagues for some action and resolution of this issue and for the greater sensitivity on related issues involving Christians. Again, I present this not as a matter of charges, "rights," politics, or even the macroissues of the Middle East peace process for whose success we all pray. Rather, it is a matter of sensitivity and doing perhaps a bit more than is owed in a given situation because that is the nature of a living relationship of two ancient peoples of faith in a world still broken. Together we need to begin to take the steps necessary to enable us better to work together toward the mending of the world.

NOTES

1. Rabbi Schindler's colleague Albert Vorspan takes a humorous look at the internal Jewish discussions surrounding the papal visit of 1987 in his *Start Worrying: Details to Follow* (New York: UAHC Press, 1991), pp. 24–28.

2. *The New Republic*, vol. L, p. 315.

3. Paul Blanshard, *American Freedom and Catholic Power* (Boston: Beacon Press, 1949), p. 4.

4. John J. Kane, *Catholic-Protestant Conflicts in America* (Chicago: Regnery, 1955), p. 4.

5. Ibid., p. 40.

6. Ibid.

7. R. A. Billington, *The Protestant Crusade* (New York: Rinehart, 1952), p. 148.

8. George Weigel, "Forgotten Treasures, Unexplored Problems," in the symposium on "American Catholic Social Thought," *U.S. Catholic Historian*, vol. 5, no. 2 (1986), pp. 235–239.

9. David J. O'Brien, "Social Teaching, Social Action, Social Gospel," *U.S. Catholic Historian*, p. 198.

10. R. Emmet Curran, S.J., "Confronting the Social Question: American Catholic Thought and the Socioeconomic Order in the Nineteenth Century," *U.S. Catholic Historian*, pp. 165–193.

11. Ibid., p. 199. For the texts of these and later relevant social and economic statements, see Hugh J. Nolan, *The National Pastorals of the U.S. Bishops*, 4 vols. (Washington, DC, 1983) and *Origins* (Washington, DC: Catholic News Service).

12. On the development and method of social policy in the United States Catholic community as influenced by papal social teaching from Leo XIII to Paul VI, see the essays by Monsignor Francis J. Lally; Archbishop J. Francis Stafford; Monsignor George G. Higgins; Rev. J. Bryan Hehir; and Rev. John T. Pawlikowski, O.S.M., in Eugene Fisher and Daniel Polish, eds., *The Formation of Social Policy in the Catholic and Jewish Traditions* (University of Notre Dame Press, 1980) and also those in its follow-up volume, *Liturgical Foundations of Social Policy in the Catholic and Jewish Traditions* (1983). These volumes, the result of formal dialogues between the Synagogue Council of America and the National Conference of Catholic Bishops, contain insightful essays by Jewish counterparts and remain valuable for Catholic-Jewish understanding.

13. Annette Daum and Eugene Fisher, eds., *The Challenge of Shalom for Catholics and Jews: A Dialogical Discussion Guide to the Catholic Bishops' Pastoral on Peace and War* (New York: UAHC/NCCB, 1985). For the ecumenical study, see Ronald White and Eugene Fisher, eds., *Partners in Peace and Education: Text and Documents of the Roman Catholic/Presbyterian-Reformed Consultation IV* (Grand Rapids, MI: Eerdmans, 1988).

14. There were, for example, very different viewpoints between Catholics and Jews with regard to the Spanish Civil War of the 1930s. And, as has been reflected in various studies, for example, the editorial positions of one diocesan paper, *The Brooklyn Tablet*, in that period and beyond, the controversy also spilled over into attitudes with regard to other foreign issues like "isolationism" and the question of a Jewish homeland. See Esther Yolles Feldblum, *The American Catholic Press and the Jewish State, 1917–1959* (New York: Ktav, 1977). Perhaps ironically, given the controversies spurred by American Jews and Catholics, the Franco regime, while Fascist, was not anti-Semitic and, indeed, was responsible for providing refuge for many Jews during World War II. See also Trudi Alexy, *The Mezuzah in the Madonna's Foot: Exploring 500 Years in the Paradoxical Relationship of Spain and the Jews* (New York: Simon & Schuster, 1993).

15. John Paul II, "To the Jewish Community of Australia," November 26, 1986, cited in E. Fisher and L. Klenicki, eds., *John Paul II on Jews and Judaism, 1979–1986* (Washington, DC: U.S. Catholic Conference/Anti-Defamation League of B'nai B'rith, 1987), p. 96.

16. Catholics have been invited to reflect on the significance of the "religious attachment" between the people Israel and the land of Israel in the *Declaration on Catholic-Jewish Relations* of the U.S. Catholic Bishops (November 20, 1975) and again in the Holy See's *Notes on the Correct Way to Present the Jews and Judaism in Preaching and Catechesis in the Roman Catholic Church* (Commission for Religious Relations with the Jews, June 24, 1985). It is in this context that the 1985 *Notes* comment: "The permanence of Israel (while so many ancient peoples have disappeared without trace) is a historic fact and a sign to be interpreted within God's design."

17. "Israeli/Palestinian Agreement," statement of Archbishop John R. Roach, chairman, International Policy Committee, U.S. Catholic Conference, September 10, 1993.

18. For the history, documents, and papers of the International Catholic-Jewish Liaison Committee, see its volume *Fifteen Years of Catholic-Jewish Dialogue, 1970–1985* (Rome: Lateran University/Vatican City State: Libreria Editrice Vaticana, 1988). On the American dialogue, see E. Fisher, J. Rudin, and M. Tanenbaum, eds., *Twenty Years of Jewish-Catholic Relations* (Mahwah, NJ: Paulist Press, 1986).

19. It should be noted that eleven volumes of such archival documents have already been published by the Holy See, covering the years 1939 to 1945, under the title *Actes et Documents du Saint Siège Relatifs à la Seconde Guerre Mondiale* (Vatican City State: Libreria Editrice Vaticana, 1965–1981). Catholic scholar John F. Morley has taken a critical look at the material in his *Vatican Diplomacy and the Jews during the Holocaust, 1939–1943* (New York: Ktav, 1980). As the English language editor of the series, Rev. Robert Graham, S.J., has pointed out, however, Morley did not include the last two volumes of the series, which came out after Morley had concluded his study for New York University.

20. For recent scholarship on Coughlin, see Mary Christine Athans, B.V.M., *The Coughlin-Fahey Connection: Father Charles E. Couglin, Father Denis Fahey, CSSp, and Religious Anti-Semitism in the United States, 1938–1954* (New York: Peter Lang, 1991).

21. National Catholic News Service, November 17, 1938.

22. Gershon Greenberg, "American Catholics during the Holocaust," in *Peace/Shalom after Atrocity*, Proceedings of the First Scholars' Conference on the Teaching of the Holocaust (Greensburg, PA: Seton Hill College, The National Catholic Center for Holocaust Education, April 1989), pp. 37–51.

23. *Victory and Peace: Statement Issued by the Archbishops and Bishops of the United States* (Washington, DC: National Catholic Welfare Conference, November 14, 1942), p. 4. Gerhart Riegner reassesses his own stance on the issues in his *The Efforts of the World Jewish Congress to Mobilize the Christian Churches against the Final Solution* (Jerusalem: World Jewish Congress, June 1982).

24. Cited in *P.M.*, May 25, 1943. For a brief survey of the literature on the Catholic church in the period, see Michael R. Marrus, *The Holocaust in History* (Hanover and London: University Press of New England for Brandeis University, 1987), pp. 179–183, and John T. Pawlikowski, O.S.M., "The Vatican and the Holocaust: Unresolved Issues," in M. Perry and F. Schweitzer, eds., *Jewish-Christian Encounters over the Centuries* (New York: Peter Lang, 1994), pp. 293–312. On the larger historical context, which is vital for understanding yet often missing in discussions of the Holocaust, see Anthony Rhodes, *The Vatican in the Age of the Dictators, 1922–1945* (New York: Holt, Rinehart & Winston, 1973). The difficulties faced by American Catholics and the National Catholic Welfare Conference in organizing to save fellow Catholics during World War II are narrated by Haim Genizi, "Catholic Hesitations and the Catholic Committee for Refugees," in his *American Apathy: The Plight of Christian Refugees from Nazism* (Ramat-Gan, Israel: Bar Ilan University, 1983), pp. 137–171.

25. Philip Friedman, *Their Brothers' Keepers* (New York: Crown, 1957), pp. 72ff.

26. Leon Wells, "The Righteous Gentiles," in *Holocaust Literature: A Handbook of Critical, Historical, and Literary Writings* (Westport, CT: Greenwood Press, 1993), p. 155.

27. Eugene Fisher, "Dreaming Together: Christians and Jews in the Twenty-First Century," *Thought* (New York: Fordham University Quarterly, vol. LXVII, no. 267, December 1992), p. 446.

28. For documents, commentary, and annotated bibliography of the dialogue, see Eugene Fisher and Leon Klenicki, *In Our Time: The Flowering of Jewish-Catholic Dialogue* (New York: Paulist Press, 1990); Eugene Fisher, *Faith without Prejudice: Rebuilding Christian Attitudes toward Jews and Judaism*, 2d ed. (New York: Crossroad, 1993); and D. Efroymson, E. Fisher, and L. Klenicki, eds., *Within Context: Essays on Jews and Judaism in the New Testament* (Collegeville, MN: Liturgical Press, 1993).

29. Fisher, "Dreaming Together," p. 447.

30. For interactive Jewish and Christian perspectives on that history, see the paired essays in Eugene Fisher, ed., *Interwoven Destinies: Jews and Christians through the Ages* (Mahwah, NJ: Paulist Press, Stimulus Books, 1993) and *Jewish Roots of Christian Liturgy* (Mahwah, NJ: Paulist Press, 1990).

31. *God's Mercy Endures Forever: Guidelines on the Presentation of Jews and Judaism in Catholic Preaching* (Washington, DC: National Conference of Catholic Bishops, 1988), publication no. 247-0.

32. The reader may recognize this final portion of the essay as being excerpted from my address delivered at the 1992 UAHC Biennial in Baltimore and reprinted in *Interreligious Currents*, Spring 1992 (New York: UAHC Department of Interreligious Affairs), pp. 2–3.

33. A recent editorial in *The Jewish Week* (December 2–8, 1994), p. 4, makes the case from a Jewish point of view that "it is time to reevaluate our...opposition to a voucher system. This is no longer an Orthodox issue."

In our search for allies, none of us requires, and *we* certainly do not look for, ideological congruence, for a full agreement on each and every issue facing our nation and the world, before we join forces with others. We Jews can, for example, disagree with the Roman Catholic bishops on abortion and birth control but still work with them full-heartedly on such burning issues as nuclear disarmament and economic justice. We can disagree with many of our Protestant colleagues on matters affecting the Middle East but still join them in the quest to achieve racial harmony and overcome world hunger.

Aye, these issues require the united response of the entire religious community, do they not? Consider our demeanor as a nation: Here we are, the wealthiest country on earth; yet millions of fellow Americans are living in debasing poverty, fully one-sixth of all children, nearly half of all African American children—and they have lost the faith that this is a society that gives a damn for them.

Here we are, with medical technology and savvy that brings the ailing to our hospitals from all over the world; yet fully one-third of our own people are without medical insurance, without the ability to receive care from the hospital and medical professionals of their choice.

Here we are, able to project military force to the farthest reaches of the globe; yet we are unable to safeguard our own city streets.

We are only the eleventh among the developed countries in per capita-giving of foreign aid—and apart from military aid, we are dead last. And then we look with pity and despair upon swollen bellies, shrunken limbs, hopeless poverty, and senseless violence—look with pity and despair rather than with a sense of deep personal responsibility and *teshuvah*, with soul-felt repentance.

The so-called political or economic matters are religious in their essence—and in their solution. The dichotomy between the "secular" and the "religious," between "activism" and "commandment" is diminishing to the point of irrelevance in our world. And we in the religious community should stand together at the forefront of the struggle to integrate politics and the spirit as we turn this century.

Rabbi Alexander M. Schindler
Christian-Jewish Dialogue
Chicago, Illinois
November 1990

CHRISTIAN-JEWISH RELATIONS IN AMERICA

JOAN BROWN CAMPBELL AND JAY T. ROCK

In the face of difficult issues, we have consistently been stimulated by Rabbi Alexander Schindler, whose thoughts and actions are rooted in a passionate and unapologetic religious commitment. We have come to depend on his leadership. Again and again he calls us to the kind of renewed engagement with the world that we seek to maintain in our own lives and to foster in our community.

In this, as in many things, we Christians and Jews are not so different. It seems that our churches and synagogues now are searching and having discomforting family struggles regarding what it is we are "called" to do. Most of us are willing to confess that we need guidance about how to be faithful to God in these times.

Rabbi Schindler's vision has provided light for us all. He has repeatedly called us to remember the past, to respond to the sufferings of the past, but to live in the present—in our own historical situation. In that spirit, we offer these reflections on the history of relationships between the Protestant and Orthodox churches and the Jewish community in the United States—on the importance of this history in shaping our partnerships today.

Historic Roots

A thorough history of Protestant-Jewish relations in this country would have to begin in the revolutionary or prerevolutionary period. It would trace the ways in which small Jewish communities worked together with much larger Christian communities to create the economic, social, and political institutions and arrangements of a new nation. Such a historical survey would focus less on the Christian-Jewish relationship itself than on the ways both communities have been weavers of the complex fabric of United States history and society.

Looking at our relationship in this broad historical light helps us understand ourselves and appreciate our roots among the many peoples that have a part in this society. In analyzing why we perceive each other as we do, we may find that how we supported or did not support each other at defining moments in our communal history still affects our expectations and assumptions—and thus our relations with each other.

In an insightful article "The Other and the Almost the Same," in *The New Yorker* magazine, Paul Berman shows how the history of such moments of perceived presence and absence as partners in each other's struggles contributes to the particularly tense current situation in African American-Jewish relations. The strong connections between liberal Jews and blacks during the civil rights struggles from the 1910s and 1920s (with the involvement of some Jews in the work of the NAACP) through the 1960s had as one of their roots the perception of shared histories that linked the communities in kinship and solidarity. As is painfully evident in the communities' responses to Louis Farrakhan and the Nation of Islam, this perception has broken down. Engagement with and against each other in the complexities of concrete interactions has fostered both "an acknowledgment of similarity and ...an acknowledgment that similarity contains a difference." This has led to the kind of highly charged relationship between people who are "almost the same." Berman notes: "The American Jews and the African Americans are who they are because of long centuries of a past that can be put to different uses but cannot be overcome. It was the past that made the blacks and the Jews almost the same, and the past has the singular inconvenience of never going away."

Berman's article helps us see that it is important to reflect on the long period in American history in which many and varied alliances existed, prior to the current period of self-conscious and organized Jewish-Christian relations. He writes: "During slavery times—when Jews counted for half of 1 percent, or even less, of the American population—a small number of Jews participated in the slave trade, along with vastly larger numbers of Christians and Muslims; and a small number of other Jews participated in the abolitionist movement."[1] The historical record, then, checks those who might want to glorify or demonize our relationship.

Seen in this light, Protestant-Jewish relations in the United States are both more complex and less set apart from the web of social relations than they are often presented to be. In fact, we are talking about relations between Jews and Anglo-Saxon Protestants, Jews and German Protestants, Jews and African American Protestants, and also about Jews and American Orthodox Christians of Russia and Eastern Europe, Greece, the Middle East, etc. Each of these relationships begins at a different period in American history, and each has distinctive content and dynamics; the stories are full of nuance and complexity.

Our understanding changes when we know, for instance, that Jews and African American Christians took important roles in the westward expansion of the United States or that crypto-Jews were among the earliest Spanish settlers who came into what is now New Mexico. More importantly, how we view each other and the possibilities for future cooperation is intimately connected to our understanding of the conditions through which our communities became players on the stage of American history, as well as to our ability to talk openly about the shifting patterns and fortunes of our involvements. Thus, it is impossible to understand Jewish-Christian relations without frequent recourse to the historical record.

From Mission to Sisterhood

Amidst this rich history, it is notable that American Jewish-Protestant relations in and of themselves had little significance until very late in the nineteenth and early twentieth centuries. The changes that led us to build self-conscious relationships were long in coming and require more study.

The slow change in the attitude of the churches toward interfaith relations is reflected in their thinking about mission. In a recent talk, Hans Ucko, secretary for Christian-Jewish Relations, World Council of Churches, noted that the missionary conference of 1910 in Edinburgh left "little room for any other understanding of mission than one of frontier mission, of reaching the unreached and having the unreached name the name." Again in the mission conferences of Jerusalem (1928) and Tambaram (1938), one heard "this voice of nothing but Christ: 'Christ is our motive and Christ is our end. We must give nothing else and we can give nothing more.'" (Jerusalem) Even after World War II, at the founding of the World Council of Churches in Amsterdam, the strong denunciation of anti-Semitism as "sin against God and man" was placed in the context of a discussion of "Barriers to Overcome" to successful mission, including mission to Jews! American Protestants were involved in these events and shared in this kind of thinking.

On the other hand, a self-conscious desire to build bridges between faiths motivated Protestants and some Jews to organize and take active roles in the World's Parliament of Religions of 1893. In opening remarks, its chairman, John Henry Barrows, welcomed participants to "the first school of comparative religions, wherein devout men of all faiths may speak for themselves without hindrance, without criticism, and without compromise and tell what they believe and why they believe it."

To find the roots of this new relational impulse would require a detailed inquiry into the cultural history of this period.[2] The impulse must have derived at least in part from the academy and from the maturity in the United States of several schools of universalist thought. It was probably nourished as well by the more aggressively democratic impulses of the new industrialism, fueled by its demonstrated ability to link advances in engineering with various old and new schemes of Manifest Destiny. The mass immigrations of European peoples, including Jews, in the later decades of the nineteenth century brought many immigrants who arrived with great enthusiasm for the idea of a society based on individual rights and equality, invigorating varying commitments to liberalism and universalism in our society.

The World's Parliament of Religions in 1893 included only one Muslim representative and no Native Americans. Diana Eck notes: "Native American religiousness was clearly not seen as a religious perspective at all.... On September 16, 1893, while the parliament met, six and one-half million acres of Cherokee, Pawnee, and Tonkawa reservation lands were opened for homesteader settlement, and 50,000 settlers rushed to claim homestead lands on that day alone. Nothing of the trampling of native peoples was mentioned in the parliament." Only two African Americans addressed the parliament. There were few women and few representatives of Asian religions. This was an event involving Christians, primarily white Protestants, and Jews like Chicago's Rabbi Emil Hirsch.[3] In Eck's analysis:

> The Parliament was dominated, on the whole, by Christian participants with a universalist fulfillment theology—the view that Christianity represents the flower and fulfillment of the religious hopes and aspirations present in other faiths.... As for the relation of Christianity to other faiths, the Parliament was very cautious.... Despite the dominance of Christian discourse [however], the spirit of the Parliament was really something quite new.[4]

Taking shape out of this same swirl of cultural and historical forces, other manifestations of this new spirit of building intentional interfaith relations came into being around the United States. Notable among these were efforts to deal with the problems and prejudices encountered by European immigrants to the United States; to address the increase of social discrimination against Jews, Catholics, and others after the 1880s; and to respond to the growing problems of our urban centers. This period saw the creation of church organizations to assist in the resettlement of immigrants, as well as the organization of the Hebrew Immigrant Aid Society. Volunteers of America was founded in 1896. Christians in this period undertook a wide array of new ministries in our cities, and Jews began such communal service organizations as the American Jewish Committee, the Anti-Defamation League, and the American Jewish Congress. Cooperation in countering prejudice and promoting tolerance eventually gave rise, in the 1920s, to the idea of

Brotherhood Week and to the first intentionally Christian-Jewish organization in the United States, the National Conference of Christians and Jews, founded in 1928.

Twenty years later, following World War II, the Protestant churches of the United States were working together through Church World Service to provide material relief to the people of Europe and to resettle refugees, including Jews. In 1938, the Federal Council of Churches had attempted to call public attention to what was already happening to Jews in Germany. In 1950, when the National Council of Churches was brought into being out of these and other cooperating Christian institutions (with twenty-nine original member churches), it was involved in Christian-Jewish relations of this most practical sort.

But it was not until some years after the war that the ecumenical movement, motivated as it still was by a kind of evangelical fervor, became aware of its relationships with Jews and other non-Christian communities and began to move toward programmatic and theological relations.

Intentional Dialogue

In November 1990, the twelfth National Workshop on Christian-Jewish Relations was held in Chicago. Over 1,000 people attended this gathering, indicative of the extent to which Christian-Jewish relations had become institutionalized in America since 1950. The Office on Christian-Jewish Relations of the National Council of Churches was again one of the national sponsors of this Workshop.

Leontine Kelly, an African American woman and United Methodist bishop, told a story that spoke powerfully of the depth and roots of our relationship: When as a youngster she and her family had moved into the parsonage of her father's church in Cincinnati, they discovered that it was connected by a tunnel to a building on the campus of the Hebrew Union College. A Christian-Jewish connection had kept open the underground railway!

This story bridges the considerable gap of time and context between the life-and-death efforts of escaping slaves and abolitionists helping them and the hotel ballroom full of contemporary Christians and Jews. On one hand, it is a moving reminder of what we can do together and of the shared history out of which the intentional Christian-Jewish dialogue and relationship of the last thirty years has emerged. It reminds us that this relationship is rooted in our American soil and in the shared struggle for justice. On the other hand, Bishop Kelly's story urges us to look at the present stage of our relationship with an ever-critical eye and to ask continually whether we are doing together what we can and should.

For many in our churches, it has been the encounter with the enormity of the Holocaust and advances in theological reflection of the sort represented by the Second Vatican Council that have led to significant engagement with the Jewish community. For many others, such intentional relationship flows out of the civil rights and antiwar struggles of the 1950s, sixties, and early seventies and the significant alliances and coalitions of that time. A number of leaders of the National Council of the Churches of Christ (NCCC) and Jewish colleagues marched and prayed together in the South and elsewhere; some were involved in the activities of organizations like Clergy and Laity Concerned.

It was not until 1973, however, that the National Council of Churches obtained assistance from the Lilly Endowment and opened an Office on Christian-Jewish Relations. (In that same year, the first National Workshop on Christian-Jewish Relations was held in Dayton, Ohio.) The Rev. William Weiler, an Episcopal priest, provided staff assistance and, with an Advisory Committee on Christian-Jewish Relations, began to work with Jewish colleagues to build relationships and create educational opportunities and resources to nurture Christian understanding of Jews and Judaism. Twenty-one years later, the Christian-Jewish Relations Committee is part of the Council's Working Group on Interfaith Relations. It provides educational resources, consultation to local or regional groups in building Christian-Jewish relationships, and special attention to issues of Christian theology and practice, rooted in regular consultation and dialogue with national Jewish organizations, including particularly close ties with the Union of American Hebrew Congregations.

In the 1970s and eighties, the politics of the Middle East often dominated the discussions in Christian-Jewish meetings. This was particularly true in the years surrounding the Council's adoption of its Middle East Policy Statement in 1980. Careful attention was given to the voices of Israeli and American Jews, among others, through the long process of study and development that resulted in this policy statement. The statement's clear support for the Jewish state was often overlooked in the light of its position that the PLO had to be a partner in the self-determination process of the Palestinian people. Today it seems fair to say that one result of the frank discussions and disagreements over public stances on Israel and the Palestinians is that our Christian-Jewish relationship has moved beyond pretense and superficiality to a mutual exchange rooted in honesty and self-disclosure.

In the 1980s, two significant and related developments contributed to this new stage of Christian-Jewish understanding. The first found expression in the churches' attempts to help its members understand and commemorate the Holocaust. A number of churches affiliated with the National Council of the Churches of Christ have added Yom Hashoah to their liturgical calendars. The NCCC Committee on Christian-Jewish Relations, under the direction of the Rev. David Simpson, worked closely with the Department of Interreligious Affairs of the Union of American Hebrew Congregations, the Southern Baptist Convention's Department of Interfaith Witness, and the National Conference of Catholic Bishops' Secretariat for Catholic-Jewish Relations to create a packet of educational and liturgical resources for Christians to use in commemorating the Holocaust. (These have now been revised and expanded in the booklet *Christians and the Holocaust*.) Joint commemorative services and study of the Holocaust have further deepened Jewish-Christian relations.

The second development is the reassessment of Christian self-understanding vis-à-vis the Jewish people. Sharing in the spirit of the Second Vatican Council's *Nostra Aetate*, and the guidelines and notes that clarify its significance, a number of the NCCC-member churches have addressed the anti-Judaism that can be found in much of traditional Christian theology. The United Church of Christ, the Presbyterian Church (U.S.A.), the Episcopal Church, the Christian Church (Disciples of Christ), and the United Methodist Church have all, in various ways, made this sort of theological reevaluation available to their members. The Evangelical Lutheran Church in America has also issued a remarkable declaration on the anti-Semitism of Luther. These churches have tried to articulate the uniqueness of God's revelation in Jesus Christ while also clearly affirming God's authentic revelation to and continuing covenant with the Jewish people.

Because of this kind of work within the Christian community, and because of the intentional programmatic relationships that have led to the creation of resources like the UAHC-NCCC's *Thinking and Working Together: Study and Action Suggestions for Jewish and Christian Congregations*, we live in a new era of Christian-Jewish relationship in the United States. We are freer to learn about each other in depth, as well as work together for social justice; correct misperceptions and incorrect teaching and preaching; and develop relationships that include rather than exclude who we are as religious persons.

Healing and Shared Commitments

A number of concerns and possibilities mark this new stage of our relationship. One important need is to include the whole of our communities in our dialogue. In contrast to the fifties and sixties, Christian-Jewish relations today do not often include African American Christians. Other groups within the Christian family, as well as in the Jewish family, do not yet participate in this relationship. In the dialogue, we will need to deal with the racism as well as the anti-Semitism. Moreover, we will need to do more than invite into the dialogue those who are not now participating; we will need to go out into our communities, to listen to the concerns that our relationship needs to include, and to engage those not yet involved in consideration of the issues and possibilities of our relationship.

Second, it is now more than ever possible and necessary to share the *life* in our traditions. We need to let each other know how Christianity and Judaism affect our daily lives. Why do we continue to be Jews or Christians? What is the joy and vitality that our traditions give us? If we can share with each other the meaning of our commitments and actions, if we can invite each other to witness the sources of our own religious growth, we will have relationship that includes the emotional and convictional core of who each of us is. We need to cultivate this depth of connection in the areas of theology, spirituality, and action.

Third, it is very important that we continue to attend to the healing and repair that remains to be done between our communities. Unavoidably, Rabbi Schindler's idea of Judaism again becoming a "missionary faith" calls to our minds the exclusivist zeal and real harm that have been visited on Jews and other peoples by Christian missionaries in many times and places. We must continue addressing the damage that has been done and attend to the ongoing healing process in which we are now engaged. We Christians will need to continue moving beyond the stage of statements and implement a positive and accurate understanding of Jews and Judaism in our educational and liturgical lives and in our theology. We will need to continue strengthening our support for the peace process in the Middle East. And *together* we will have to confront issues that require a healing approach among our people today: the possibilities and limits for sharing in prayer, as well as the difficult issue of interfaith marriage. Our community just by virtue of its size is involved in what Rabbi Schindler terms the Jews' "fear of self-extinction." But we wholeheartedly agree with his call that we do not "respond to the suffering of the past by living in the past." We have no choice but to attend to healing in the present.

Finally, might we not consider together what are our separate missions as Jews and as Christians, as well as what is our joint mission? As religious persons in this society, do we have a mutual witness to give? Are there not religious and moral insights that we can contribute and articulate out of our traditions for United States social renewal? How do we understand and what can we contribute to our society's struggle to come to terms with religious and cultural pluralism? In all of these we are convinced we can do much together.

We desperately need, as Rabbi Schindler reminds us, to "wedge open the doors of the world's conscience." We welcome the partnership we can have in the work of redemption.

Blacks and Jews are kindred in spirit. Our commonalities exceed our differences by far, especially when it comes to our aspirations.

We share a vision of a just, generous, and open society. We both recoil against the stench of bigotry. We both wish to see government help to solve social inequity. We vote more alike than do any other racial or religious groups....Ours are the two American peoples who are committed to the idea of change in our country, who see the American dream not in the valley of the status quo but on Martin Luther King's mountaintop.

Only our common enemies, the enemies of freedom, rejoice when we square off against each other. Too much was lost during the era of our face-off! No longer do we stand on the ground of a socially progressive era. Indeed the ground on which we have stood in the past is crumbling beneath us.

Six years of trickle-down Reaganomics have deepened the sense of danger and despair in America. Six years of assault on social welfare programs have raised the poverty indices of the black urban underclass to unpardonable levels. Six years of an adversarial justice department, of relentless federal attacks on municipal affirmative action have poisoned the public consciousness against blacks and other minorities. Far-right demagoguery has infected the wounded places of America with racism and anti-Semitism both.

And we Jews and we blacks stand frozen in a wrestler's clench when we should be surging forward like two running backs on the same team. Aye, we Jews and we blacks sit like a couple of Jonahs in the belly of a whale when we should be doing God's work together, calling great cities—nay, a great nation—to repentance.

Rabbi Alexander M. Schindler
Centennial Address
Central State University
February 3, 1987

BLACKS, JEWS, AND FARRAKHAN

JULIUS LESTER

It is troubling that so many people listen to Louis Farrakhan. If no one listened, his would become a voice in the wilderness. But listening transforms monologue into relationship. Farrakhan's audiences are predominantly black, but blacks are not his only listeners. Jews listen, too, and with an almost compulsive fascination, making it unclear which group has the more intimate relationship with Farrakhan.

Relationship offers confirmation of identity and affirmation of self. Farrakhan confirms and affirms identity for both blacks *and* Jews. Because he does, blacks and Jews are mesmerized by what are, in essence, nothing more than simplistic nationalist ravings, angry harangues, crude anti-Semitic diatribes, and historical ignorance. (I use Farrakhan to refer not only to the individual but also to the other purveyors of black anti-Semitism.)

Before exploring what Farrakhan confirms for blacks and Jews, two illusory truths must be addressed: The black anti-Semitism of the past two decades is new and blacks and Jews share a common oppression.

The black-Jewish coalition of the civil rights era is put forward as the shining paradigm of what was and what could be again. As significant as that alliance was, it never represented the *only* relationship between blacks and Jews. The black-Jewish coalition was between the elites of both peoples; at the grass roots level, however, there was never an alliance. Black anti-Semitism has deep roots as shown in the following tale from Zora Neale Hurston's introduction to her classic collection *Mules and Men*.

> When God created people, He didn't give them their souls. God knew that the soul was very powerful and He wanted to wait until people were strong enough to hold their souls in their

bodies. God kept the soul beneath the skirts of His garment and, one day, a white man walked past God and, just as he did, a little breeze lifted up the hem of God's skirt and some light from the soul streamed out and it was so bright that the white man got scared and ran away. Next day, a black man was walking past God and he got curious about the soul. So he went over and tried to peek under God's skirt and the light and warmth from the soul was so powerful that it knocked him over and he ran away. A few days later, along came the Jew. He was walking past God when a big wind came and lifted up God's skirt. The Jew saw the soul gleaming brightly and streaming with lights of many colors and he ran and grabbed the soul. Well, the soul was so powerful that it knocked the Jew down and rolled him over and over on the ground. But the Jew wouldn't let go. That soul knocked him up in the sky and back down on the ground, but the Jew still wouldn't let go. The Jew hugged the soul so hard that it broke into a lot of little pieces. The white man and the black man came and picked up the little pieces and put them inside and that's how man got his soul. But, one of these days, God is going to make the Jew divide that soul up fair so everybody gets equal amounts.[1]

The tale is the black folk response to the concept of Jews as the Chosen People. Just as Christians and Muslims asserted their election to supplant Jews and be God's *new* chosen people, so Louis Farrakhan states:

This I want the Jews to know, and we want the world to know: ...they are not the chosen people of God....

The Holy Koran charges the Jews with taking the message of God and altering that message and giving the people a book written by their own hands, saying that the book is from God....The Jews...fed a corrupted light through this book and were the father of false religions and false religious practices. They cannot be considered the friend of God, doing such evil.

I am not anti-Jew. I am pro-truth, but, in this serious hour, the truth must be told so that the true people of God may come up into the view of the entire world. These that have stolen our identity, these that have dressed themselves up in our garments must be defrocked today that the world may see who are the true and chosen people of Almighty God.[2]

Farrakhan's agenda is not only political; it is theological (but questions of identity always are). That is why statements condemning Farrakhan have not only been ineffective but have increased his credibility among blacks.

Moral appeals are effective only when speaker and listener belong to the same "moral community." (My use of this phrase is taken from Professor Laurence Thomas's important new book, *Vessels of Evil: American Slavery and the Holocaust.*) Thomas observes that "the moral expectations...people have of both themselves and others...are generally tied to the consensus of the moral community in which they live and with which they identify."[3]

The black-Jewish coalition of the civil rights era succeeded because blacks and Jews shared a vision of a moral community where racial integration and equal opportunity were the agreed-on values and goals. Blacks and Jews no longer reside in the same moral universe, and, especially since *Roe* v. *Wade*, the nation itself has ceased to be a cohesive moral entity. The ethnic wars of the Balkans are a paradigm for our time. Black-Jewish conflicts are mesmerizing because they are not so much about blacks and Jews as they are about struggles between radically different moral communities for possession of God's soul.

At one time it was thought that blacks and Jews were denizens of the same moral community, allies and compatriots in the land of oppression. In her seminal work *In the Almost Promised Land: American Jews and Blacks, 1915–1935*, Professor Hasia Diner found striking illustrations of the Jewish identification with blacks in the Jewish press.

> The situation of the Negroes in America is very comparable to the situation of the Jews...in Russia. The Negro diaspora, the special laws, the decrees, the pogroms...the Negro complaints, the Negro hopes are very similar to those we Jews...lived through.[4]

Jews saw themselves specially suited to be advocates for blacks. "Many of us were oppressed in Old Russia as were the Negroes in free America. We can understand them better and, therefore, we sound their appeal wide and quickly."[5]

It is remarkable that Jews did not automatically opt for assimilation in the face of withering anti-Semitism from the dominant society but chose instead to empathize with and act on behalf of the oppressed. The integrity of Jewish involvement in the civil rights movement should not be questioned or denied. That the motivation for that involvement was not as pure as some today would like to think does not mean it was Machiavellian, either. The motivations were complex, combining genuine empathy and self-interest, which also, however, characterized the motivations of the blacks in the alliance.

Jews felt a "real bitterness" about anti-Semitism, Diner writes, but were "afraid to vent the full extent of their anxiety" directly. They did so "through the problems of blacks." Jews also saw themselves as "cultural bridges between the white and black worlds because they understood both." As whites, they could move more easily in the wider society, but, as members of an oppressed group, they understood blacks. "Because of that empathy, *the black experience had become extremely personal to Jews.*" [emphasis added][6]

An essential element of secular and liberal religious Jewish identity became bound to blacks. Jews had taken blacks into the nexus of their emotions, never dreaming that blacks had not done the same.

> "Being good" to blacks, dealing sensitively and sympathetically with them, was perceived as a natural outgrowth of the Jewish tradition, and as ethnic group leaders they [Jews] had a real stake in the preservation of that tradition. They believed that their efforts and concerns for American blacks set Jews apart from other Americans, apart from Christians. This became, in effect, *the American version of the "Chosen People" notion, the American adaption of the message from Mount Sinai.* [emphasis added][7]

Ironically, for many Jews, Farrakhan's anti-Semitism provides a sense of Jewish identity that had been missing. When Farrakhan comes to a campus, membership increases in Jewish student groups. He has caused more Jews to embrace their birthright than has any rabbi.

For blacks, anti-Semitism expresses a deep resentment at the Jewish presumption of shared oppression. What was true to some extent in the early decades of this century is not true at the century's close. Today blacks see Jews as white because, in a white society, white skin is an advantage, even if you're a Jew.

But Jewish success cannot be attributed only to skin color—or education and hard work—as Farrakhan astutely pointed out in a speech at California State University at Northridge:

> ...success is not a mystery; success is not by chance....When you find a synagogue, next to it you find a school. What is going on in there?...They're teaching their people from the tradition. The school is teaching them the history of themselves and their culture so that no matter where Jews go, they remain intact. Jews know who they are, they know their origin in the world, they know their history. But the black has been deprived of such knowledge....[8]

The black-Jewish alliance was doomed to implode because the elements of shared oppression were never as great as the differences. No difference is more profound than Jewish certainty about the Jew's place in history and before God. Regardless of how an individual Jew may feel about being a Jew, the solidity of Jewish history, culture, and religion are incontrovertible. It is the very absence of confidence in the solidity of life itself that marks the gulf between blacks and Jews.

Laurence Thomas expands on Orlando Patterson's concept of "natal alienation." This is the condition that results when "the social practices" of a society "forcibly prevent" members of an ethnic group "from fully participating in and thus having a secure knowledge of their historical-cultural traditions," as well as denying them "full membership in the society." The alienation is total because the group has "neither equality nor their historical-cultural traditions."[9]

Blacks of every economic class and educational level respond to Farrakhan because he makes visible the natal alienation all blacks know.

> What is the problem? The problem is the fear on the part of those in power of the rise of black men and women to the destiny that

Almighty God has called us to....Today in America, the black male is under siege. Today in America, because of hate, not taught by Farrakhan, but *hate that has been bred into black men and women for self and for their own kind and for their origins in the world. We have been made to hate ourselves, our color, our hair, our features, our origins. So that to destroy one another is to destroy what we hate. So that today black young men are the No. 1 destroyers of self....* [emphasis in original]

Now these black people that are so disrespected by the world and so disrespectful of self have a divine destiny. You're a wonderful people, destroyed, but, even in your destruction, there is a beauty that emanates from you that makes you like the salt of the earth....*You are the only people that don't have a native language that ties you to Africa and your original roots—you ain'ts got it. Why? How did you lose your tongue? You lost your tongue because you lost your mother. Mother gone, father gone, a motherless child sees what? A hard time. This is what the slave master did. See, what they want to show is* Schindler's List. *I ain't got no problem with that; I have no problem with that....You don't have nobody to tell your story. So don't get angry because* Schindler's List *is out there. Nobody wants to talk about what happened to black people. And because I said that the holocaust of black people was 100 times worse than the holocaust of Jews, they were angry with me for even comparing this....* [emphasis in original][10]

Thomas points out that people who suffer from natal alienation are "without a narrative" or "set of narratives that defines values and positive goals and fixes points of historical significance and ennobling rituals that cannot be readily appropriated...the narratives of a people define their conception of the good."[11] In other words, the narratives of a people establish the foundations and parameters for their moral community.

Much of black anti-Semitism is the expression of envy of the Jewish narrative and the painful longing by blacks for a healing narrative of their own.

Professor Gerald Early, chairman of the Department of African and Afro-American Studies at Washington University, wrote of a trip he took to Israel with a group of blacks. After visiting Yad Vashem, the black delegation wondered why blacks had not done more to enshrine the memory of slavery as Jews had the Holocaust, why blacks lacked museums devoted to their history, why blacks were not as tightly organized as Jews seemed to be. Early answers: "While in Israel I learned this about the black American mind: that *blacks are in awe and jealous of the enormous achievements of Jews* and, as we see it, their privileges; and *we feel inferior to them.*" [emphasis added][12]

Neither alliance nor dialogue is possible when one group feels inferior to and shamed by the other, when one group is driven with self-hatred and perceives itself as abandoned by God, if not wholly rejected, while the other knows the pride of accomplishment and has a narrative that tells them they are God's Chosen.

Laurence Thomas argues that the depth of black natal alienation is demonstrated by the black acceptance of Christianity because "the acceptance of the religious traditions of one's oppressor [is] the most telling sign of natal alienation possible."[13]

Minister Farrakhan speaks to natal alienation by creating narratives that bestow an African-American tradition in history and an African-American identity before God. Part of that narrative is described by C. Eric Lincoln in *The Black Muslims in America*:

> The true believer who becomes a Muslim casts off at last his old self and takes on a new identity. He changes his name, his religion, his homeland, his moral and cultural values, his very purpose in living. He is no longer a Negro....Now he is a Black Man—divine, ruler of the universe, different in degree only from Allah himself....His new life is not an easy one: It demands unquestioning faith, unrelenting self-mastery, *unremitting hatred.* [emphasis added][14]

Farrakhan's other narrative strategy is devaluation of Jews, which is not mutually exclusive from the one Lincoln describes. If one lacks a narrative that gives a definition of the good, a narrative that, at least, gives a definition of the evil is preferable to no narrative at all.

The Jewish sense of moral community wants blacks to condemn and reject Farrakhan for his anti-Semitism. But the black sense of moral community, particularly among the young, needs the moral autonomy that comes when a community chooses its own leader. The power to choose one's own leader is a greater moral imperative for blacks than is repudiating anti-Semitism. To be in possession of one's identity means to have the power to make one's own choices, even wrong and despicable ones.

That so many blacks listen and respond to Farrakhan indicates a frightening nihilism rampant in black America. Farrakhan fills the void with a narrative of hateful anti-Semitism, historical lies, and appeals to black superiority. Only a people desperate to the point of disintegration could take Farrakhan seriously. If blacks were to pause, they would realize that their active and passive support of Farrakhan creates the climate and gives permission for whites to be as publicly hateful of blacks as Farrakhan is of Jews. The black infatuation with anti-Semitism can only result in a more virile antiblack racism.

But the black-Jewish conflict is more than a turf war between two minorities. Blacks and Jews are merely acting out the most serious moral crisis in the nation's history, a crisis in which the nation finds itself without a moral community and with a weakened narrative.

For all the changes wrought during the sixties, none is so much with us as the loss of a sense of moral community. In different ways, the assassinations of John Kennedy, Malcolm X, Robert Kennedy, and, most especially, Martin Luther King, Jr., killed the national faith that the good would always prevail. It would not be too much to argue that something of the good in ourselves died when those men were murdered. If the consequence of goodness is assassination, why would anyone, black or white, want to do ever again what was right and what was good?

The sense of belonging to a moral community was further eroded by our loss of faith in the office of the American presidency. Lyndon Johnson lied about United States involvement in Vietnam and had to leave office; Richard Nixon tried to cover up a burglary, lied to the American people, and left office rather than risk impeachment. The office of the presidency lost its moral authority—and none of the succeeding holders of the office was able to restore it—and such matters as Irangate undermined it further.

Moral authority and a sense of a moral community have been replaced by a politico-religious fundamentalism that cuts across racial, class, and religious boundaries. Pat Robertson, Jerry Falwell, the ultra-Orthodox rabbinate, and Louis Farrakhan have much in common because each sees the world as an Armaggedon with the Chosen (themselves and God) on one side and the Rejected (everyone who is not with them) on the other. Each offers a narrative of fear and exclusivity posturing as religious righteousness.

Since the day blacks arrived involuntarily on these shores, they have confronted the question Where do we fit? That is now the question facing the nation. Where do any of us fit anymore? What is our moral community and what is the good?

Farrakhan presents one set of answers, and Jewish attacks on him are not only ineffective but counterproductive. It is not Farrakhan's speech that should be silenced; rather, we—blacks, Jews, and whites—must be given something else to listen to, namely, a narrative that gives us all an image of the good, the true, and the beautiful, an image in which we can see ourselves as belonging not only to the good but to one another, too.

What might that narrative be? Perhaps it is one some blacks and some Jews and others tried to create in the sixties, a narrative that saw as the good not race but community, the "beloved community," as it was called then. It was a vision of a society where the needs of individualism would be balanced by the needs of community, and community was not only those of my race or religion or region but those who shared an inclusive vision of humanity that extended beyond the immediacy of one's personal issues, that eschewed the elevation of one's group as the apotheosis of humanity.

Farrakhan offers an ugly and hateful vision. It is no longer sufficient to express our moral disapproval of him and that vision. It is time we offered an alternative vision. If we do not, we accede moral authority to those who in their self-hatred hate us all.

NOTES

1. Zora Neale Hurston, *Mules and Men* (New York: Harper & Row, 1970), pp. 19–20.

2. *The New York Times,* June 29, 1984.

3. Laurence Thomas, *Vessels of Evil: American Slavery and the Holocaust* (Philadelphia: Temple University Press, 1993), p. 71.

4. Hasia Diner, *In the Almost Promised Land: American Jews and Blacks, 1915–1935*

(Westport, CT: Greenwood Press, 1977), p. 76, quoting the Yiddish *Forward*, July 28, 1917.

5. Ibid., p. 71, quoting the Yiddish *Forward*, June 4, 1930.

6. Ibid., p. 113.

7. Ibid., p. 238.

8. *Boston Jewish Times*, November 12, 1993.

9. Thomas, *Vessels of Evil*, p. 150.

10. *Boston Globe*, March 13, 1994.

11. Thomas, *Vessels of Evil*, p. 156.

12. *St. Louis Post-Dispatch*, July 25, 1993.

13. Thomas, *Vessels of Evil*, p. 159.

14. C. Eric Lincoln, *The Black Muslims in America* (Grand Rapids, MI: William B. Eerdmans Publishing Co., 1994).

The author wishes to thank David Kanell of Lyndon State College, Lyndonville, Vermont, for his research assistance.

There is a striking parallel between the centrifugal forces of ethnic nationalism fraying the Soviet Union and the current climate of racial and ethnic assertiveness disuniting our own society. Moscow and Crown Heights may be oceans apart, but the same ill vapors pollute the atmosphere.

To be sure, none of the American states is likely to secede from the United States of America, but we do face the threat of a multiculturalism run amok, of the understandable quest for recognition perverted by the less admirable quest for power. A nation is enriched when groupings of divergent backgrounds seek to preserve their distinctive heritage and identity, when numerous threads of languages and cultures are interwoven to form one tapestry. But when these groupings confound culture with politics and identity with power, the fabric of society begins to unravel.

In his new book *The Disuniting of America*, historian Arthur Schlesinger, Jr., bemoans the splintering of a once homogeneous America into a host of heterogeneous enclaves competing for power, each exalting its own identity while demonizing others. He asks the crucial questions: "The national ideal had once been E pluribus unum. Are we now to belittle unum and glorify pluribus? Will the center hold? Or will the melting pot yield to the Tower of Babel?"

This, alas, is what is happening in our land. The public classroom has become a combat zone for competing interests battling over multiculturalism. On campus, racial and ethnic isolation intensifies and is given the garb of academic respectability by the pseudoscientific rantings of a Michael Levin and a Leonard Jeffreys. In the inner city, the Martin Luther Kings and Bayard Rustins have been succeeded by the Farrakhans and Maddoxes; builders of bridges are being displaced by those who construct barricades and bunkers.

Soon we will not be able to talk to one another at all. Was not this the ultimate causative factor of Crown Heights...disparate communities unwilling, unable to communicate with one another? And if the silence continues and voices of responsibility are not raised, the reviling chants of Brooklyn will be heard all over this land, and more blood will be spilled.

Rabbi Alexander M. Schindler
"Dear Reader"
Reform Judaism
Winter 1991

AMERICAN PLURALISM AND JEWISH INTERESTS

LEONARD FEIN

Jewish insiders are troubled. They're worried by declining Jewish numbers, by a fiscal crisis that threatens Jewish agencies and institutions, by an apparent resurgence of anti-Semitism, by Israel's failure to live up to its mythic expectations. Jewish outsiders, by way of contrast, are bored. They're bored by the community's pre-occupation with survival (to what end?); they're bored by all the talk about Jewish compassion (where's the evidence?); they're bored and alienated by the gap between the thundering Jewish past and the petty Jewish present.

Neither side is getting it right, not about its own condition, not in its perceptions of the other.

For the insiders, this year's crop of crisis is merely a surrogate for a brooding underlying problem they are loathe to name and often incompetent to confront—a growing recognition of Jewish aimlessness, a loss of purchase on the future, a sense that the formulas that have worked more or less effectively until now are tired, that yesterday's rhetoric bears little relationship to today's reality.

You don't have to be Jewish to be demoralized these days. Just yesterday, the curtain was raised on a sweet new world, old walls—literal and figurative—suddenly tumbling down. Eastern Europe, Nicaragua, South Africa, and more—all the sore and ugly spots healing overnight. Or so, for a moment, it seemed. And now it turns out that it was just a tease, less the beginning of a successful new play starring Havel, Mandela, et al., more a tantalizing peekaboo. We did just fine with the "out with the old" part, but we're still inept with the "in with the new." (It remains to be seen how far-reaching the change in Israel's relationship with its Arab neighbors in general and its Palestinian neighbors in particular will be and also how deftly we will respond.)

And, meanwhile, here at home, the slide continues, and the gloom spreads. We blame the president, the Congress, the citizens, Japan, whomever; the problem is not who's to blame but whether anyone knows what to do. The schools, the hospitals, the highways and bridges—all part of a new American roulette in which there's a bullet in every chamber, and each day we wait to learn where the gun is pointing when fate pulls the trigger. All that, plus the sham, the hype, the lies. A new administration causes a brief surge of hope, and the hope may yet prove warranted. But, for the time being, it is hope against hope. The American house is a shambles.

No, you don't have to be Jewish to be demoralized these days. But it does help, for to the litany of general misery there's our own dismal addendum.

What is it that disturbs and unnerves America's Jews (by which I mean, generally, "the organized community") these days? There is the National Jewish Population Study, which informs us that about half the new marriages in which there is a Jewish partner involve only one Jewish partner. There are the continuing reports of anti-Semitism, not only in Poland, in Lithuania, and in Rumania, but also in Crown Heights and at CUNY and UCLA, and all across the good old U.S.of A. There's the new fiscal crisis, a compound of the recession and Operation Exodus, government cutbacks, and, perhaps, some less ephemeral, more systemic causes, which together leave the agencies and institutions of our own community reeling. And then, of course, there's Israel, where the good news has yet to displace the chronic disappointments in its political processes, governmental competence, religious behavior, and so forth.

But beyond these sources of unease, there's a darker demoralization, a growing sense of aimlessness, even foreboding. Back in the 1960s, it was generally supposed that American Jewry was winding down, that we were finally going to be seduced by the open society. And then, quite suddenly, there was an explosive renewal of interest, involvement, commitment. Jewish studies programs sprouted like mushrooms after a rain; *chavurot* moved from the fringes to the mainstream; new magazines, new museums, new momentum everywhere, a genuine resurgence of the Jewish appetite. It became almost fashionable to be Jewish. Not any longer. The adrenaline high experienced by the community in the aftermath of the Six Day War has long since worn off, and now, reluctantly, some truths we'd hoped our frenetic activity would allow us to avoid have become blatant and relentless. Specifically: What connects us to one another?

Religion? A Gallup poll shows that 53 percent of America's Jews regard religion as "not very important," while only 30 percent hold that it is "very important." (The comparable figures for the general American public are 14 percent and 55 percent.) The only religious principle that unites American Jews is that *if* there is One, there is only one, not three, with the emphasis on "if." Beyond that, those Jews who claim to believe tend to believe in a God who bears only a vague resemblance to the God of Jewish history and tradition. It is a measure of our religious confusion and distress that so many religiously indifferent Jews are prepared to accept the claim of the Orthodox to superior religious authenticity. We continue to behave as if in religious matters, more is better, hence most is best; accordingly, the Chasidim are the bearers of the true tradition. Regarding them as most authentic (rather than as merely most photogenic), we feel ourselves inauthentic—and, for the most part, instead of struggling towards our own authenticity, we abandon the quest.

The pursuit of justice? Back in the 1950s, when Marshall Sklare and Joseph Greenblum did their study of "Lakeville" (a pseudonym for Highland Park), they found that most Jews placed a far higher value on devotion to "all humanitarian causes" than to either Jewish ritual or Jewish belief. A "good Jew," 93 percent of them said, was one who leads "an ethical and moral life." But if that's the gist of it, what do you say to the kids when they observe that you don't have to be Jewish to be ethical? (I call this the "Ethical

Culture Question," and it is almost invariably the very first question I am asked when I conclude a speech in which I urge Jews to get on with the pursuit of justice.)

Then there's the disconcerting fact that this isn't the 1950s; in the 1990s, even if we define ourselves as a fellowship in justice or ethics, our actions appear to have only a casual relationship to our definition of ourselves.

Community? Some people contend that a voluntary group doesn't need an ideology; it's enough that it offers its members consolation, a dependable oasis of support in a world amok. And there's surely some truth to the argument: A Judaism of manifestos and marches alone can't make it; alongside belief, there's simple kinship, the special warmth of those who share a language, a past, some holidays, and some responsibilities—perhaps, also a destiny.

But if the past is unknown, the language unspoken, the destiny optional, the responsibilities avoidable, then the community of kinship is attenuated. More important, it is a community, if at all, selected rather than inherited; in that sense, it is an artificial construct rather than an organic product of human (subspecies: Jewish) nature. It may—it must, if it is to survive—nurture its adherents, but that is only a necessary condition. It is not yet sufficient because those who choose to be Jews are, indeed, "adherents," Jews-by-choice.

That is the sea-change in the American Jewish condition. Two hundred years after the Emancipation, Judaism has finally become, in fact as well as in theory, an option. We now truly enter the age of Judaism-by-consent. And the question, therefore, becomes: To what have we consented when we say "I do"?

The traditional answers of organized American Jewry are barely adequate today, and they are likely to diminish in their appeal tomorrow. Those answers focus on our activity on behalf of Israel and our concern with anti-Semitism. But as "pro-Israel" is generally defined, it reduces to check writing and petition signing; however worthy, even urgent, such activities may be, a Judaism of consent wants to be something more than a political action committee or a lobby. And as to anti-Semitism, it is simply not enough to shout "Never again!" "Never again" tells us what to avoid, but it says nothing about what to embrace.

The defense of Jewish interests, including Jewish lives, is an

obvious implication of saying "I do" to Judaism. But Jewish interests are not self-defining, and it is inadequate to define them, as
they often are defined these days, by a two-item Jewish agenda. It is
simply too stingy a definition for a people that announces itself as
partner in the work of Creation, as a religious civilization, or as
committed to an "ism" so embracingly grand as Juda*ism*. Such a
definition opens up too wide a gap between our grand (some might
say grandiose) claims and our actual behavior.

Why not, then, make more modest claims? It's time, perhaps, to
set aside the dreams we've claimed to dream, to walk a bit more
humbly with ourselves and with our God.

But then, of course, the question would become, "Why bother?"
Why say "I do" ourselves or care a whit whether others say it if all
we mean is that we have enlisted in a volunteer fire department,
ready in the name of decency to respond when there's an alarm,
but otherwise disengaged?

These days, many people insist it is time for Jews to turn from
their soft universalistic values to tough particularistic interests.
There is a new parsimony to Jewish life, rationalized in a variety of
ways, a focus on muscles rather than morals, and it betrays not only
our heritage but also the very interests it so often asserts—and the
reason is that *the Jewish people has no higher and more urgent interest
than the energetic pursuit of its values*. The pursuit is not only our
purpose but also our method. From time immemorial, we have
declared ourselves a people of moral distinction (or, at least, of
moral ambition). A hundred years ago we used to tell our children
that if one day we were an empowered people, we would be the
children of Isaiah and Amos. Now that we are empowered here,
and empowered in Israel, our children, the best of them, come to us
and ask, "Now that you can be who you said you would be if only
you could be, are you?" We cannot answer them by referring them
to our words; today, it is our works and not our words that provide
the best evidence. And if there turns out to be no truth in Jewish
self-advertising, if all we have become is a partnership in *chutzpah*,
then our children will walk away from us disdainfully or will simply
be swallowed up in the credibility gap, the gap between words
and works.

In short: If until now we have leaned on crutches that have lately
come to feel inadequate, it is time to learn to stand on our own. But

we are afraid. In order to stand, you have to stand *for* something, and we do not any longer know for what we stand.

◆ ◆ ◆

What are our values? For what do we stand?

One version: Lately we have come to understand, both from our own experience and from the unfolding experience of other nations (particularly the Eastern European nations), how urgently men and women everywhere—notwithstanding that this is the end of the twentieth century, notwithstanding the emergence of the global village—respond to the call of the tribe. Serbs vs. Croats, Palestinians vs. Jews, Hindus vs. Muslims—the tribal imperative has not been stilled and will not be stilled, not there and, for better *and* for worse, not even here.

"Even" here because this nation's great contribution to the human experiment has been its assertion that the tribe is not the primary or the inevitable source from which personal identity derives. Instead, we have said, and by and large meant, that identity is for the individual to pursue and define.

That superficially simple assertion is, in fact, an American revolution, a stunning deviation from the general human tradition. But to assert that the tribe is not central here is not to suggest that we have "solved" the tribal problem; we may know what the tribe is not, but we are left with the question of what the tribe is. Is it an atavistic loyalty to be overcome—that is, to be melted in the universal American pot—or is it a separate family room in the American house?

To that question, America has offered confused and confusing answers. It was not until 1908, when Israel Zangwill's play by that name was first produced, that the term *melting pot* entered the vocabulary. But the idea of the melting pot—essentially, the idea that in this nation there is no place for the hyphenated American—had long been accepted. Thomas Jefferson had worried that immigrants would "infuse [legislation] into their spirit; warp and bias its directions; and render it a heterogeneous, incoherent, distracted mass." John Quincy Adams insisted that new immigrants "must cast off the European skin, never to resume it. They must look forward to their posterity rather than backward to their ancestors." Woodrow Wilson claimed that "a man who thinks of himself as belonging to a particular national group has not yet become an American."

But it was Zangwill himself who defined the theory most enthusiastically. Here is an excerpt from the key speech of the hero of *The Melting Pot*, David Quixano:

> America is God's crucible, the great Melting Pot where all races of Europe are melting and reforming! Here you stand, good folk, think I, when I see them at Ellis Island, here you stand in your fifty groups with your fifty languages and histories, and your fifty blood hatreds and rivalries, but you won't be long like that, brothers, for these are the fires of God you've come to—these are the fires of God. A fig for your feuds and vendettas! German and Frenchman, Irishman and Englishman, Jews and Russians—into the crucible with you all! God is making the American.[1]

However inflated his language, Zangwill captured the prevailing American doctrine. To Jews, it promised a society that would ignore their Judaism. True, it asked for our cooperation: It would disregard our Judaism if we ourselves would not insist upon it; it would not treat us as Jews if we would not behave as Jews. That, at least, is how very many of us came to understand the implicit American contract. And if there were, here and there, vestigial elements of Jewishness that simply would not go away, we argued eloquently for their trivial nature; in the things that mattered, we were no different from the others:

> Hath not a Jew eyes? Hath not a Jew hands, organs, senses, dimensions, passions? Fed with the same food, healed by the same means, warmed and cooled by the same summer and winter as a Christian is? When you prick us, do we not bleed; when you tickle us, do we not laugh; when you poison us, do we not die?[2]

As, however, Glazer and Moynihan observed in 1963, "The point about the melting pot is that it did not happen.[3] Ethnicity was too stubborn; race too intractable; the group, the tribe, too basic a form of human and social organization.

Most of those who thought about such things viewed the facts of enduring ethnic and racial separateness as disturbing atavisms, indications of how far our practice had yet to go in order to comport with our theory. Yet there was a minority view that argued that the way to close the gap was not to modify the practice but to alter the theory. The principal author of that view was Horace Kallen, and the doctrine he proposed was called "cultural pluralism."

In 1913, Kallen claimed that America is "a democracy of nationalities," a federation of ethnic groups. It was and should remain a symphony orchestra, each section contributing its own distinctive quality to the larger whole—a whole that would thereby be larger than the sum of its parts.

The idea of cultural pluralism has had a hard time for unlike the melting pot—"into the cauldron with you" and once made American, unalloyed, American forever—cultural pluralism depends on a delicate balance. It may be—it is—difficult to imagine a melting-pot society in which people emerge from the cauldron naked of all their past, innocent of earlier affiliations, unwilling to sing, and unable to remember the songs of their folk. But it is a hundred times more difficult to imagine a society in which the group is regarded as legitimate, yet does not become a prison, a trap.

In the same *Merchant of Venice* in which Shylock so eloquently argues for our essential sameness, he argues also for our difference: Bassanio invites Shylock to dinner, but Shylock, who observes the laws of *kashrut*, declines: "I will buy with you, sell with you, talk with you, walk with you, and so following, but I will not eat with you, drink with you, nor pray with you."

In point of fact, it is exceedingly difficult to walk, talk, buy, and sell with people without eating, drinking, and praying with them— and it is equally difficult to refuse to eat, drink, and pray with people and yet expect them to be willing to walk, talk, buy, and sell with you. Yet it is precisely such a balance that cultural pluralism requires.

As America becomes more and more multicultural in fact, truly the world in miniature, it must finally clean up its theoretical act and ask what it is that it wants to be. In theory, it could revert to the doctrine of the melting pot, but, in practice, it is already too late for that. As much as they may yearn to breathe free, the new generations of immigrants will not accept that they are the "wretched refuse" of the "teeming shores" of Europe or Asia or Africa or Latin

America. Like Yehuda Amichai's Jews, Americans are "a geological people with rifts and collapses and stratá and fiery lava." Nor, for that matter, is there any longer a dominant WASP culture to which to aspire and then assimilate.

No regrets. Pluralism in all its manifestations—cultural, political, intellectual, economic—is at the heart of the American genius; it would be foolish to abandon it. But note that multiculturalism and pluralism are not identical: Pluralism is not about demography; it is not simply a synonym for diversity. Pluralism is meant to describe not only the existence of a variety of groups but also the manner of relationship of those groups to one another. Pluralism describes a social arrangement that offers space to groups smaller than the whole but insists that the boundaries that mark off the separate spaces be permeable.

That arrangement has a rich, albeit uneven, history in the United States, both as aspiration and as achievement. Reviewing the American experience with pluralism, we are reminded of both the joys and the difficulties it offers. The images are easy enough: Let there be an American mosaic. But a mosaic needs grout to hold it together, and it is by no means clear that if you allow people their own space, their own group identity, their own place in the pluribus, they will still attend the claims of the unum.

Plainly, that is the fear with which we live today; it is specifically the fear of those who have chosen to campaign against the doctrine of multiculturalism, which is not quite merely this generation's version of Kallen's cultural pluralism.

It is, at least, interesting and, perhaps, instructive to cite in this connection from an unpublished memorandum of a meeting convened in the waning days of 1938 by Felix Frankfurter. The American Jewish Committee had just completed the first public opinion survey on anti-Semitism, and the results were so worrisome that Frankfurter invited a small group to review the findings and propose remedial actions. At the conclusion of a two-day conversation, Frankfurter made a proposal summarized by the rapporteur of the meeting:

> Frankfurter stressed the importance of creating new materials
> that would help destroy the illusions and myths now surround-
> ing the Jews and bring out the affirmative aspects of the

contributions to American democracy made by Jews, as well as other groups. Although America had been peopled and developed by a constant stream of immigrants from different lands, no good literature on this basic aspect of American civilization is now available. He said that at the present time most of the literature on various immigrant groups is either dull, monographic truck or pietistic essays. What really remains to be done is to rewrite American history in terms of the dynamics of its group ingredients. Everyone agreed and thought that the American Historical Association should be urged to sponsor such a project. Max Lerner and others thought it important not only to have first-class historians do the job but to have it done in such a way that the material would percolate through the whole educational system—public schools, parochial schools, etc. The National Education Association should be urged to get behind such a project.

Now, more than fifty years later, we are, at last, on the verge of adopting the Frankfurter recommendation. But it is important to understand the fundamental difference between Frankfurter's motives and the motives of the contemporary multiculturalists. Frankfurter believed in America, and he believed in rationality. He assumed that if we were all exposed to one another, we would come to like and respect one another more. He was not particularly concerned with the preservation of a distinctive Jewish identity, a Jewish space, in this country; he was concerned, instead, with making the melting pot work better, specifically making it work better for Jews by reducing the anti-Semitism that prevented Jews from "melting," and he thought the curriculum he proposed would accomplish that.

The current press for multiculturalism comes from a different and a more melancholy background. The critical difference between Kallen's cultural pluralism and today's multiculturalism is that the latter comes largely from people who have given up both on the melting pot and on cultural pluralism itself. Many of the advocates of multiculturalism have concluded that the boundaries are simply not permeable. It is not the Jewish experience that provides their model; it is the black experience, the ghetto imposed rather than chosen, the boundaries marked by high walls rather than by modest street signs, identity assigned rather than elected.

And all this is in a nation becoming, in strictly demographic terms, more and more multicultural every day, less and less European white in its composition. We, the Americans, enter this new phase of our history ill-prepared, either behaviorally or theoretically, to deal with it. And we, the Jews, the people of both Zangwill and Kallen, whose experience with America, despite all the confusions, has been so benign, are not well situated at this time to take a leadership role in defining the new social understanding that awaits development. The jewel in the crown of Jewish contributions to American society is surely our invention of the field of intergroup relations. (Rarely has so Disneyland a term been assigned to so Lebanese—or is it Yugoslavian?—a phenomenon.) But the agenda of Jewish intergroup relations agencies has been diverted, as so many of us as individuals have also been, into an agenda overwhelmingly oriented to action on behalf of Israel. I do not suggest that such action is not wise or not warranted; I submit merely that where once the focus of our intergroup relations agencies was on intergroup relations, that focus has shifted and is now driven by our concern for Israel.

Nor is our preoccupation with Israel the only thing that inhibits our commitment to intergroup relations. We are also preoccupied, not to say obsessed, with anti-Semitism; the amount of time and energy we invest in combating anti-Semitism is out of proportion to its incidence in this country. (I say that knowing full well the risk I run in saying it, since the obsession touches us all, and Jews are ever reluctant to let go the sense of threat; it has become a central aspect of our identity.)

Broadly, there are two approaches to the battle against anti-Semitism, real or imagined, and only one of them contributes to a pluralistic America. The one approach emphasizes the particular interests, rights, entitlements of the Jews; the other speaks to the kind of America that would be hospitable to Jews—that is, to the quality of intergroup relations in America and not merely to the character of America's response to its Jews. Insofar as our agencies feel, whether out of genuine conviction or because it's the surest fund-raising device, an obligation to focus on anti-Semitism per se, they tend to neglect the larger context of intergroup relations.

That is unfortunate on a variety of counts, not the least of which is that it is probably the less effective way to fight anti-Semitism. The principal inhibition against the expression of anti-Semitism is what we call "civilization." The heart may be filled with lust, the belly with envy, the mind with rot—but there are the norms of civilization to interrupt the connection between anti-Semitic instinct and anti-Semitic behavior. There is the rule of law, the essential ingredient of a decent society—and there are also the norms of civil society. Perhaps Hobbes was right: Left to our own devices, we'd soon make all this a jungle. But we are not left to our own devices. We grow up as members of societies, and we infer what is right and what is wrong from what those societies teach, both formally and informally. That which strengthens the institutions of civil society weakens the prospect of anti-Semitism. And who among us would argue that the institutions of civil society are these days being strengthened, that the civic culture is in good health?

In the United States, the principal defining characteristic of civil society is pluralism. And pluralism is the preeminent societal mechanism for inhibiting anti-Semitism. Only in a pluralistic society does the system protect the integrity of groups smaller than the whole; only there are groups not merely tolerated but cherished. If pluralism is well, Jews and Judaism can thrive; if pluralism withers, Jews and Judaism suffer. And if the field of intergroup relations languishes, pluralism withers.

More bluntly still: Jews can survive anti-Semitism. But America cannot survive either the insistent universalism of the melting pot nor the balkanizing particularism of the extreme multiculturalist position—the position adopted by those who are responding, not to the sustaining remembrance of things past nor to the energizing call of dreams shared, but to the brute fact of having been locked out of the system. Power tends to corrupt; so, equally, does powerlessness.

If, as seems inevitable, multiculturalism is the new dispensation, Jews must make sure to be at the table where it is translated from theory into curriculum to ensure that it is not merely a response to racism—a response to racism and a surrender to it—but is, instead, an assertion of both the pluribus and the unum, of the pluralism upon which we depend.

✦ ✦ ✦

And now for the connection between all this about pluralism and the question of what we stand for.

We are asked two questions, and we are meant to live in response to both: the question that arises out of our particularism, "If I am not for myself, who will be for me?" and the question that points us towards universalism, "If I am only for myself, what am I?"

This is not simply ancient blah-blah from the mouth of a moralistic rabbi. I like to think that Rabbi Hillel was a savvy teacher and knew precisely what he was saying. He knew that in a heterogeneous society, it is the very first rule of politics that nothing can be achieved without working together with others, without forming coalitions of groups that are prepared to support one another's critical requirements. None of us can, whether as a matter of our own self-interest or as a matter of our own and the larger society's values, hide behind the gates and hedges of our own neighborhoods. If we think for a moment that we can establish impermeable boundaries between ourselves and others, if we think for a moment that our own privilege can exist independently of what is happening behind the ghetto's walls or that the chaos within those walls can be contained, what we will surely and quickly learn is that chaos knows no boundaries.

There's something else Hillel foresaw: In a pluralistic democracy, the ends are the means. What we have is all process; the process is the substance. None of us will live to see the end of the game; all there is for us is the way in which the game is played, the search for usable (rather than final) truths.

And Jews, notwithstanding our fatigue, our diverse resentments, our current overload, and all the rest, are especially well advantaged to make that crucial point and to make it in the only way that counts—by living it. Which is to say that if what America (the world, too) needs is a model for how groups can live with each other and of how individuals can retain personal autonomy without having to reject the claims of the group, the Jews, with both our interests and our values at stake and with our remarkable history in this land to draw upon, can take a leadership role in defining the model.

Is that not something for which to stand? But surely, it will be said, a commitment to pluralism is not grand enough to inspire us, we who were to have been the relentless pursuers of justice, menders of a fractured world. Can a social arrangement, no matter how attractive, be adequate to a people with so thundering a past and so sacred a mandate? Are sociologists to be the new prophets? Is the end of days merely about good fences and good neighbors?

And why not? "Each with its own god, we with ours," it is written; that's how to ascend the holy mountain. Maybe finding the balance between particularism and universalism is not the whole of a Jewish agenda, but in a world where much of the agony owes to confusion about the relationship between the two, and for a people the whole of whose history can be read as an effort to reconcile their competing claims, it's not an implausible place to start—or restart—the mending.

NOTES

1. Israel Zangwill, *The Melting Pot: A Drama in Four Acts*, rev. ed., reprint of 1932 ed. (New York: Arno Press, 1975).

2. Ibid.

3. Nathan Glazer and Daniel P. Moynihan, *Beyond the Melting Pot: The Negroes, Puerto Ricans, Jews, Italians, and Irish of New York City* (Cambridge, MA: MIT Press, 1963).

don't know how many of you have read the opinion of Jerusalem's Chief Rabbinate this past fall to the effect that those Jews who listen to the *shofar* in a Conservative or a Reform synagogue have *not* fulfilled the *mitzvah* that bids us to hearken to the *shofar*'s sound.

In a like vein, a preeminent American halachic authority, Rabbi Moses Feinstein, recently ruled that when a Reform or a Conservative Jew has an *aliyah*, "his blessing is not a blessing"; whereas when an Orthodox Jew approaches the Torah, though he regularly violates the Sabbath, "his blessing is a blessing." And why? Because, according to Rabbi Feinstein, the latter, though a sinner, believes in God while the Reform or Conservative Jew does not.

What arrogance, what brazenness! To presume to know just which rites and prayers are or are not acceptable to the *Ribono shel Olam*; to claim the clairvoyance to look into a man's soul and to judge his feelings for God!

The judgments of the Jerusalem rabbinate and their like are manifestly destructive of Jewish unity. They read out of the Jewish fold four-fifths of the world's Jews. And then these very judges turn around and accuse *us* of not being sufficiently heedful of the *k'lal*, knowing full well that we are pledged to peoplehood and pluralism, that we accept all segments of the Jewish people without questioning their authenticity.

You will understand that I am not speaking against Orthodoxy as such. Rather I am denouncing a politicized Orthodox establishment that has—as my teacher Eugene Mihaly reminds us—"resisted and, with rare exception, fanatically fought every creative impulse and movement in modern Jewish life" from the Haskalah to the renascence of the Hebrew tongue, from Chasidism to liturgical reform to Zionism. Yes, Zionism, too, for the State of Israel "was and is today given only grudging and post facto acquiescence by the leading halachic authorities, the *poskei hador*."

It is *this* Orthodox establishment that we must resist with a greater vigor, especially in Israel. We cannot be content any longer merely to ward off those recurring efforts to reduce our status there still further by amending the Law of Return. We must move ahead toward that fuller equality, which is our entitlement as Jews, by challenging inhibiting laws and restrictive procedures and by pressing for the passage of remedial legislation.

Rabbi Alexander M. Schindler
State of the Union Message
Toronto, Canada
November 1979

THE NATURE OF RELIGIOUS PLURALISM IN ISRAEL

S . ZALMAN ABRAMOV

The creation of a Jewish state in its historic homeland caused a major crisis in the traditional culture of the Jewish people. If the term *traditional culture* suggests the Orthodox religious tradition of the Jewish people as crystallized in the pre-Emancipation period and regarded as "normative Judaism," contemporary Israel cannot be considered as a "continuation of traditional Jewish culture." That culture afforded a way of life for a community of faith; its norms were prescribed by a code of laws, and its behavior was regulated by the minutiae of that code. What is equally significant is that Jewish tradition regarded *galut* ("exile") as a divinely ordained condition, a deserved punishment for transgressions committed by past generations. Even as *galut* was divinely ordained, so would redemption from the travails of *galut* be an act of divine grace to be brought about by a Messiah. God's advent cannot and must not be accelerated by human activity; in fact, such activity in itself is a rebellion against the divine scheme.

Consequently, in contemplation of traditional culture, the creation of a Jewish state by a human rather than divine agency was a break with that culture. In one further respect, Israel constitutes a break with normative Judaism. From a community of faith, characterized by strict adherence to Judaism as traditionally interpreted, the Jews have been transformed into a pluralistic society in which traditional Judaism is no longer the dominant spiritual force and where varieties of Judaism, both religious and secular, compete for influence and acceptance. This break, however, does not imply a departure from Judaism. In Israel, in particular, we witness an attempt to revitalize Judaism, both by reestablishing a link with the preexilic past and by distilling from the totality of our history the essence of the Jewish spirit so as to make it meaningful to the modern age and compatible with the needs of a people that is charged with the responsibility of maintaining a sovereign state.

Following the exile of the Jewish people in the second century, there had developed a religious culture adopted to the circumstances of an exilic condition. Now in the early stages of our reentry into history, we are groping towards molding a new tradition, deriving its inspiration from a distant past as well as from significant elements of the rich tradition that has accumulated throughout the generations. While this development constitutes in many respects a break with the exilic past, it, nevertheless, is an innovative continuation of Jewish culture, responding to the revolutionary transformation in the condition of the Jewish people in the modern era.

Contemporary Israeli ethos and culture do indeed incorporate values different from and even conflicting with important elements in traditional Judaism. That Israel is a democracy is in many respects at variance with *halachah*, which repudiates the principle of peoples' sovereignty and their authority to legislate. Traditional Judaism sees no need for legislation, which is set out in the divinely ordained *halachah* and lends itself to interpretation by persons versed in this legal tradition and committed to its divine origin.

Rabbi Zadoc Kahn, the Orthodox chief rabbi of France at the close of the nineteenth century, was helpful to Herzl in his initial steps on behalf of Zionism. However, he rejected Herzl's suggestion to join the Zionist movement for, as an Orthodox Jew, he could not conceive of a Jewish state based on anything except *halachah*. "If the state is theocratic as it once was," he reasoned, "what will become of the freedom of thought? And if it is a secular state, how will it be Jewish?" The Jewish people eventually rejected a theocracy and opted for a secular state, which, nevertheless, is Jewish because its population consists predominantly of Jews committed to being Jews.

The reality of a Jewish state is a source of embarrassment and divisiveness within the Orthodox community, and the gulf is still unbridgeable after a half-century of Jewish statehood. The ultra-Orthodox wing (*charedim*) denies any religious legitimacy to the Jewish state because its birth was brought about by transgressions of the Divine Law. Consequently, although residing in Israel, the *charedim* view themselves as dwelling in *galut* and treat the government of Israel as an alien authority. Democracy is irrelevant to them, and the organizational constitution of Agudat Israel makes Israel a classical theocracy. Like their like-minded counterparts in *galut*, they, too, take advantage of the democratic process to secure their particularistic interests.

The Orthodox—adherents of the National Religious Party and generally referred to as *dati'im*—accord to the State of Israel full religious legitimacy and view it as "the beginning of redemption." Unlike the *charedim*, the *dati'im* offer prayers for the well-being of the nation; their sons serve in the army; and they celebrate Israel Independence Day. In brief, the Orthodox have become fully integrated into the manifold structures of the state. While the *charedim* regard the Jewish people as a mere community of faith united in its commitment to the halachic code, the *dati'im* are committed also to the nationalistic dimension and accept democracy as a basic principle on the national level as well as in their internal party structure. They successfully employ the democratic process, particularly in order to secure "religious legislation." Their most notable achievement was the prevention of the enactment of a written constitution and of a bill of rights.

While the *dati'im* assert that the *halachah* is compatible with the requirements of a modern state, they also experience at times a good deal of uneasiness. Thus, for example, in the operation of public services like power stations or police duty, the *dati'im* insist that on the Sabbath their followers be replaced by secular or non-Jewish employees, thereby admitting that without secularists or non-Jews, the *halachah* is not adequate to meet the needs of a modern state. Thus, we note that within Israeli Orthodoxy there is a sharp ideological rift between the *charedi* and *dati* camps and further fragmentation within these groups. Pluralism, more than any other feature, characterizes the Orthodox world of Israel.

A person who is pious in his own way, believes in God, leads a righteous life, or is an adherent of a non-Orthodox religious denomination is regarded by the *dati'im* as a *chiloni*, a "secularist." This term, less derogatory than *apikoros*—which was the term used in the early years of this century—began to be applied by the Orthodox to describe not only assimilated Jews but also all non-observant Jewish nationalists, including the militantly antireligious elements that were then vocal among Jewish socialists in Eastern Europe and Labor Zionists in Palestine. Thus, all who were not Orthodox were lumped into one category: secularists. One of the more notable achievements of Orthodoxy is its success in attaching to all shades of non-Orthodox opinion the label of secularist, thus implying that there is no Jewish religion other than the Orthodox. From this it logically followed that secularism was the only ideological alternative to Orthodoxy since there was no religious alternative to Orthodoxy. The *dati'im* have thus been relieved of the need to justify their position in dialogue with non-Orthodox religious trends or to engage in a meaningful discussion with the secularists, for they have no common ground with either. Orthodoxy has thus been recognized as the only legitimate expression of Judaism in Israel and, therefore, is entitled to exclusive control of all religious offices. Thus, a clear line of demarcation was drawn between the secularists and the Orthodox, with the latter secure in their enjoyment of an ideological and institutional monopoly of (the Jewish) religion.

To be sure, secularism has been firmly grounded in Zionist theory and practice. Even those who maintain that the century-old Jewish renaissance—which encompassed the revival of the Hebrew language and literature, the return to the cultivation of the ancient soil, and the ingathering of the exiles within a reconstituted commonwealth—could not have been brought about without a messianic impulse admit that Zionism was essentially a form of secular nationalism. It was the nationalist movements in Italy and in central Europe in the second half of the nineteenth century— movements that were liberal and secular—that stimulated the early stirrings of Zionism. To Herzl and his associates in the creation of political Zionism, as well as to Ahad Ha-Am, exponent of cultural Zionism, the new and essentially secular nationalism was an expression of the imperishable Jewish urge to survive in a period when the cohesion of the Jewish people as a monolithic religious community had begun to give way. Zionism was in open revolt against the heretofore unchallenged traditional view that *geulah*, the redemption of the Jewish people, culminating in a return to Zion, would come about in God's own time and that any attempt to force the Divine Hand by bringing it about through a human agency was an act of sacrilege. Even the false messiahs of the past, including Shabbetai Zvi in the seventeenth century and Jacob Frank in the eighteenth, claimed divine authority for their pretensions. The founders of Zionism advanced no such claim.

For its part, Zionism did not purport to act in pursuance of a religious authority or to achieve a religious goal. To Herzl and his associates, Zionism meant the end of the homelessness of the Jewish people. To Ahad Ha-Am, a Jewish state was a means of assuring the survival of Jewish culture, which he conceived in terms of the ethical teachings of the ancient prophets. While the Zionist movement freely borrowed religious and traditional symbols in its educational and propagandist activities and also incorporated certain religious rituals into its system of national festivals, it remained essentially secular. Even the revival of the Hebrew language and the consequent return to the Bible and the sources of Jewish culture in their original tongue did not alter the basically secular character of Jewish nationalism.

If we examine the term *chiloni*—a term that refers to the predominant majority of the people—it appears that this majority is not quite as *chiloni* ("secular") as the term might imply. If secularism implies atheism, animosity towards religion, rejection of rituals and observances, then it is a misleading description of the attitudes and practices of the so-called secularists.

The great majority of those who make *aliyah* from Islamic countries are traditional Jews who have their children educated in state religious schools. However, their traditionalism, in terms of their behavior, is different from the Orthodoxy of the Ashkenazic communities. They have not associated themselves with the extremist wing of the ultra-Orthodox Natorei Karta; they have not been involved in acts of violence, nor have they been identified with excesses in the name of religion. On the whole, they are far more tolerant of nonobservant Jews than are Orthodox Jews of European origin. They also exhibit a visible transition from observance to nonobservance. This change is part of the general disintegration of their patriarchal way of life, which characterized the Oriental communities in their lands of origin.

While no definite figures are available—indeed, the nature of the subject does not lend itself to statistical accuracy—it can be estimated that close to 30% of the total Jewish population in Israel may be classified as Orthodox, about 20% as nonreligious, and about half as neither Orthodox nor nonreligious but favorably disposed to some degree of traditional observance. Together with the nonreligious, this large group is categorized by the Orthodox as *chilonim*, "secularists," though its general attitude to traditional observance is not at all negative. While a person may be incensed at the imposition of some of the halachic rules that run counter to his moral feelings, he may still participate in varying degrees of ritual observance, whether it be occasional visits to the synagogue or adherence to the dietary laws. The mood of this significant segment is summed up by a well-known student of Israel's religious landscape:

> They are not willing to commit themselves to a religious way of life, but they want to retain a good deal of the religious tradition. They prefer to be inconsistent rather than to break completely with Judaism. This attitude represents a synthesis of opposition to a total commitment to religion together with an equally strong attachment to the religious traditions of Judaism.

Several years ago the Louis Guttman Israel Institute of Applied Social Research carried out an extensive in-depth survey of "Beliefs, Observances, and Social Interaction among Israeli Jews." It concluded:

> ...the rhetoric of secular and religious polarization generally used

to characterize Israeli society is highly misleading.

> ...Israeli society has a strong traditional bent, and, as far as religious practice is concerned...there is a continuum from the "strictly observant" to the "nonobservant," rather than a great divide between a religious minority and a secular majority.

> Israeli Jews are strongly committed to the continuing Jewish character of their society, even while they are selective in the forms of their observance. They believe that public life should respect the tradition but are critical of the "status quo" governing state and religion.

The study shows that 14% of Israeli Jews define themselves as "strictly observant"; 24% say they are "observant to a great extent"; and approximately 40% report that they are "somewhat observant." An overall analysis regarding a gamut of observances from three important domains (Shabbat, *kashrut*, and holidays) shows that 95% of all Jews observe at least one of these. Thus, as opposed to the 20% of those who define themselves as totally nonobservant, empirically only 7% do not perform any of the observances. Between 80% and 85% observe some *kashrut* rules and 92% affix *mezuzot* to their doorposts. *About 70% favor granting the Reform and the Conservative the same status as is by law conferred on the Orthodox.* Thus, the great majority repudiate the monopoly of religious affairs held under exclusive control of the Orthodox establishment.

If we deduct the 14% of the strictly observant and the 20% who report that they are nonobservant, 66%, two-thirds of Israeli Jewry, are committed to varying degrees of religious observance, ranging from "observant to a large extent" to "somewhat observant." These data support the conclusion of this study that "there is a continuum from the 'strictly observant' to the 'nonobservant,' rather than a great divide between a religious minority and a secular majority."

To be sure, the practice of observances is not of itself a firm indication of the level of religiosity of its practitioners, but it does point to a wide religious pluralism. If one were to draw a comparison between North American Jewry and Israeli Jewry, one could suggest that Israelis who define themselves as "observant to a large extent" would fit nicely into the Conservative category, and the "somewhat observant" would generally fit the Reform mold. In

Israel, as in North America, the Conservative and the Reform far outnumber the Orthodox. Thus, it can be asserted that the great majority in Israel in terms of observance can be classified as either Conservative or Reform, and so they meekly submit to the term *chiloni* imposed upon them by the Orthodox.

There is, however, a basic difference between religious pluralism in North America and in Israel. In the former, the state is not involved in religious matters. In Israel, the state has set up an established religion for the Jews, which is headed by a rabbinate that exercises jurisdiction in matters of personal status and is staffed by Orthodox rabbis who adjudicate in accordance with the *halachah*. Thus, in contemplation of the law of the land, Orthodoxy is officially recognized as the only legitimate Judaism.

The reasons for the failure of the *chilonim* to rise up against the excesses of Orthodoxy are numerous and call for a separate treatment. Suffice it to point out that what draws Jews in North America to join a synagogue is largely a desire for ethnic identification. In the all-embracing Jewish society of Israel, a synagogue is only one of many foci of Jewish identification. Thus, the urge for an association with a congregation, so important in the Diaspora, is absent in Israel.

The activities of the religious parties, although they represent only 13% of the current Knesset membership, are strategically well placed to deter the government from making any concession to non-Orthodox religious formations or from relaxing some of the rigors of Orthodox practices.

The religious parties, including the National Religious Party, cannot accord legitimacy to Israel as a Jewish state unless certain religious elements are incorporated into its legal and administrative system. They contend that for them the separation of religion from the state is ruled out by the very nature of the Jewish people, which is a community of faith as well as an ethnic and national entity. To achieve their objective within the framework of a democratic society, the Orthodox have resorted to political action. Thus, the issue of religion in Israel has shifted from the spiritual-ideological plane to the political plane and has led to considerable strife. It is regrettable that so far the authentic ideological confrontation between the Orthodox and other trends has been minimal.

From time to time, and at times quite often, there arises an outcry against Orthodox positions and utterances. The protesters focus on rabbinical insistence on observing the minutiae of ritual and on rabbinical indifference to moral issues. Their attitude to ethical norms is in many respects the great divide that separates the Orthodox from the Conservative, Reform, and others. In the view of the Orthodox, that which at any given time is considered to be ethical cannot warrant a restriction or modification of halachic rules. The *halachah*, being metahistorical, cannot yield to prevailing notions or intellectual fashions. The rules prohibiting a *kohen* from marrying a divorcée or prohibiting a young childless widow from remarrying without the humiliating ceremony of *chalitzah*, or the tragic fate of a woman who obtained a divorce from the rabbinic court but is unable to remarry because her husband refuses to deliver to her the bill of divorcement personally may indeed constitute hardships, but the submission to these and other hardships is an act of obedience to the Divine Law and in that sense only is an ethical act. In the view of the *chilonim*, however, any halachic rule cannot restrict or negate a human right, except for reasons that pass the test of moral criteria.

Thus, in Israel, unlike in North America, the stress on ethical values rather than on ritual draws the demarcation line between Orthodoxy and its ideological opponents, be they the Conservative and Reform denominations or the *chiloni* public in general.

The incipient Reform and Conservative congregations in Israel have so far failed to make a significant contribution to an ideological debate. Lack of an effective leadership is one of the causes. Instead of concentrating on enlightening public opinion by stressing the ethical rather than the ritual aspect of Judaism, the emphasis was placed on legal action in the court of law. In this field, valuable work was done by the Reform movement, often successfully, in contesting administrative acts of the government and its agencies, be it in matters affecting Reform institutions directly or human rights generally. This activity, valuable in itself, has had a limited impact on public opinion. On the other hand, issues of principle that agitated public opinion did not receive the attention they deserved.

Thus, when we survey the Israeli landscape, we discover in the realm of religion a highly diversified society representing a colorful spectrum of religious varieties. The great majority of Israelis are tradition-oriented, and the term *chiloni* applied to them is a misdescription of their authentic attitude. This majority has so far failed to evolve a proper vocabulary to articulate its ideas, let alone create institutional frameworks for collective action.

It must also be borne in mind that with Israel being beset by security problems, the issue of religion, vexing and burdensome as it has often been, did not loom large on the national agenda. Consequently the treatment of the religious problem was not a result of a consistent policy but a patchwork of ad hoc arrangements aimed at resolving a recurring crisis.

No clear-cut policy on the religious issues can be formulated as long as the grand debate on the future of Israel's frontiers splits the nation. Therefore, serious national problems cannot be dealt with. Once peace is achieved, Israel will have to face a series of domestic issues, which so far have been subordinated to the problems of national security. This will lead to a realignment of the political forces in response to a new reality. Only then will the nation be free to focus on internal problems, and undoubtedly the problem of religion will loom large on the national agenda.

· II ·

IN THE IMAGE OF GOD

Healing, Ethics, and Tikkun Olam

I want to urge a heightened encounter with Jewish texts in all of our educational endeavors, texts that at present we more often teach about than teach.

Encountering a text can be a religious experience. So are we taught in *Seder Eliyahu Rabbah*:

> *Kol hamchadesh divre torah al pif*
> *dome kefi shemashmi'im min hashamayim.*
>
> Whosoever interprets a text in a new way,
> it is as if it were revealed to him from heaven.

Reading a text, interpreting it anew, is a transforming experience. We approach the text, and soon the text begins to reach out to us, to envelop us, until we almost become the text.

Altogether, I am afraid that our movement has taken too literally the rabbinic teaching *lo hamidrash ha'ikar elo hama'aseh*, that the essential thing is not study but deeds. True enough, study without action is denounced as a vanity, yet deeds, however good, when detached from Torah study are trivialized and denied their Jewish moorings.

We Reform Jews are easily deterred by the word *obligatory*. But I do not speak of the coercion of religious authority. I speak rather of the coercive power of truth itself: the truth that our patriarchs and matriarchs discovered in lonely places and in encounters that forever changed their lives; the truth that generations of commentators, in safety and in peril, in exile and in Jerusalem, debated and expounded and applied to the details of daily life; the truth that only life itself can ultimately teach and that Judaism posits as a core spiritual perception: that life is a holy unity, a single web of meaning.

When this perception of unity leaps off a page of Scripture or rabbinic commentary—when we drink it deeply with our eyes—it goes directly to the heart. There it resonates with all those feelings of wonder and compassion stored since our childhoods, and it gives rise to the irrepressible *mitzvot* commanded by the life force itself.

The Talmud proclaims that each day God regrets the creation of this world of ours, and each day a destroying angel is set forth to revert it all to chaos. But when God sees young children studying the Torah, when God sees would-be sages studying with their masters, the heavenly rage transforms to compassion, and the world once again is spared. This reprieve is earned not by prayer, mind you, not by deed but by study, by the encounter with the text.

Rabbi Alexander M. Schindler
State of the Union Message
Baltimore, Maryland
November 1991

LET US MAKE MAN

EUGENE MIHALY

In tribute to Rabbi Alexander Schindler, dear friend and colleague, creative and imaginative *darshan,* whose inspired leadership personifies the ancient rabbinic wisdom: "Redemption comes little by little and progressively increases." (*Midrash on Psalms* 18:36)

The biblical account of creation is a literary marvel. Reading the first chapter of Genesis as a scientific or historic account of the origin of the universe or of man—the approach of the literal fundamentalist—inevitably vitiates the biblical text and reduces it to a ludicrous irrelevancy. In contrast, talmudic literature repeats four times, "Whatever a faithful, pious scholar will teach"—whatever he will discover in a text, derive from or bring to it—"Moses heard it at Sinai." That is to say, Scripture must be approached as the inspired poetry that it is.

In addition to their high literary merit, the biblical myths concerning the origin of the species reveal, as classical legends often do, some of the profoundest aspects of man's perceptions and insights, man's deepest longings, apprehensions, and fears—those lurking on the edge of our conscious awareness or even those hidden in the deeper layers of our psychic labyrinth. This is true not only of the primary stratum of the legend, as it appears in biblical context, but of the many layers of exegesis, of exposition and interpretation, as each sentence, every word and letter, was prayerfully rehearsed, studied, and minutely examined through the centuries.

Join me for a session of the ancient academy in Lydda in southern Palestine. We shall not learn much about the origin of the cosmos or the evolution of homo sapiens. But we may learn something of intellectual history and gain a deeper insight into ourselves and the goals and ideals that motivate our actions and attitudes.

It is the beginning of the third century. The leader of the session is the eminent scholar Rabbi Joshua ben Levi, renowned for his homiletic acumen and the imaginative parables with which he illustrated his keen exposition of Holy Writ. The text is the Hebrew Bible, Genesis, chapter 1, beginning with verse 26: And God said, "Let us make man in our image, after our likeness...."

Though I attribute the entire discussion to the teachers of antiquity, what follows is my inference, not the actual interchanges of the ancient rabbis. We listen and hear not with a third-century but with a twentieth-century ear. We inescapably bring ourselves and our own apperception to the classic text. Just as Moses, according to the well-known legend, could not comprehend all the intricate profundities that Akiba, many centuries after Moses, quoted in his name, so would Rabbi Joshua ben Levi and the other rabbis I quote find much of what I attribute to them incomprehensible. Nevertheless, it is all implicit in their biblical exegesis, waiting to be discovered as we engage the text in serious, creative dialogue.

◆　◆　◆

"Note, dear colleagues and students," Rabbi Joshua begins his discourse, "that the text before us is in the plural, 'Let *us* create...in *our* image, after *our* likeness.' Throughout the chapter, God is the sole actor. All creation is the handiwork of God. 'He stretched out the heavens alone and spread out the earth,' the prophet Isaiah emphasizes. What is the possible meaning of the plural 'Let us'? We know that nothing in Scriptures is fortuitous or superfluous. Every letter, each jot, is there by design, carefully arranged by a Divine Intelligence to teach a significant lesson. It would seem that by resorting to a discordant, even shocking, use of the plural, the Divine Author would bid us to pause and search more deeply to discover the profounder nuances hidden in the biblical text.

"Even more disturbing than the plural formulation," Rabbi Joshua continued, "is the radical change in the mood of this part of the narrative. The text before us is a prologue to the creation of man. First 'God said, "Let us create man..."' and only after this declaration of intent does God proceed with the act, 'So God created man....' This is the only instance in the entire series of reported events when an act is preceded by a statement of intent. Throughout the narrative the Creator acts by decree, decisively, without hesitation or pause: God creates, separates, fashions, brings forth, and forms. The repetitive refrain is, 'God said...and there was....' But when we reach the climax of the drama, the culmination of the entire process—the creation of man—the certain, decisive stance of the Hero of this awesome cosmic enterprise abruptly changes. Instead of the expected joyous enthusiasm that the arduous task of creation was about to reach its highly successful conclusion, we discern a hesitancy, a certain ambivalence perhaps—as if the Creator had misgivings, not quite convinced of the wisdom of what He was about to do. God seeks reassurance and asks for counsel: 'Let us make man.' We hear it almost as a question, 'Shall we?' What hazards, risks did the omniscient Creator perceive that caused Him to hesitate? Why was He apprehensive? What was His doubt, His dilemma? And to whom did He, could He, turn for advice?"

Many of the assembled students and scholars had previously considered and struggled with the incongruous use of the plural in the text. A number had actually been confronted by the devotees of the numerous heretical Gnostic sects, who cited this very verse as a proof-text for their doctrine that man was created by evil powers—

by the demiurge and his demonic legions. Some of the students were also aware that the early Church Fathers interpreted the plural form of our text christologically, as referring to the logos and the trinity. The members of the academy perceived Rabbi Joshua's question not as an abstract, exegetic nicety but as a vital problem that affected their core Jewish belief and commitment.

After a brief interval, Rabbi Joshua resumed his exposition: "The problems we raised were, of course, many times noted and discussed by our predecessors, of blessed memory. Some understood the phrase 'Let us make...' as the plural of majesty. Others regarded our verse, along with the entire chapter, not as a description of remote origins, of the beginnings of the universe or of the first human being. All of that is beyond the ken of mortals. Didn't Ecclesiasticus caution many centuries ago, 'Do not pry into things too hard for you or examine what is beyond your reach....Do not busy yourself with matters that are beyond you; even what has been shown you is above man's grasp....' The primary purpose of the account in the first chapter of Genesis is to teach some important ethical lessons—proper rules of conduct—so that human beings may fulfill their creative potential. Our teachers thus understood the verse 'Let us make man in our image, after our likeness...' as an ongoing and ever-present call addressed to each man and woman as they are about to be married. The verse charges each bride and groom to fulfill the most exalted of human tasks: 'Let us make man!' God pleads with each couple, 'Take Me as your partner and together let us create a human being.'

"Rabbi Jonathan, to cite another example, explained our verse as follows: 'When Moses recorded the events of each of the six days of creation, as God dictated, and he heard the phrase "Let us make...," he protested. "Master of the universe," Moses said, "why do You provide this opportunity for attack, this misleading excuse to the heretics?" But God insisted. "Write precisely as I say it, Moses, and let him who chooses to err do so. It is his option—the hazard of freedom. But those who expend the effort to understand this verse in its proper context will perceive the deeper lesson implicit in My use of the plural with its implication that I consulted with other, lesser creatures before I created man.'

"'You well realize, Moses—you experience it daily as the faithful shepherd of a mixed multitude of former slaves—that the descendants of Adam are not of equal stature. Some are more powerful, brighter, and more skilled than others. The stronger will inevitably be tempted to exploit the weaker—lord it over them—and treat them with contempt. "Why bother to consult the powerless, ignorant masses?" the privileged self-righteously exclaim. "Of what use or value can the opinion or advice of the hoi poloi possibly be? They are incapable of judging what is for their own welfare. They are oblivious to their true self-interest. It is our burden, our painful ethical duty, to lead the herd and even coerce them, if necessary, to do what is good for them."'

"'My use of the plural "Let us make man...," God told Moses, 'is the response to every tyrant, to all those who would deprive man whom I created in My image of his freedom, of his inalienable right to be consulted and to participate in all matters that affect his welfare and his destiny. I intentionally humble Myself, Moses, I risk heretical misunderstandings of My nature and omnipotence to set the example and to teach this indispensable lesson. Before I created man and granted him dominion over all creation, I assembled every celestial and terrestrial creature—from the ministering angels to every animal and lowly bush—and sought their advice and consent: "Let us make man...." I would not act without their participation. I promulgated this central, ethical principle prior to the creation of the first human being as a guiding principle for all times. This act of Mine, Moses, establishes the inherent right, the ethical duty to rebel against those who enslave and deprive those who bear My image of their inherent human dignity.'

"This lesson that our teacher derived from the text before us," Rabbi Joshua emphasized, "is only one of hundreds of insights our fathers bequeathed to us as our precious heritage. We are blessed, indeed, that we are the heirs to this rich patrimony. Scriptures in their broadest sense—the biblical texts as interpreted and deepened by centuries of devoted study and search—are our moorings, which protect us against the vogue, the superficial. But we are obliged to be more than passive transmitters of an age-old inheritance. Each successive generation is urged to confront the text anew and to discover its meaning in light of the ever-changing perceptions of reality, to assure that our Testament is alive and relevant in each age.

"I suggest for your consideration," Rabbi Joshua proceeded with his discourse, "that the plural of 'Let us make man' and its implied ambivalence are intended to convey an inner struggle within the Godhead itself—an internal debate between the divine attributes of justice and of love and compassion. Man, the creature God was about to fashion, the capstone of creation, would differ essentially from all others. He would be made in God's image—sentient, endowed with freedom to choose between good and evil. He will be largely responsible for his own destiny—beyond the control of his Creator.

This was indeed a hazardous venture, which required the most careful deliberation. The attribute of justice foresaw that this self-aware creature would, in his arrogance and pride, delude himself that he is omnipotent. He will rebel by challenging and seeking to replace the Creator. He will thus destroy not only himself but all other creatures as well. The attribute of mercy and compassion argued, however, that though mortal man will inevitably stumble, he also has the capacity to repent and change his ways. He will learn from his mistakes and ultimately achieve his potential as a partner in an ongoing creative process.

"This internal debate within the omniscient Mind of the universe may be compared," Rabbi Joshua elaborated, "to a father's ambivalent attitude as he experiences the development, the progressive maturation, of his son. On the one hand, the parent encourages and delights in the independence, the self-reliance of the child. On the other hand, the loving father is also apprehensive and full of trepidation that his progeny will make the wrong choice and harm himself. The father is, therefore, reluctant to let go, fearful of the consequences of self-assertion and independence. Nor does the parent always react sympathetically to the competitiveness, the rebellion—often in the form of hostile rejection—as the son strives to achieve his own identity and ego integrity. This is what our teachers termed 'the *pain* of rearing offspring.' Only a mature, compassionate perspective resolves the conflict and enables the parent to loosen the restraints, to let go, and lovingly to help the child's wholesome development into adolescence and maturity.

"Our text communicates a similar struggle within the Godhead, a debate between the attributes of stern justice and forgiving, embracing love. 'Let us make...,' and the hesitancy it conveys, picture the painful dilemma. The verse 'So God created man...' indicates the resolution. Man was created; he survives, often by the skin of his teeth; he has a future because the divine attributes of love, compassion, and mercy predominated and are operative in the world. This is our faith, our commitment—our eternal hope."

Rabbi Joshua concluded his discourse with the standard formula of praise, comfort, and consolation. Now the other members of the academy would add their responses to Rabbi Joshua's questions and his interpretations of the biblical text.

✦   ✦   ✦

After a short recess, Rabbi Joshua called on his devoted disciple Rabbi Simeon, the outstanding member of the prominent Pazzi family of Tiberius, who had achieved wide renown as far distant as the academies in Babylonia. "I have been enlightened, inspired by the brilliant insights of our beloved and revered teacher, Rabbi Joshua," Rabbi Simeon began. "May I be privileged to sit at his feet for many years to come and be the beneficiary of his wisdom and his amazing erudition. I have long been troubled by the problems in our text that our teacher so lucidly analyzed. My understanding of this verse 'Let us make man,' with all due deference and respect, differs, however, from that of our mentor and guide. My explanation combines elements of the two views we heard in the opening discourses: that of Rabbi Jonathan, that God consulted with all creation; and that of Rabbi Joshua, that the plural indicates an inner debate, a struggle within the Godhead.

"I picture the situation in a different light. When God was about to create man," Rabbi Simeon explained, "the ministering angels became highly agitated and disturbed. An ancient tradition preserved through the centuries—included in part in the various books of sacred Scriptures—suggests that the angelic hosts formed contending parties, opposing groups. Some insisted that man be created; others, with even greater vehemence, argued against the creation of man. The dramatic, celestial debate was vividly described centuries ago by the Psalmist (85:11): 'Loving-kindness and truth met [in combat]; mercy and truth embraced [in struggle].' Love said, 'Let man be created. He will perform acts of loving-kindness.' The angel of truth opposed the creation of man. 'He is full of lies and deceit,' truth argued. Mercy joined love in favor of creating man since he is capable of deeds of compassion and mercy. Peace, however, strongly objected since man is full of contention and strife. The vote was a tie—a standoff between love and mercy who were for the creation of man and truth and peace who were opposed. God was stymied; His grand design was about to be frustrated. In order to break the impasse, so the Book of Daniel (8:12) informs us, God 'cast truth down to earth,' and He created man.

"When the heavenly hosts saw what happened to their cherished and respected colleague, they cried out in protest: 'How can You so embarrass "truth"! Is not his name inscribed in Your seal—the designation by which You identify Yourself?' To pacify His irate angelic hosts, and to mitigate the harshness of His act, God decreed, the Psalmist (85:12) reports, 'Let truth spring up from the earth.'

"The obvious message of this ancient legend," Rabbi Simeon explicated, "is that the celestial debate and the vote were a mere formality, a strategem. In His eagerness to create man, God resorted to subterfuge. When He failed to enlist a majority for His proposed venture by legitimate means, He eliminated a negative vote by banishing 'truth.' He was thus able to proceed with His favorite project, the creation of man.

"Such an interpretation would be appropriate if we were confronted by one of the numerous myths about the pagan idols, the inhabitants of the Roman pantheon. It is, however, blasphemy to attribute such capricious acts to the Master of the universe, our God and the God of our fathers. Is it conceivable that the God of justice and compassion would resort to chicanery and deceit? Heaven forfend!

"No! The ancient reconstruction of the celestial scene prior to the creation of man preserved by our sacred tradition must be understood in light of our encounter with the Divine," Rabbi Simeon passionately pleaded, "in terms of our historic experience and our millennial search. From this perspective, the debate between the angels of truth and peace and [the angels of] mercy and loving-kindness that resulted in truth being expelled from the heavenly realm—demoted to the terrestrial sphere, destined ever to reach upward by 'springing up from the earth'—this legend in the form of an elaborate metaphor conveys profound insights into the nature of man, his possibilities and his limitations.

"Consider, my colleagues and teachers," Rabbi Simeon continued, "that the being whom the Creator was about to fashion was to be a combination of matter and spirit, dust from the earth and an immortal soul, a fusion of the terrestrial and the celestial. These two elements, which constitute man's essential nature, are in continuous creative tension with each other. Man's destiny inherent in his very makeup is to reach for the stars and yet be earthbound, inescapably chained by his finitude and his mortality.

"His material nature, earth man, driven by the insatiable desires of the flesh, seeks the satisfaction of its lust and the immediate gratification of its senses. Unreflective, driven by blind instinct, the flesh wants it all, wants it now. Yet simultaneously this same creature, soul man—this spiritual being—yearns for, longs for, expends untold effort and sacrifice to achieve a society of truth, justice, and peace; a perfect world, egalitarian, where 'each man shall sit under his vine and under his fig tree and none shall make him afraid'; a blissful state when death shall be banished forever, 'and God will wipe away tears from all faces.'

"What is often overlooked, at times consciously obscured, is that just as sensual man, driven by blind, uninhibited instinct, seeks immediate fulfillment of his voluptuous passions, so does spiritual man, driven by his lofty ideals to which he clings with fanatic dogmatism. And they are both equally illusory, unattainable, and fatal.

"In the material, sensual realm, man's attempt to achieve the ultimate here and now is expressed in delusional fantasies of apocalyptic orgasm, 'polymorphous sexuality'—a vision of man as unrepressed, unsublimated eros. While in the spiritual domain, this intense passion for the ultimate—the ideal—takes the forms of imminent messianism; 'the millennium is at hand'; 'the heavenly Jerusalem is about to descend'—'Utopia is here!' Whether in the physical or spiritual realms, this fascination with, this passion for the absolute—this utopianism—is vain, tragic—lethal. The lamb may be enticed to lie down with the lion, but the result will inevitably be ever fewer lambs.

"Let us now return to the legend with which I began," Rabbi Simeon urged, "and let us analyze it in the light of our discussion. In His omniscient wisdom, the merciful Creator surely perceived that the angel of truth—absolute, unbending, ultimate celestial truth—would not only object to man's creation, since he cannot by his very nature fulfill truth's expectations, but that this heavenly being would be a continuous threat to man's survival. Absolute truth, as long as it is enthroned on high, will remain the ideal—

always beckoning, tempting, judging. But man, limited by his mortality and his carnal passions, is destined to fail. Celestial truth will forever remain beyond man's reach. As a last resort, therefore, as an act of love and compassion, in order to give man a chance for survival, God reluctantly cast truth to earth. Henceforth, terrestrial truth—not absolute, stern, uncompromising, but a truth that considers man's foibles, his weaknesses, his irresistable temptations—will be the ideal. Truth will continue to ascend, challenging mortals to rise ever higher—but it will be a compassionate, understanding, earthly truth.

"Similarly, heavenly peace, perfect tranquility, absolute serenity—the final reconciliations of man and man and man and nature—are beyond human attainment. Such an ideal, given man's need for power, his passions, his acquisitiveness, would ultimately be his doom. Yes, this frail mortal is capable of and will perform acts of mercy and loving-kindness. They, therefore, consented to man's creation. These attributes—love and mercy—are not absolutes. They do not require a denial of man's essential nature. They are relational. They involve specific, limited acts in man's relation to his fellow human beings. Peace, however, is an absolute. As long as it remains in its pristine state, a peace as envisioned by the prophets for the end of days—in a postmessianic, redeemed world—such an absolute, idealized state is not only beyond the reach of mortal man, but it may cause his destruction. Occasions will arise when unprincipled demagogues, bloodthirsty, vicious tyrants will have to be restrained and disciplined. Rebellion and strife may on occasion not only be justified but may be the ethical means—the imperative—to preserve peace and pursue it.

"Peace did not share the fate of truth. It retained its place in the celestial realm. But after truth ceases to be an unattainable absolute and becomes a reality that may be progressively realized in an unredeemed world, peace, too, may become an achievable goal—not the ideal, messianic peace, but one for frail mortals who will falter and fail but will learn to appreciate the merit of partial achievement. Our tradition does teach that the Messiah recedes as he is approached—but he appears a little at a time.

"You will recall," Rabbi Simeon concluded, "that when Abraham our patriarch pleaded for the cities of Sodom and Gomorrah, he confronted God with the question 'Shall not the Judge of all the world do justice?' Our tradition, however, understood Abraham's statement not as a question but as a command: 'The Judge of all must not do absolute justice!' And our sages elaborate: 'Abraham said to God, "If You desire a world, You cannot have absolute justice, and if You want justice, You cannot have a world. Yet You grip the rope at both ends and pull it taut. You want a world and You want absolute justice. If You do not let go a little, the world will not endure."'"

Rabbi Joshua rose from his seat after Rabbi Simeon concluded his remarks. He embraced his beloved disciple and kissed him on the forehead. Rabbi Joshua turned to the assembly and said in a barely audible whisper—as if he were praying—"Had we come to hear only Rabbi Simeon's exposition, it would have been more than enough. Happy are we, blessed are we, that such scholars are in our midst."

APPENDIX
GENESIS RABBAH

8:3 "Then God said, 'Let us make man in our image, after our likeness....'" (Gen. 1:26) With whom did He counsel? Rabbi Joshua ben Levi said, "He counseled with the works of heaven and earth...."

8:5 Rabbi Simon (Simeon ben Pazzi) said, "When the Holy One, blessed be He, was about to create man, the ministering angels formed themselves into [contending] groups and parties. Some of them said let him [man] be created, and some of them said let him not be created. As it is written in Scriptures, 'Loving-kindness and truth met [in combat]; mercy and truth embraced [in struggle].' [The rabbis understood *tzedek* as mercy, charity.] (Psalms 85:11) Loving-kindness said, 'Let him be created for he does acts of loving-kindness.' Truth said, 'Let him not be created because he is all lies.' Mercy said, 'Let him be created for he does acts of charity.' Peace said, 'Let him not be created for he is full of strife.' What did the Holy One, blessed be He, do? He took truth and cast it down to earth. The ministering angels said to the Holy One, blessed be He, 'Why do You disgrace Your seal? Let truth arise from the earth.' This is what is written in Scriptures, 'Truth shall spring up from the earth.'" (Psalms 85:12)

8:8   Rabbi Samuel bar Nahman said in the name of Rabbi Jonathan, "When Moses was writing the Torah, he wrote the creation of each day. When he came to this verse, 'And God said let us make man in our image, according to our likeness,' he said before Him, 'Master of the universe, why do You provide an excuse for the heretics!' He [God] said to him, 'Write, and he who desires to err, let him err.' The Holy One, blessed be He, said to him, 'Moses, this man whom I have created, shall I not cause both great and small ones to descend from him? When a great man will come to ask permission from one less than he, he may say, "Why should I ask permission from one less than I?" They will then answer him, "Learn from your Creator who created all that is above and below, yet when He was about to create man, He counseled with the ministering angels."'"

49:25   Rabbi Levi said, "The Judge of all the world must not act with the demands of [absolute] justice. If you desire a world, there cannot be justice; and if you desire justice, there cannot be a world. You grasp the rope at both ends: You want a world and you want justice. If you do not let go a little, the world will not survive." [The above is a comment on Genesis 18:25. Rabbi Levi understands Abraham's rebuke when God was about to destroy Sodom not as a question but as an imperative, a command: "God, You must not do justice!" R. Levi vocalizes the letter *hei* in *hashofet* as a definite article.]

Indeed, wherever I go on this great continent, I find people whose principal reason for identification with our movement is our commitment to *tikkun olam*, to Jewish social justice. This is as true of converts—Jews-by-choice—as it is true of born Jews.

Let there be no doubt about it. Reform religious action has returned to the Jewish fold numerous idealists, young and old, whose prophetic yearning had no prior Jewish expression, who knew only the language of universal activism. It has helped to rear a generation of Jews for whom there is no schizophrenic division between the real world and the world of Jewish devotion, who understand that *tikkun olam*, the quest for justice and peace, is indeed the work of Judaism.

Now as far as Jewish education is concerned, it appears that our children find that above everything else the concept of *Judaism as a pathway of action* makes their Jewish identity plausible. Take away social action, and you take away the driving force of NFTY. Take away social action, and you deflate the sense of purpose and community that makes Reform camping a transformative Jewish experience.

Being free to choose or not to choose Judaism in our era of voluntary Jewish identification, our children want to know just *why* they should choose to be Jews. And most of the answers we give them apparently are not sufficiently persuasive.

The one argument that carries the day with most of our young people is, "We want you to be a Jew because we Jews have a special vocation, and that is to pursue justice."

We dare not separate social action from Jewish education, for we teach our children Torah not only to know Torah, nor even to teach Torah, but above all to *be* Torah.

As the Berditchever Rebbe taught:

> What does it amount to that they expound Torah! A man should see to it that all his actions are Torah and that he himself

becomes so entirely Torah that one can learn from his habits and his motions, and even from his motionless clinging to God.

Rabbi Alexander M. Schindler
Sermon at Washington Hebrew Congregation
Washington, D.C.
June 11, 1994

DOES GOD HAVE A CONSCIENCE?

HAROLD M. SCHULWEIS

By authority of the Heavenly Tribunal and of the Court below with divine sanction and with the sanction of this holy congregation, we declare it lawful to pray together with those who have transgressed.

This preamble to the *Kol Nidre* declares the interdependence of heaven and earth, the unity between the law above and the law below, the dignity and power of the holy congregation. It is a proclamation that proceeds not with a prayer but with a legal formula recited three times and ending with the stark declaration, "Our vows to God shall not be vows, our bonds shall not be bonds, and our oaths shall not be oaths."

How strange to begin a day of solemn resolutions with the nullification of oaths. Jews honor their vows. We are told, "Be not rash with your mouth nor let your heart be hasty to utter a word before God." (Ecclesiastes 5) A vow in Judaism is sacred. As it is stated in the Bible, "When you make a vow to *Adonai* your God, you must pay it without delay. Be careful to keep any promise you have made with your lips." (Deuteronomy 23:22)

The rabbis teach, "Your yea shall be yea and your nay nay." How then dare we begin the Day of Atonement with the nullification of our vows to God? What in the tradition gives us the power to annul, to absolve, to nullify, to release?

The following three texts from the Book of Numbers reinforce the annulment formula. The first is "And the congregation shall be forgiven"; the second is "Pardon the iniquities of this people"; the last is "God said I have forgiven according to thy word." These texts refer to the report of the sins of the people in the desert. Now that the Israelites have left the bondage of Egypt, they do nothing but murmur, complain, and yearn to return to the fleshpots of Egypt. They are unable or unwilling to take destiny into their own hands and implement the command to enter the Promised Land of Canaan. In the absence of Moses, they construct a golden calf to worship.

Angry with this ungrateful people, God declares, "How long shall I bear with this evil congregation that keeps murmuring against Me?" And after the insult of the golden calf (Deuteronomy 9), God says, "I have seen this stiff-necked people. Let Me alone that I may destroy them and blot out their name from under heaven." *Heref mimeni veashmidem.* God has sworn to destroy this people, and "if God, Ruler of the universe, has proposed an oath, who can nullify it?" (Isaiah 14:27)

How did the sages understand this exchange between Moses and God? Consider the imaginative rabbinic reconstruction of the encounter as reflected in the Talmud (*Berachot* 32) and Midrash (*Shemot* 43:4). When Moses heard God say, "Let Me alone that I may destroy them," he considered God's peculiar diction. What does it mean when a powerful, omnipotent God cries out to be let alone? Who is holding God back? Who can stop God? Moses understood the hint. He seized hold of God's garment and would not let God go. Moses insisted, "I will not let You go until You forgive and absolve this people." God cannot abandon the people to whom God has given God's word. What did God expect of the Israelites whom God had brought into Egypt, where they were forced to live as slaves and where they were raised in an atmosphere of idolatry and superstition? God was moved by Moses' defense.

God replied to Moses, *Kevar nishbati.* "I have already sworn; I have already taken an oath. What can I do but keep it?" Moses answered, "Ruler of the universe, did You not teach us that if some-one takes an oath, that person can consult a scholar who may absolve the oath? Come to me, Ruler of the universe, and I will absolve Your oath." Thereupon, Moses wrapped himself in a prayer shawl and sat down. God stood before the seated Moses who asked God, "Do you regret Your oath?" And God answered, "I regret the evil that made Me issue that oath." Then Moses replied, "You are absolved, God. There is no oath and there is no vow." And God said, "I have forgiven according to thy word." God forgives according to man's word. Man's word can override, even exonerate, God's oath. Therein lies the stunning use of the biblical verse included in the prayers recited after the *Kol Nidre*: "I have forgiven according to thy word." The power of that word is drawn from the fount of conscience.

Certainly the tradition is not saying that compared to Moses, God is weak or wrong. Rather the rabbis are propounding a unique conception of God. God is not the Grand Inquisitor. The God of Israel does not declare, "Obey Me, follow Me blindly, bite your tongue, shut your mouth, bind your hands, and bend your knee." Instead, God affirms, "I am the loving God who breathed into you a free spirit. I have created you with a mind and with a heart. I am not Pharaoh."

Therein lies a distinctive aspect of Jewish spirituality. Believers do not grovel before a divine authority but stand before God with the moral dignity of those who know themselves to be loved as people created in the image of God.

A Religion of Obedience?

In comparative religion classes, college students are presented with the God of Judaism as an imperial, inflexible, wrathful Commander who gives orders. Judaism is quintessentially a faith of obedience. This was the caricature that the New Testament drew of Judaism, depicting it as a legalistic system devoid of the spirit of love. From Spinoza and Moses Mendelssohn to Kant, Fichte, and Hegel, the legacy that Judaism is nothing but a polity of laws that demands obedience was promulgated. That subservient characterization of Judaism has been internalized even by Jews who think of Judaism as an authoritarian, legalistic tradition. The late Jewish philosopher

Professor Yeshayahu Leibowitz avers that "the Torah and the prophets never appeal to man's conscience, for such an appeal is always suspect as a possible expression of idolatry. In fact, the term conscience is not to be found in the Hebrew Bible. The guidance of conscience is an atheistic, indeed, an idolatrous concept." He goes on to contrast conscience with the *halachah*, which as a religious instruction does not tolerate the concept of ethics. ("Commandments" in *Contemporary Jewish Religious Thought*)

That portrayal is widespread, distorting, and hurtful. It ignores the heroic divine-human relationship. It eviscerates the unique theistic humanism of the Jewish stance before God. Moses' nullification of God's vows is not the first or the last time that the prophets or the rabbis exposed the moral nerve of our faith. Examine the following stunning rabbinic commentary in *Bemidbar Rabbah* 19:33, which is rarely taught, preached, or explained but which exemplifies the radical character of Jewish faith.

In this commentary the conflict is about nothing less than the wording of the Ten Commandments, recorded both in the Book of Exodus and the Book of Deuteronomy. "I, *Adonai* your God, visit the iniquity of the parents upon the children and the children's children unto the third and fourth generation." Many rabbis were uneasy about this hereditary punishment. In their moral imagination they envisaged Moses rising before God to argue, "Ruler of the universe, Terah, Abraham's father, worshiped idols, but Abraham discovered and loved only one God. King Ahaz was a cruel king, but his son King Hezekiah was a man of great spirit. King Amon was wicked, but his son King Josiah was a righteous leader. Is it fair that the righteous be punished for the sins of their fathers?"

How, according to the rabbinic account, did the Ruler of the universe respond to Moses' critique? God says, "Moses, you have instructed Me. *Limaditani. Ani mevatel devarai umekayem devarecha*—I shall nullify My words and confirm your words. Moreover, your instruction, Moses, will be recorded in your name in the statement 'Parents shall not be put to death for children, nor children be put to death for parents. People shall be put to death only for their own sin.'" (Deuteronomy 24:16)

The implications of this confrontation are far-reaching. God does not shut Moses up. He does not dismiss him as a mere mortal cipher nor declare his challenge as hubris. Neither God nor the tradition resents Moses' moral challenge to God as insubordination, treason, or *lèse-majesté*. Moses rests his argument on God's morality. God is therein fulfilled. God's relationship to God's people is like that of a parent. Moses' moral assertiveness is what every father and mother hope to see in their own children. Moses appeals to God in the name of God against God. Moses knows that the God within God will not sanction injustice. The God whom Moses is appealing to has, as it were, a conscience. God recognizes in the protesting voice of Moses' conscience God's own voice. In much the same manner as there is a law within law, *lifnim meshurat hadin*, there is a God within God.

Whom is Abraham addressing in the classic remonstration at Sodom? "Will you indeed sweep away the righteous with the wicked? . . . Far be it from You to do after this manner. . . . Shall not the Judge of all the earth do justly?" (Genesis 18:23-25) Abraham appeals to no third force, only to the God within God. It is for this reason that the rabbis extol Abraham's challenge over that of Job. Job sought to appeal to another power besides God to adjudicate the quarrel between them. "Would there were an umpire between us, that he might lay his hand upon us both." (Job 9:33) But Abraham trusted God's own moral sense to render justice fairly, despite God's earlier decision to destroy the citizens of Sodom. (*Baba Batra* 16a)

Note well that in this and in other confrontations, the prophetic conscience that is critical of kings and governments and even divine laws does not end in anarchy or lawlessness. The result of Moses' critique is not anomie but a deep responsiveness of the law to moral conscience: "I will nullify My decrees and confirm yours. Your instruction will be recorded in your name in My book." Conscience yields a heightened sensibility that is crystallized in Jewish law. Those who rush to call conscience heresy fail to appreciate that conscience is the motivation and the energy of a nobler law. Those who are nervous about the elevated status of conscience forget that it is the Jewish conscience that has kept Jewish law alive, responsive, and spiritually refined.

Law and Conscience

"The law of the land is the law." (*Baba Kamma* 113a) The duly constituted authority must be obeyed. In a balanced view there is no schism between law and conscience in Judaism. Law and conscience are not enemies. Judaism knows from its long history that without law anarchy takes over. There is no civilization without rules, regulations, and structure. The fear of *hefkerut*, "anomie," led to the counsel in the rabbinic aphorism "Pray for the welfare of the state, for were it not for the fear of government, people would swallow up each other alive." (*Pirke Avot* 3:2)

One cannot live without law, but law that is not invigorated by the fresh air of moral conscience stagnates. Based on Leviticus 19:2, Nachmanides observed, "You can be a scoundrel within the letter of the law," *naval bereshut hatorah*. Legality stripped bare of moral conscience can become a sophisticated art for circumventing the purpose of the law. Exclude conscience from your legal behavior and *halachah* can be turned into a mask of idolatry.

Consider the role of Jewish sensibility in the decisions of law rendered in one of the celebrated cases cited in the Talmud. (*Baba Metzia* 83a) Some porters accidentally broke a barrel of wine that belonged to Rabbah bar Huna. The rabbi seized their garments and the workers promptly went to Rav to complain about the seizure of their property. Rav ordered Rabbah to return the porters' garments. The verdict surprised Rabbah and he asked the judge, *Dina hachi*—"Is this the law?" The judge answered, "Yes." To support his ruling, the judge quoted the verse from the Book of Proverbs 2:20, "Ye shall walk in the way of good people." Later the workers returned to the judge. "We are poor men," they said. "We have worked all day and are in need. Are we to get no wages?" And Rav, the judge, turned to Rabbah, the owner, and said, "Go and pay them." Rabbah was surprised at the verdict and asked, *Dina hachi*—"Is this the law?" And the judge answered, "Yes, it is the law." And Rav defended his decision by citing the latter part of the same verse above from the Book of Proverbs—"Keep the paths of the righteous."

We can imagine Rabbah's chagrin at Rav's ruling. Does the *Mishnah* not state clearly that "they may not show pity in a legal matter"? (*Ketubot* 9:2) Can a ruling on monetary matters be based on the abstract moral sentiment of a verse in the Book of Proverbs, to "walk in the way of good people" and "keep the paths of the righteous"? After all, the Bible itself admonishes in Exodus 23, "Do not give preference to the poor man in law." Surely the porters were responsible for the breakage and the owner had the right to seize hold of their garments as security. Without the leaven of conscience, that counterargument could well hold water. But Maimonides included the ethical ideal "You shall walk in God's ways" (Deuteronomy 28:9) as one of the halachic 613 *mitzvot*. Rabbi Isaac of Corbeil similarly included the ethical goals "And you shall do the right and the good" and "You shall be holy" among the mandatory 613 commandments. (Aaron Lichtenstein, in Marvin Fox, ed., *Modern Jewish Ethics: Theory and Practice*, Ohio State University Press, Columbus, Ohio, 1975) At the heart of the teleology of the Torah is conscience.

The Marks of Conscience

What is this "word" by virtue of which God forgives and people can annul oaths? We have identified it as conscience. But what is conscience? From where does it come and to whom does it belong?

There is no word for conscience in the Bible or the Talmud. For that matter, there is no word for religion in the Bible. Yet surely the Bible is a religious book and just as surely conscience is the governing spirit that hovers over Jewish law and lore. Still, there is no entry for conscience in the Jewish encyclopedia.

There is a mystique about conscience and it is difficult to define. But we can identify some of its marks in sacred writings and in the inner witness of our lives.

One of the salient characteristics of conscience is its peculiar inner compulsion. Some issues cannot be evaded. Situations arise to which we respond not out of submission to an external authority but out of assent to an inner authority. Positions must be taken despite our awareness that they may not be in our best self-interest and will not redound to our fortune or popularity. Even during those times when we possess the ring of Gyges—when we know that we are invisible, when we feel that we can get away with something, when we think that we can cut corners without anyone being the wiser for it—we will not deny the inner imperative to act against the grain. When suffocated, the still small voice produces a restlessness that finds no relief. We experience something of the inner compulsion described by the prophet Jeremiah, who, having been released from the stocks for speaking out against the immoral policies of the king, is warned to hold his tongue. He cannot. "If I say that I will not speak anymore in God's name, then there is in my heart a burning fire shut up in my bones, *ke'esh boeret atzur beatzmotai*, and I am weary holding it in, and I cannot, *velo uchal*." (Jeremiah 20:9) This "I cannot" indicates something beyond the subjectivity of the self. It intimates a sense of transcendence, an identification with something larger than the interest of the calculating self. Conscience is experienced not as something alien beyond the heavens or the seas but "the word [that] is very nigh to you in your mouth and in your heart that you may do it." (Deuteronomy 30:14) It is the transcendent character of conscience that enables Moses to speak to God not as an antagonist but as a person who is at one with the God within God.

The exercise of conscience is a sign of transcendence made immanent. It confirms the reality of the divine breath blown into the nostrils of the self. Gershom Scholem observes that the Chasidim make an attempt to prepare "the Torah of the heart," which is a term that comes closest to the idea of conscience. He cites a chasidic interpretation of a passage in Deuteronomy 17:18,19 about the king of Israel: "And he shall have written for himself in a book a copy of the Torah . . . and it shall remain with him, and he shall read it all the days of his life. . . ." This chasidic interpretation explains that the king was to read the Torah inscribed within. The heart of the king was nurtured and cultivated by the collective conscience of the people as revealed in the Torah.

The sense of transcendence experienced in conscience typically runs counter to self-advantage. Conscience responds to the needs of those who are the least likely to return the favor. The target of conscience is directed toward the powerless, the pariahs of society, the members of the submerged community.

The sense of transcendence experienced in acts of conscience yields a deeper awareness of the self. It is not simply the discovery that we have a conscience but that we are our conscience. In conscience lies the recognition of the authentic self and its closeness to the God of conscience. The moral intuition points beyond the immanent self to the transcendent character of the divine image.

Jewish Conscience Learned

We are not born with a conscience. We are born into a community of conscience. Individual conscience is not innate or isolate. It draws on the collective conscience of universal principles, the basic attitudes of a tradition. Conscience is cultivated by family, friends, teachers, and the community of faith with which we identify. Conscience is a process that evolves and is subject to change. It is cultivated early, developing from all kinds of experience. I recall a few early accounts that particularly impacted upon my moral sensibilities.

I remember myself as a small child who was sent to the grocery store to buy something and received more change than I was due. I recall my hesitation. Having finally decided to return the money to the grocer, who barely acknowledged the heroism of my deed, I returned home and blurted out what I had done. Everything depended upon how Papa and Mama would respond. Would they regard me as a naif who knew nothing about taking advantage of my good fortune or would they praise me for doing what was right? My parents never knew how significant to the shaping of my character their response to my confession was.

I also recall that my father never crossed a picket line. Any man holding a picket sign was an *arbiter*, a "working man." Papa wasn't poor or a worker, but for him crossing a picket line was an act of treason. Decades later, my son Seth and I went to see a particular movie. When we arrived at the theater, we discovered that it was being picketed. I couldn't cross the picket line. My son understood.

Whether Papa was right or wrong about not crossing a picket line is arguable. Surely there are strikes that should not be honored. But the function of conscience is not to tell us in detail whether a strike is good or bad. Conscience doesn't tell us everything. It doesn't tell us how to vote on a tax bill or a health plan. But conscience does raise a red flag. It calls attention to people, conditions, and ends that are often neglected. Whatever the issue that calls for resolution, conscience does not allow us to overlook the homeless, the hungry, the beaten, and the stranger in our midst. Rabbinic conscience reminds us that all these people are God's special children. Conscience may not tell us which remedies are best, but it does not let us forget the underlying moral purpose of the act that we are contemplating. Conscience stirs up ultimate questions that bear on such decisions as: Who are we? What moves us? What makes us cry? What motivates us to sacrifice?

Conscience cultivates moral sensibility, which can be taught. A third personal recollection that impacted upon my moral sensibilities is of a Bible class that was given at the Talmudic Academy High School. The late Rabbi Samuel Mirsky was interpreting a biblical verse in class. He sang out the verse: "When you lend your neighbor any manner of loan, you must not go into his house to seize his pledge. You must stand outside." (Deuteronomy 24:10, 11) And then the rabbi repeated the last phrase: *Bachutz ta'amod*, "You must stand outside, while the man to whom you made the loan brings the pledge out to you." "Why?" the rabbi chanted rhetorically. "Why must I stand outside when I am the creditor and my pledge, my money, is inside?" He answered, "You may be the man's creditor and he may be your debtor, but you must respect the debtor's dignity, his privacy." And the rabbi went on, "And if the man is poor, you shall not sleep with his pledge when the sun goes down." The rabbi continued, "And if you take your neighbor's garment as a pledge, you must restore it to him." (Deuteronomy 24:12, 13) Rabbi Mirsky explained why: "For that is his only covering. It is the garment for his skin. Where shall he sleep? 'And when he cries unto Me, I will hear him for I am a compassionate God.'"

Rabbi Mirsky was not teaching socialism or capitalism. He was cultivating conscience in the course of transmitting the *neshamah* of the law. The law has a heart, a goal, a conscience. Whenever I consider the source of individual conscience—even when it runs counter to a law or authority—I know that it is not orphaned. It is parented by the collective conscience of a tradition mindful of the law within the law and the God within God.

The Individual and Collective Conscience

The individual Jewish conscience is not created ex nihilo. It develops within the womb of community. The dialectical interdependence of individual and collective conscience, for example, is not coincidental to the understanding of the political behavior of Jews. Their voting behavior continues to bewilder sociologists and political scientists who observe that while most socioeconomic, religious, and ethnic groups vote their economic self-interest, Jews with incomes of Episcopalians vote like Puerto Ricans. There are Machiavellians who sneer at the folly of Jews whose voting patterns continually favor foreign aid, bills on civil rights, and welfare proposals that do not benefit their own people. Most recently even the sharpest critics of Jews were incredulous that the first and loudest voices of protest against the ethnic cleansing of Bosnia were those of officials of Jewish organizations. What an irony that it was Elie Wiesel, the Holocaust survivor from Hungary, who turned to the president of the United States at the dedication of the United States Holocaust Memorial Museum and called upon his good offices to intervene in the slaughter of Bosnians and their neighbors. The irony lies in Wiesel's urging intervention on behalf of Croats and Muslims who have shown little friendship for Jews or Israel. Croatia's pro-Nazi puppet state and its vicious anti-Semitic Ustashi movement slaughtered thousands of Jews during the Holocaust. Muslims were anti-Zionist during the Holocaust and today do not make the Jewish heart sing for joy. What induced officials of major American Jewish organizations to meet with Clinton administration officials and members of the Senate to protest the inaction of the American government? Surely not self-interest. It was because Jewish conscience triumphed over the urge to get even with the sons and daughters of the Croats and the Muslims. So, too, Jewish conscience has led Mazon, the Jewish Response to Hunger, to supply fifty million dollars in food and medicine not only to Jews in need but to non-Jews as well.

Since Jewish conscience is not inborn, it can perish. Jewish conscience is not in the DNA. However warm the hearts of the ancestors, the children's hearts can become hardened, coarsened, and cold. Jewish conscience can weaken and die. When conscience dies, the soul of the Torah dies. The Meiri explained why the Talmud compares the death of a person to the burning of a *Sefer Torah*. When a Torah is burned, we tear our garments; when a person dies, we also tear our garments, for there is Torah in the human heart. "Love of man," Rabbi Abraham Isaac Kook wrote, "must erupt from the sense of *chesed* [loving-kindness], not out of

Today I want to talk to you not so much about the massive social and economic problems of our world but rather about the more personal ethical choices we are called upon to make. Events of the day compel me to do so, for the present-day plague of ethical nihilism has scarcely passed us by.

People credit me for conceiving and crystallizing the idea of "outreach." In fact, Judaism had such a program eons before I came on the scene. *Lech-Lecha* states it quite clearly, as God reaches out to Abraham and bonds him to the covenant through the ritual of circumcision. "Walk in My way," says God, "and be blameless." *That* was Judaism's original outreach program. It consisted of exemplary moral conduct that might provoke others to say: If this is how they are, this is something I covet and want to be.

But how far from "blameless" have we become? The piteous fact is that the casual question that Jews ask about people in the news, "Is he Jewish?" is nowadays asked more often with worry than with pride. The grievous fact is that of late Jews are being named more often as indicted public officials and businessmen than as Nobel Prize winners.

Some may argue defensively that only one or two of the Jews caught up in the recent notoriety have significant ties to the Jewish community. Such an argument makes a virtue of our ineffectiveness! Besides, some of this ethical decay has contaminated our very own community's bone and marrow. The drug-and-drink, pleasure-and-oblivion culture is alive and well in many Jewish homes...the epidemic of divorce and of legally intact but spiritually failed marriages afflicts us, too...the tides of abuse, of exploitation, of prejudice...the quest for instant gratification...the furious frenzy of greed—*all* these plagues include as participants—or should we say as victims—an unseemly number of Jews.

Now, I know full well that this lawlessness and corruption is widespread in our land and touches every level of our society. Look and see: Not even the holier-than-thou TV evangelists are impervious to the moral malaise of our age! Still, we must ask: What has happened to our once profoundly ethical Jewish community? What are the sources of our degradation and shame?

We must find a way to recover the Jewish sense of noblesse oblige. We must return to the prototype of our outreach effort that bade us win adherents not by precept but by example. And we must recapture that ethical self-esteem that led to Rabbi Stephen Wise's proud reply to an American lady who tried to impress him with the information that one of her ancestors had witnessed the signing of the Declaration of Independence: Wise held his leonine head high and majestically rejoined, "My ancestors, madam, were present at the giving of the Ten Commandments."

Rabbi Alexander M. Schindler
State of the Union Message
Chicago, Illinois
November 1987

JEWISH ETHICS IN THE DAILY LIFE OF THE JEW

JACK STERN

A preliminary note: It is appropriate that these reflections on Jewish ethics be included in this tribute to Rabbi Alexander Schindler. It was his presidential address during the 1987 Union of American Hebrew Congregations Biennial Assembly in Chicago that sparked the formation of the Ethics Task Force. The quality of his leadership and his character have strengthened the ethical underpinnings of Reform Judaism and provided it with a sturdy model of a *moreh tzedek*, a "teacher of righteousness."

✦ ✦ ✦

I once addressed the following questions to students in a confirmation class: "How many of you have cheated on school papers or exams?" Most hands were raised. "How many of you cheat with some regularity?" A few hands went down, but most remained up.

When I asked the students to explain how they accounted for their cheating pattern, their answers included the following:

> Because everybody does it.
>
> So I can get better grades, which will help me to get into a better college.
>
> I only cheat in classes in which I don't like the teacher.
>
> Cheating doesn't hurt anyone except yourself.

The distance is short between the answers of those sixteen-year-olds and the perceptions that permeate much of contemporary society. The following question was asked in a Time-CNN poll: "Do you believe that there is less truth-telling in government than there was a decade ago?" Seventy-five percent answered yes. The current wisdom is that almost everyone lies. Regarding the conduct of business affairs, Meir Tamari writes: "Our acceptance of previously low standards of business ethics, development of 'gray' areas in morality, and social pressure for an even higher standard of living further blur the distinction between permitted and forbidden actions."

This blurred distinction between "permitted and forbidden," between right and wrong, between good and bad, keeps chipping away at the bedrock of our society—and at the bedrock of our Jewish existence. The "blurred distinction" cannot hide from the ethical commandments of the Torah, the ethical (and passionate) pronouncements of the prophets, the ethical laws and precepts of the Talmud, the ethical principles of modern Zionism, and the centrality of ethical values in Reform Judaism. It cannot hide from the long-standing and proud Jewish claim that we were the ones who taught the world about the one ethical God, that we delivered the ethical message of that God to all of humankind: "It has been told you, O man [not 'O Jew'], what is good and what *Adonai* requires of you—to do justly, to love mercy, and to walk humbly with your God."

This ethical message to humanity begins with the Jewish account of universal human origins as it appears in the biblical saga. (I am grateful to Dr. Eugene Borowitz and to Rabbi Joseph Soloveitchik, *zichrono livrachah*, for my understanding and further exploration into this account.) Man and woman (later to be called Adam and Eve, who are prototypical of all humankind) are not the only creatures who make their appearance on the sixth day. The animals of the field were created before Adam and Eve entered the cosmic scene.

From this juxtaposition of animals and humans derives an essential Jewish teaching about the nature of being human (and ultimately about being ethical): In some respects we are not unlike our animal relations. Centuries before Darwin, the Midrash suggested that primordial man and woman had tails like monkeys, but God removed them "out of respect for human dignity." And the Talmud would later contend—centuries before Sigmund Freud—that human beings share four instincts with the creatures of the animal kingdom: hunger, sex, power, and possessiveness.

Thus the Talmud acknowledges our primal instinctual drives, which it labels our *yetzer hara*, our "evil instinct." At the same time, however, such instincts are not condemned per se because without the aggressive energy they produce, homes would not be built, children would not be conceived, and business ventures would not be undertaken. What the tradition warns against—and commands against—are not the instincts, which are part of who we are and how we were created, but rather the animalistic expression of those instincts. Not animal sex. Not the animal power of the jungle. Not the animal hoarding of material possessions. Not the animal lunging for food. (Rabbi Soloveitchik has suggested that the recital of a blessing before eating constitutes a human declaration that we are able to hold the hunger instinct in check and take time out to say a prayer.)

It is this capacity, which the Talmud calls our *yetzer hatov*, our "good instinct," to rise above our own animal selves and to set limits and tame our own primal urges that constitutes the basis of the ethical dimension of human experience. It is this other aspect of ourselves, this *tzelem Elohim*, this "image of God," that not only becomes counterpoint to our animal nature but also supersedes it. It generates all of those extraordinary qualities that make us human: our capacity to create and to love, our capacity to reason and plan for the future, and, most of all, our capacity to live as moral and ethical human beings. It allows us, consciously and deliberately, to distinguish between what makes us animal and what makes us godlike, between what is hurtful and what is helpful, between cen-teredness on self and concern for another, and between the primal self and the ethical self. Goaded by the *tzelem Elohim*, we confront moral issues and make moral choices, set limits and say no to our own animalistic and instinctual pushes, and make room for moral and ethical values in our day-to-day lives.

It is the *tzelem Elohim* that enables Adam, the prototype of all humanity, to be on the same wavelength with God and thus be addressed by God. Adam is told to tend the garden. He is told from which trees he may eat and which are off-limits, what is permitted and what is forbidden. And Adam, with his *tzelem Elohim*, is capable of responding to the God who addresses him. Adam can obey the directive, ignore it, or even defy it. He can stand before God or he can hide. This ability, distinctively human, to be addressed and to respond or not to respond is what accords us our moral freedom, what allows us to make moral decisions. We can choose "what is right and good in the sight of *Adonai*" (Deut. 6:18), we can choose something else, or we can make no choice at all—which is also a choice. What makes any behavior ethical or unethical in any given situation is determined by my response to what is ethically com-manded in that situation. The question thus becomes: What is the *mitzvah*, the "commandment," that applies to such a situation?

If I were an Orthodox Jew, those commandments (*mitzvot*), both ritual and ethical, would all be laid out for me in the 613 *mitzvot* of the Torah and all the subsequent rulings in the Talmud. Since such *mitzvot* and rulings represent "the word of God from Mount Sinai," it is incumbent upon me to comply with them accordingly.

For the liberal Jew, however, these *mitzvot* and rulings constitute not the literal words of God but the inspired words of the Jewish people at a given moment in history to articulate what they believed the God of the covenant wanted them to do, ritually and ethically. Since we live during another time in history, we are entitled to be selective in our compliance with the traditional *mitzvot*: to accept ("do not wrong the stranger"), to reject ("an eye for an eye"), or to create anew (gender equality). The indispensable requirement, however, is that we make such selections out of knowledge and commitment, not out of ignorance and inconvenience.

But even with the accepting, rejecting, and creating anew, the liberal Jew embraces, no less than the Orthodox does, the *idea* of *mitzvah*, of being commanded. Our question is: In this situation, what response on my part, what course of action is "right and good in the eyes of *Adonai*"? Our response to that question, with all of its imperative urgency, with all that our ancestors have taught us, and with all that we have learned since, bears testimony to our ethical responsibility.

Does this mean—this accepting, rejecting, and creating anew—that for liberal Jews there can be no ethical absolutes that transcend factors of time, place, and historical or personal circumstance? Does this mean there are no ethical values—caring, compassion, love—that can be labeled "eternal" or "permanent"? My response would begin with the tradition of Orthodoxy itself. Even with its insistence upon the eternal and permanent validity of the Torah, Orthodox Jewish tradition has always made room for modification of those original ethical mandates. "An eye for an eye," commanded in the Torah, was later interpreted to mean monetary compensation according to the value of an eye. Times had changed, society had advanced to a higher ethical level—and so had the old ethical commandment. The Torah labeled homosexuality an "abomination," a totally unethical mode of behavior. But times have changed, and society is learning more about homosexuality and is moving to a different and more informed level of understanding. And even though contemporary Orthodoxy has not yet modified the ancient absolute ethic, the day of reconsideration may not be too far distant.

And how absolute do such values as caring, compassion, and love deserve to be? Were those who loved Hitler (and many did) living out an ethical value? Are those who refuse to honor the parents who abuse them violating an ethical value? Or should it not be, as Rabbi Soloveitchik has taught, that no emotion—including caring, compassion, and love—can itself be called ethical until we know to what end, what object, or what recipient these emotions are directed? By such definition, the love directed to Adolf Hitler was flagrantly unethical. By such definition, disloyalty to abusive parents (by reporting them to the authorities) may be the most ethical course of action possible.

What we sometimes proclaim as absolute ethical values may, in fact, simply serve as guiding ethical principles. As with any such principles, the attempt is to make them operative in specific situations with the clear understanding that they will operate differently from one situation to the next. Perhaps the closest we come to an unwavering principle that deserves the label of an "absolute" value is articulated in the Genesis saga of creation: "And God created man in the divine image, in the image of God did God create him; male and female God created them." (Gen. 1:27) Whatever other values may be applied to a life situation, the bottom-line ethical question, derived from this fundamental ethical value, is: Do my own response and my own behavior affirm—or ignore or denigrate—that sacred God-image in another human being? What makes cheating, slandering, or abusing unethical is not only what each does to weaken the fabric of the community but what each does to disparage the image of God in that human being and, therefore, God as well. Conversely, when my behavior validates the worth of another human being, when it imparts strength, support, comfort, and hope, then I am affirming the God-image in that person and God as well. Then my behavior fulfills the ethical mandate.

But even more than that. Besides the person I have cheated, slandered, abused, or harassed, I have produced a second victim. My unethical act has sullied the God-image in myself and has, therefore, rendered the act doubly unethical. (In instances of slander, the Talmud cites three victims: the slanderer, the one slandered, and the one who listens to the slander.) But when I fulfill the *mitzvah*, when I provide the hope or help to enhance the life of another human being, I, too, am enhanced. And my *mitzvah* is doubly ethical.

But what of those situations where the ethical direction is less than clear? What of those situations when our crisis of conscience is not between right and wrong but between right and right, not between good and bad but between good and good? A classic example from Jewish tradition follows:

> Two men are traveling through the desert and one of them has a
> flask of water. If he alone drinks the water, he will reach the

town; but if both of them drink, they will both die (*Sifra* on Lev. 25:36)

One teacher, Ben Petura, said both should drink and die rather than one should live while the other dies. Rabbi Akiba said that the man who has the flask is entitled to drink the water and live. (Neither said that the man who has the flask should give it to the other man.)

How in our own day do we confront the conflict between the two "rights," concern for self and concern for another? How do we resolve the issue of an employee who has served loyally over the years but now is physically unable to function at standard efficiency? How do we address the issues of privacy and confidentiality when they entail a disease like AIDS? How do we decide whether or not to have a life-sustaining apparatus removed from a loved one who is terminally ill? How do we decide upon the "right" course of action when there are two—or more—"right" courses of action, all of which give due regard to the God-image both in the other and in ourselves?

Each time we confront such a conflict, we turn to related case precedents in traditional Jewish law (*halachah*), which may or may not be of help. In each situation, we turn to the compendium of Jewish ethical values that have been forged out of millennia of Jewish experience. In each situation, we take into account the various people involved and the various possible consequences of one course of action or another. But, ultimately, the litmus test of our ethical responsibility is the asking of that same question: In this situation, however complex, how in my best judgment does the one ethical God (however differently God may be perceived) call upon me to proceed? The very asking of the question acknowledges that the standards are God's and not our own because when the ethical standards are derived from our own human selves, however noble, or from our human communities, however idealistic, we run the risk of fixing the ethical standards to fit our own imperfect behavior. We run the risk of constant self-justification, of doing only what is right and good in our own eyes rather than in the eyes of God. Not the question: What do I expect of me? but the urgent question: What does the one ethical God expect of me?

It was the question that Adam failed to ask when he ate from the forbidden tree and when he and Eve went into hiding, and when they came out. It was Adam's (and our) failure to exercise his sense of responsibility by putting the blame elsewhere: "The woman you put at my side, she gave me of the tree and I ate." And Eve followed suit: "The serpent duped me, and I ate."

Their primordial pleas of self-defense persist until our own day: from people who rob other people, who murder other people, who rape other people. "Don't blame me. Blame my parents, who abused me; blame TV violence, which goaded me; blame society, which deprived me; blame pornography, which aroused me."

But the Bible had an answer for Adam and Eve and all their blaming successors. God calls Adam to account for his failure to assume responsibility—and Eve, too, and the serpent, too. They could run away from their responsibility but not from their accountability. The tradition insists all are held ethically accountable, which is what Rosh Hashanah and Yom Kippur are all about. We are all confronted with the divine question:

> Adam, where are you?
> Eve, where are you?
> What have you done—
> or not done?

Adam and Eve, with all their capacity to respond and with all their ethical power to set limits on their own primal instincts, failed the test and got themselves ousted from the garden. And thus does it proceed: Cain murders Abel and fails the test; the generation of the flood—"full of corruption and violence"—fails the test; and Noah, who survives the disaster as humanity's only hope for an ethical future, simply gets drunk and passes out—and fails the test. And, finally, the people of Babel were so fired up with their primal push for power that they built a tower to storm the heavens and take over from God—with not even an awareness of an ethical test. The *yetzer hatov* has succumbed to the *yetzer hara*.

Then what happens, according to the biblical saga, is what happens in any large organization when a task needs to be accomplished and the membership at large fails to accomplish it: A committee is appointed and is especially charged with the ministration of that particular task. God now needs a committee, and

Abraham is called to serve as chairman with Sarah as his partner. The committee, henceforth to be known as "a people" or "a community," will enter into a covenant with the one ethical God and will commit itself to rescuing the failed task of ethical responsibility and to teach the world what the world has thus far refused to learn. The community will be expected to model itself into "a kingdom of priests and a holy people," and no small part of the modeling will consist of making the right ethical choices.

From Leviticus 19:

> When you reap the harvest of your land, you shall not reap all the way to the edges of your field, or gather the gleanings of your harvest.... You shall leave them for the poor and the stranger: I am *Adonai* your God. (vv. 9, 10)

> You shall not defraud your neighbor. You shall not commit robbery. The wages of a laborer shall not remain with you until morning [because one is entitled to them on the same day that one works]. (v. 13)

> You shall not insult the deaf, or place a stumbling block before the blind.... (v. 14)

> You shall not take vengeance or bear a grudge against your kinsfolk. Love your neighbor as yourself. I am *Adonai*. (v. 18)

> You shall rise before the aged and show deference to the old.... (v. 32)

> When a stranger resides with you in your land, you shall not wrong that neighbor.... (v. 33)

> You shall have an honest balance, honest weights.... (v. 36)

The proposition that undergirds all these laws is that when a Jew acts unethically, he or she is doubly accountable: as a human being who has failed his or her own ethical potential—like Adam and Eve, Cain, Noah, and the people of Babel—and as a Jew who has turned his or her back on the holy ethical "calling" of the Jewish people, the community that defines its very existence by its ethical standards. When a public official has been found guilty of corrupting the position of public office—and that person is a Jew; when a stockbroker is found guilty of insider trading—and that person is a Jew; when an employer exploits employees or harasses them—and that employer is a Jew; when a family member abuses a spouse or a child—and that family member is a Jew; when a Jew behaves only with the primal push of the *yetzer hara* and without the limits of the *yetzer hatov*—in each of these cases that Jew has reneged on responsibility to that very community that, by definition, is expected to set the ethical example for the rest of society. We are sensitive when Jewish names are linked to public scandals because that's not the way it's supposed to be—as the Yiddish axiom phrased it: *Paast nicht fur a Yid,* "It's not befitting a Jew." As one commentator wrote: "Even when Jews are no more ethical than anyone else, they think they ought to be."

Granted that to live as a Jew is to live day to day as an ethical human being. Granted that to live as a Jew is to claim membership in a community that defines itself by its ethical standards and by its historic covenant with the one ethical God. Granted that you have to be ethical to be Jewish. But what of the other question that some Jews—and not just teenagers—will ask in reference to their daily lives: Do you have to be Jewish to be ethical? Now that Christianity has formulated its own ethical system, now that Western secular civilization has come to subscribe to the so-called Judeo-Christian ethic (even when it doesn't live up to it), now that we have increased knowledge of the ethical components of the Eastern religions, why can't someone simply live life day to day as an ethical person without a label or brand name?

Do you have to be Jewish to be ethical? What about Mother Theresa? What about those Christians who live as ethical exemplars, or, as they say, "very Christian"? And what about those Righteous Gentiles, like Oskar Schindler, who risked their lives to save Jews and whose names and memories are commemorated at Yad Vashem in Jerusalem? And what about all those born Jewish who do not belong to a synagogue and do not connect in any way with the Jewish community, who neither deny nor affirm their Judaism, or those who simply say that their religion is being an ethical person and living an ethical life?

Do you have to be Jewish or do you have to *live* Jewishly to be ethical? The answer, of course, is no, but that's only the beginning of the answer. To continue the answer we turn to the world of literature. The late Isaac Bashevis Singer was once asked in an interview: "You wrote on such universal themes—love, death, sexuality. Why must you make your writing so Jewish? Your language, your style, your characters, your settings—why do they have to be so Jewish?" And Singer answered: "Because every writer needs an address, a place where he lives and from which he writes. What gives a work passion and authenticity are those personal landscapes."

A good Christian can be ethical from his or her own Christian landscape just as a Jew can be ethical from the Jewish landscape. The more intimately we are connected to our respective ethical landscapes, to our own roots, our own cultures, our own families, our own traditions, our own covenants—the more passionately and authentically can we live our ethical lives.

Following are some glimpses into the Jewish ethical landscape. They were formulated in ages past—before advanced technology, before corporations, before labor unions. However, the ethical thrust of those dicta—in which the God-image in every person is acknowledged, in which a measure of respect and sensitivity is accorded to all parties in a transaction—bears urgent timeliness for our own moment in history.

The Ethics of Honesty

One must not promise to give something to a child and not give it to him [her] because thereby he [she] is taught to lie. (Talmud, *Sukah* 46b)

The shopkeeper must clean his [her] measures twice a week, wipe his [her] weights once a week, and clean his [her] scales after every weighing. This refers to moist goods, but it is not necessary for dry goods [because dry goods will not affect the balance]. (*Sifra* 91b)

The punishment of the liar is that he [she] is not believed even when he [she] speaks the truth. (*Avot de-Rabbi Nathan* 45b)

Ethics for the Marketplace

For the merchant:

It is both good and honest to do everything necessary in order to show the consumer the real value and beauty of an article. However, for one to cover and hide a defect in the article is nothing less than deceit and is forbidden. (Luzzatto, *Mesillat Yesharim*)

For the consumer:

One may not ask "What of the price of this thing?" if he [she] has no intention of purchasing it. (*Baba Metzia* 4:10)

Ethics for the Workplace

For the employer:

You shall not abuse a needy and destitute laborer, whether a kinsfolk or a noncitizen in your communities. You must pay that person's wages on the same day, before the sun sets, for the person is needy and urgently depends on it; else the person will cry to *Adonai* against you, and you will incur guilt. (Deut. 24:14-15)

For the employee:

Just as the employer is directed not to deprive the poor worker of wages or withhold them when they are due, so the worker is directed not to deprive the employer of the benefit of work by idling away time, a little here and a little there, thus wasting the whole day deceitfully....Indeed, the worker must be very scrupulous in the matter of time. (Maimonides, *Mishneh Torah*, "Laws concerning Hiring," 13:7)

The Ethic of Tzedakah

In the early nineties, a newspaper item reported that the United Jewish Appeal, which is supported by the American Jewish community (constituting less than 3 percent of the general population), raised more money ($668 million) that year than was raised by any other charity in the United States—surpassing even the Salvation Army ($649 million). Such an achievement, I would propose, derives directly from the Jewish ethical landscape. Even the vocabulary itself: In the general culture, the act of giving money to the needy is designated by the term *charity*—from the Latin *charitas*, which means "caring" or "loving." The other term is *philanthropy*, from the Greek word that means "love of humanity." Both terms imply a sentiment, what my heart moves me to do.

By contrast, the Jewish ethic of giving is termed *tzedakah*. It does not designate a deed we may feel like doing but a deed, a *mitzvah*, we are required to do, expected to do—which is what the term *justice* implies and which is what *tzedakah* literally means. It is the justice we owe the community to keep it from being destabilized by poverty. It is the justice we owe the poor people themselves because, according to the Jewish ethical landscape, many of them are where they are not because of their own doing but because they were forced into that poverty or the wheel of fortune turned against them and put them there. Conversely, those of us who are able to claim a measure of material well-being arrived at such a fortunate condition either because we were born into it or because, in addition to our own hard work, the wheel of fortune turned in our favor.

Consequently, according to the Jewish ethical landscape, since what we possess is not only ours but ultimately God's, we owe it to God and to God's impoverished children to share with them something of what we possess. Furthermore (and this may not sit well in some of the discussions regarding public welfare payments), according to the Jewish ethical landscape, there is even a sense of entitlement that goes with being poor—entitlement not only to financial support but also to respect and dignity. The story is told of the *shnorer*, the "professional beggar," who went to the affluent Lord Rothschild for his yearly handout and was met by Rothschild's secretary.

> Shnorer: I've come for my annual contribution.
> Secretary: Here are fifty rubles.
> Shnorer: Every other year I get a hundred rubles. Why only fifty this year?
> Secretary: Because this year Lord Rothschild is marrying off two of his daughters, and the expenses are enormous.
> Shnorer: You tell Lord Rothschild for me that he should marry off his daughters on his own money, not mine.

To do what is expected of us, what justice demands of us is what makes it *tzedakah*, and that is why the United Jewish Appeal collects more money than the Salvation Army.

The Ideal Ethic

From the Babylonian Talmud:

Some porters carelessly dropped a barrel of wine they were carrying for Rabbah bar Chana. As a penalty, he took away their coats. The men went to Rav and complained, and he ordered that their coats be returned.

"Is that the law?" Rabbah asked (knowing he had the law on his side).

"It is," answered Rav, "because Scripture says: 'That you may walk in the way of good men.'" (Proverbs 2:20)

After their coats were returned, the workmen said, "We are poor men who worked all day, and we are hungry. Are we not entitled to get paid?"

"Pay them!" Rav ordered.

"Is that the law?" asked Rabbah, astounded that he should be ordered to pay people who carelessly destroyed his property.

"It is," came the answer, "for it is written: 'And keep the paths of the righteous.'" (*Baba Metzia* 83a)

The episode illustrates the ideal ethic from the Jewish landscape. It is labeled *lifnim mishurat hadin*, "beyond the line of the law." According to the law and to the ethical principle upon which it is based, the porters could have been held responsible for their negligence. But the ideal ethic moves beyond fairness and justice and responds to the plight of the hungry porters. It ascends to the level of "more than fair," of "compassionate beyond justice." It ascends to a level that ordinary human beings may not always be able to achieve, but for every Jew it adds yet another step in the process of making ethical decisions.

How are such ethical values transmitted from one generation to the next? How do children learn to respond ethically in their own daily lives so that they will eventually take their place in the adult community as ethically responsible human beings who confront moral issues and work their way toward moral courses of action?

The beginning of an answer comes from those heroically ethical non-Jews who risked their lives to save Jews from the Holocaust. Three characteristics were shared by the rescuers: Their parents had served for them as models of ethical behavior; they, the rescuers, tended to be people of action, doers rather than talkers; and they tended to see themselves as somewhat set apart from the company of their peers, less conformist and more independent.

One way, therefore, to foster ethical responsibility and moral strength in the daily lives of children growing up is both to create a climate in which such traits can thrive and to ensure that the children encounter, through example and education, the ethical values that permeate their own Jewish landscape.

How then does all this—the *tzelem Elohim*, the *mitzvah*, the landscape, the ethical decision making—become incorporated into the daily life of the Jew? My answer comes from a personal experience of many decades ago when I was serving a congregation in the Deep South. The civil rights movement had not yet gained any significant momentum, and the pattern of racial segregation was still in force. During the High Holy Days (which was my first encounter with the congregation), I delivered a sermon on the ethical theme of human equality as derived from the Jewish belief in God. After the service an officer of the congregation told me how impressed he was with the sermon. A few weeks later I presented to the congregation's Board of Trustees a proposal for a day-long institute to be held in the temple for all the clergy of the community. The first response was from the man who had complimented me on the sermon. "The idea is fine," he said, "but, of course, you will make sure that the white clergy will sit on one side of the sanctuary and the Negro clergy on the other." Taken aback, I blurted out my startled retort: "I don't understand what you're saying. A few weeks ago you praised what I said about human equality, and now you're saying this!"

What he then said directs us to the heart of Jewish ethics in the daily life of the Jew: "The principle is wonderful. You just have to watch out when you get specific."

The reality of Jewish ethics is a resounding rejection of that man's warning. To the exact contrary, the general admonishment to do "what is right and what is good in the eyes of *Adonai*" is but the first step in the process (and even the Ten Commandments, which are essentially general principles, are not much farther along the way). The key is to get specific: In *this* specific situation; in *this* business deal; in *this* interaction with my customer, my patient, my client, or my colleague; in *this* family conflict—in each of these cases, is there an ethical ingredient that deserves to be factored into the final decision?

There is no promise of easy answers because other factors may be present, too. And sometimes there can be more than one ethical factor, which can be at odds with one another. Now we are getting specific, and we are asking the questions that only the *tzelem Elohim*, the "image of God," is capable of asking: In this specific situation, what does the one ethical God require of me? And how shall I respond to that requirement? Where shall I turn in my Jewish landscape to guide me and bolster me in my response?

We begin with a dual decision. We must live our lives as moral and ethical human beings by tapping the energy of our own ethical and moral selves, and we must carry the ethical banner of the Jewish people, which is at the core of our Jewish existence. And then it impels us to get specific with each day's issues, each day's decision, and each day's ethical *mitzvah*. When that continues to happen, say our Jewish mystics, as *mitzvah* is added to *mitzvah*, we are performing the most sublime of all *mitzvot—tikkun olam*, the "repairing of the world," the removal of its ethical imperfections, its poverty, violence, bigotry, corruption, and abuse. The more repairs we make, the closer we bring the Messianic Era.

And when God calls to us (as God does every day), "O man, O woman, where are you?"—there will be no need to hide.

As rabbis we must be concerned not just with the well-being of our congregations as a whole or even only with that majority of our people who are reasonably well-involved and well-served. Our care must extend also to those who are disabled in body or spirit.

Our tradition enjoins us to do so. In the *Mishnah*, tractate *Sanhedrin*, we are taught: "If a man saves a single life, it is as though he has saved the world." This familiar teaching proclaims the sanctity of each human life.

It also contains a more subtle, almost mystical implication that each single life is a microcosm of the whole world. Within each life and each family are all the elements of war and peace, love and hate, cooperation and competition, creativity and destructiveness that shape events in the world at large.

The *Sanhedrin*'s dictum also warns us—and here is the lesson I choose to emphasize today—never to overlook the saving of a single life in the course of trying to save the world.

It's always so much easier to save the world. It's easier to sign a petition for a nuclear freeze than it is to quit smoking cigarettes, though both are matters of survival. It's easier to demand justice for all than it is to deal justly with those who stand near. It's easier to vote for a resolution on Ethiopia than it is to give succor to a neighbor who is out of work and out of hope and who despairs that there is anyone who gives a damn for him.

Thus does the *Mishnah* remind us: Save the single soul, and you will save the universe.

This matter applies to the smaller world of our Union family as well. Here, too, we must care for not only the many but the one. Our success must be measured not only by how we respond to vast groupings of congregants but also by what we do or fail to do for those who are far fewer in number, the solitary souls, the lost souls, the disabled in body or in spirit.

Rabbi Alexander M. Schindler
Report to the UAHC Board of Trustees
Bal Harbor, Florida
November 30, 1984

ON BEING A JEWISH DOCTOR

BERNARD LOWN

Thinking of Alex Schindler evokes in my mind the image of a fellow physician who is oriented to healing the fractured human spirit. In an age of specialization, Alex concentrates on Jews. Rabbis and doctors are not far apart; both are dedicated to the art of healing. While their methods are strikingly different, their goals are shared—to make life endurable and, perhaps, even livable. In the case of doctors, the focus is on physical and psychologic ailments. For the rabbi, the aim is to enhance the spiritual dimension, thereby easing the existential angst provoked by the utter emptiness of a materialist society. Ivan Turgenev wrote, "The soul exists within us and perhaps a little about us; it is a weak glow that the ancient night eternally tries to snuff out." Resuscitating that weak glow is the rabbi's prime mission, a supreme healing function. Body and soul are separate only as a metaphysic artifact. The doctor aiming to heal can, therefore, not be unmindful of the spiritual dimension. Medicine, if properly practiced, is never far removed from the rabbinate. It would not be farfetched to suggest that many good doctors are but clerics in disguise.

These ruminations lead me to ask why the medical profession has such a large percentage of Jews. The rabbinic aspect of medicine is no doubt a factor. Ingrained deeply in the Jewish mind-set is a love of the book, a consummate curiosity, a yearning to touch the godliness in the human face, a craving to explore life's meaning, and a sense of mission to serve the wider community. These qualities find challenge as well as fulfillment in medicine.

The tragic Jewish experience over the ages may be a more significant explanation for attracting a disproportionately large number of our faith to medicine. From the very beginning of the diasporic ordeal, Jews made their mark by doctoring. For people who were wandering, medicine was a kindly calling. For a people frequently coerced to be on the run, to uproot at short notice as the price of surviving anti-Semitic hordes or pogroms, the tools of medicine were few, hastily assembled, and easily carried. Medicine permitted mobility; one was not burdened with merchandise that could be robbed while transported over dangerous highways. Healing herbs and lotions were available everywhere. One could readily set up shop anywhere. The practice was international, and the skills were universally applicable. When anti-Semitism grew venomous in Spain, the great Maimonides moved his practice to Egypt, achieving there prompt recognition and acclaim.

Professional skills were based almost exclusively on the human senses, finely honed by experience. In those days, the sick person was threatened more frequently by a doctor's ignorance and dogma than by the disease. Jews had few justifications for exhibiting either. As a social outcast, his life constantly imperiled, the Jewish doctor had to exercise the therapeutic restraint counseled by the first teacher of medicine, Hippocrates. He believed that a physician's role was to assist nature, deeming it the greatest of all healers. In medieval times there was no more effective approach to illness.

Medicine was also sought as a profession as it enabled an outcast Jew to gain intimacy with the powerful and aspire realistically to the highest rungs of society. No other way existed for immunizing against the virulent virus of anti-Semitism, always on the ready to rampage and to murder. This was the only existing occupation for protecting kith and kin. While rulers, potentates, viziers, and the like could dispense with money lenders, only at their life's peril could they rid themselves of their Jewish physician.

Once Jews gained some civic status after the French Revolution, they flocked to medicine. Nowhere was this more evident than at the very hub of the medical world, nineteenth-and early twentieth-century Vienna. The creativity of Jewish doctors conferred on the city distinction as the world's medical capital. The vital contributions made by Viennese Jewish physicians were momentous, launching many of the subdisciplines of medicine as we know them today. Jewish physicians excelled in every sphere from anatomy to roentgenology. Three earned the Nobel Prize in medicine: Rudolph Bárány, Karl Landsteiner, and Otto Loewi.

From the inception of the Nobel Prize to the advent of Hitler, Germans won 30 percent of all prizes, more than any other nation. German Jews, constituting but 1 percent of the population, garnered 30 percent of these. Even more remarkable is the fact that they won 50 percent of the prizes in medicine.

Since World War II the largest impact on global medicine has been made by American physicians and scientists. Among them the role of Jews has been dominant and extraordinary. This is the more remarkable since the ready entry of Jews into medicine was severely restricted until about forty years ago. When applying to medical schools in the early 1940s, I was rejected nearly everywhere, notwithstanding having graduated summa cum laude and having been first in my class. Harvard Medical School turned me down because as the dean confided, "We already have our quota of your people." Yet, at the present time, probably a third of the faculty at Harvard Medical School is Jewish. While the United States now dominates in winning the Nobel Prize in medicine, perhaps half or more of these prizes have been won by Jews.

It is sad to reflect that in this modern age of unprecedented freedom for Jews, rabbi and physician have come to a parting of ways. This is not because rabbis have steered a different course; it is physicians who have changed direction by increasingly abandoning their mission of healing.

Medicine is currently in profound crisis. The paradox is palpable. Notwithstanding enormous scientific achievements, never before in this century has the image of physicians been in more disrepair and their counsel more suspect. At a time when physicians have the most to offer in curing disease and prolonging life, the public is growing ever more suspicious, distrustful, and even antagonistic to the profession. At this writing, the doctor is in less repute than in any era except, perhaps, during biblical times when, according to

Ecclesiastes, "He that sinneth before his Maker let him fall into the hands of a physician."

No profound social transformation results from a single or simple cause. The introduction of ever more sophisticated technology is certainly one reason for the discontentment with the medical profession. Compared to the sharp images provided by ultrasonography, magnetic resonance imaging, computerized tomography, endoscopy, or angiography, a patient's history is regarded as confused, subjective, and seemingly irrelevant. Furthermore, it takes a good deal of time to elicit a full history. Technology has become an efficient substitute for the time that should be spent with patients.

The teaching of Hillel, "In a place where there is no man, strive to be a man," is no longer hallowed. It seems that the medical profession has indulged in a Faustian bargain. A 3,000-year-long tradition, which bonded doctor and patient in a special affinity of trust, has been replaced with treating, caring is being supplanted by managing, and the art of listening is taken over by technologic procedures. The distressed afflicted person is frequently absent from the transaction. The doctor is guided by scientific insights and uses ever more sophisticated technologic tools. No one would question that complex diseases for the first time can be diagnosed and effectively treated. But the majority of problems brought to the doctor have to do with symptoms arising from the rough-and-tumble of living. Though the complaints focus on particular organs, they stem from an aching heart, impervious to any modern instrument. Yet, these are not hidden from an ear cultivated to listen for the inaudible sigh, nor are they concealed from an eye sensitive to the unshed tear.

To heal requires the fullest exploitation of science guided by an art that addresses the indissoluble link between mind and body. Mind is the living, sensate, self-conscious individual, charged with feelings, agitated by fears, seeking from the physician optimism and empowerment not only to cope with illness but to cope with the ordeals of living. For medicine to fulfill its calling, science and art must be inseparable. The rabbinic calling needs reinstatement. This thesis needs frequent repetition. While it receives lip service at every medical school commencement, in practice it is fouled by inattention.

The downward traverse of the image of the medical profession is also hastened by an extraordinary reductionist hubris that is taught to young medical students. A simplifying conception is purveyed, which views a sick person as merely a repository of malfunctioning organs or deranged regulatory systems never refractory to some technical fix. Within this constellation the doctor is an exacting scientist engaging in an act of discovery. Gravitating in this direction were not only new philosophic notions of illness but powerful economic incentives as well. Society places a much higher premium on uses of technology than on listening or counseling. An hour in an operating room or with some invasive procedure is financially rewarded more than tenfold compared to an hour spent conversing with patients or family.

This approach is damaging to both doctor and patient. In addition to obviating discourse, it focuses on the acute and emergent. It is completely indifferent to disease prevention or to health promotion. Since preventive medicine, though the most cost-effective approach to illness, is time intensive, it is completely neglected. Diligent prevention invariably plays second fiddle to heroic cures. Human apostasy reappears in every age, each worshiping its own uniquely wrought golden calf. The situation will continue to deteriorate until doctors abandon technologic idolatry and reconnect with their tradition as healers.

Since Jews constitute a significant intellectual force in American medicine, how is one to account for the trajectory of health professionals away from their humanitarian moorings? One does not find Jewish physicians on the ramparts in that valiant struggle to assert medicine's ancient sacred compact with human beings. But do we Jews not pride ourselves on being people of the Book? In the words of Isaiah, are we not committed to be a "light unto the nations"? Being Jewish relates little to having a sensitized palate for gefilte fish or attending services on Fridays. George Steiner captured the essence: "Whatever can explain the mystery of Jewish survival, the roots of that mystery are ethical or they are nothing." Where then are the voices of Jewish doctors? This question may surprise some. After all, Jews have happily integrated into the American melting pot. Why should they hew to higher standards than anyone else? Why make waves?

How is one to account for the disjuncture in the medical profession in general and among Jewish doctors in particular? Like any complex social phenomena, no answer can be sought in simple explanations. One factor no doubt relates to the schizophrenia in modern life between individual values and social practice. The commodification of human relations affects Jews and non-Jews alike. Jewish doctors are as much a product of a technologic consumer culture as are other professionals. Market values replace the sacred and the spiritual. All succumb to the profitable deal. As Rabbi Leonard Beerman sermonized one Yom Kippur: "The landscape of every city is dominated by the high-rise buildings of commerce. These are our real cathedrals and synagogues; it is there we worship, there you will find the common religion of all Americans." The deep roots of Jewishness are weakening, overwhelmed by the eloquent forces of consumer culture as they confront the reticent forces of community ties.

History affords not only despair but also hope. Whenever historic forces emerge that diminish our rich millennial heritage, counterforces soon are mobilized to offer resistance. When the odds are overwhelming, Jews do not disdain from attempting the miraculous. Alex Schindler's lyrical words address this very issue: "For as Maimonides taught, miracles are not the things that awe us with a sense of the impossible. Miracles, rather, are those events that stretch our sense of the possible. Miracles are not transcendent, not otherworldly. They are simply the achievements of people in this world who proceed in faith to deal with life not merely as a personal quest for happiness but as a communal quest for *worthiness*." [Schindler's italics]

My own life in medicine, now extending over more than four decades, has taught me that the miraculous is achievable when the essential motif for living adheres to the "quest for worthiness." For me, it means bringing to medicine my Jewishness. Einstein summarized it well in a letter written shortly before his death: "The most important human endeavor is the striving for morality in our actions. Our inner balance and even our very existence depends on it. Only morality in our actions can give beauty and dignity to life." This is the essence of our Jewish heritage that must suffuse all our actions; this in my mind is living up to the injunction of Isaiah to be a "light unto the nations."

As a small boy growing up in a Lithuanian *shtetl*, I believed in the indispensability of Jewishness for being either a rabbi or a doctor. The only two doctors attending the entire community were Jewish. The unique qualities of Jewishness to doctoring have been widely acknowledged. In 1992, in a posthumously published book, *Intoxicated by My Illness*, Anatole Broyard, former literary critic of *The New York Times*, wrote: "My father was an old-fashioned Southern anti-Semite. He insisted on a Jewish doctor when he developed cancer of the bladder. A Jewish doctor, he believed, had been bred to medicine. In my father's biblical conception, a Jew's life was a story of study, repair, and reform. A Jewish doctor knew what survival was worth because he had to fight for his."

Coming from several generations of rabbinic forefathers, I imbibed a Jewish tradition that has not been so much steeped in prayer and formal observance as in relating Jewishness to *tzedakah*, to the ancient precept that "a person possesses what he gives away." Jewish doctors are the heirs to a rich tradition that was delineated by Maimonides in the twelfth century: "May I never consider him merely a vessel of disease." To go beyond the sickness and embrace the afflicted human being requires cultivation of an art in every way as important as the science the physician brings so proudly to the bedside.

The following experience illustrates how my rabbinic genes helped shape a philosophy of healing rather than treating. The latter focuses on a malfunctioning organ system; the former helps a distressed human being. The event I am about to describe is especially relevant to this essay. It deals with a problem that has preoccupied Alex Schindler for over fifteen years, when he first preached his imaginative Outreach program. What I am about to relate happened more than twenty years ago.

◆   ◆   ◆

Mr. Sam D. is a burly, heavyset man from the Midwest. Self-made, comfortable, kindly, and affable, his only extracurricular activity other than golf is the synagogue where he is president. He seeks medical advice for recurrent atrial fibrillation, a disorder of the heartbeat in which the pulse is rapid and irregular. Though the palpitation may be unnerving, the condition is largely benign. For Mr. D. the paroxysms of arrhythmia are proving increasingly disabling. Accompanying him on each visit is his wife, Rachel, a largely speechless witness. She must have been a beauty at one time. Raven-black hair now with a dab of dye, nicely chiseled features, high cheekbones, deep-set olive eyes austere and sad, always looking away as though more than momentary eye contact would provide insight into a deep cavern better left unexposed. Her figure is scrawny, tensely coiled like a tight steel spring, with a cigarette defacing a voluptuous lipsticked mouth. She extends a limp, cold, moist hand that refuses to grip or make human contact. She never talks but defers to her husband. He weighs about two hundred and fifty pounds; she would not tip the scale at one hundred. Much unspoken warmth is reflected in their relationship, which is now approaching thirty-five years.

A careful history divulges no psychologic problems. They have three devoted children at various stages of university education. In retrospect, I remember her wincing when Sam discusses the family. It did not register at the time. I succeed for a while with various antiarrhythmic drugs, but success is only temporary. Over several years I come to know them well and respect their unpretentious, small-town dignity. Each visit leaves a tingle of discomfort that hidden somewhere is a burning hot coal. Attempts to identify the source of the heat are consistently rebuffed. One day, as I implore her once again to stop smoking, she—insisting that it is impossible—abruptly and impassively lets drop, "You should know we have four children, not three children." I sit bolt upright in the swivel chair that leans back close to a large picture window extending from floor to ceiling and overlooking a parking lot six stories down. My voice is tinged with excitement and irritation.

"Tell me about it. How come you waited so long?"

"My husband forswore me never to mention her name. For him, she is dead. Many a night I cry myself to sleep."

"I don't understand. Your daughter died?"

"No, she is very much alive."

"Do you see her?"

"No, even when she writes to me, I hide her letters."

I grow more perplexed with each drawled response. This is not an easy-flowing conversation. Every phrase is a veritable tooth extraction.

Sam's return from having an electrocardiogram ends the sputtering dialogue. She has a guilty, furtive, fearful look. Though aroused and brimming with curiosity, I restrain from pursuing the subject and wait six months until the next return visit.

I make a point to see Rachel alone. She again beseeches me not to raise the subject with her husband. She fears his having a stroke or doing her physical harm for divulging the family secret that certainly is no secret, as everyone in their community must know about it. Apparently, this daughter had been her husband's favorite. Bright, quick, temperamental, opinionated, she invariably twisted her father around her little finger. She began to date a non-Jewish boy while in high school and when she graduated, they eloped and settled in Cleveland. Sam, on learning of this event, sat *shivah* for a week, had a nervous breakdown, and, after recovering, ordered that every scintilla of remembrance of his daughter be removed from their home. When he discovers a letter from his daughter, he has a violent temper tantrum. He may even have hit Rachel. She is evasive about this.

One time, in exasperation, I make a more frontal assault. Sam and I had become friends. "I can't help you unless you are aboveboard with me. I sense something is troubling you deeply, and yet you are ashamed to talk to me. If a doctor is denied the facts, he has a fool for a patient."

He thereupon relates the facts as earlier outlined by his wife, but with much more anger and tearfulness. His daughter, married to a non-Jew, deliberately rejects her Jewishness. With Israel threatened, how is this permissible? If his daughter does not wish to be Jewish, then she is not his child. On each subsequent visit we discuss the problem but without progress. His medical situation deteriorates; he does not adhere to the anticoagulant medication and experiences a small stroke. We are getting into a crisis situation. I have the feeling that his life is becoming unbearable, and he is committing a slow self-immolation that goes unrecognized by all concerned, including the victim.

It is a late autumnal afternoon, gray and dismal. I am swiveling restlessly in front of the large picture window that amplifies the drab outside melancholy. I am rocking to and fro, frustrated, angry at the whole world for my inept helplessness. And then out of the blue without seeming provocation, I begin to shout: "I don't know why I am wasting my time with a miserable human being like you. You make me sick with your self-pity, but more so with what you have done to your daughter, to her family, to your wife, to your other children, and to yourself. You are ruining life for all. It is mind-boggling what a selfish man you are. According to the Jewish religion, God can forgive sins committed against God, not sins committed against other human beings." I quaver with apprehension. Who is the maniac talking through my mouth—a veritable biblical Bilam's ass? He lurches forward like a massive football tackle, eyes bulging, breathing stertorously with neck veins corded. I can visualize myself being shoved backward, shattering the plate glass, and plunging six stories down to the asphalt parking lot. His emotionless robot of a wife begins to weep hysterically as though a dam had given way. Limbs flailing, she shrieks as during an exorcism. I am drenched with perspiration, anguish, and remorse. Why such an idiotic outburst on my part?

It is improper of me, and yet, like a wound-up marionette, the spring is still taut and it has to unwind, for it knows not how to stop once released.

I continue, "If you had any decency, you'd drive directly to Cleveland, right now, knock on your daughter's back door—you do not deserve the front entrance. On bended knee, ask her forgiveness. Only she can relieve you of the burden of sin, not God."

Had I gone psychotic, pretending to be a Jeremiah, the ancient prophet of the strong word? Is there no balm in Gilead? There is a loud sob; his huge body is convulsing. He rises slowly, suddenly weighed down with grief and age. He leaves the room, his wife, even more shriveled, following behind. I am overwhelmed with guilt. Yet another motif is welling up, a warm liquid excitement. A thought is nudging, "It's OK; this is what healing is all about—it sometimes takes pain to lessen pain."

When the next appointment rolls around, I am excitedly astonished to learn that the visit is being kept. Sam is a chastened but much relaxed man. He did exactly as I had urged. He went to Cleveland and begged his daughter's forgiveness. The festivities are unending, and he does not stop exuding excitement as he talks about his little grandson. The two families are now inseparable. He looks back on the past few years as a mad aberration he would rather forget. The atrial fibrillation has ceased to be a problem.

✦ ✦ ✦

Reflecting on the above experience two decades later, I am not as proud as I was at the time. The fact that the outcome was favorable does not convince me that the means were proper. Poor means are never sanctioned by good intentions nor justified by good results. Was this the only way to have him reconcile with his daughter? Would gentle persuasion over time have achieved a similar outcome? The provocation of such a storm of emotion could have done him great harm physically as well as psychologically. What truly happened is that I lost complete control. Indeed, I acted as though "possessed." This is absolutely no justification for improper behavior. It is a costly part of nearly every doctor's education. Patients are the unwitting guinea pigs of a doctor's inexperience. I draw comfort from Heinrich Heine's deathbed reflection, "God will pardon me. It is His trade."

Alex Schindler will be pleased to learn that the family has been reconciled. The grandchildren are being gathered into an ancient fold. This story is also related to make clear the dimension of healing, which to be effective must be attentive to matters ailing the human spirit—what may be designated as the rabbinic dimension of medicine. Patients crave this outreach to their souls. In their heart of hearts, there is hope that their doctor commands the sacred repository wherein life's secret is concealed.

Jews celebrate the Passover festival by retelling the story of the Exodus from Egypt. The accounting of the ten plagues is a dramatic element of that story. You surely remember it:

> Bloody, polluted waters...a vast sudden increase in the number of pests and parasites...skin diseases and other lingering ailments...failed crops in a poisoned land...darkness that blackens the day...a dying generation of children.

These are the plagues that devastated the land of Egypt. The biblical poet ascribes this devastation, this fearsome destruction of the laws of nature to the hands of a wrathful God.

Alas, we have learned over the past two decades that our own technology when misapplied with Pharaonic arrogance is perfectly capable of wreaking devastation on a scale fully parallel to the plagues that afflicted Egypt.

Let us as Jews utilize the memory of slavery in Egypt to fashion a Jewish response to the degradation of God's creation. The place on which we stand, this planet Earth, is holy, and we must never countenance its despoilation.

Rabbi Alexander M. Schindler
Joint Appeal by Religion and Science
for the Environment
Washington, D.C.
May 11, 1992

RELIGIOUS LEADERSHIP
AND ENVIRONMENTAL INTEGRITY

CARL SAGAN

Intelligence and tool making were our strengths from the beginning. We used these talents to compensate for the paucity of the natural gifts—speed, flight, venom, burrowing, and the rest—freely distributed to other animals but denied to us. From the time of the domestication of fire and the elaboration of stone tools, it was obvious that our skills could be used for evil as well as for good. But it was not until very recently that it dawned on us that even the benign use of our intelligence and our tools might—because we are not smart enough to foresee all consequences—put us at risk.

Now we are everywhere on Earth. We have bases in Antarctica. We visit the ocean bottoms. Twelve of us have even walked on the Moon. There are now 5.5 billion of us, and our numbers grow by the equivalent of the population of China every decade. As we were commanded in the Book of Genesis, we *have* subdued the other animals and the plants (although we have been less successful with the microbes). We have domesticated many organisms and made them do our bidding. We have become, by some standards, the dominant species on Earth.

And at each step, we have emphasized the local over the global, the short-term over the long. We have destroyed the forests, eroded the topsoil, changed the composition of the atmosphere, depleted the protective ozone layer, tampered with the climate, poisoned the air and the waters, and made the poorest people suffer most from the deteriorating environment. We have become predators on the biosphere—full of arrogant entitlement, always taking and never giving back. And so we are now a danger to ourselves and the other beings with whom we share the planet.

Imagine humanity as a village of 100 families. Then, 65 families in our village are illiterate, 70 have no drinking water at home, 80 have no members who have ever flown in an airplane. Seven families own 60 percent of the land and consume 80 percent of the available energy. They have all the luxuries. Sixty families are crowded onto 10 percent of the land. Only one family has anyone with a university education. And the air and the water, the climate and the blistering sunlight are all getting worse. What is our common responsibility?

The wholesale attack on the global environment is not the fault only of profit-hungry industrialists or visionless and corrupt politicians. There is plenty of blame to share. The tribe of scientists has played a central role. Many of us didn't even bother to think about the long-term consequences of our inventions. We have been too ready to put devastating powers into the hands of the highest bidder and the officials of whichever nation we happen to be living in. In too many cases, we have lacked a moral compass. Science from its very beginnings has been eager, in the words of René Descartes, "to make us masters and possessors of nature" and to use science, as Francis Bacon said, to bend all of nature into "the service of man." Bacon talked about "Man" exercising a "right over Nature." It is not long ago that we heard about "conquering" nature and the "conquest" of space—as if Nature and the Cosmos were enemies to be vanquished.

The religious tribe also has played a central role. Descartes and Bacon were profoundly influenced by religion. The notion of "us against Nature" is a legacy of our religious traditions. In the Book of Genesis, God gives human beings "domination...over every living thing," and the "fear" and "dread" of us is to be upon "every beast." Man is urged to "subdue" Nature, and the word "subdue" was translated from a Hebrew word with strong military connotations. There is much else along similar lines in the Bible—and in the medieval Christian tradition out of which modern science emerged—as well as some less central mitigating language.

Of course, both science and religion are complex and multi-layered structures, embracing many different, even contradictory, opinions. It is scientists who discovered and called the world's attention to the environmental crisis, and there are scientists who, at considerable cost to themselves, refused to work on inventions that might harm their fellows. And it is religion that first articulated the imperative to revere all living things.

True, there is nothing in the Judeo-Christian-Islamic tradition that approaches the cherishing of nature in the Hindu-Buddhist-Jain tradition or among Native Americans. Indeed, both Western religion and Western science have gone out of their way to assert that Nature should *not* be viewed as sacred.

Nevertheless, there is a clear theme that the natural world is a creation of God, put here for purposes separate from the glorification of "Man" and deserving, therefore, of respect and care in its own right, not just because of its utility for us. A poignant metaphor of "stewardship" has emerged, especially recently—the idea that human beings are the caretakers of the Earth, put here for that purpose and accountable, now and into the indefinite future, to the Landlord.

The methods and ethos of science and religion are profoundly different. Religion frequently asks us to believe without question, even (or especially) in the absence of hard evidence. Indeed, this is the central meaning of faith. Science asks us to take nothing on faith, to be wary of our penchant for self-deception, to reject anecdotal evidence. Science considers deep skepticism a prime virtue. Religion often sees it as a barrier to enlightenment. So, for centuries, there has been a conflict between the two fields—the discoveries of science challenging religious dogmas, and religion attempting to ignore or suppress the disquieting findings.

But times have changed. Many religions are now comfortable with an Earth that goes around the Sun, with an Earth that's about 4.5 billion years old, with evolution, and with the other discoveries of modern science. Catholicism, mainstream Protestantism, and Reform Judaism are. Orthodox Jews and fundamentalist Protestants and Muslims, as far as I can tell, have still not made their accommodation. But no matter how comfortable a given religion may be with modern science, and no matter whose responsibility the current environmental crisis mainly is, there's no way out of it without understanding the dangers and their mechanisms and without a deep devotion to the long-term well-being of our species and our planet—that is, without the central involvement of both science and religion.

In the last few years, scientists and the leaders of many of the major faiths worldwide have joined together to address the world environmental crisis. In the United States a vigorous effort is under way by a consortium of Roman Catholic, Protestant evangelical, mainstream Protestant, and Jewish religious leaders—with Rabbi Alexander Schindler playing a vital role.

"We believe a consensus now exists," they write, "at the highest level of leadership across a significant spectrum of religious traditions, that the cause of environmental integrity and justice must occupy a position of utmost priority for people of faith. Response to this issue can and must cross traditional religious and political lines. It has potential to unify and renew religious life."

I have long admired Rabbi Schindler for his concern for justice, for the depth of his knowledge, for his kindly demeanor, and for his courage—the latter demonstrated not only by his citations for valor and bravery in action in World War II. How many Jewish leaders urge their fellow rabbis to "stop romanticizing" Orthodoxy? "Where it alone prevails," Schindler has stated, "stale repression, fossilized tradition, and ethical corruption often hold sway." And so it is not surprising that Rabbi Schindler, almost alone among the religious leaders, has had the courage to state forthrightly what one of the major impediments is in repairing the environment on which all of us depend. In a meeting of the Joint Appeal by Religion and Science for the Environment, held in the United States Capitol in May 1992, Schindler stated that our recent ecological disasters "are the price of profit, the price of corporate thinking about human values, the price of a materialism so corrosive that it can rupture an oil tanker's hull or a nuclear reactor's containment vessel." The problem, he says, is "greed, that corrosive materialism of our time that we as religious leaders must join forces to counter."

Schindler describes how in preparation for that ecumenical meeting in the Capitol, "a broad range of Jewish leaders gathered to launch a major effort seeking to involve the Jewish community in the national drive to protect the environment. Several hundred leaders were in attendance, and every conceivable stream of Jewish life, religious as well as secular, was represented. With a unanimity uncommon in our midst, we agreed that the 'ecological crisis hovers over our many other vital concerns' since the threat to the environment is global, endangering all human life."

The cause of protecting the planetary environment is strengthened and enriched for having the support of Rabbi Alexander M. Schindler.

· III ·

SWORDS INTO
PLOUGHSHARES

War and Peace

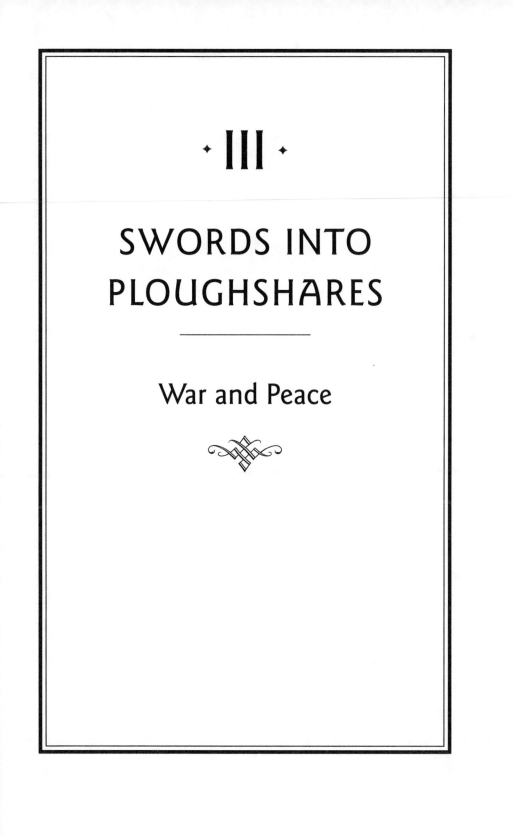

Once again we are assembled in this sanctuary.
Once again a sacred service of remembrance summons us
here.

Not that we really need this *hazkarah* lest we forget.
We need no reminders...we remember too well.
Memories come...to interrupt our sleep...to still our laughter...
to fill our silence with the voice of the past.

Our memories are haunting, hurting...they still make us stagger.
The pavement sinks under the feet, the walls spin 'round,
the world reels.
We cannot stop it even if we would.
We cannot pluck the remembrance of the *Shoah* from us,
its anguish pierced too deep.
The bitterness has eaten into our sinews,
dissolved our flesh into festering sores,
reduced the very spirit of our lives to sparkless,
blackened ashes.

And our response to all these aching memories is silence.
It must be that, it always will be that—a silence.
For our speech has been stifled by darkness,
and our suffering is of a kind that has no tongue.
The martyrology of the Jew is one long stillness,
an endless silent scream reaching to the heavens—
where God was silent, too.

And yet we must speak, for we are the spokesmen of the dead.
It is our duty to testify in their behalf,
ever to remind the world that it was not God, but brutal men,
who brought darkness to the human soul.

Those who lived through and outlived this evil do not need to

speak; the yellow badge is burned on their flesh for all to see.
But their ranks are thinning;
   the generations come and go.
Memory fades.
And there are those who have determined to wipe its slate
   to make it seem as if these things had never been.

So we must speak and meet and write,
   however faltering our tongue and unavailing our speech.
And we begin this task as did our forebears
   with words hallowed by centuries of our martyrdom:
Yitgadal veyitkadash shemeh raba...
Magnified and sanctified be the name of God.

It has been ordained that this prayer be repeated six million times.
People must never forget why this is so.

Rabbi Alexander M. Schindler
Warsaw Ghetto Uprising
Thirty-third Anniversary Commemoration
Congregation Emanu-El
New York, New York
April 25, 1976

IS THE HOLOCAUST COMPARABLE TO OTHER GENOCIDES? THE HOLOCAUST— FIFTY YEARS LATER

YEHUDA BAUER

Some of our contemporaries in the Jewish world have taken the position that anyone who tries to compare the Holocaust to other examples of genocide is committing a kind of sacrilege or an act of antisemitism, heaven forbid, as though the Holocaust or its memory were something sacred and the Holocaust itself an absolute that cannot be compared to anything. If that is the way the term *uniqueness* is understood, then I would strongly differ: first, because the Holocaust was murder, and no murder is sacred; second, because the memory of the Holocaust in our minds is the memory of horror, of suffering, of loss, and there is nothing sacred about this terrible sadness; third, because if the Holocaust is unique in the sense of incomparability, then it is outside of human history, caused by some extraterrestrial, extrahuman agency, God or Satan or both, and all we can do is to look at it because it is absolutely, and in principle, inexplicable. All attempts, then, of looking at the reasons and the motivations of the actors in that tragedy is pointless because the Holocaust, in this view, is assumed to have taken place outside of human comprehension. That, indeed, is the position taken by many of the Orthodox and all the ultra-Orthodox.

If, on the other hand, it is agreed that the Holocaust is an event that falls within the parameters of human history, then, from a historian's point of view, the term *uniqueness* as applied to the historical events we call the Holocaust can have a number of meanings.

The first is the trite statement that every historical event is unique in the sense that no human action is ever exactly the same as other actions to which it may be similar; hence, *every* event is unique, and so is the Holocaust, but not more so than any other event.

The second meaning could be that the event we are discussing is the product of such an unusual combination of circumstances that it has absolutely no precedent with which it could be compared, and though the theoretical possibility of a repetition is not excluded, its probability or plausibility is negligible; one may, therefore, assume that for all practical purposes the event has neither precedent nor the possibility of repetition. This approach has a close affinity, it seems, to the Orthodox/ultra-Orthodox view, although it is presented overwhelmingly by non-Orthodox Jews.

The third possible meaning is that the event has only partial precedents but includes aspects that, as far as we know today, are unprecedented; and there is the possibility of repetition in the future, which is proved by the fact that the basic conditions that created the event have not disappeared.

The first trite statement can be ignored—it is not *that* kind of uniqueness we mean when we discuss the Holocaust. The other two interpretations, as applied to the Holocaust, imply that what is unique is the character of the plan to annihilate the Jewish people and its possible connection to what is called "genocide." But if uniqueness is to have any meaning, it can only be derived from a comparison with other cases of genocide. Otherwise, the term *uniqueness* becomes meaningless. Any attempt, therefore, by Jews who see themselves as the guardians of the memory of the Holocaust to deny the legitimacy of comparisons is a self-defeating exercise. If you don't compare, you cannot argue for *any* kind of uniqueness.

To be able to discuss the two basic approaches I have mentioned, we must first define our terms. What do we mean by Holocaust? To my mind, the Holocaust (*Shoah, Churban*, Judeocide, call it what you will) was the attempt to annihilate the Jewish people totally, down to the last person, on the basis of an ideology that saw them as a satanic force whose very existence endangered humanity as the Nazis understood it. However, by extension, Holocaust would then be any such attempt, past, present, or future, to annihilate totally a people, an ethnic group, or a racial group. Contrary to some colleagues of mine, I would not include in this definition religious or political groups because individuals belonging to such groups have, in theory at least, the option of changing their outlook or their religion, thus escaping annihilation. Members of ethnic, national, or racial groups have no such choice. Genocide, I would argue, belongs to the same genus as Holocaust. However, genocide differs in that it involves, in all known cases, selective mass murder without a plan for total annihilation. Genocide is the attempt to wipe out an ethnic, national, or racial group by depriving it of its identity by a variety of means, in all cases using oppressive force.

Let us address the argument that the conditions that produced the Holocaust are so unusual that they have in practice no precedent and cannot in practice be repeated. What were these conditions? I would argue for five basic conditions: an ancient hatred, a brutal dictatorship, a bureaucracy that is not only willing to execute directives from above but is eager to show initiative and drive in acting within a consensus created by the dictatorship, a technology that enables the Holocaust to be committed efficiently and thoroughly, and a war or an armed conflict under whose shadow massive murder is possible.

Let us assume a hypothetical situation in the future in which a relatively powerful state is ruled by a dictatorship that is convinced that a minority, either a territorial one within or adjacent to that state, or an ethnic or racial group dispersed within the state, endangers the very existence of that state. If there is a general or regional conflagration of hostilities, such a state will, under present-day conditions, be able to execute a plan of total annihilation of the targeted population, provided there is a reasonably long history of animosity between the majority people and the minority. Since 1945 we have seen a number of Holocaust-like situations. It is not so difficult to envision a situation in which the Muslims of Bosnia, turned into refugees by the "cleaning" process, having nowhere to go because the European states refuse to accept them, might be completely wiped out by the Serbs and the Croats, though that is *not* the present situation. There is indeed an ancient animosity in that area based on historical situations (Turkish rule over Christian Slavs and the emergence of Slav-speaking "collaborators" with the Muslim conqueror); there are the elements of a brutal dictatorship; there is a military bureaucracy in place; and there is a suitably advanced military technology. But, of course, there is no Holocaust situation there at present.

There have been several such cases in the last fifty years, and one must, I think, conclude that Holocaust situations have become possible in our time and age.

Another part of the same argument is that the uniqueness of the Holocaust lies in our impossibility to comprehend it, whereas all, or almost all, other historical events can be comprehended. This one cannot because we cannot put ourselves in the place of the victims, and we most certainly, so the argument goes, cannot put ourselves in the place of the perpetrators. The response to this argument must surely be that, unfortunately, sadism, murder, and the suffering they bring have been with us since the beginning of recorded history and most probably before that. The murder of children, the most horrible tortures, and acts of extreme sadism are not what make the Holocaust unique: They have been there before. Nor is the number of the victims of the Holocaust or their proportion in relation to the total number of Jews unique: The numbers of Chinese murdered by the Maoist regime or the numbers of Russians killed by the Nazis are in sheer quantity larger, and the proportion of Armenians killed by the Young Turkish regime in relation to the total Armenian population is probably at least about the same as that of the Jews. The method of gassing, which was applied by the Nazi murderers to about one-half of the Jewish victims, was used prior to that on German mentally and/or, supposedly, genetically sick persons; and later, while no less than 95 to 96% of the gassed victims were Jews, thousands of Gypsies and some Russians and Poles were gassed, too.

Moreover, if we cannot understand the victims, we really cannot have any access to history because it is full of victims of murder, torture, and sadism. For the individual Jewish victim, the experience was not one of massive killing; it was a very personal, tremendously intense experience of the suffering of *one* person, of *one* family, of *one* community. In recorded history, there are uncounted millions like these. We cannot re-feel the suffering. But we can empathize, approach the suffering, and understand it as much as we can understand any human emotion or the pain of another human being. Within limits, we can understand the victim because many of us have the subjective urge to identify and understand. Modern techniques of communication make this understanding more practicable.

It has been argued that while it may be possible to understand the victim, it is impossible for a civilized and sensitive human being to understand the mass murderers, the perpetrators. "I will never be able to *understand* Himmler or Heydrich because I am incapable of being either of them; I cannot empathize with them; I do not possess the drives that made them into what they became"—that is the argument.

This statement, I believe, is fallacious. It reaches back into the German historicist school of the previous century, whose members Dilthey and others argued for a differentiation between explanation (*erklaeren*) and understanding (*verstehen*). It is argued that *explaining* the behavior of the perpetrators is a possibility but penetration into their psyche, what made them "tick," is ultimately impossible because the element of a putative identification with them, which would be the primary building brick of *understanding*, is missing. But as we have learned from psychologists as well as from historians, human beings *are* capable of the widest range of actions and reactions to real situations; God and Satan, as symbols of what we call "good" and "evil," dwell potentially within the human psyche of *all* humans, at least in embryonic form. Himmler could have, in different circumstances, lived out his life as a chicken farmer in Bavaria; Heydrich might well have taken on a musical career or returned to the armed forces of a democratic Germany, even after having been fired from the German navy. There must be huge numbers of potential Himmlers and Heydrichs in every society, unknown to themselves and to others. The societal framework that would enable their capacity for murderous actions to manifest itself does not exist, hence their anonymity. We all have bits of Himmler and Heydrich in us, and the fact that we so vociferously deny it shows how scared we really are of our own potentialities.

If we are, then, capable not only of explaining the Holocaust but of understanding it, we can no longer argue that this particular horror is inexplicable while all the others are explicable. In effect, the second argument would lead us into an absolute uniqueness that would exclude the Holocaust from all human consideration. As we have seen above, this is the position of all ultra-Orthodox and many Orthdox Jews.

Let us return to this extreme position now. It is a well-known fact that traditionally religious Jews in past ages—and in those times this meant *all* Jews—ascribed to themselves the guilt for disasters that happened to the Jewish people at the hands of others. Disasters occurred *mipnei chataenu*, "because of our transgressions." This was certainly an effective way of solving the troubling question of chosenness by an all-powerful and just God on one hand and the obvious suffering, powerlessness, and humiliation of the supposedly "chosen" people on the other. In all past ages, the answer was that the Jews had not followed God's command in the way they should have, and the logical conclusion was that if they now did, no further harm would befall them. Very often rabbis and others pointed their finger at certain people, certain groups, or certain attitudes or customs associated with Jews and saw in these the transgressions for which the whole community was being punished. Basically this has not changed in our own day; some of our contemporaries are engaged in the same search for sins the Jews may have committed—sins for which punishment resulted at the hands of an angry deity. The root cause for this self-accusation was a theology that argued that all things, good and bad, came from God, and in the end—because God was good and just—the purpose of punishment and castigation was educational, i.e., intended for the good of the sufferer. The perpetrators of atrocities against the Jews were seen as scourges sent by the Almighty to implement God's wishes, from Nebuchadnezzar to Hitler and beyond. In this way, all autonomy seemed to have been taken from these perpetrators; they could not really have acted differently because they were just instruments in the hands of a wrathful deity. At the same time, however, and not very logically, these same perpetrators were evil beings who would in the end be punished for their evildoing, whether in this world or the next.

We can see this attitude in the writings of the great teachers of contemporary ultra-Orthodoxy, e.g., the Lubavitcher Rebbe or the previous Satmar Rebbe. The Lubavitcher, Menachem Mendel Schneerson, did not accuse the Jews of specific transgressions, though there is a broad hint that Reform and assimilation were the main culprits. He simply states in his book *Emunah Ve'Mada* the "fact" that God acted like the surgeon who cuts off a rotten limb to cure the patient. Large numbers of devout Jews were killed, together with others, because God punished the Jewish people by striking its face (*panim*), the pious Jews being the *pnei hador*, the "face of the generation." In this way, the theological requirements are met; God is the source of both good and evil, but responsibility is laid at the door of the Jews themselves, who were granted a free will to make the moral choice.

A similar attitude is taken by the late Joel Taitelbojm, the Satmar Rebbe, in his book *Vajoel Moshe*. Rescued by the Zionist Kastner in Hungary, Taitelbojm accuses the Jews of Zionism, which stands in contradiction to God's command not to rebel against the nations and not to "climb the wall," i.e., to return to the Holy Land prior to the coming of the Messiah.

One can find similar explanations not only among the ultra-Orthodox but among some of the Orthodox leaders as well. Important and indeed brilliant minds such as former British Chief Rabbi Immanuel Jakobovits have argued that while it is futile to guess why God has punished the Jewish people in such a terrible way, clearly it was the sins of the Jews that brought about the disaster, again pointing the finger at Reform.

From a general Jewish perspective, not excluding the Orthodox one, the question arises how *any* transgression could have "caused" the murder of between one and one-and-a-half million Jewish children under the age of thirteen who obviously were not responsible for any sins. The Jewish tradition has, after all, long ago rejected the formula that visits the sins of the ancestors unto the children and has instead adopted the rule that people be judged by their *own* sins. There is no way out of this dilemma in the terms these people use except to say—which they also do—that one cannot ask questions like these because God's ways are inscrutable. There is a clear contradiction between that statement and the attempts at explanation in the spirit of *mipnei chataenu*. Yet both these contradictory statements are continually made.

The explanations offered lead to a conclusion that ultra-Orthodoxy, of course, utterly rejects: If, indeed, God is responsible for both good and evil and a million innocent Jewish children were killed, then God must be evil; if God is just, then God is not all-powerful.

In addressing this dilemma, Rabbi Irving Greenberg has argued for a new covenant between the Jewish people and God, based on the recognition that the Jews have a responsibility to help a just God who is not all-powerful. This formulation raises the difficult question: Why pray to a powerless, *nebbach* God?

In comparing the Holocaust with other genocides, Orthodoxy and ultra-Orthodoxy have no problem at all: There can be no comparisons because the Holocaust happened to the Chosen People and thus acquires, in principle, a metahistorical quality.

Another consideration that makes the Holocaust incomparable for many Orthodox and all ultra-Orthodox is the view that the Holocaust is a clear sign of the *chavlei Mashiach*, the turbulence preceding the Messiah's arrival. Throughout the ages, whenever a major disaster occurred to the Jewish people, it served as a clear sign of the imminent coming of the *Mashiach*. The worse the disaster, the more fervent the belief in the proximity of redemption. (In present-day Israel another aspect has been added: Victories and successes are also interpreted as a sign of the approaching end of the days, "the beginning of our redemption.") This eased the psychological trauma of the disaster but also removed the believers from any contact with reality because no *Mashiach* is in sight. This dangerous pseudo-Messianism (which is shared, by the way, by the other monotheistic radicals, Christian and Muslim, in their own terms) not only constitutes a danger to the body politic of the Jewish people but also further accentuates the metahistorical quality of the Holocaust in the eyes of the ultra-Orthodox, thus making any comparisons with similar events blasphemous.

For a non-Orthodox Jew the questions are much more difficult. We have already seen that it is not brutality or sadism that makes the Holocaust unique, nor is it any sign of chosenness because millions upon millions of others were butchered by enemies in past ages and in our own times, and they were not chosen peoples (though most peoples and tribes do consider themselves chosen in one form or another). God has to be put in brackets, so to speak—whether one accepts God's existence or not—because clearly the Holocaust, like other genocides, was the work of human beings, and God's action or inaction becomes irrelevant to the discussion. The issue is put squarely into our laps: Are genocides comparable? If so, what does that teach us about the propensity of humans to enact these events? And if they have such a propensity, is there anything special about the Holocaust that emerges from a comparison between it and other genocides?

The answer, clearly, is that while the Holocaust is comparable to other genocidal events, there are several factors that make it qualitatively different. One must immediately warn the reader that this difference does not imply that the Holocaust is more extreme in the sense that it is "worse" than other genocidal events. There is no moral distinction between mass murder and mass murder. The life of a Jew killed in Auschwitz is not more or less valuable than the life of a Russian villager killed by the Germans, an Armenian killed by the Turks, or a Cambodian killed by a Pot Pol executioner. However, the Holocaust is, first, more extreme in the sense that the intention of the murderer is to annihilate a group in its totality. Anyone born of three or four Jewish grandparents was sentenced to death for the crime of having been born—and that, to my knowledge, has never happened before. Second, the motivation of the Nazi perpetrator was purely ideological; that is, it bore no relation to the reality of the Jewish people: Jews were considered to be satanic and out to rule the world through a conspiratorial cabal; they were considered a criminal antirace whose criminality was hereditary. The enemy of Nazism was not the real Jew—though he/she was the real victim—but an abstract, totally illusory construct called International Jewry, of which every *real* Jew was an obedient subject. This, again, has vague precedents but no real parallel. Third, the Holocaust affected a very important minority, the Jews. This is a thought that has to be stated carefully because it is so easy to misuse and misunderstand.

The Jewish heritage is, undoubtedly, one of the pillars of Western, Northern, and Christian-Muslim civilization. The other main pillar is classical Greece. But the modern Greeks are remote descendants of the ancient Greeks in culture, in language, in customs, in philosophy, in art, etc. The Jewish heritage has also undergone tremendous changes, but the contemporary expressions of Jewish civilization, split and divided and fragmented as it is, are the results of a continuous development down to this very day. The stories, legends, histories, modes of expression, and much more have had a continuity stretching over thousands of years. Modern Western civilization attempts to follow the footsteps of the prophets, agonizes about the observance of the Ten Commandments, uses the Jewish experience as a paradigm. Moral values aspired to in the West—rather unsuccessfully—originate to no small measure with the Jews.

The fact that the Holocaust hit the Jews, the visible continuation of a civilization that is so basic to Western self-understanding, challenges the legitimacy of that civilization. From a Christian point of view, there is called into question the credibility of a faith that worships a savior who came nineteen hundred years ago to preach a gospel of love and who died in expiation of human sins and nineteen hundred years after his arrival and his sacrifice, his people are murdered by baptized Gentiles. The murder of the Jews can perhaps, or arguably, be viewed as a rebellion of the sinful son against the Jewish father-figure in Western culture. It is to me not at all surprising that not a month passes without yet another play, a film, a TV series, a work of art, a piece of fiction, etc., about the Holocaust. Holocaust has become a *code* in Western civilization, a paradigm in many complicated ways.

Compared to the many other instances of genocide, these three points of difference make it unique because in so many other cases the practical issues predominate. The Spaniards murdered Indians for gold and silver; the settlers in North America murdered Indians because the former coveted tribal land; the Young Turks wanted to annihilate the Armenians in Turkey to create a pan-Turkic empire stretching from the Bulgarian border to Kazakhstan, and the Armenians were in the way. The Gypsies' life-style and the Gypsies themselves were a nuisance in Nazi eyes. In none of these cases do we see the kind of universalist ideology imagining an enemy that did not really exist at all and yet had his supposed representatives everywhere in the shape of the real Jews. Wherever there was a genocidal ideology, it served as a rationalization for material, economic, political, or historical reasons relating to real situations: Mesoamerican and South American Indians did have access to gold, and later they could serve as slaves on Spanish plantations; North American Indians were the masters of lands and forests; Armenians, who were a people with their own ethnic and national aspirations, sat on land that had been theirs for millennia and was coveted by the Turks; Gypsies were, in part, a wandering people that had not been absorbed in a civilization that rejected them. And none of these people whose sufferings *are* comparable to those of the Jews occupied the place that the Jews did in Western civilization. The tragedy of the Jews was, and is, that Jews are important for the cultures in which they live. They don't want to be, but they are. And they have to make their peace with that fact.

Jewish opposition to such comparisons is typically defensive. The only way future disasters of a genocidal character can be successfully avoided is by opening the field to a realistic discussion of human societies that are in essence of equal worth, have important similarities as well as dissimilarities, and whose tragedies have elements that can be compared. Qualitative uniqueness in one case or another does not contradict such an approach.

Intellectually, I affirm the rightness of reconciliation between German and Jew. But too many bitter memories restrain my heart from following my mind.

Jewish custom prescribes that Holocaust Remembrance Day be marked in the month of April...it is a most unlikely time to mark so somber and melancholy an occasion. After all, April is the first full month of spring, the time "when the air is calm and pleasant," so Milton wrote, "and it were an injury and sullenness against nature not to go out and see her riches and partake in her rejoicing."

As individuals, we can well do that; we can go out into the public gardens and rejoice, roll up our sleeves to feel a little springtime warmth; but as Jews, rolled-up sleeves all too quickly remind us of those numbers tattooed on the arms of death camp inmates.

As individuals, we can rejoice in April showers and breathtaking rainbows; but as Jews, we cannot hear of "showers" without shuddering, nor view a rainbow without thinking of the Nazi killers who shattered its radiance, who took its colors and pinned them to our hearts: yellow for Jews...red for communists...brown for Gypsies...pink for gays...and on and on through the spectrum of murdered souls.

As individuals, we can hearken to the Song of Solomon: "Arise...my fair one, come away!" But as Jews, we are mired in agonizing memories and cannot come away. We cannot see a meadow without thinking of mass graves. We cannot see a dancing butterfly without recalling the poem of a twelve-year-old Jewish girl inmate of Theresienstadt who said of her captivity that she "never saw another butterfly."

Oh, would that we *could* forget. But quick forgetting is not the reality of a people who lost one-third of their number in half a decade; who lost one and one-half million of their children, innocent, guiltless all! Quick healing is not the reality of a people for whom nature itself was defiled by Nazi murderers who sowed bones instead of seeds in the month of April.

I suppose we will never forget, nor should we. But somehow we must muster the strength to follow what faith and reason dictates: to respond to those many Germans, especially the young among them who recognize the past for what it was and are resolved never to countenance its return.

Rabbi Alexander M. Schindler
Lecture at the College of the Holy Cross
Worcester, Massachusetts
April 7, 1992

GERMANY, THE JEWISH COMMUNITY, AND RECONCILIATION

ALBERT H. FRIEDLANDER

Half a century ago, Germans and Jews stopped talking to each other. It was not a true, healing silence in which the survivors of the Holocaust could have found a way into a future where later generations could have begun a halting dialogue. Jews and Germans thought they *were* talking to each other with accusations from one side and defense from the other. But, in fact, they were no longer communicating. It was not the problem of English, Polish, Hebrew, French, or Russian being spoken on one side and German on the other side. Rather, quite simply, the terms had lost their common meaning. In a post-Auschwitz and postreligious world, words like "guilt," "responsibility," "atonement," and, certainly, "reconciliation" had taken on new meanings. Whatever meaning had once been assigned to these words belonged to a new frame of reference, new paradigms of thinking. The concepts had to be renegotiated.

Even before Chancellor Helmut Kohl had moved towards the right in order to squeeze out the narrowest of victories as the leader of Germany, he had challenged any notions of guilt or responsibility for the past and had thus become a respectable person defending the German national spirit. While Kohl is sensitive to the feelings of Jews and is concerned about German anti-Semitism, his mistakes on Bitburg and in other areas show his own inability to speak to world Jewry and to come to terms with the language necesary for a Jewish-German dialogue.

I find it difficult to think about Germany. One cannot make a rational assessment of this schizophrenic land, torn apart by rapid changes that follow one another with blinding rapidity—a land that still struggles to rid itself of a past that came to an apparent end more than a half century ago but still refuses to go away. The unresolved guilt of the Nazi period still resides in the land, no matter how often the people and the land celebrate the "grace of being born after the event." Encapsulated traumas reside in the body politic, and the children's teeth are still set on edge because the fathers have eaten sour grapes.

East Germany and its regime fell, and five new states joined the Greater Germany as the Berlin Wall fell, but the dowry East Germany brought to the marriage was a new guilt. Over 200,000 East Germans had worked for the state police and had betrayed their friends and family out of fear or out of greed. They had not been the Nazis of the past; they had not killed (well...not many had gone that far). But the "Stasis"—part-time members of the state police—had kept a corrupt government in power and had themselves been corrupted. At a time when Nazi trials are still creaking through the courts, one begins to think about trials for the Stasis, for the leaders who had betrayed them, and for the little people who lacked courage and decency.

Can one try a whole country? An argument is taking place involving the intellectuals and the pastors as well, even those who appeared to be the leaders of the modest resistance that had taken a stand against the Communist regime. Who is there left to judge? And who is innocent? And, somehow, does all this not bring back that dark past of another dictatorship, one that was greater in evil and perhaps as persuasive in letting the multitude enter a dark valley in which they ceased to be human beings?

In looking for guides, directives, and attempts to deal with the problems besetting the Germans today, one must examine the teachings of the German theologians and the history of Jewish life in Germany, East and West, after World War II. East Germany (the German Democratic Republic or DDR) had been more difficult to explore until recently because access was basically denied to outsiders. The Jewish community in East Germany, a small minority of less than a thousand, was almost a protected species. The head of the Jewish community in Magdeburg once remarked to me: "If I call the mayor of the city and tell him that a stone has fallen out of our cemetery wall, I can observe a whole team of workers the next day, carefully repairing and repainting the whole wall!" Yet the same man had great difficulties in procuring ritual objects for his congregation, and the gift of my *talit*, "prayer shawl," and prayer book was gratefully accepted. The Communist state was firmly against religion, but the few remaining Jews were showpieces used to demonstrate the humanity of the state.

In an article on Jewish life in East Germany before and after the fall of the Wall, Stefan Schreiber of Humboldt University in East Berlin observed that in 1953 the Jewish community (registered members of the synagogues) officially cut off all links with their co-religionists in the West. It was the summation of the anti-Jewish and anti-Zionist developments in Eastern Europe, including the murder of anti-fascist Jewish leaders in the USSR, the Slansky Trial in Prague (1952), and Stalin's attack on the "conspiracy of the Jewish doctors" in Moscow (autumn 1952). It was also a "necessary" answer to the appeal by Rabbi Peter Levinson and community leader Heinz Galinski in West Berlin (January 15, 1953) that the Jews of East Germany come to West Germany. While some East German Jews did leave at that time, the bulk remained. Many of the Jews who had returned to East Germany from abroad after the war had done so out of conviction for a socialist future. They could have had more material comforts in West Germany, but they truly believed in a political philosophy that often saw them hounded out of jobs in the West, which had a great fear of "the Communists in our midst." Recognizing that artists and writers (the Eisler brothers, Arnold Zweig, and others) had returned out of political conviction, the DDR treated these persons as political assets. However, after the fall of the East German government, a deep revulsion set in as people learned how much those in power had stolen from the powerless. At that point, hatred erupted against the betrayers, including those who had led the Jewish communities and, therefore, had been members of the state apparatus. They were viewed with the deepest suspicion, treated as "collaborators," assumed to have been part of the Stasi machine, and cast into the wilderness. Many of the best and most decent Jewish leaders were suddenly out of office, out of work, out of favor.

When the Wall fell, the Jewish community of East Berlin and of the rest of what is now called the "five new lands" rejoined the West German Jewish community. To some extent, it must be said that they were, in fact, taken over. Outstanding Jewish leaders, like Dr. Peter Kirchner of East Berlin, practically became nonpersons, tainted by the role they had played within the old power structure. Also, of course, there was the dynamic leadership from the West that had swept aside all of the old Eastern structure. The Zentralrat der Juden in Deutschland, then led by Heinz Galinski, took over all leadership functions by October 1990.

As the focus of German Jewry shifted to the West, a *Kulturkampf* engulfed the community, drawing battle lines between the different segments: religious Jews against secular Jews; the new Russian arrivals—almost a majority—against those who had settled in earlier. The simple fact that where there are four Jews there are five opinions still makes it difficult for a community to exist in a present overshadowed by the past. From the outside, as the old nationalism grows stronger, comes the challenge: Can Jews be counted as Germans? In a German society where Herr Schoenhuber's Republican party gained 10 percent of the vote in Baden-Wuerttemberg and a number of seats in that parliament, questions are raised for the future of minorities in Germany, particularly the Jews. Franz Schoenhuber's star role has ended, but the malady lingers on.

The major issues for Jews living in Germany today are the relationship to Israel and, of course, the emergence of a new anti-Semitism, whether open or concealed. In the five new lands, the relationship to Israel has changed markedly and a dialogue has developed that has been enhanced through group journeys to Israel, as well as the recognition of "Righteous Gentiles," those who at great risk helped Jews during the Nazi period. On January 22, 1990, Yad Vashem granted six former East German citizens recognition as "Righteous Gentiles," whose names will be preserved in Jerusalem (the act of recognition took place in Berlin). And, during its last days, the Volkskammer of the German Democratic Republic confessed the guilt of Germany and gave full recognition to the State of Israel.

The one remaining, disturbing aspect of Jewish life in the eastern part of Germany is the effect of East German attitudes on the new totality of Germany. To put it quite simply: There is a wave of anti-Semitic feeling coming out of the eastern part of Germany. This statement seems strange when one recognizes that the DDR had officially made anti-Semitism a crime. But there is all of the undigested past to consider. The DDR had found an easy solution to cope with the Nazi past: "We were the Communist opposition against Hitler, the good guys. Look at Erich Honecker: ten years in a Nazi concentration camp! The Nazis all stayed in West Germany, holding official positions there. Let them pay compensation to the victims—we had nothing to do with it!" The fact that many good Nazis became good Communists was ignored.

The West Germans had at least tried to work out the problems of the past and had succeeded in many ways. Now, the burden of that first guilt has reappeared, together with a strong nationalism and xenophobia. Moreover, the new guilt, the Stasi problem, confronts them with almost the same questions regarding the past: "Should justice be done, or is it better to cover it all up, to forgive and forget? So many East Germans cooperated with their government and spied on their families—but it wasn't quite like the old Nazi days. Why should justice be seen to be done? That black Ossie dog sitting by the supermarket—was he one of the dogs on the Wall? But he was just doing his duty; so were we all, so were we all."[1]

In the miles of Stasi files, there is really no one whose name might not appear. There is also "disinformation" in those files, a fact that cannot be discarded automatically. In a world of paper, one can start false paper chases. Even East Germans who escaped early and fought the Communist regime from the outside are sometimes suspected now in that uneasy world where fear of the neighbor has suddenly been reenforced by the fact that everybody seems to have betrayed everybody else!

The five new lands are now being exploited in many ways, with carpetbaggers moving in to take a major share of the economic growth that will undoubtedly occur. Most of the charity work done by Jews and non-Jews in Germany—support to art, religion, or other worthwhile enterprises—centers on the development of that area. Even the gigantic profit machine of the German economy has begun to falter as it tries to deal with the tasks that reunion has brought. Confronted with a higher tax bill, the citizens of Germany have challenged the Christian Democrats and Chancellor Kohl. And, suddenly, the emphasis for new development and growth is all directed towards the eastern lands. Now, as ever, the Jews of eastern Germany are a barometer of the political climate. The growth of anti-Semitism has always shown the flaws of systems that do not acknowledge the rights of minority groups. To that extent, as Professor George Steiner of Cambridge University has shown, the Jews remain the conscience of the world.

✦   ✦   ✦

Since World War II the Jews of West Germany have lived a quiet, problematic life among a people who tried to eradicate them from the earth. Until recently, when the coming of the Russian Jews changed the pattern, there were about 30,000 Jews in West Germany who had established a *modus vivendi* that avoided publicity whenever possible. Now, suddenly, with the influx of Russian Jewish families whose children fill the religious schools and appear in the synagogue for bar mitzvah celebrations, long dormant communities have revived. A new more hopeful picture is emerging, but it is too early to evaluate its impact on German Jewry.

A positive sign for the future is the *Arbeitsgemeinschaft Juden und Christen am Kirchentag*—a dedicated group of Christian and Jewish scholars who present important programs every two years at the *Kirchentag* of the Protestant Church in order to gain an insight into the achievements and the great problems that exist at the very top of the German-Jewish confrontation. When these *Kirchentage*—the major assemblies of Protestantism that attract over 200,000 participants every two years—developed, there was initially no role for the Jews. What did *Jews* have to contribute to Christian meetings? Gradually, it became apparent to the Church that the Jewish roots of Christianity *and* Auschwitz were major items on the agenda.

We have spoken of the "double guilt" that rests heavily upon Germany these days, the inheritance of the Stasis and of the Nazis. And any assessment of intellectual, moral, and philosophical thinking after the darkness must occupy itself with this situation. It is in that context that the dialogue between Jews and Christians and between Jews and Germans becomes understandable.

Where there is crime, there is guilt. Christian theologians often take the stance of speaking for God and of forgiving. Yet the best Christian theologians are very much aware of Dietrich Bonhoeffer's teaching concerning the "easy grace"—and those who transgress and sin must be given the chance to atone rather than cashing in a letter of indulgence from their religion. I insist upon coming back here to my own approach—which is suspicious of systems—of suspecting a completely formed theology that gives answers to all the situations; the general rules of the Ten Commandments must be applied by us to individual situations. Those teachers whom we find address something within us, our own individual intuition, and our own intellect must then determine our actions.

But we know so little in this world! Can't we rely on experts? Here, in the area of contemporary history, shouldn't we at least be given guidance by the historians? Historians only offer pictures that suit the contemporary mood. Histories are like fashion modes, changing constantly. The Dutch historian Johan Huizinga stated: "History is the intellectual form through which a culture gives an accounting to itself of its past." Yet one cannot give an image of the past "as it truly was"; the historian selects a few facts of the million available; and what he or she chooses depends on personal mood and the endemic feelings of the environment out of which the historian operates.

The picture of history with which West Germany, after World War II, portrayed itself was a most efficient model. It was called "anti-Communism" and promised security, continuity, and integration after a time of upheaval. As the historian Eberhard Jaeckel points out, this permitted the ex-Nazis to find room for themselves in this image. They had been *good* anti-Communists, even if they had been wrong about everything else. Those who had been passive and had not fought the Nazis could now catch up by fighting Communism. And, in the fifties, this historical construct became a matter of faith, supported by the intellectuals:

> The end result was the totalitarianism theory: Both dictatorships had been the same, and since one had disappeared and the other was a present, actual threat, public opinion concentrated upon it.[2]

A new historical paradigm arose in the sixties when the earlier perspective clearly needed to be corrected. As time passed and the crimes of the Holocaust became better known, Nazis and Communists could no longer be equated. An attempt was made to uncover that darkest period of German life. It was an uncomfortable time for many, but there was the genuine attempt to understand, aided by the media, which showed films about the Holocaust.

In the eighties, the historical image changed again. "It's time to draw a line under the past," said Helmut Kohl, speaking for the nation. A bit of the earlier approach reemerged as Helmut Kohl enlisted Ronald Reagan in honoring the fallen SS soldiers buried at Bitburg. The battle of the revisionist historians now took place in 1986. Led by the respectable historian Ernst Nolte, it was an attempt to bring the Nazi crimes out of the realm of the demonic by comparing and equating them with Soviet actions and subsuming them under the normal excesses of war. In the end, the revisionist historians lost that battle, although they are still very much with us. Professor Jaeckel summarizes it in this way:

> The *Historikerstreit* [battle of the historians] ended with the victory of those who neither wanted an end to the debate [about the Holocaust] nor [the establishment of] parity between racial and class murder. In a way, the "totalitarianism theory" had been replaced by the "convergence theory." Democracy and Communism develop towards each other as the latter reforms; Fascism had been the true evil of the century. If one became too anti-Communistic, he was considered a reactionary and not attuned to the spirit of the time.[3]

Then East Germany collapsed, and the picture had to be revised again. West Germany became the great united Germany; and the Communist crimes—mass graves and the use of concentration camps in East Germany as convenient places of killing and enforcing Communism—moved to the foreground:

> All public thinking now concentrated itself upon the crimes of the DDR. The thought of a tribunal arose, a second Nuremberg. Once again, as in the time of de-Nazification, one had to justify one's past....Documents were needed....Whether one should do this exactly as in the past or precisely for that reason differently, the patterns are the same. The Germans conduct themselves like the Allies cleaning up after 1945. It is almost as if they enjoy to be, finally, the victors.[4]

The historical portrait of the former East Germany is now far darker than ever. Erich Honecker, once recognized as a resistance fighter who served a decade in a concentration camp, had become another Eichmann to be hunted across Eastern Europe until his death in South America. In Stuttgart, the court declared its inability to further prosecute Nazi war criminals; meanwhile, the trial of the guards of the Berlin Wall is moving forward rapidly. And the historians and the general populace again fell into the trap of trying to compare two pasts with each other, in a sense, trivializing the greater crime. By equating Stasi with Nazi and East Germany with the Third Reich, the Nazi crimes were again reduced to normal acts of war. As Professor Juergen Moltmann, the leading German theologian, had stated, Auschwitz could only happen in a time of war, but it surpassed all that has ever happened in a war. And as the Israeli educator Edna Brocke, who lives in Germany, also pointed out, this does not guarantee that Auschwitz cannot happen again in a different framework. The world can be brutalized to a point where genocide becomes a way of controlling population growth and of solving economic problems. New theories of government can arise; but the old theories must not be compared in a way that distorts and destroys past realities.

We should *not* expect repentance from the grandchildren of the Nazi perpetrators, but we can expect them to accept responsibility for the bitter inheritance given to them. There is far less anti-Semitism in Germany today than there is in the surrounding lands.

And the somewhat sad history of the Jewish community that has slowly reestablished itself in this part of Europe also testifies to Jewish hopes that there is a future for Jewish life in Germany. Those who retreat from that knowledge and simply insist that the Jews should leave that poisoned land are abandoning part of the Jewish community; they are also abandoning Germans who could and should be partners in the conversations with those who live after the darkness and need to reach out to us so that the past will not return as the future. This is why reconciliation must begin on both sides of our encounter in post-Auschwitz history. Many Jews in America cannot break out of the frozen stance of "we cannot forgive or forget." This is understandable, but it keeps them from self-analysis and from the necessary task of looking at a new world, two generations later, where all must work together in an attempt to keep Auschwitz from repeating itself in the twenty-first century.

NOTES

1. See A.H. Friedlander, *Riders towards the Dawn* (New York: Continuum Press, 1994), pp. 168–169.

2. Eberhard Jaeckel, "Die doppelte Vergangenheit," *Der Spiegel*, vol. 52, 1991.

3. Ibid.

4. Ibid.

It is recorded in the Book of Genesis that when our father Abraham breathed his last, his sons, Isaac and Ishmael, "buried him in the cave of Machpelah." Isaac and Ishmael mourning together at their father's tomb! Isn't it always thus? A common tragedy draws erstwhile foes together.

We descendants of Abraham—Muslims and Jews—who live here in America are better able to reclaim our common heritage and to engage in fruitful dialogue than we are in our father's house. It is the great tragedy of contemporary life, is it not, that at the cave of Machpelah, there in ancient Hebron, Muslim and Jew are still incapable of dialogue, or even of peaceful silence.

America both facilitates and makes necessary our dialogue. The effectiveness of that dialogue, however, will be due to something more than a receptive environment or a political imperative.

It will be due in the first instance to our willingness to be honest with ourselves, to engage in what the Jewish tradition calls a *cheshbon hanefesh*, a self-reckoning of the soul. Every journey to our fellow men and women is first a painful journey inward to our own existence: a confrontation with our own past and present imperfections, a wrestling match with the demons in our own soul.

Second, the effectiveness of our dialogue will depend on our willingness to be honest each within our *own* communities. The wounds inflicted by the fulminations of a Farrakhan or a Meir Kahane cannot be assuaged by caution or polite silence. "Death and life are in the power of the tongue," the Bible instructs us, and the Talmud adds that "silence is tantamount to a confession, to an admission of guilt." Jews, alas, do not need Scripture to understand the importance of speaking out against hatred, whatever and wherever its source; centuries of persecution have engraved that on our hearts.

Third and finally, the effectiveness of our dialogue will depend on our willingness to be honest with one another, on the resolve not to say only what we think will please the other to hear but always to tell the truth as we perceive it, to assert our convictions with passion, even as we remain respectful of our disagreements.

Rabbi Alexander M. Schindler
Jewish/Muslim Convocation
Chicago, Illinois
March 26, 1995

ISAAC AND ISHMAEL, ABRAHAM'S PROGENY (GENESIS 21) A MIDRASHIC PARADIGM FOR MODERN JEWS

NORMAN J. COHEN

Unlike many in the generations that preceeded us, who were immersed in the texts of the tradition and as a result intimately knew their power, we modern Jews must find a path back to our biblical and rabbinic moorings. The challenge that we as modern, liberal Jews face is clear: how to reclaim the texts of the past in an authentic way for ourselves and our children; how to be energized by the words of Torah as our grandparents and great-grandparents were in their day.

For me, the path back to the text has been the process of *midrash*, the attempt to find contemporary relevance and meaning in the ancient words of Torah. It enables us as readers to take seriously the texts of our people's past, yet in a creative way reach beyond the context in which they were shaped. Therefore, *midrash* is built upon a dialectic that informs our search as Reform Jews; a tension with which we resonate: to hear the words of tradition and try to understand the message shaped by our early forebears, while demanding that they speak to us in a contemporary voice as well. *Midrash*, based on the Hebrew root *darash*, literally means to seek, search for, or demand contemporary significance from the timeless words of Torah.

There is no passage in the Torah more relevant today for the Jewish people than Genesis 21, the story of the birth and future promise of Isaac, which is set against the relationship between Abraham and Ishmael. The tension implicit in the biblical account raises questions regarding how Ishmael is to be seen and treated, even as Isaac is the link in the chain of tradition extending from his father, Abraham, to his son, Jacob. It is especially poignant as a paradigm for our attitude as Jews, descendents of Isaac, toward non-Jews in general and our Arab brothers and sisters in particular. In light of the struggle for peace in the Middle East, it behooves us to listen to the words of this ancient text and, in the process of opening ourselves to it, to be touched, taught, and perhaps even transformed by it.

Isaac's Birth and Circumcision

At the outset of Genesis 21 we are told that Sarah bore a son to Abraham. (v. 2) Isaac is Abraham's *ben zekunim*, the "son of his old age," which most probably indicates his special affection for him. Isaac was the guarantor of his future, the insurer of his immortality. Then the text continues in a somewhat redundant manner: "Abraham gave his newborn son, whom Sarah had borne him, the name of Isaac." (v. 3) By underscoring that Isaac was born to Sarah (and not Hagar), we understand that he is special and set apart from his half-brother, Ishmael. Isaac is the one who will carry the covenant. The irony, of course, is that for as much as Isaac and Ishmael are different, there is an affinity between them. Isaac is named Yitzchak, from the root *tzachak*, because his parents laughed at the thought of his impending birth. (Gen. 17:17; 18:12) Yet, Ishmael is described as the *metzachek*, the one laughing or playing. (v. 9) We see that the two sons of Abraham are described by the same Hebrew term.

Isaac is circumcised when he is eight days old (v. 4), as God had commanded Abraham. (Gen. 17:12) Isaac is the one to bear the sign of the covenant on his flesh; he is the *ben berit*, the "son of the covenant." But Ishmael is also circumcised, albeit when he is thirteen years old. (Gen. 17:23ff.) Ishmael's circumcision, however, is set in the context of the promise that Sarah will give birth to a child, Isaac, who will be the father of a great nation. (Gen. 17:16) But upon hearing God's promise, Abraham, who cannot believe that he and Sarah are young enough to conceive a child, pleads with God: "Oh that Ishmael might live by Your favor!" (Gen. 17:18) At the precise moment of the prediction of Isaac's birth, Abraham focuses on his other son, Ishmael, about whom he is concerned and for whom he prays. The fact that in Genesis 17 the dialogue shifts back and forth, focusing on one son and then the other, clearly stresses the relationship and the tension between them.

In the same way God stresses that Sarah will give birth to Isaac through whom the covenant will be maintained (Gen. 17:19) and, having heard Abraham's plea, immediately adds that Ishmael will also be blessed. And the blessing? God will make him fertile and exceedingly numerous; he will be the progenitor of twelve tribes and become a great nation. (Gen. 17:20) God's promise concerning Ishmael sounds familiar: to be fertile and numerous; to father twelve tribes; and to become a great nation. This is the essence of the promise accorded his brother, Isaac. Both will produce twelve tribes, powerful and strong. Yet, let us not confuse the two brothers; the comparison will go only so far. The covenant will be established through Isaac. (Gen. 17:21) The parallelism between Isaac and Ishmael and at the same time the tension between them, because of the predictions of their future, are made abundantly clear in this narrative.

We learn that Abraham was one hundred years old when his son Isaac was born to him. (Gen. 21:5) The emphasis is clear: Isaac is his, Abraham's son, the only son of the covenant that he has. And now that Sarah has borne Isaac, she remarks: "God has brought me laughter; everyone who hears will laugh with me," *yitzchak li*. (v. 6) Bearing a son at her age is no longer a laughing matter for her; rather, it is a source of true joy. Furthermore, the phrase *yitzchak li* can be read as "Yitzchak (Isaac) is mine!" Again, it is Isaac, the one who will carry the covenant, who is important, not Ishmael. And Isaac's primary position is made even clearer when Abraham holds a great feast on the day that Isaac is weaned. (v. 8) Now that Isaac was considered a viable infant, the whole clan could celebrate his life. Yet one could ask how Ishamel, then thirteen years old, must have felt standing on the side watching this spectacle. Why, he must have asked, didn't his father mark any of the important moments in his life? Was he not Abraham's son, too? Did his father not love him?

After the weaning celebration, Sarah saw Ishmael playing, *metzachek* (v. 9), and became furious. Why did this aggravate the situation? Why now, of all times, would Sarah become upset because of Ishmael? Now, at the very moment of her heightened joy at the realization that Isaac would surely live, why should Ishmael matter? What was he doing that upset her? The verse states that Sarah saw only one thing: Ishmael was *metzachek*. That was her sole focus. The word here clearly ties in with *Yitzchak*, Isaac, to whom *metzachek* also refers in a later narrative. (Gen. 26:8) That this same word is used in reference to both Isaac and Ishmael and that Isaac's name is based upon this same root show that Sarah is concerned about one thing and one thing only: the affinity between her son and the child of the Egyptian handmaid. Ishmael's presence and closeness to Isaac pose a real threat in Sarah's eyes, especially since she is aware of Abraham's positive feelings toward his first-born son. (v. 11) Both sons are precious in Abraham's eyes, and this presents a threat to Isaac's inheriting Abraham's position.

And so Sarah orders her husband to "drive the slavewoman and her son from the house, for the son of that slave shall not share in the inheritance with [her] son, Isaac." (v. 10) She would not deign to call either Ishmael or Hagar by name. In Sarah's eyes, Ishmael is nothing, certainly not worthy of mention in the same breath as Isaac, her son and Abraham's heir. But how was Abraham to feel? How should he react to the thought of losing Ishmael, with whom he surely had built a close relationship over thirteen years? How would Abraham, the father, respond to Sarah's request, which was tantamount to murdering his child? We learn that the matter distressed Abraham greatly because it concerned his son. (v. 11) As Isaac is "his son" (v. 5), so also is Ishmael. While Sarah might have viewed him as nothing more than a child of an Egyptian slave-woman, Abraham saw Ishmael as his own flesh and blood and loved him as he loved Isaac. More than all the other misfortunes that befell Abraham in his life, the banishing of Ishmael was the most painful thing that ever happened to him. (*Pirke de-Rabbi Eliezer* 30)

Then why does he listen to Sarah? What prompts him to drive his firstborn son from his house although he feels great love for him? It appears that it is God's response to his concerns and his love for both his sons that give him the courage to heed the request. In a very supportive manner, God urges Abraham not to be distressed over Ishmael or Hagar, for it is through Isaac that his future will be sealed. (v. 12) God also reassures Abraham that Ishmael will be the progenitor of a great nation because he, too, is Abraham's seed. (v. 13) Like Isaac, Ishmael is his *zera*, his "seed," and as such his future is guaranteed as well. It is God's guarantee that Ishmael will not only live but flourish that enables Abraham to fulfill Sarah's request.

Perhaps, the guarantee regarding Ishmael explains why it is necessary for God to test Abraham futher in the Akedah. (Gen. 22) One more trial is needed because God has to know if Abraham is willing to put his son's (Isaac's) life on the line without an explicit guarantee that he would be spared. God told Abraham to take Isaac to the land of Moriah and offer him as a sacrifice there on one of the mountains that God would show him. (Gen. 22:2) It must have seemed to Abraham that God's previous promise of making his progeny as numerous as the stars in the sky (Gen. 15:5)—a prophecy that was to be fulfilled through Isaac—was now obviated. In sacrificing Isaac, Abraham would be giving up his own future and immortality. At Moriah, God would know exactly how deep was Abraham's faith.

Ishmael's Banishment: Will He Survive?

The parallelism and the close connection between the Akedah in Genesis 22, Abraham's final test, and the banishing of Ishmael in Genesis 21, Abraham's penultimate test, are underscored by the fact that Abraham rises early in the morning to fulfill both commands. (Gen. 21:14 and 22:3) Perhaps his desire to demonstrate his zealous fidelity to God makes him rise earlier than usual. It is more probable, however, that Abraham on both occasions was restless and could not sleep. His ambivalence and fear at what he was about to do forced him out of bed early. In both cases, the father in him would not allow Abraham to linger in bed, as if a casual day's labor awaited him.

Therefore, having received God's guarantees about the future of both Isaac and Ishmael, Abraham rose before dawn, took some bread and water, placed them over Hagar's shoulder, and sent her into the wilderness, together with his firstborn son. (v. 14) Had he given her enough food and water to reach an oasis, or was he an accomplice to the murder of both the maidservant and the child? As Abraham watched them make their way into the wilderness outside of Beer-sheba, what exactly was going through his mind?

Even more difficult for us to perceive is how Hagar and Ishmael felt. Driven from the only home they had known, now disoriented and wandering in the desert, what might they have thought about Abraham, whom they always believed had cared for them? Displaced from their home, their future in doubt, fearing they might not survive the heat and the aridity of the desert, they must have felt a deep animus for Abraham, the patriarch of the nation of Israel. They were not unlike their descendants, today's Ishmaelites, who feel that they, too, have been driven from their homes by the heirs to Abraham's covenant.

To be sure, history teaches that many Palestinians voluntarily abandoned their homes at the outbreak of Israel's War of Independence at the behest of the leaders of the Arab world, who guaranteed that in a matter of days they would drive the Jews into the sea. Then the Arabs who had left their ancestral homes would return to the land of their fathers and mothers and inherit the possessions of their former Jewish neighbors. However, this view of history is not held by today's descendants of Ishmael. The refugees in the camps in Gaza and the West Bank, not far from where Abraham dwelt with Sarah and Isaac, can only feel that their land and homes have been taken from them and they have been driven unjustly into the wilderness to struggle for survival—like Hagar and Ishmael—with little hope for the future.

And when the water was depleted, Hagar began to panic, fearing the worst: the death of her son. Feeling absolutely helpless, unable to bear watching Ishmael die, she cast the child away from her. Placing Ishmael under a bush, she moved far from him, raised her voice, and burst into tears. (vv. 15–16) She was resigned to the fact that both she and her son would die, as they were nowhere near a watering hole.

But God could not abandon the boy, who like Isaac had to fulfill his destiny to become a great nation. (v. 18) Although it was Hagar who had cried out in despair, God heard the voice of Ishmael—*yishma El*, "God heard"—as the Divine hears the voices of all humanity, and God responded to the plight of Abraham's firstborn son. For an angel (*malach*) of God called to Hagar, saying, *Mah lach, Hagar*? "What troubles you, Hagar?" as if the word play in the text was teaching us that God indeed had sent Hagar her own angel (*malach Hagar*), thus calming her fears and telling her that the Divine had heard the cry of the child where he is. (v. 17) God understood his plight and would show his mother that she possessed the strength to save him. It was not enough for Hagar to raise (*tisa*) her voice in anguish (v. 16); now she had to raise up (*se'i*) the child. The angel instructs her literally to strengthen her hands for the sake of the boy; she had to realize that she had the power to insure his survival. (v. 18)

God had opened Hagar's eyes to her own strength, and she saw a well that would save them. (v. 19) In the Hebrew text, *Vayifkach Elohim et eneha, eneha* means "her eyes." However, *ayin*, in additon to meaning "eye," can also mean "well." God, indeed, had opened the wellsprings of her own being, enabling her to see the nearby well. Although the well, the source of their redemption, was there all the time she was sitting a distance from Ishmael, only now could she know it existed. So she filled the water skin and let her son drink. The text here emphasizes that God was truly with Ishmael (not only with Isaac), and as a result Ishmael would live. (v. 20)

Like his mother, Ishmael's contemporary descendants are learning that they have the ability to insure their own survival and take responsibility for it. They, too, can shape a positive future for their children if they can see that the desert can flourish like an oasis. They are not only Abraham's children but also God's children, and, as such, the power in the universe that makes for wholeness is as much a part of them as it is a part of their Israeli brothers and sisters. Though we believe in our unique role as descendants of Isaac and his son Jacob, we recognize that God hears the cries of all peoples and responds accordingly.

The Aftermath
The Family Can Come Together Again

Although Ishmael had been banished from Abraham's tent and dwelt in the wilderness of Paran (v. 21), Abraham did not lose contact with him. After all, Abraham loved Ishmael deeply, and banishing him with his mother was the most difficult thing Abraham ever had to do. Therefore, Abraham occasionally went to visit Ishmael in the desert, showing continuing concern and affection. (*Pirke de-Rabbi Eliezer* 30) Abraham would never lose contact with Ishmael.

Once, after Ishmael's marriage to his second wife, Fatimah, Abraham arrived at Ishmael's camp in the heat of the day to find her at home. Tired and a bit faint from the journey, he asked her for some bread and water. Without realizing who the visitor was, she gave it to him. Abraham then arose and prayed to God on behalf of his son; thereupon, Ishmael's house was filled with bountiful blessings. When Ishmael returned home, his wife told him about the stranger and about what had transpired. He immediately knew that his father still loved him. And Ishmael longed to see him again.

Perhaps Ishmael did see his father, Abraham, on a continuous basis. It is told that Keturah, the woman whom Abraham married toward the end of his life (Gen. 25:1), was, in fact, Hagar. What evidence do we have? The text emphasizes that Abraham "*again* took a wife," indicating that he married the same woman a second time. (*Pirke de-Rabbi Eliezer* 30) Remarrying Hagar, Abraham began to reconstitute his relationship with his son Ishmael as well. The irony, of course, is that it might have been Isaac who brought his father back together with Hagar, the mother of his step-brother, since Isaac had been in an area geographically close to her. We are told that Isaac had come back from a place named Beer-lahai-roi, the "Well of the Living One Who Sees" (Gen. 24:62), the very area in the desert to which Hagar had fled when Sarah mistreated her before she gave birth to Ishmael. (Gen. 16:14) It is most poignant to contemplate that following the remarriage of Abraham and Hagar, the family was together again and Isaac and Ishmael were no longer estranged.

It is, therefore, not very surprising that when Abraham dies, both

Isaac and Ishmael come to the cave of Machpelah to bury their father. Although he must surely have known that Isaac had inherited his father's position and wealth (Gen. 25:5), Ishmael loved his father and simply had to return to pay his respects to him, no matter how painful. One can imagine the scene as it unfolded that day in the field of Ephron the Mittite, facing Mamre.

Isaac stood near the cave, gazing toward the southwest from where Ishmael would come. In the distance, he could see the sand clouds indicating that a caravan was approaching. He knew this had to be Ishmael, and he began to tremble ever so slightly. Would he recognize his half-brother after all these years? Surely time will have taken its toll. And will Ishmael harbor a grudge against him because of all that had happened over a score of years before? But, above all, Isaac tried to think of the words he would say. What do brothers say to each other that can enable them to fill the chasm of time, distance, and life experiences? As the camels approached, Isaac saw Ishmael get down. Looking up, Ishmael caught sight of Isaac. As their eyes met, Isaac saw a smile appear on his half-brothers's face. The years vanished as they embraced, kissed each other, and cried together. Isaac had not realized that when brothers meet after years of separation, if there is love in their hearts, words are not necessary. The smiles on their faces said it all.

Can Isaac and Ishmael come together and live in peace with each other? Can the wounds of the past be healed as the memories of struggle for position and power fade? Can the children of Abraham embrace as they stand in the fields of Hebron and contemplate living together once again? Perhaps, it is not merely a dream to envision their descendants as a family unified again after so many years of strife. After all, they were the sons of the same father who loved them both though he caused each of them so much pain. And, perhaps, they always knew deep in their hearts that one day they would meet and embrace.

A Rabbinic and Contemporary Postscript

The midrashic tradition on Genesis 21 upon which we have drawn indicates that the rabbis struggle with the tension between their particularistic and universalistic concerns. Even at times of heightened concern for Jewish survival, they exhibited compassion for other people and for humanity in general. They did not see themselves existing in a world of only their Jewish brothers and sisters; their world was one in which Jews had to live in peace with their neighbors.

For example, in the context of severe Roman persecution in the third and fourth decades of the second century C.E., the question is asked: "What is the most important principle of the Torah?" (*Sifra, Parashat Kedoshim*, on Lev. 19:18) Rabbi Akiba responds by citing the Golden Rule: "Love your neighbor as yourself." (Lev. 19:18) It is clear that linguistically the word for "your neighbor" in Hebrew, *re'acha*, means "your fellow Israelite," since it follows upon terms such as *amecha*, "your people" (v. 16), and *achicha*, "your brother." (v. 17) Rabbi Akiba, stressing the unity of the Jewish people in the face of a threat to its survival, insists on Jews being concerned for their fellow Jews. When our survival is on the line, our particular needs, in his eyes, are not only totally justified but essential.

Shimon ben Azzai demurs, however, and offers a counter-suggestion regarding the *kelal hagadol shebatorah*, the most important principle of the Torah. He cites Genesis 5:1,2: "This is the book of the generations of Adam.—When God created humankind, God created the [human being] in the Divine's likeness; male and female [God] created them." For ben Azzai, the most important focus was not the Jewish people nor our particular covenantal relationship with God, no matter how important it is. Rather, he underscores the importance of every single human being who is created in the image of God. The implication of this principle, which overshadows our particularistic concerns, is that we have an obligation to relate positively to each and every human being, for we are all children of the Divine. Muslim and Jew, Arab and Israeli—all are brothers and sisters.

At the time of Roman persecution of their people, when even their future survival was in doubt, the rabbis, through the voice of ben Azzai, remind all of us of the vision of Israel's prophets: the people of Israel secure in their land, yet living in peace with their fellow non-Jews around them. When we most expect them to be concerned only about Israel's future, they show us that it is dependant on our ability to see the "other" as our brother or sister.

So, too, does today's Israeli long for a time when our people will not only be secure in its ancient homeland but also when we,

Abraham's progeny, can live peacefully side by side with Abraham's other children. In this regard, recall the words of one kibbutznik following the Six Day War (paraphrased from the collection *The Seventh Day*, Charles Scribner's Sons, New York, 1971):

> When the fighting began, and the mountains around Ein Gev [on the Golan Heights] began to spit fire, a group of our reconnaissance troops on one of the hills next to the Syrian border was busy...putting out a fire in a field belonging to an Arab peasant. "A field is a field," said one of the Israelis. Could anything be more paradoxical? And yet, it seems to me that behavior like this really symbolizes [who we are as Jews]. Our feelings are mixed. We carry in our hearts an oath that binds us never to return to the Europe of the Holocaust; but at the same time, we don't want to lose that Jewish sense of identity with the victims.
>
> We, it is true, do fight...and do hit back...for we have no choice. But we dream of a time when we will be able to stop...when we be able to live in peace [with our Arab brothers and sisters].

We pray with all our strength that that time will come speedily and in our day—and that we have already witnessed its first signs.

What a wondrous moment it was in the history of our people: erstwhile bitter enemies crossing the swollen rivers of hatred in order to sow the seeds of peace!

It was but a moment, only the beginning of a long and arduous journey. Still, it held forth the promise of a strategic turning point in Arab-Israeli politics, a turning point more sweeping than was Sadat's dramatic journey to Jerusalem.

It was a moment that allowed us to dream great dreams—of Israel as the Hong Kong of a new Middle East, of Jews and Palestinians joining forces to build it, to create a united continent of great tolerance and real freedom, of science, of education, and of understanding.

Much nurturing must be given if this tender shoot of peace is to come to its full flowering. Wreckers of the peace abound, as do its doubters, and they must be countered.

They speak of the unconscionable risk that Israel is taking for peace, and risk it doubtlessly is. Israel is trading materiality for mere words on paper. But is that risk really unreasonable?

Israel may be trading land for peace, but it certainly is not trading its strength for peace. Israel's defense forces constitute the fourth most powerful military force in the world today. From the security perspective, the Oslo Plan is heavily weighted in its favor. Therefore, the risk, such as it is, is hardly inordinate! As Leon Wieseltier so elegantly reminds us, "When the lion lies down with the lamb, it is the lamb, not the lion, who lies down anxiously."

True, the Palestinians retain the power to unleash destruction in the streets. But in the absence of peace, the stones and knives of terrorists were scarcely stayed and their rockets were never silenced. Those who would rely on force alone tried everything to quell the *intifada*—war, killing, the expropriation of land for new settlements, collective punishment, mass deportations, and even counterterror. Yet nothing availed.

And so there was a serious risk also in permitting the present state of affairs to fester. The status quo sowed the seeds of endless conflicts. It corroded the Jewish and democratic character of the State. It was a demographic time bomb ticking away at Israel's vital center and threatening to shatter its very being.

And what better time to take the risk for peace than now? For it is now that the Jewish state is in full command of the peace process, with leaders whose peacemaking skills match their military prowess, and whose security arrangement is more favorable than what Menachem Begin accepted at Camp David. It is now that the Arab powers understand that the real threat they face is not the steady achievement of Zionism but the rampaging golem of Muslim fundamentalism. It is now that the influx of Jews to Israel from the former Soviet Union has upset the demographic contest the Palestinians had expected to win. Therefore, it is now that we must speak up for peace, loudly and clearly, now and throughout the unfolding of this remarkable, soul-stirring process.

Rabbi Alexander M. Schindler
"Dear Reader"
Reform Judaism
Winter 1993

VISION OF A
NEW MIDDLE EAST

SHIMON PERES

We cannot build our future on the ruins of an old order. We are part of a process of perpetual change, which compels us to replace outdated concepts with an approach tailored to new realities.

Such major events as the collapse of the Soviet Union, the end of apartheid in South Africa, and the Israel-PLO agreement have all occurred without the intervention of armies or superpowers. These classical instruments of history have become irrelevant. Today a nation cannot gain wealth through military might. An army cannot effectively defend its territory because the range of missiles exceeds the size of the country. The significance of "strategic depth" has been reduced. Science has no borders, technology has no frontiers, information penetrates iron curtains.

The classical defense strategy was based on three factors: time, space, and superiority. All three have lost their value. If a missile can traverse the distance between the United States and Russia in six minutes, what is time? If a missile can fly over mountains, rivers, deserts, and fortifications, what is space? And if a single bomb can destroy a city, what is superiority? All the classical strategies need to be changed and new solutions found. To achieve peace, we must first acknowledge the futility of war. The Arabs cannot defeat Israel on the battlefield. Israel cannot dictate the conditions of peace.

Confronting Fundamentalism

We no longer confront enemies; we confront problems. Yesterday's enemies could be targeted with guns. Today an army is no match against militant fundamentalism. Instead, we must confront the root causes of this spreading tide.

The prolonged Arab-Israeli conflict has led to the misery and poverty of millions of Muslims who, in frustration, have rejected the modern state and immersed themselves in a mystical fundamentalism. This development now threatens the stability of our region and jeopardizes global interests.

There are a billion Muslims—one-sixth of the earth's population. If they become impoverished and bitter, embrace fundamentalism, and acquire nuclear weapons, they can destabilize the world. This unsettled population is now undergoing an inner struggle that has more to do with protesting poverty and basic freedoms than with religious matters. In *Anna Karenina*, Dostoyevski says that all happy families are happily alike, but every unhappy family is unhappy in a different way. So it is with fundamentalism; it gives voice to the diversely rejected. Israel must be viewed in the Muslim world as part of the solution, not the problem, if we are to overcome the most pernicious threat to peace: the spread of Khomeinism.

The Price of Dominating Others

Not only has war become purposeless, but the desire to govern and control another nation is no longer feasible. To govern today is to pay for the poor, to control the desert, to be a policeman fighting a lost cause. When an Israeli soldier with an automatic weapon cannot defeat a Palestinian youth holding a stone, the soldier no longer has a purpose.

Israelis and Palestinians must learn to see each other as people, to understand each other's desires, doubts, hopes, and fears. Breaking the psychological barrier is the precondition for success in our quest for peace. The problem of Jewish settlements is one of relations, not borders. If relations between the two communities improve, it would not be an intrusion for 600 or 700 Jews to live in proximity to 120,000 Arabs (as is the situation in Hebron). To achieve this we must develop strategies of information, delivering images of hope for peace and prosperity to counter those of hate and fear.

A Regional Community of Nations

Regional organization is the key to peace and security. It will promote democratization, economic development, national growth, and individual prosperity. Our ultimate goal is the creation of a regional community of nations with a common market and elected centralized bodies modeled on the European arrangement.

Improved relations will slow down the arms race. The nations of the Middle East have poured hundreds of billions of dollars into armaments. Had there been peace, much of that money would have raised the living standard of the Arabs. No single nation in our part of the world will stop buying arms unless disarmament is regional. And foreigners will not invest here unless the entire region becomes stable.

Political victories that are not accompanied by economic benefit stand on shaky ground. Regional economic development in the new Middle East requires disarmament, which would save 30 billion dollars annually; water resources management, in order to stop desertification (water does not respect frontiers, rivers do not follow borders, and rain does not go through customs); biotechnology, to increase food production; more extensive transportation and communications systems; expanded tourism; more foreign investment; and the creation of a regional bank.

The Middle East regional security system will be structured around two types of mutual obligations: nation to nation (bilateral) and nation to region (multilateral). The bilateral approach is necessary to extinguish the fires of the old conflicts, but it alone will not bring about a durable peace. The entire region must achieve a greater level of individual freedom as well as higher education and living standards.

The structure best suited to the limitations and possibilites of the area is a Jordanian-Palestinian-Israeli "Benelux" arrangement for economic affairs. A separate Palestinian state would be received with unease, either overtly or covertly, among Jordanians and would face fierce opposition from Israelis. Further, there would be widespread doubt as to whether a separate Palestinian state could actually survive and develop.

The Moral Dimension

For us, Israel is not just a territorial homeland; it is a permanent moral commitment. The Jewish people have never sought to dominate another people. Because of the dynamics of conquest, a nation that forces itself on another loses the will to abstain from oppression.

Great empires that once dominated the Jewish people have disappeared from history; yet we survive. What force has sustained us? We have placed morality above physical might. God fashioned us as a small figure with an abundant spirit. The key to Israel's permanence remains the moral judgment of its leaders, for that is the highest degree of wisdom.

I am optimistic that Israel and its neighbors will achieve true peace in my lifetime. When my book *The New Middle East* was published in 1993, only 6 percent of the Israeli public supported my ideas; now the number has grown to 61 percent. Nobody, not even I, believed the peace process would move ahead as fast as it has. All my life, I never knew what one could do with pessimism. It's a waste of time. I prefer to dream.

I found in Rabbi Alex Schindler the wisdom of Jewish morality and the depth of Jewish commitment. He is a profound leader and a trustworthy friend, who has paved a way for Jewish existence to enter a new century without losing the moral purpose of our genesis.

NOTE

This essay is based on passages from *The New Middle East* by Shimon Peres (New York: Henry Holt, 1993) and on an interview with Israel's foreign minister by Aron Hirt-Manheimer.

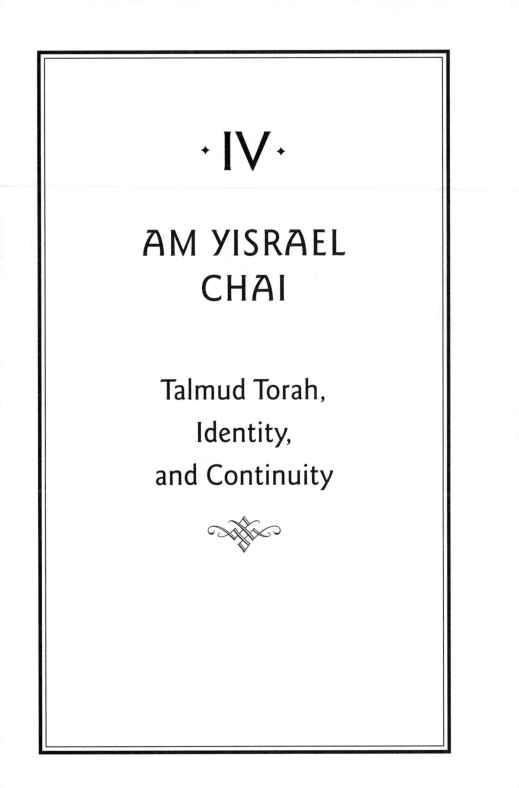

·IV·

AM YISRAEL CHAI

Talmud Torah, Identity, and Continuity

Jewish education is the primary purpose of a congregation's striving. The *Shema* is the cornerstone of its liturgy, is it not? The very word *shema* means "listen...learn." And at the core of this prayer is the commandment to take the "words that I command you this day" and "to teach them diligently to your children." *Talmud Torah*, the "study and the teaching of the Torah," is the transcendent ideal that the synagogue enshrines. Thus, every aspect of the congregational program must be bent to serve this end, the bulk of its resources applied to it. Only then will its center hold.

Jewish education is not limited to the classroom by any manner or means. It must penetrate every other room and activity of the temple's life. In the sanctuary, prayer and study must be intertwined. Conversionary programs are of scant value if they involve merely the imparting of labels lacking substance. Social action loses all force if its religious rootage is not probed, its religious motivations left unexplored. In a word, all temple activities—from committee meetings to conversation within the temple's halls, from social events to the letters and bulletins we send out—should be seen and seized as means to further the Jewish educative process.

Nor is the transmission of Judaism the domain of the professional teaching staff alone. All professionals and lay leaders, too, must engage in this process. *Nolens volens*, they are engaged in it anyway because our children internalize their values primarily by identification with the ego ideal, that is to say, they take their clue not so much from what people say but from what they do.

And so the manner in which we conduct the temple's affairs, how we approach one another, how we comport *ourselves*, the kind of people we single out for leadership or choose to honor otherwise—all these and more teach our children a good deal about those values we affirm ourselves and see our synagogues enshrining.

Rabbi Alexander M. Schindler
NATE Convention
Chicago, Illinois
December 26, 1988

TALMUD TORAH AND THE JEWISH FUTURE

ALAN D. BENNETT

The More Torah, the More Life

Jews who cherish the Jewish future recite with the Sinai generation, "Our children are our surety!"[1] They expect education to be the enabling, saving instrument. Across the continent communities are betting the bank on Talmud Torah's ability to extend continuity. Is that realistic? Can education promise a worthwhile future? If so, what kind of education? For what kind of future?

Biblical generations taught their children and transmitted faith in the covenant and its Author. Talmud Torah worked at that time and for a few thousand years after. Does it still? The 1990 Jewish Population Survey states that we're losing Jews. Without Jews, no Judaism. End of the Jewish road. Have we placed too much faith in the redemptive power of education? Abraham Joshua Heschel expressed his doubts when he wrote: "None of us can rest content with his intellectual, moral, or spiritual state of living. The disease from which we all suffer is *intellectual* as well as *spiritual illiteracy*; *ignorance* as well as *idolatry of false values*. We are a generation devoid of learning as well as sensitivity." The cause? The "vapidity of

religious instruction" complicated by the "trivialization of education." [emphases in original][2]

Did Heschel exaggerate? If not, why expect otherwise of Talmud
Torah now? What magic invests education of the 1990s with the
power of salvation? The sixties were simpler times compared to
three decades later. If education failed of purpose then, why will it
work now? After all, Talmud Torah was, at least in liberal circles,
modern. If it fell short, it did so despite Dewey. Jewish schools
rejoiced in activities curricula and life experiences. Education was
so child-centered that some called it "juvenile Judaism." (Heschel
was wrong in this. Judaism, not education, was trivialized.)

Furthermore, Talmud Torah was ineffectual despite our sages.
Pondering the assertion that study outweighs righteousness,
Maimonides concluded, "Study in all cases takes precedence over
practice since it leads to practice, but practice does not lead to
study."[3] That view led to fine textbooks, challenging workbooks,
and influential teaching materials. Education did aspire to transmit
Jewish knowledge and wisdom so that another generation would
live as Jews. We've been disappointed. Why?[4]

The answer, in part, is that an appropriate social setting to
actualize traditional values—religion, practice, family learning—
was gone. The self-contained, self-reinforcing, Jewish-validating
community lived only in nostalgia. Liberated Jews joyously traded
shtetl restrictions for vaunted riches of the *Goldeneh Medineh*. Brass
rings on the beguiling slide to assimilation were more appealing
than demands of a transplanted *kehillah*. Our predecessors signed a
Faustian pact. We inherit the consequences.

Something New under the Sun

Some tried to harmonize tradition with modernity, as in the New
York *Kehillah*. Insistent forces, like war and immigration, weakened
hopes for such a future. In the end, the model from another time
and place could not withstand the dislocating political and social
changes Jews confronted. Arthur A. Goren states:

> [Judah] Magnes came to understand that under the free
> conditions of American life, ethnicity was but one of many
> attachments shared by group and individual. Only some leaders

would continue the elusive pursuit of "organic community." ...
But most Jews remained interested in the minimum of separation from the larger society necessary for maintaining their
Jewish identity. They would be content with a more modest
vision of community.[5]

What is the "modest vision" now? How can it protect Judaism?
What kind of education will fulfill the vision on which the Jewish
future rises or falls? On a continuum of beliefs, all options may
work at some time for some Jews, and strength may lie in variety.
But where on a spectrum between Orthodoxy and secularism is the
critical-mass number that will live as Jews in the next millennium?
The vision has to comprehend that Jews are free not to be Jewish
in a society that makes that easier all the time. That same freedom
fosters unparalleled Jewish diversity. Emancipation and Enlightenment carry high price tags. The open society, despite lingering anti-
Semitism, is good for Jews. Although it engenders religious
uncertainty, it nurtures the reemergence of a Jewish polity that,
says Jonathan S. Woocher, is "a faith for the ambivalent American
Jew." This new way of being Jewish, "civil Judaism," is "a religious
posture and an activist program that faces a series of ongoing
challenges: Teaching Jews how to live in two civilizations; penetrat-
ing the structures of national and organizational life with the power
of Jewish values; ensuring that the Jewish people endures for its
work of *tikkun olam* in a world that assaults both the people and its
faith; reaffirming the Covenant in a time when it is difficult even to
speak of God...." Civil Judaism also includes being a "bridge
between the sacred and the profane."[6] Civil Judaism suggests that
this bridge continues to expand as diversity and complexity
increase. Talmud Torah for the future will have to recognize that
truth as well.

Manifestly, Jewish diversity is nothing new. What is new, believes
Jack Wertheimer, is a fragmentation among Jews in religious
behaviors and public discussions about Judaism. These are in the
context of "division in American society and religion in general....
[However] American Judaism...must contend with some uniquely
Jewish dilemmas...a yawning chasm between the religiously
committed and the indifferent; the four major denominations are in
conflict with one another and each is divided internally; there are

Jews who choose to remain on the margins of official Judaism and reject all denominational religion; there are issues that unite some Jews across denominational lines to join in ideological combat against other Jews...."[7]

Wertheimer cautions against writing off the Jewish people because its creativity, resilience, dynamism, and high quality of Jewish life are powerful counterfoils to decline. Yet his conclusion is somber: "Tensions over religious questions thus intrude into all spheres of Jewish communal life...color social relations between Jews of different denominations and outlooks...undermine the ability of the American Jewish community to act in concert regarding domestic issues...exacerbate estrangement between American and Israeli Jews. It is no longer possible—or wise—to dismiss religious polarization as peripheral to Jewish life. The divided world of Judaism imperils the unity of the Jewish people in America."[8]

What do such glimpses of the future mean for Talmud Torah? What new education will carry liberal Judaism into the next millennium?

Torah—For All Generations

Civil Judaism, despite wanting to ameliorate and arbitrate the divisiveness Wertheimer describes, is itself potentially a source of internal competition. At the same time, it frames a fruitful discussion about where Jewishness and the Diaspora meet. This tension, which has a long history, was described by Hutchins Hapgood in his turn-of-the-century seminal chronicles, which are instructive for insights about acculturation. The following could have been written about today's boys and girls:

> Even before he begins to go to our public schools, the little Jewish boy finds himself in contact with a new world that stands in violent contrast....With his entrance into the public school, the little fellow runs plump against a system of education and a set of influences that are at total variance with those traditional to his race and with his home life. The religious element is entirely lacking.[9]

Bernard Reisman says similar conditions prevailed in the Jewish context thirty years later: "What they were supposed to be learning in Hebrew school and how it was being taught were at variance with their newly absorbed American values and aspirations. How could it be otherwise since their teachers were predominantly reared in 'the old school' and still committed to it?"[10] (Dissonance was evident in many spheres. For example, young Jewish men who came to America encountered, when their wives joined them, a separation of two centuries, not two or three years. Ghetto divorces and desertions were frequent. Acculturation transforms.)

Jewish education in the New York, Old World-type *cheder* could not overcome countervailing, outside forces. Yet, something persuaded most young Jews to remain in the fold. For, as Nathan Glazer observes, institutional, if not religious, life was strong in the twenties and thirties. "The future, it then seemed, would see the rapid dissolution of the Jewish religion....Jewish students had moved much farther from any religious position than the Catholic and Protestant students. More were atheist, more agnostic, fewer accepted any traditional religious formulations...." These were on the way to becoming secular and institutional, not religious, Jews. Judaism, as theretofore understood, was endangered despite a burgeoning education system in synagogues and in community-sponsored schools.

As a matter of fact, Glazer continues, "Jewish education, like all of Jewish life, was much better organized in this period than at any time before....But this Jewish education often had nothing to do with the Jewish religion...[which] was only one of a number of contending influences in the Jewish community." A myriad of cultural, philanthropic, and political activities—socialism, Zionism, Yiddish movements, philanthropic associations, benevolent societies, defense organizations, the Jewish Center movement—offered ways to be Jewish in other than the religious sphere. These were "so rich and variegated and vigorous...that a number of Jewish thinkers, in particular the philosopher and liberal Horace M. Kallen, proposed that the future Jewish life of this country should be built on all the varieties of Jewish expression that had come into existence and not only on Judaism...a community in which...religion would be only one of the possible expressions of Jewishness."[11]

Which visions of Judaism should Talmud Torah serve: religious, ethnic, secular, civil? All of them and more? Despite ninety years of

Jewish education, religion appears to be weak; to many Jews it is inconsequential. How does that affect Talmud Torah and the future?

Judaism resides in a special people with a shared history and institutions and a worldview that embraces variety. This "positivism," reviewed by Albert Schoolman about thirty years ago, "affirms the existence of an American Jewish community that is aware of its many-faceted culture, with elements of philosophic and religious, ethical and social, artistic and aesthetic involvements that endow it with the characteristics of an ethnic civilization." He went on to say that Jewish educators of all groups, with some modification, affirmed that concept.[12]

Seen this way, education was effective because diversity has been facilitated in "the total functioning of this way of life in all its relationships...[by] a multiplicity of organizations, of social agencies, and services."[13] Moreover, synagogue membership is not plummeting; Jewish communities boast committed and hard-working Jews who fulfill *tikkun olam* for the benefit of Jews and non-Jews; Jewish books and magazines abound and are read by Jews; large numbers of young men and women are choosing to become Jews. These are not signs of a failed system.

Talmud Torah of the past succeeded in that we are here, speculating about these things as Jews in a Jewish context. But, for many, it failed to preserve traditional religious indexes of Jewish survival like law, ritual, and regular prayer. That's because vectors external to Talmud Torah's reach also shape Judaism. This is our historical process: The Jewishness that survives is the outcome of a syncretism of inherited value-system and host mores. Judaism is receptive to its environment—Sumerian, Aristotelian, Hellenic, Islamic, Christian, European, and North American. From the sacrificial Canaanite wheat-wafer to Chanukah gift-giving, Judaism was cast and recast by the unique value-stance of its historical travelers—the Jewish people. This religio-social process, except in times of persecution or enforced isolation, permitted and even encouraged contact with the "others."

Abba Hillel Silver viewed the nineteenth-century Enlightenment as "a determined effort...by leaders of both Western and Eastern Europe...to achieve the two-fold objective of adjusting religious laws and customs to the needs of modern life and of reestablishing freer contact with other cultures...to abolish the walls of partition that external intolerance and internal shrinking had erected...to facilitate contact with the surrounding world, where a new spirit of freedom and tolerance was then making itself manifest."[14] Creative adaptation, while not unique to Judaism, is for Judaism one secret of survival.

New World experiences advanced the process—with an important difference. By the twentieth century, adaptations and adjustments by previous generations had weakened traditional roots. Jews who emerged from turn-of-the-century New York ghettos stood on the shoulders of nineteenth-century European ghetto Jews, but they saw a sparser landscape. Jews who fashioned—and then left—America's gilded ghettos planted in Jewish religious soil dramatically poorer than that of their immigrant forebears. Each succeeding, freer, rebelling generation grafted its Judaism on increasingly vestigial roots. How long before there's nothing left to nurture the new? Can Talmud Torah for the future slow, halt, or reverse the process?

Know before Whom You Stand

In an increasingly free, multi-ethnic, multi-racial, multi-religious, multi-whatever social fabric, Judaism became but another among the multitude of threads. Inclusiveness and anonymity made it easier not to be Jewish. Most Jews found it incrementally more convenient to ignore the spiritual demands of the ancestral religion.

Charles E. Silberman finds a paradox here. That same openness makes today's Jews freer to be Jews than Jews ever were. Fears of anti-Semitism are diminished, and most Jews don't feel compelled to be quiet and invisible to avoid attracting attention. Jews comprise a significant political, economic, and social force. Individual Jews occupy important business and government positions. Someone who wants to be Jewish and public in this generation can be so in ways that Jews one or two generations ago could not.[15]

If it's easier to be Jewish now, what's the problem? Why do so many warn that Jews are not expressing their religion? One reason is that large numbers lack the knowledge and skills to live as the Jews they'd like to be. These are the "Jews of North America [who] live in an open society that presents an unprecedented range of opportunities and choices. This extraordinary society confronts us with what is proving to be a historic dilemma: While we cherish our freedom as individuals to explore new horizons, we recognize that this very freedom poses a dramatic challenge to the future of the Jewish way of life. The Jewish community must meet the challenges at a time when young people are not sure of their roots in the past or of their identity in the future."[16]

It's not that they escaped Talmud Torah. Most received some Jewish education at some time in their young lives. (That's true today as well.) But when children experienced prayer, it was usually in an academic context of practicing "special Hebrew," not as a pathway to faith. God was absent from curricula, teachers were squeamish about their own relationship to God, or both. *Mitzvah*, "commandment," and *Metzaveh*, "Commander," were referents, for the most part, only in the arena of *tikkun olam*, which was, preferably, "social action." Observances were frequently taught as "things some Jews do" or as folk mores, hardly ever as expressions of *berit*, "covenant." The milieu for *Tanach* was more often "Bible stories" than encounters with the Divine in history. Hebrew was "to know the blessings" or for "modern conversation," hardly ever the values-conveyor of a people. Feeling good *about* being Jewish had priority over *being* Jewish and responding to life in Jewish ways.

In the mid-seventies some educators like Daniel B. Syme started challenging prevailing views. Why can't God be in the curriculum? Why aren't rituals presented as God's will as much as bonds with ancestors? Why aren't Holocaust faith-heroes—Anne Frank, Leo Baeck, Janusz Zorczak, Yossele Rakover, and a host of others—held up as affirmations that God was present to some during the *Shoah*? Why don't teachers and rabbis discuss understandings of God so children and adults can connect their religious ideas to Jewish models?

But the voices were few and out of sync with the times. Thus, many of today's parents don't nurture Judaism in their home because of the inadequacies of their own Jewish instruction in the ways of their religion. Now, correctives such as family education parallel child-parent studies, and basic Judaism courses address past failures. How can we assure that past mistakes are not repeated in Talmud Torah for the future?

Some of what appears to be failure may, in fact, be part of the Jewish adaptive process: The open society, no longer demanding energy for survival, liberates energy for difficult, ultimate questions, the kind Egon Mayer asks: "What do we believe? Why do we want to be apart from others as a culturally distinct entity? How do we relate to those with whom we differ?"[17] The questions persist.

Train the Child

School and society are symbiotic. A perpetual debate strikes at the fundamental purpose of education: Should schools guard and preserve the culture, transmitting the social order as it is, or should they initiate change in the order that creates and sustains them? Sometimes a search for a philosophy of education is overtaken by events outside schools and beyond their control. Sputnik's flaming launch brought American educational reform without a lot of debate. No systematic analysis preceded black and other ethnic studies on American campuses. Japanese business competition sent educators scrambling to find the formula for preparing successful American competition. When events drive educational change, schools may appear to be preparing learners to live in an open-ended society. In reality, pragmatism not rationality is at work, and schools are followers not leaders in social change. Education serves society's socializing needs. Education's missions are defined and shaped by society's other instruments.

In 1953, on the occasion of the thirtieth anniversary of Reform's Commission on Jewish Education, Solomon Freehof wrote: "The changes in Jewish life, affecting the work of our Commission, have been immense." Noting the disruption of education with the destruction of European Jewry, the rebirth of Israel and Reform's shift towards Zionism, the change in Reform's emphasis from doctrine to ceremony, the growing eagerness for traditional observances, and the increasing rabbinic interest in Judaism as law, he concluded, "All that we teach is a vehicle for our ultimate spiritual and ethical purposes."[18]

Talmud Torah for the future depends on "spiritual and ethical," i.e., religious, purposes. But where do you begin to define purpose for a community in which fewer than 30 percent attend religious services weekly or monthly and nearly 25 percent never attend; nearly 30 percent usually or sometimes have a Christmas tree; 50 percent of marriages involving one Jewish spouse is a mixed marriage, and, in those homes, 72 percent of the children are being raised with no religion or in a religion other than Judaism?[19]

In the thirtieth-anniversary publication of the Commission on Jewish Education, Emanuel Gamoran emphasized education's responsibility for curriculum and texts reflecting all viewpoints. Nevertheless, he cautioned that "any system of Jewish education that is worthy of the name will operate with the three concepts of God, Israel, and Torah. And the classic Jewish dictum from the Kabbalah 'Israel and the Torah and the Holy One, blessed be He, are One' is a reflection of the true Jewish spirit."[20] Under his directorship, the Commission's publications included all three aspects. But, as Gamoran acknowledged, what a school uses—and how—depends on what the congregation believes Judaism ought to be.

Reform's dilemma about telling Jews what to do is not new. Past efforts evoked little response among those who believed Reform's validity grows with its distance from Orthodoxy. There were notable anticipations of the spirituality movement: Abraham J. Feldman, *Reform Judaism: A Guide for Reform Jews* (New York: Behrman House, 1956); Frederic A. Doppelt and David Polish, *A Guide for Reform Jews* (Chicago: Jennie Loundy Memorial Fund, 1957); W. Gunther Plaut, ed., *A Shabbat Manual* (New York: Central Conference of American Rabbis, 1972). These, followed by the CCAR's *Gates* volumes starting in the seventies, signaled new directions. Education's response was too slow. We need Talmud Torah that reacts more quickly to new realities and will help, in its way, to fashion the future.

Both These and These

The Divine, Peoplehood, Law—these comprise the traditional essence of the Jewish spirit. Jews emphasized different aspects and discovered new meanings in each in a variety of times and places. Consistent with its own tradition, the Reform movement persists in that inexorable process. New spirituality seminars seek to restore *emunah*, "faith," to our people; published guides[21] describe what a Reform Jew should do; *mitzvah* is one of the many "gates" to God. A religious spirit for liberal Jews is shaping as religious reawakening stirs a generation pursuing its roots. The search requires that we reexamine who we want to be. Gamoran spoke of God, Israel, and

Torah as "concepts." Aren't they, rather, realities? How we perceive these and other formative values will determine the content of Talmud Torah for the Jewish future.

We are proud of our synagogue schools, as well as of our youth programs, camping, family education, cradle-to-grave learning, day schools, Israel experiences, and the like. Each is an exciting aspect of Talmud Torah. Each contributes to a viable, productive future. But it starts with schooling, as Alice Goldstein and Sylvia Barack Fishman conclude from the data: "Informal educational experiences...function primarily as *complementary* rather than *alternative* forms of Jewish education. Jewish camps and youth groups are much more likely to be frequented by children and teenagers who have *also* received formal Jewish education. Moreover, children who receive more formal Jewish education are dramatically more likely than those with less formal education to participate in Jewish youth groups and camps." [emphases in original][22]

Talmud Torah demands coordinated, driving purposes motivated by religious commitment and grounded in postmodern realities. Education begs to reflect the "true Jewish spirit" of the Jewish future. Survival requires that spirit to be embedded in faith. Reform's emerging religious visions must systemically and consciously animate its Talmud Torah so that it may articulate its own contribution to that future. Absent that and fifty years hence others will wonder why Jewish education failed again—if, indeed, there will be enough committed Jews to wonder.

NOTES

1. *Tanchuma Vayigash*, cited in C. G. Montefiore and H. Loewe, *Rabbinic Anthology* (Philadelphia: Jewish Publication Society, 1960), p. 219.

2. Abraham J. Heschel, "The Values of Jewish Education," in David Weinstein and Michael Yizhar, *Modern Jewish Educational Thought* (Chicago: College of Jewish Studies, 1964), p. 24. Heschel was neither the first nor last to proclaim the failure of Jewish education. Thus Samson Benderly, 1913: "There are about 1,000 *cheder*s in this country...half of them in New York City....No one, not even among the most optimistic or the most Orthodox, doubts that the *cheder* is a complete failure....Its inherent defects, which in the atmosphere of Russian Jewish life were already noticeable but bearable, are a terrible anomaly in the new environment." (Reprinted in Lloyd P. Gartner, *Jewish Education in the United States* [New York: Teachers College, Columbia University, 1969], p. 135.)

Heschel's lament was repeated often in assessments of Jewish education. Especially vociferous was the assertion that Jewish education was like the Platte River, a mile wide and an inch deep. (Alexander M. Dushkin and Uriah Z. Engelman, *Jewish Education in the United States* [New York: American Association for Jewish Education, 1959])

3. *Hilchut Talmud Torah* 1:8.

4. While this essay focuses on children and, more narrowly, on schooling, Talmud Torah should be understood broadly as Jewish learning for all ages in many settings. In 1964, Alexander M. Schindler, then director of Reform's Commission on Jewish Education, warned about the dangers of neglecting adult Jewish learning, which, he demonstrated, has deeper roots in Judaism than does education for children. (*National Association of Temple Educators News*, vol. IX, no. 3, November 1964) Shoshana Cardin (*Jewish Telegraphic Agency Daily News Bulletin*, 6/30/93) appealed for various ways to encourage Jews to choose to be Jews. Don't blame the apostates, she asserts. Blame institutions that are failing to attract them.

5. Arthur A. Goren, *New York Jews and the Quest for Community* (New York: Columbia University Press and Philadelphia: Jewish Publication Society, 1970), p. 252. Magnes's view that ethnicity is a component of Jewishness has been widely held. That may no longer be the case. Jonathan Sarna suggests that "the Jewish community has been mistaken in its belief that its ethnic identity is 'innate and immutable, passed on from one generation to the next....The larger society no longer recognizes Jewishness as an ethnic category at all.'...And beyond the question of recognition, ethnicity is increasingly ignored. It is not only Jews who are intermarrying, but all ethnic groups." (*Jewish Telegraphic Agency Daily News Bulletin*, 6/30/93) If this view is correct, we will have to reexamine the tasks of Talmud Torah, as well as the rationale and method of outreach programs.

6. Jonathan S. Woocher, *Sacred Survival: The Civil Religion of American Jews* (Bloomington: Indiana University Press, 1986), p. 200. Woocher's position as executive vice president of the Jewish Education Service of North America makes this a particularly important book. Its insights illumine the emerging role of federations in the new education.

7. Jack Wertheimer, *A People Divided* (New York: Basic Books, 1993), p. xviii.

8. Ibid., pp. 195–196.

9. Hutchins Hapgood, *The Spirit of the Ghetto* (New York: Funk & Wagnalls, 1902), p. 23.

10. Bernard Reisman, "Needed: A Paradigm Shift in Jewish Education," *Jewish Education*, vol. 60, no. 2, Summer 1993 (New York: Council for Jewish Education), p. 29.

11. Nathan Glazer, *American Judaism* (Chicago: University of Chicago Press, 1957), pp. 84 ff.

12. Albert Schoolman, in Graenum Berger, *The Turbulent Decades*, vol. II (New York: Council of Jewish Communal Service, 1981), p. 1055.

13. Ibid.

14. Abba Hillel Silver, *Where Judaism Differed* (New York: Macmillan, 1963), p. 367.

15. Charles E. Silberman, *A Certain People* (New York: Summit Books, 1985), pp. 246 passim.

16. *A Time to Act: Report of the Commission on Jewish Education in North America,*

1990, p. 25. The report identifies "a substantial number of Jews [who] no longer seem to believe that Judaism has a role to play in their search for personal fulfillment and communality."

17. Egon Mayer, "For U.S. Jews, an Age of Anxiety," *New York Times*, 9/19/93.

18. *30th Anniversary: Commission on Jewish Education* (New York: Union of American Hebrew Congregations and Central Conference of American Rabbis, 1953), pp. 3 ff.

19. *Looking Towards the 21st Century: Facts and Issues for Jewish Education* (New York: Jewish Education Service of North America, 1993), p. 23. A fascinating comparison, even allowing for methodological differences, is with 1935 data noted by Nathan Glazer in *American Judaism*. Then, 72 percent of men and 78 percent of women, ages 15–25, had attended no religious service during the past year.

20. Emanuel Gamoran, cited in *30th Anniversary: Commission on Jewish Education*, p. 13.

21. Simeon Maslin, ed., *What We Believe...What We Do...* (New York: UAHC Press, 1993); *Shaarei Shabbat* (New York: UAHC/CCAR, 1993).

22. Alice Goldstein and Sylvia Barack Fishman, *Teach Your Children When They Are Young: Contemporary Jewish Education in the United States*, Research Report 10, 1993 (Center for Modern Jewish Studies/Brandeis University and Jewish Education Service of North America), p. 4. This report and Report 8 (*When They Are Grown They Will Not Depart: Jewish Education and the Jewish Behavior of American Adults*, 1993) are based on the National Jewish Population Study of 1990.

Our vitality as a religious community is assured by a massive stone in our institutional altar, the North American Federation of Temple Youth. NFTY was founded during the last week in December 1939 and quickly grew to become a very creative affiliate. Tens of thousands of our young people have participated in its activities, and their lives have been transformed by the experience.

Wherever I go on this continent of ours, I find NFTY alumni. They are our rabbis and cantors and educators and administrators. They are the lay leaders of our congregations and their most devoted members. And whenever they speak of their NFTY years, a dreamlike, wistful gleam illuminates their faces.

NFTY has spawned many programs of great worth: junior youth groups and activities for its alumni on campus; the Eisendrath International Student Exchange program; Bible tours and archaeological digs in Israel; the NFTY Mitzvah Corps, bringing religious action to life in Puerto Rico and Mexico and to the ghettos of America. A group of NFTY song and dance leaders even toured Russia this past summer to help rekindle the Jewish spark among Soviet Jews.

To this day, the Reform movement sends more teenagers on summer programs to Israel than does any other youth movement in the world. Indeed, without NFTY, there would be no Kibbutz Yahel, no Kibbutz Lotan, and no Mitzpe Har Halutz in the Galilee; these very settlements lend primary credibility to Israel's Progressive movement.

Most notable of all, NFTY brought the Union's camp program into being, and it remains the most effective vehicle for the transmission of Judaism at our command. By a magic all their own, our camps make Judaism come to life in the hearts of our children.

Rabbi Alexander M. Schindler
State of the Union Message
New Orleans, Louisiana
November 1989

NFTY AND JEWISH IDENTITY

JEROME K. DAVIDSON

A national religious institution develops a youth program hoping to maintain the commitment of the coming generation. It is rare indeed that the youth movement itself becomes the driving, pace-setting force, ultimately giving direction to the entity that created it. Such has been the remarkable role of the National (now North American) Federation of Temple Youth (NFTY) in the amazing growth and development of the institutions of Reform Judaism in the past half century.

In 1939 the creators of NFTY, who brought together a country-wide organization of the young people of Reform synagogues, pioneered the concept of a denominational youth movement that became the pattern for Conservative and Orthodox Judaism. Local temple youth groups, called "Young Folks Temple Leagues," had already been established in a number of congregations for several decades primarily for young adults of postcollege age. However, by the mid-forties NFTY had officially become a high school organization with the goal of maintaining the affiliation of teenagers following the conclusion of their formal religious school education. While that in itself would have been no small achievement, it is hard to imagine that these pioneers could have envisioned that their creation would not only assure the continuity they sought but, at the same time, would produce generations of the movement's leadership. More astoundingly, NFTY would impact profoundly upon the very nature of Reform Judaism through the next decades—its worship, ritual traditions, social commitments, and educational priorities. When 3,000 delegates attend one of the Union of American Hebrew Congregations biennial conventions, now the largest organizational Jewish gathering in the world, an overwhelming portion of the rabbis, cantors, educators, lay leaders, and members are there as a result of the motivating influence of their experiences at summer camps, at weekend city conclaves, and in local temple youth group programs. Most of the songs they sing, including much of the liturgical music; the powerful social action themes they passionately support; and the rituals that bind them together first inspired them when they were part of NFTY.

The transformation from organization to movement and from a federation of youth groups to a revolutionary new Jewish experience for teenagers began when NFTY initiated its programs in a camp setting. It was the plan of Rabbi Samuel Cook, who became national director in 1946, for NFTY to bring representatives of local temple youth groups to ten-day or two-week camp sessions where young people were to learn how to become youth group leaders. At these National Leadership Institutes, as they were called, the teenagers were to share the powerful discovery that Judaism could become an exciting, motivating force for them. The results were dramatic, not only in training young people to return to their temples as leaders of youth groups, but in instilling in them an awareness that Judaism need no longer be simply an intellectual subject studied in a formal religious school setting but rather an emotionally fulfilling part of their youthful lives.

Reform Judaism was not first in the Jewish community to discover the educational value of the camp experience, but Reform's ingenious utilization of the camp opportunity and its extension into year-round programming were pacesetting. Jewish educational camping began with the Cejwin Camps founded in 1919 by Albert P. Schoolman, an early proponent of the utilization of "modern" methods in Jewish instruction. He and his colleagues were persuaded by the advocates of progressive education that camps created an environment in which personal development as well as learning could be effectively promoted. Samson Benderly, regarded as the "father" of modern Jewish education, wrote these prophetic words decades ago: "Even if the camp may not succeed in imparting a great fund of Jewish knowledge, it can implant a love for and an interest in things Jewish and arouse in the child a desire for Jewish knowledge."[1]

As Jewish camping developed in the 1920s and 1930s, early emphasis was placed more on the Americanization of the children of immigrants than on the Jewish nature of the experience.

However, by the 1940s a variety of Jewish camps had developed—Zionist, Hebrew-speaking, Yiddish-speaking—and in the fifties Federation and denominational camping as well began to utilize the great potential of the experience to help young people strengthen their Jewish identity in creative and emotionally appealing ways. The "melting pot" agenda became a search for "roots."[2]

In response to a newly felt need to strengthen Jewish identity, the Conservative movement established Camp Ramah in 1947, and the Reform movement established the Union Institute in Oconomowoc, Wisconsin, in 1952. The Conservative leadership regarded Ramah as a summer opportunity for Jewish young people to study texts, experience an environment of Jewish living, and at the same time serve as a recruitment center for the Jewish Theological Seminary. However, in developing its own unique approach, the Reform movement's first step into camping created a quite different kind of institution, which was to influence profoundly the nature of its youth movement far into the future.

The Union Institute was in part the achievement of Rabbi Herman Schaalman, who, along with several other German-born rabbis, had been exposed to camping in the Jewish boy scout movement in Germany. Representing the Jewish Chautauqua Society, he had also experienced the remarkable impact on teenagers of a Methodist summer youth camp in Iowa. Schaalman, with the strong support of Reform Jewish lay leader Joseph Ackerman of Chicago, clearly recognized that the Reform movement could enhance its work with high school students in a similarly informal camp setting, utilizing the participation of rabbis in significant numbers as the Methodists had done so successfully with their clergy. Rabbi Samuel Cook, who developed the NFTY National Leadership Institutes a few years before, renting facilities in Decatur, Michigan, and Haverford, Pennsylvania, had pressed UAHC leadership for a Reform camp for several years. Now he brought his highly successful program to Oconomowoc. Soon the Union Institute became the first in an expanding UAHC camp enterprise that today comprises nine countrywide locations. Cook and Schaalman shared in understanding the value of the informal interaction between rabbis and youth, in the willingness to be experimental in programming, and in a sensitivity and responsiveness to the special nature of young people.

Schaalman, who was later to become president of the Central Conference of American Rabbis, expressed his view of the early camp program's immediate and remarkable success:

> The vision was...to develop fond emotional responses to Judaism, to make Judaism exciting, vibrant, beautiful—maybe even to some extent romantic in the sense that we really wanted to have the whole person involved rather than just merely the educational aspect. And so singing and being in touch with nature, having outdoor services and campfire sessions... imprinted themselves on our young people...which left a deposit of something exciting and beautiful.[3]

That enduring "deposit" was made possible by the development of an approach to educational camping that the NFTY National Leadership Institutes fine-tuned over subsequent years. By encouraging the participation of creative and inspiring rabbis, young and old, along with rabbinic students and some exceptional religious school educators, the youth camps became astounding phenomena within the Reform movement. High school students would return to their congregations from a NFTY event so charged with enthusiasm that the synagogue's young people and the congregation as a whole soon felt the impact. These young people insisted on changes within the religious school. They advanced the approach of informal education even in formal classroom settings; they presented creative youth services to adults, now amazed with this new youthful fervor; and they began to talk about becoming rabbis in a denomination whose rabbinic leadership had come almost exclusively from outside the movement.

It is interesting to note that the rabbis leading the National Leadership Institutes and the conclaves, which quickly spread to every region of the expanding national organization, had instinctively learned to utilize the principles of informal education and social psychology that were being developed and generally accepted during the preceding several decades. John Dewey, one of the most renowned proponents of progressive education in the 1930s, established the principles of instruction that represented the direction in which Reform Jewish camp education would move. As expressed by Bernard Reisman in his report *Informal Jewish*

Education in North America, Dewey's progressive education sought

> to correct the inadequacies of traditional education, replacing
> imposition from above with expression and cultivation of indi-
> viduality, rejecting external discipline in favor of free activity,
> learning from experience instead of learning from texts and
> teachers, and rather than preparing students for a remote future,
> the time orientation of progressive education focuses on the
> opportunities of present life.[4]

At the same time social psychologists were beginning to
understand how and why informal education could achieve so
successfully what formal teaching had not. In a rabbinic thesis, *The
Religious Attitudes of Reform Jewish Youth*, presented at the Hebrew
Union College in Cincinnati in 1958 when the NFTY camp program
was enjoying the height of popularity and success, I researched the
subject of value acquisition by the adolescent. Then as now, the
single most significant factor in the literature was clearly seen to be
the peer group, the power of group approval. Kurt Lewin's
pioneering research broadened the concept to the teaching of all
ages, recognizing the potential of the small group for influencing
human behavior and education. Lewin and his colleague Paul
Grabbe in their article "Conduct, Knowledge, and Acceptance of
New Values" suggest that when the individual accepts belonging-
ness to a group he accepts a new system of values and beliefs.
Through the creation of the "we-feeling," new values can be taught,
but the teaching is done through the dynamics of the group. This
occurs most effectively when guided by an instructor using
discussion techniques rather than a more traditional lecture
approach.[5] As Margaret Mead put it, "Groups of people can do a
thing better when they themselves decide upon it."[6] Such a
group-oriented approach became the hallmark of the NFTY
experience in camp and city—not only to teach Judaism but, as we
shall note, for the very operation of the camp program and the
youth movement itself.

Students of adolescent psychology affirm the validity of another
aspect of the NFTY experience as it developed in these early years at
the Camp Institutes. The critical role of the rabbis, regarded as so
important by Rabbis Cook, Schaalman, and others from the very

beginning, probably had greater significance than the earliest camp leaders realized. Young people establish their ideas and values through, in addition to group forces, identification with an older admired individual. They imitate the values of the person with whom they identify, with an image they want to emulate. Values are then "caught" rather than taught, becoming an important part of a young person's system of ethics and morals. Thus the dynamics of identification play a powerful role in a teenager's struggle to find direction and meaning. This is precisely what happened during the camp sessions where rabbis especially attuned to the needs and feelings of young people became effective role models and remained so for years to come. I, along with many other rabbinic colleagues whose decisions to enter the rabbinate were clearly influenced by the camp experience, can trace both personal goals and values to these much admired teachers.

Another dynamic whose power caught many of the first rabbinic leaders by surprise was the depth to which young people were moved by dramatic ceremony. High school boys and girls, who would say they had never been particularly inspired by synagogue services, suddenly found themselves profoundly touched by worship out-of-doors, by campfires, and by evening friendship circles when faculty and campers would express their thoughts with great feeling. When darkness had settled over the camp on a Saturday evening, the *Havdalah* service, with its brightly burning flame, its wine, and fragrant spices, became so inspiring a ritual with which to end the Sabbath day that these young people took that ceremony home where it became part of Reform Jewish observance, an occurrence most rabbis believe would never have happened were it not for its exposure at camp.

Here, too, students of adolescent psychology discussed the phenomena of dramatic ceremony in the process of developing values and loyalties in this population group. Irene Josselyn explains:

> During the entire period of adolescence, the individual is more responsive to all stimuli. The sunset, which in preadolescence was meaningful only as a signal to return home for dinner, now at adolescence becomes an aesthetic experience. It becomes beautiful, depressing, or stimulating. Trees, which previously were of value only for climbing, now take on symbolic meanings.

Music, which was a matter of rhythm or melody, is now associated with all the emotional turmoil of the individual.[7]

It is not surprising, therefore, that ritual and ceremony that are dramatic and make use of natural settings have a great emotional appeal to the teenager. The skillful use of this environment, the blending of Jewish ritual and worship with the beauty of nature, of the sunset, of darkness itself, creates a sharing experience that intensifies not only loyalty to the group but to the Jewish faith. The group's singing of both religious and folk material, directed by skilled cantors and song leaders, creates a melodic, almost magical bonding among these young people and their rabbinic and other adult instructors and advisors.

Thus peer influence, identification with teachers whom they greatly admired, and the creative and dramatic use of the camp setting created a passion and loyalty among Reform Jewish teenagers for the NFTY movement and for their religion that most of the young people would never have believed would become a consuming part of their high school lives.

From the earliest NFTY Camp Institutes it was Rabbi Cook's conviction that the young people themselves must be given the responsibility to develop their own programs. The rabbinic "deans" and faculty of the first several annual summer Institutes, whose confidence in the young people matched that of Rabbi Cook, truly understood the potential of the camp environment as a setting for the development of teenagers in roles of Jewish leadership. Together they created the concept of the camp as a model temple youth group, "Instygroup," led by the young people. The goal, as described by Eleanor R. Schwartz, then associate director of NFTY and later director of the National Federation of Temple Sisterhoods, was to "motivate the students to see themselves as the movers and doers."

Among the rabbis and leaders most responsible for shaping the nature of the Camp Institutes were Eugene Borowitz, Abraham Cronbach, Maurice Davis, Albert Friedlander, Erwin Herman, Irving Levitas, Eugene Lipman, Alexander Schindler, Robert Schur, Eleanor Schwartz, Jack Stern, Arnold Jacob Wolf, and Albert Vorspan.

Aside from the classes taught by the many rabbis Samuel Cook brought together, every aspect of the camp's daily activity was carried out by the work of committees of young people: program, social action, worship, publicity—the very committees a functioning local youth group would be encouraged to develop. Though an adult "advisor" would oversee, young people serving as chairpersons would guide the committees' plans as the teenagers created their own worship, evening-program activities, and projects that united the camp in a community-action endeavor. Each young person would have an opportunity to share in the processes of creativity, organization, execution, and evaluation. Thus the resulting program or activity grew out of the feelings and ideas of the teenagers. While faculty helped them build the vital bridges between their thoughts and Jewish values, texts, stories, and experiences, they owned the product. They had given an idea life and developed it into a meaningful Jewish expression of their feelings and aspirations.

A worship service once focused upon the unlikely theme of "God in the Newspaper." Participants found articles in the daily press that dealt with issues important to them, concerning which they felt Judaism ought to have something to say; they added prayers to the basic structure of the service that expressed the values and needs they thought a particular situation inspired. An evening program on civil rights, so dominant a theme in the sixties and seventies, linked the teenager's perception of personal feelings of exclusion, of being left out, to the pain of racial discrimination, all in the context of the Jewish ideal of human unity. Thus Judaism became real for these young people, answering the question they would so often ask, "I'm Jewish, but what difference does it really make?"

The overall program was also chaired by teenagers, working with rabbinic deans, yet very much involved in every aspect of scheduling and decision making, representing to the larger camp community that the Institute was indeed a youth enterprise.

In reflecting on the effectiveness of empowering the young people in this way, Eleanor Schwartz suggests that the program was successful because the leaders "trusted the kids with Judaism, bridging the gap beetween religion and the reality of their youthful lives. In addition, the communication, respect, recognition of partnership, and genuine affection that developed between the rabbis and the teenagers linked the *bimah* and the congregation, which they had previously perceived as distant and out of reach. All this they brought home with them."

Indeed, Judaism at the camps became an intimate, immediate experience in an ideal community setting. Pressures of home and school were replaced by an all-consuming participation in Jewish living. Hebrew designations for programs and events, constant sensitivity to Jewish ideals, and the sharing of close friendships with rabbinic leaders, who in a home context might have seemed distant, caused many young people to become intensely committed to holding on to the experience. They passionately sought to re-create back home in their own synagogues what they had shared at camp.

The lukewarm reception their enthusiasm frequently received when they returned home was very distressing to them. Their fellow teenagers saw the youth group as but one of a multitude of competing activities, often low on the scale of priorities. Those rabbis who were bewildered by a call for changing the formal Friday evening services to become more like the experience at camp complained that young people were returning with unrealistic expectations. It was wisely decided to build into the final two days of each two-week Camp Institute a number of "back to reality" sessions to demonstrate to the young people how to bring home their ideas and integrate them effectively into a long-standing, functioning synagogue agenda. Rabbi Jack Stern commented that the hallmark of the Institute's success was that in spite of the difficulties they knew they would encounter, "the kids went home ready to go for it." In a closing friendship circle on the final night of an early Institute, one of the rabbis shared this thought: "The God of the lake and the open fields is also the God of our neighborhoods and city streets; the God we experienced through the friendships we made at camp is the God of our own families and the love we share with them; the God to whom we prayed in the outdoor chapel beneath the stars is the God we can find in our own temple sanctuaries if we continue our searching."

Indeed, the young people successfully made the transition, and that made all the difference. The major impact upon the Reform movement born out of these leadership programs is due to the emphasis that was placed from the very beginning on extending the experience to the local community. The Camp Institute was never meant to be an end in itself. The focus was always on the role the young people would play when they returned to their home synagogues. First in the individual temple, then through youth groups of nearby cities holding joint conclaves on weekends, the momentum was sustained. Rabbi Cook was not as interested in the national aspect of his program as much as he was in decentralized successful activities.

For many years, other than the NFTY National Leadership Institutes and the organization's tours to Israel, all programming was local and regional. Conclaves with one community's youth group hosting others took place throughout the school year nearly every weekend in different sections of the country. The movement's leaders discovered with much gratification that using the techniques developed in the camp setting, these weekend joint retreats in temple facilities were exceedingly effective in developing the same sense of loyalty and commitment. Nonetheless, NFTY youngsters seeking camp settings for their summer activities provided much of the incentive for UAHC regional leaders to purchase a network of camps, including NFTY's own national center, the Kutz Camp in Warwick, New York. Carefully chosen regional youth advisors followed the same youth-empowering leadership roles developed on a national level, and young people themselves took charge of the fast growing nationwide Reform youth program.

Gradually the Reform movement as a whole began to reflect the new vitality that was coming from its young people. Immediately apparent, of course, was the increase in the number of local temple youth groups in large and small congregations, whose members met with regularity, thus bringing young people back into the temple from which most had disappeared after ninth- or tenth-grade confirmation. However, the ultimate consequences of NFTY's successes reached far beyond simply holding on to teenagers during their high school years. A transformation of the entire Reform movement began to occur. Born of an age of reason, accustomed to emphasizing the rational, Reform now needed to find ways to respond to the emotional needs of its people, to bring congregants closer to each other and to God, and to answer questions of meaning and purpose. NFTY's youths, especially as they became active young adults, served as the catalysts for these changes, bringing a sense of community, spirituality, and commitment to the significant involvement of laity in charting new directions. Many factors played a role, but the young people who had experienced a new kind of liberal Judaism at camp helped a new age in Reform to unfold in the years to come. Recognizing this, Rabbi Jeffrey Salkin in his article "NFTY at Fifty: An Assessment" refers to a new Reform Jewish character that emerged in the 1970s and 1980s as the NFTY young people—now congregational leaders, rabbis, and educators—began to have a profound influence on the course Reform was to take.[8]

A clear consequence of the NFTY movement was the change in our patterns of worship. It began when, at least annually, the young people in most temples would create their own worship service modeled on their experiences at the NFTY camps, using music and themes that had special appeal to the young people of the congregation. The vitality and spirit of these services attracted a positive response from their parents' generation as well. Thus the creative liturgy movement in Reform Judaism, the far less formal approach to worship, the placement of contemporary literary sources in the text of the service, the use of guitar music, and the emphasis on congregational singing were to become mainstream. At the very least these became frequently used alternatives to the old *Union Prayerbook* service on which the previous generation had been raised.

Over the years creativity became infused in much of Reform worship. Relevancy in theme and the beauty of new melodies, many of which were created by young composers and cantors influenced by the youth movement, encouraged a far greater expression of emotion, which large numbers of adults—especially former NFTY young people who had become active congregational members and leaders—found moving and appealing. Reform's new daily and Sabbath prayer book, *Gates of Prayer*, resonates with many themes and materials from sources, Jewish and secular, not unlike those that young people discovered and developed at their Camp Institutes. A number of the rabbis responsible for this major liturgical publication had been influenced by the youth movement, having served as faculty at the camps; some, indeed, were products of them.

It has been argued that the resulting creativity eventually found in brotherhood and sisterhood services, in bar and bat mitzvah celebrations, in family worship, and in every kind of special occasion a congregation commemorates on a Shabbat eve has created a liturgical "cut and paste" chaos. Nonetheless, most Reform leaders and congregants today would concur that the vitality infused into worship in both text and music by the NFTY-inspired liturgical creativity has vastly enriched us. Early fears that the essentials of Jewish liturgy would be lost to this wave of innovation have proved unfounded. Congregations have learned to blend the traditional and the contemporary, as, for example, does UAHC biennial convention worship with which Reform Jews, nationwide and thousands strong, seem very comfortable. The liturgical openness in Reform, itself an inspiration to other movements, clearly harkens back to NFTY camp worship creativity.

In addition to profoundly shaping our Reform mode of worship, NFTY significantly influenced Reform Jewish education. As Rabbi Salkin writes:

> The mood in Jewish education shifted from formal to informal. The goals moved from cognitive to effective. Many of these innovations first emerged from the Rocky Mountain Curriculum Planning Workshops held in Colorado in the early 1970s....A perusal of the names and backgrounds of the participants in these early experiments in "the greening of Jewish education" reveals that they emerged from NFTY backgrounds.[9]

Appropriate questions have been raised as to whether Jewish education can afford to replace content with feelings. However, the innovative, project-oriented, discussion-based approaches to learning brought new life to many a stultifying Sunday school classroom. Hebrew Union College Professor of Jewish Religious Education Michael Zeldin points out that informal approaches can be effective means of transmitting knowledge; informal education and "educational" are far from mutually exclusive terms.[10] Bernard Reisman concurs: "The difference between formal and informal Jewish educational settings is diminishing and the similarities in the methodologies used...are increasing." NFTY young people surely played a role in the past four decades in inspiring Reform Jewish educators to move their rows of chairs into circles; to shift, on occasion, their classrooms to camps; to alter their teaching methods to become more experiential; and to focus on issues that are challenging and relevant to our youths. Today, Rabbi Alan Smith, present director of the UAHC Youth Department, remains an ardent advocate of the effectiveness of informal experiential education and points to its increasing acceptance and utilization by Jewish educators.

The NFTY emphasis on intimacy and participation in which everyone is up front and part of the action can be seen in various aspects of Reform synagogue life. As young people became adult leaders of our congregations, they wanted to remove the distance between pulpit and pew, rabbis and members, to feel more involved than an observer in an audience, both for worship and for learning. Thus, services in-the-round in which everyone participates became a frequent alternative on many temple worship calendars. Home-study groups with the rabbi leading a discussion in a living room setting developed as a popular form of adult education. Congregational *chavurot*, or small groups of families within congregations celebrating holidays and studying together, reflect the same intimacy that began to appear as a result of NFTY's influence on the character of Reform Jewish life.

One might suggest, as well, that Reform's strong emphasis on social action was greatly affected by a generation taught through the camp programs that religion meant action and Reform, indeed, is a verb. Rabbi Allan Smith maintains: "It was NFTY that acted in behalf of civil rights and expressed active dismay over Vietnam...the young people gave the movement the ability to jump in."[11] Thousands of young people were also directly influenced by Albert Vorspan, an Institute faculty member for many years and the long-time director of Reform Judaism's Commission on Social Action. Social action projects became a staple of local youth-group programming. Adult social action committees in which young people participated soon began to develop in nearly every Reform temple. To this day NFTY plays an important role in furthering this area of activity through hands-on Mitzvah Corps programs on behalf of the poor and homeless and through the sponsoring of youth trips to the Union's Religious Action Center in Washington, where young people learn to advocate issues on matters in which public policy might be influenced by Jewish social values.

It is also worth considering the role NFTY played in changing the position of women in Reform. Of course, cultural and political forces have brought great changes in recent years regarding the status of women in our society. Yet, it was in the NFTY camp environment that multitudes of young women, leading services and programs on an equal basis with their male teenage contemporaries, realized that they could play a significant role in the future of Reform Judaism. It is clear that many of the hundreds of women rabbis, cantors, educators, and congregational trustees in the Reform movement found inspiration and encouragement in precisely this way.

In assessing NFTY's impact on the Reform movement today, surely the most dramatic testimony is to be found in the ranks of Reform's leadership: rabbis, cantors, educators, lay leaders, and scholars. Before NFTY had developed its camps and the consequent local programs, Reform leadership came almost exclusively from other movements, the vast majority of rabbis and cantors from traditional backgrounds. Today, as it has been increasingly for several decades, nearly all rabbinic candidates at the Hebrew Union College are influenced through their involvement in NFTY programs and are inspired by their contact with rabbinic models—many with whom they became close in youth group related activities. If it is true that the vitality of a movement is reflected in its ability to create its own leaders, then NFTY is surely responsible for insuring the strength of Reform Judaism far into the future.

The president of the Union of American Hebrew Congregations, Rabbi Alexander M. Schindler, to whom this volume is dedicated, expressed for himself what must be in the minds of countless numbers of his colleagues: "NFTY was enormously significant in my own personal growth and development. Those years in the youth camps were the most joyful, creative years of my rabbinate."

Indeed, if one were to list the men and women who have played significant roles in the lay and professional leadership of Reform Judaism in the past several decades, that list would contain a preponderance of names that years before had been on the NFTY rolls as well. A recent study by the UAHC Research Task Force on the Future of Reform Judaism clearly affirms that approximately 90 percent of the movement's leadership who participated in the youth groups, camping, and Israel trips of NFTY rated these experiences as important motivations for their continued involvement in Jewish life.[12] Such is surely a profound measure of the youth movement's accomplishments.

The high quality of the NFTY program was sustained and enriched by the leadership of the national directors following Rabbi Cook's retirement: Rabbi Henry Skirball from 1963 to 1971 and Rabbi Stephen Schafer from 1971 to 1986. Each, having worked closely with Rabbi Cook for years and having been among those responsible for the growing success of the NFTY camping experience, brought valuable new dimensions to the youth movement. Rabbi Skirball encouraged in-depth Jewish study in the camps, developed the NFTY Torah Corps, and expanded the NFTY-in-Israel program to include a wide variety of projects and opportunities for teenagers throughout the entire year. Rabbi Schafer, a "natural" in the camp environment, brought into the movement many new camps in which programming flourished not only for teenagers but for children of younger ages as well. In addition, he shaped a more extensive international program for the organization. Rabbi Ramie Arian and Rabbi Allan Smith, national directors in recent years, brought their exceptional talents to NFTY and to a greatly expanded Youth Department at the Union.

It is to be hoped that the wide-ranging NFTY program will, in the years ahead, renew its emphasis on training youth leaders to strengthen their local groups and ultimately their synagogues. The vitality of Jewish religious life in the twenty-first century rests upon the ability of the synagogue to respond to the needs of American Jews for spirituality and community on all age levels. The enthusiasm and training youthful leaders bring to their home temples can not only renew youth grouping but promise new vigor and significance in synagogue life for the next generation as it did so successfully in the past fifty years.

With the conclusion of these thoughts on the import of Reform Judaism's youth movement, Rabbi Schindler's role in assuring its continued strength and effectiveness needs to be emphasized. From the start of his own participation as a NFTY Institute faculty member and dean shortly after his ordination, Alexander Schindler recognized that young people are capable of discovering great joy and commitment through sharing an exciting experience in Jewish living. Working with teenagers as they developed creative worship at camp, he came to realize how responsive they were to spiritual experiences when allowed the freedom to develop their own youthful modes of expression. Remembering those young people, he recently commented: "They were in the vanguard of a transformation of Reform Judaism. Within the camp setting we shared a magic all its own, creating models of Jewish leadership for years to come."

Throughout his years as president of the Union, Alex Schindler continued to believe in each succeeding generation of youth, advocating the funds and professional direction that the youth movement required. He encouraged innovative programming for young people in high school and college alike and always rejoiced in the Reform leadership that emerged over the years from the NFTY experience.

The NFTY motto, chosen early in the organization's history, was taken from the words of the biblical prophet Joel: "Thy old men shall dream dreams and thy youth shall see visions." Several generations of rabbis and leaders, many of whom could not be mentioned in this essay, surely realized their dreams in a youth movement that provided new vision for Reform Judaism. These dreamers "trusted the kids with Judaism," and that is what made it possible.

NOTES

1. Samson Benderly, *Jewish Education*, vol. 36, no. 2 (1966), p. 80.

2. Edwin Goldberg, "The Beginnings of Educational Camping in the Reform Movement," *Journal of Reform Judaism*, Fall 1989.

3. Ibid., p. 9.

4. Bernard Reisman, *Informal Jewish Education in North America* (Commission on Jewish Education in North America, 1990).

5. Kurt Lewin and Paul Grabbe, "Conduct, Knowledge, and Acceptance of New Values," *Journal of Social Issues* 1:3 (1945).

6. Cited in Reisman, *Informal Jewish Education in North America*, p. 10.

7. Irene Josselyn, *The Adolescent and His World* (New York: Family Service Association of America, 1952).

8. Jeffrey Salkin, "NFTY at Fifty: An Assessment," *Journal of Reform Judaism*, Fall 1989.

9. Ibid., p. 20.

10. Michael Zeldin, "Understanding Informal Jewish Education," *Journal of Reform Judaism*, Fall 1989.

It is not true that the ordination and investiture of women is a total rupture with the Jewish past, that women's liberation has no roots whatsoever in the patriarchal, hierarchical system of the Jewish tradition. The reality of Judaism is rather more complex. It offers many contradictions.

Nevertheless, even at its best, tradition speaks of women largely in relation to men, rarely in relation to God, more rarely in relation to self or to other women. Even at its best, the tradition speaks *about* women, only occasionally *to* women, and, until recently, never *bekol ishah*, in the voices *of* women.

"Now for the first time," so Rachel Adler reminds us, "opportunities have arisen for women to join in the conversation." Herein lies the transformative impact of our twenty-year-old revelation on Jewish life: The voices of women are heard in the synagogue; they have been included in the conversation.

What, more precisely, has this "joining in the conversation" meant for Judaism? Exclusion has been terminated. Inclusiveness has been established as the new order of Jewish life. It permits the female experience of life-giving and motherhood to be a part of synagogue life and thus allows the image of our God as nurturing Mother to find enthronement in our minds.

Perhaps most important of all, by "joining in the conversation," our women rabbis, cantors, and educators have also enlarged our understanding of Judaism. They bring insights unique to women in their approach to our classical texts, and, thereby, they enable us to grasp a more complete, a more fully authentic Judaism.

Rabbi Alexander M. Schindler
Celebrating Twenty Years of Women
in the Rabbinate
Los Angeles, California
June 8, 1993

WOMEN AND TRADITION
TALKING OUR WAY IN

RACHEL ADLER

Jewish tradition is often compared to a vast conversation comprised of many voices.[1] Our Bible is not a single book by a single author but an assortment of texts in different genres by different schools of authors. In Talmud and Midrash, diverse voices set forth a mosaic of legal debates, proof-texts, case law, stories, philosophies, proverbs, and prayers. Codes, responsa, and modern theologies are all communal discourses among passionately interested parties. Two of the three pillars of Jewish spiritual practice, study and prayer, are ways for Jews to add their voices to this immense conversation in which the past becomes present and the lips of participants long dead move once more.

Many of us, however, belong to groups that have become estranged from the conversation or were never included in the first place. Jewish women have always stood whispering on its periphery. There was a time when Zionists, socialists, and Enlightenment intellectuals were zestful and iconoclastic conversationalists, a time when Reform Jews rekindled the conversation, reset its boundaries, and reshaped its concerns. But today many Jews have lost not only familiarity with the materials of Jewish tradition but a sense of entitlement to engage with them. These materials are thought to belong to professional Jews like the rabbi, to pious traditionalists, or to academic experts. They have become off-limits for nonspecialists to play with, fight with, or nourish themselves from. Contenting themselves with the vague conviction that their Jewish heritage moves them to work for social justice, nonspecialists are reluctant to attempt integrating their Jewishness more complexly into their intellectual processes or their moral language.

At the same time, narrow specialization is becoming passé in the secular world. Expertise in a single defined area no longer renders any of us self-sufficient. In academe, exciting new interdisciplinary scholarship has breached the walls between disciplines. Inter-disciplinary scholarship lets us bring to bear upon a problem a wider variety of conceptual categories and methodologies than a single discipline can offer. By breaking the hegemony of any single set of categories and language, interdisciplinary methods allow more intriguing questions to be posed and richer and more nuanced answers to be offered. They also prevent the ossification of disci-plinary ideologies. Because they do not want to be excluded from the conversation, scholars from many disciplines teach them-selves this new polyglot lingua franca, plunging into the foreign waters of semiotics, symbolic anthropology, theoretical physics, or cultural criticism.

Among nonacademics, too, it is no longer possible to learn a trade that will last a lifetime. Not only do people change occupations several times during their working lives, occupations change, too. To do their jobs, people must incorporate new information and skills, often from other fields, into their work. Thirty years ago many business executives could not even type, and poets were allergic to technology, while today the butcher and the baker are as dependent upon computers as the physician and the architect.

Yet the same congregant who masters the intricacies of spread sheets or magnetic resonance imaging is terrified to dip a toe into the sea of Jewish discourse. Why is this? Demographic reports inform us that Jews are the most highly educated religious commu-nity in America. There is every reason to suppose that for Jews, continuing education and consultation across professional bound-aries are familiar territories. Why, then, can so many laypeople enter these crossdisciplinary conversations confident they will learn enough of the new lingo to converse and certain they themselves have something valuable to contribute, but these same people despair of ever learning enough to participate in the Jewish conver-sation and presume that nothing they know could enrich it or affect the other participants?[2] Why is it that in their professional conver-sations, Jewish laypeople can utilize other participants as consul-tants without fear of humiliation or infantilization, but these same people believe that before they can enter the Jewish conversation they must know everything in order not to be savagely exposed and disgraced? More important, how can those beliefs and behaviors be changed so that more Jews will want to join the conversation?

The problem is that most of us have not been taught to think of Judaism as a conversation, much less to regard ourselves as potential conversants. Laypeople tend to see Judaism as a selection of institutions that claim varying degrees of authority over religious thought and praxis. They tend to envision their own contributions as largely financial. As Jewish learners, they are resigned to being the rabbi's perpetual pupils. They would be surprised to learn how inauthoritative many rabbis feel in comparison to their teachers or their teachers' teachers. In addition, many rabbis find it as difficult as do congregants to engage with other Jews in a conversation in which all may learn and change.

The pervasive feelings of shame, fear, and mistrust among so many potential conversants attest to the need to re-form the Jewish conversation. Besides being mean-spirited, a rigidly exclusionary conversation is in danger of stagnation. Because of the proliferation of information in our world and our growing perception of the complexity and interconnectedness of knowledge, we need one another's help more than ever. A one-dimensional approach to Judaism can only be an impoverished one. Moreover, the postmodernist critique has sensitized scholars to ways in which knowledge can be used as a tool of power, constructing and validating the worldviews of some groups while distorting and disempowering others.[3] Constricted perspectives risk offending against both truth and justice. A broadly based conversation would allow us to pool the shares of Torah, which every Jew may claim as an inheritance.[4]

As a feminist Jew, I am a member of a group that has been talking its way into the Jewish conversation for the past twenty-five years. Plagued by the same inadequacies and fears as other alienated Jews, feminists have found ways to explore and articulate our portion in the Torah. The values we hold, the structures we build, the ways we have developed for approaching the materials of Jewish tradition all offer some models and means for other estranged Jews to enter the conversation.

First, we authorized our own efforts to speak. At the very foundation of Jewish feminist thought is a rejection of any distribution of authority that would disqualify women as serious participants in Jewish conversation. Most Jewish women received Jewish educations that mystified Jewish sources, esotericized the Hebrew language, disparaged spiritual experience, and fostered dependency upon a professional elite. Our revolution was to affirm that we had a perspective on Torah that the tradition did not know and needed to learn and to refuse to be shamed into silence by the magnitude of what we did not know. Faced with Judaisms that silenced, ignored, or problematized women, Jewish feminism problematized and critiqued those Judaisms.

Feminist Jewish scholars challenge the assumption of liberal as well as traditional Judaisms that their theologies and praxis adequately address the perspectives and concerns, the collective memories and lived experiences of Jewish women. We contend that all modern Judaisms have yet to reflect a reality that Jewish women inhabit interdependently with Jewish men. Moreover, we have suggested that the closed and hierarchical structures of most Jewish institutions create cultures inimical to the flourishing of Judaism. In support of these contentions, we have produced not only theologies but counterstructures, alternative organizations designed to cultivate a ground upon which broader and richer conversations can occur. These groups are both laboratories and models for the ways feminists would like to change the larger conversation.

The culture we have shaped is respectful of differing needs and commitments, constructively critical, and supportive. It prizes listening and encourages alliances across denominational lines. Crossdenominational organizing has allowed us to put vital new questions on the Jewish agenda. The International Committee for Women at the Western Wall is an example of a group whose members range from Reconstructionist to Orthodox.[5] So significant were the questions it posed about Jewish religious pluralism that its case concerning women's entitlement to pray communally at religious sites in the Jewish state was heard by the Israeli Supreme Court.[6]

The Feminist Center of the American Jewish Congress of Los Angeles is another counterinstitution whose activities are designed to reshape the Jewish conversation. For academics and writers, the Center sponsors a Jewish feminist scholars' research group in which rabbis and laypeople, women and men, examine one another's work in progress, as well as a women scholars' Talmud fellowship in which rabbis and scholars in other fields pool their expertise and study as peers. The Center's adult education program offers Jewish text classes that demonstrate a feminist methodology for engaging with texts.

Jewish skills classes offered by the Center begin with the assumption that the sacred belongs to all of us and we belong to it. In the Torah workshop, for example, people who have never been close to a Torah scroll, who may be terrified even to touch one, learn not just the isolated skill of having an *aliyah* but all the skills related to the Torah: how to dress and undress a Torah, how to roll it, carry it in procession, hand it to someone else, pick it up, and put it into the ark. By the end of the workshop, participants feel confident of their ability to be responsible for the Torah, which is the very point.

Feminist models suggest new ways to converse with other feminists or potential feminists, as well as with institutional Judaisms and with the canonical texts we all claim. As the legal theorist Robert Cover asserts, a dissident group challenges the established conversation when it lays claim to its terms and texts, redefining and reinterpreting them in a way that changes how they must be lived out.[7] When the disruptive effect upon the existing conversation can no longer be ignored, the two conversations begin to address each other (usually at the top of their lungs). Then the dominant conversation must determine whether it can widen its boundaries to include the dissidents without fundamentally compromising its enterprise, and the counterconversation must determine whether it can maintain its integrity within those boundaries.[8] For example, at a certain point in its history, Christianity became separated from the Jewish conversation, while Liberal Judaism was able to maintain its dissidence within.

The established conversation has an obvious stake in integrating any counterconversation that seems likely to carry off a large Jewish constituency. For instance, for Judaism to split off into polarized masculinist and feminist sects would endanger established Judaisms more than the integration of feminism would. The content of the counterconversation and the nature of the social context in which it occurs are important factors in determining how the boundaries will be drawn. In the early years of Reform, the integration of Jewish and secular identity was as much a concern for acculturated Orthodox thinkers as for Reformers. The only way for Orthodoxy to wall itself off from the issue was to reject modernity comprehensively. Similarly, Susannah Heschel has argued that the failure of denominational Judaism to include women fully could not go unresolved because it was paradigmatic of Judaism's incomplete adjustment to modernity.[9]

Talking one's way in cannot be accomplished merely by gate-crashing. Becoming a permanent partner in an ongoing conversation is a reciprocal process that requires problem solving and adjustment on the part of all the participants. How do newcomers become included in a conversation whose past topics, language, and categories were framed by interests and experiences other than their own? How will their inclusion change future conversations or alter recollections of conversations that took place before they arrived on the scene?

Those who join the conversation of Jewish tradition need not know everything, but they must commit themselves to learning its language and understanding the experiences and concerns that shaped it. However, long-term members must also do some learning. Genuine inclusion does not mean that newcomers shed their distinctive perspectives and experiences and swap them for ones already reflected in the tradition. If they enter, they must enter as themselves, with their own particular investments in the topics raised and the interactions that occur.

Making room for new conversants is not a comfortable process. The decibel level is often high and the standards of civility low. New contributions destabilize previous understandings and call for reevaluation. New conversation partners may expose biases lurking beneath the tradition's "objective" discourse. The very rules that govern the conversation may be placed in doubt. The conversation begins to look precarious and fragile, as if the barbarian influx is threatening to destroy it. At the same time, the stimulus of fresh ideas and new personae and the flood of emotions precipitated by the disequilibrium they bring reanimate the conversation. That is why at conferences and meetings, in periodicals and papers, people want to hear feminists, even if only to fight with them. The effort of responding to what a feminist Judaism brings revitalizes the conversation.

The methodologies and the values of feminist Judaism also have implications for the Jewish conversation. Rather than concentrating knowledge and authority in elite bodies, feminists want to distribute them as broadly as possible. At the same time, feminist group structures encourage the pooling of resources, the interdependency of roles and tasks, and the practical application of results. This encourages cooperation rather than fragmentation and conclusions that point toward action rather than irrelevant abstractions. If the Jewish conversation integrated these values and methods, many Jews who are neither rabbis nor Judaica professors would become eligible to join it. Once a Jew has acquired a basic familiarity with the terms of Jewish discourse, she or he might bring something of value to the conversation—either specific skills or information, training in critical thinking, cultural memories, or life experiences that need to be recognized and included.

I have mentioned that one of the conversations feminists have had to talk their way into is the conversation about Judaism's texts. Feminist process, structures, and institutional gains have attracted more public attention than feminist approaches to text. What constitutes a feminist reading of a Jewish text, and how does it work? A concrete example seems to be called for. In II Samuel 20 we encounter a text whose meaning is greatly enriched by an interdisciplinary feminist approach. This methodology draws upon literary, historical, sociological, anthropological, psychological, and theological perspectives. Its goals are to illuminate character, text, and context; to take note of the impact of gender upon text; and to discover how the text can become a source of spiritual nourishment and a catalyst for our internal or communal transformation as a holy people. In II Samuel 20 we will see how the text is opened up when we examine the assumptions about gender that have affected its interpretation.

II Samuel 20: The Case of the Mysterious Negotiator

The Context of the Story

The two books of Samuel comprise a history of Saul's and David's reigns from the point of view of the Davidic court. The world of the story we are about to examine is complicated by political intrigue, rapidly shifting alliances, and multiple revolts. Its setting is the turbulent reign of David. The loose confederation of Israelite tribes is tenuously united under its second monarchy. It is a time of structural transition from the decentralized rule of clan leaders, charismatics, and village elders to a form of government in which power is consolidated, centralized, and funneled down through a complex hierarchy.[10]

At the time of the story, members of the houses of David and Saul are still jockeying for position. David has unseated Saul's dynasty, and David and his followers are killing off Saul's potential heirs. David's own son Absalom has attempted to seize the throne. His rebellion was put down, and now another revolt is being fomented by a clan leader from Saul's tribe, Sheba ben Bichri.

A key figure in the suppression of these rebellions is David's nephew Joab ben Zeruiah, the commander of David's army. The amoral Joab functions as a Davidic id, committing all the murders that would be convenient or prudent but morally objectionable for a righteous king. After David has concluded a peace with Abner ben Ner, Saul's first cousin and commander of the opposing forces,[11] Joab assassinates him. It is Joab who contrives the military tactic that finishes off Bathsheba's husband Uriah, as well as some other unfortunate warriors.[12] Against David's explicit orders, Joab kills David's son, the rebel Absalom, instead of taking him alive. David indicates his displeasure by appointing the former commander of the forces of Absalom, Joab's first cousin Amasa, as Joab's superior. While Sheba ben Bichri's rebellion is gaining momentum, David is still cleaning up after Absalom's revolt. Returning to his palace in Jerusalem, David sequesters the ten concubines with whom Absalom had slept in his attempt to supplant his father. They are placed under guard to live out their days "in living widowhood." Let us bear them in mind so that we can juxtapose their status and situation with those of the other woman we will encounter in the chapter.

A Murderer Hunts a Rebel

Early in the chapter Joab murders his new commanding officer, Amasa. The former rebel general has been assigned to rally the men of Judah and join with Joab's forces to pursue Sheba ben Bichri, but he is late in returning. His delay, the king complains, has allowed the rebels to escape into fortified towns from which it will be difficult to dislodge them. It is possible that Amasa's tardiness has aroused suspicion about his loyalty. When Amasa appears, Joab, pretending to greet him with a kiss, stabs him in the belly. Dragging the bloody corpse off the road, Joab seizes control of the united forces and sets off to corner Sheba ben Bichri in the walled city of Abel. There he mounts a siege and begins battering the walls of the city.

Enter the Wise Woman

At this point an unusual female character appears in the story. The text refers to her as an *ishah chachamah*. There are two such women in II Samuel, one in chapter 14 and one in chapter 20, both portrayed in interactions with Joab. In both stories it is clear that an *ishah chachamah* is called upon for her special skills in rhetoric and political negotiation. But what is an *ishah chachamah*? The Jewish Publication Society *Tanach* translates the term as "clever woman." But *ishah chachamah* could also mean "wise woman." How did the JPS decide when the root *chet-chaf-mem* means clever and when it means wise? Cleverness is shallow, while wisdom is deep. Cleverness is manipulative, while wisdom is spiritual. According to the JPS, God endowed Solomon with wisdom, not cleverness (I Kings), and the beginning of wisdom—not the beginning of cleverness—is the fear of God. (Psalms 11:10) But the *ishah chachamah* is labeled clever rather than wise.

The evidence of this story, however, suggests that *ishah chachamah* is a title for a societal role, such as a counselor or a city elder, and is not merely a personal attribute.[13] Consider the city's political situation. Abel is protecting a rebel leader from a besieging commander who is notorious for exceeding his orders. Calling from the rampart, the *ishah chachamah* boldly summons the besieger not by honorific, title, or patronymic, but by his ungarnished first name: "Tell Joab to come near so I can speak to him." When he approaches, she repeats the familiarity: "Are you Joab?" and receives the curtest possible response, *Ani*, "I am." Only then does she use the mollifying language of diplomacy: "Hear the words of your maidservant." Joab replies laconically, "I, *Anochi*, am listening."[14]

Now, as we know from other biblical references and from archaeological research, a walled city is a fairly complex social organization.[15] Other texts make reference to formal leadership structures, *zekenim*, "elders," or *amei ha'aretz*, "the people of the land," who hold decision-making power. Is it credible, then, that in the midst of a crisis, a single inhabitant—especially a female—could spontaneously open negotiations with the commander of the besieging forces? Is it not more reasonable to assume that the wise woman has the authority to initiate a parley and that the assailants have recognized her as the designated negotiator?

Gender and the Language of Diplomacy

Having captured Joab's attention, the wise woman frames her statement in the ornate rhetoric of formal oratory, which the JPS translation utterly fails to capture. It should sound something like this: "In ancient days, they were wont to say, 'Let them inquire at Abel and so shall the matter be resolved.'" The weighty profundity of the repetitive infinitive absolute verb form with its internal alliteration, *daber yedaberu, shaol yeshaelu*, combined with the old proverb attesting the city's oracular reputation, gives the sentence an antique grandeur. Through her rhetoric the wise woman is presenting herself as the living embodiment of the ancient oracle of Abel. From this authoritative position she condemns Joab's mission: "I represent the peace-abiding and loyal of Israel; you seek to annihilate a mother city in Israel. Why will you swallow up the inheritance of YHWH?"[16]

The first striking feature of this passage is that the woman refers to herself as *Anochi*, the rarer, more emphatic form of "I." We might translate *Anochi* as "I myself." Out of 359 biblical speakers who use this term, only twelve are women. The most frequent user of *Anochi* is God. The literary contexts for *Anochi* seem to be occasions of self-assertion or gravity. Its additional syllable slows the rhythm of the sentence in which it is used, lingering upon its subject and conferring a certain authority upon her or his utterance. What is puzzling to translators is that the wise woman follows her *Anochi* with plural nouns: "I am *shelumei emunei Yisrael*, 'the peace-abiding and faithful of Israel.'" If she is presenting herself as the representative of the city, she might be using the plural to identify herself with her constituents. In that case she is saying, "We are observing our peace covenant and keeping faith with David. It is you who are engaging in unlawful violence here."

The wise woman accuses Joab of trying to annihilate a city that is a mother in Israel, *ir ve'em beyisrael.* Now one of the biblical terms that means towns is *banot,* "daughters." For instance, Numbers 21:25 refers to the great city of Heshbon and its outlying villages as "Heshbon and all her daughters." While land is always imaged as feminine in the Bible, there are two special senses in which cities might be mothers. Fortified cities are havens. Villagers would have sought protection in them from an invading force. Also cities may have been economically linked to their villages, sustaining them by providing market centers and buyers for agricultural produce. The expression "mother in Israel" occurs only twice in the Bible, here and in reference to Deborah. (Judges 5:7) In both contexts the mother is the source of safety and security, and in both instances it is a female political figure who invokes this powerful image. Metaphorically the wise woman accuses Joab of matricide.

For someone representing a city under siege in which the leader of a rebel clan is indeed ensconced, the wise woman takes a surprisingly aggressive position. Its effect upon Joab is equally interesting. He backs off, vehemently denying the charges. *Chalilah, chalilah,* he says, which the JPS renders demurely as "Far be it, far be it from me to destroy or to ruin! Not at all!" while the Anchor Bible says, "I'll be damned if I'm going to afflict anything or destroy anything! It's not like that." The reader is surely taking these protestations with a grain of salt, however, for she or he recalls that the chapter opened with Joab's disemboweling his commanding officer. Employing a diplomatic fiction, Joab explains the situation as if the wise woman were unaware of Sheba's political importance: It is merely that this fellow has rebelled against the king, he explains. If you hand him over, we'll just go away.

The wise woman makes a startling response. Before consulting with anyone, she promises, "His head shall be thrown to you over the wall." Only then does she go to the entire city "with her wisdom," that is, with her counsel that Sheba be beheaded. The JPS translation, "The woman came to all the people with her clever plan," belittles both her wisdom and her authority, and "clever plan" is a rather nonchalant description of a proposed execution. But why did the wise woman insist on the execution in the first place? After Abel had extended hospitality to Sheba, why was she so adamant that his blood had to be on their hands alone? After all, Joab had promised that she need only surrender Sheba as a prisoner to end the siege.

Clearly one indication of the wise woman's wisdom is her unwillingness to rely upon Joab's promises. It seems that Joab's reputation had preceded him. Faced with a commander who murders in defiance of peace treaties and explicit royal orders, the wise woman has decided that a closed door is the most prudent policy. It is also an effective one. The promised head is thrown over the wall, and Joab's army does indeed depart. But the city's execution of Sheba is also a political statement that enables the wise woman to restore the delicate equilibrium her city maintains with the throne. Abel has not joined with the rebel in war, but its unilateral act of execution suggests the faithfulness of an ally rather than the obedience of a subject. The latter reflects the shaky and ambiguous relations between the northern tribes and the Davidic monarchy. And indeed, the next time a northern rebel blows the *shofar* and proclaims Sheba's call to arms, the king will be David's grandson, and the kingdom will be split.

Questions to Ask a Sacred Text

When people study this story with me, they often ask, "Why didn't I learn about this woman before?" There are many reasons. First, the text has predestined her obscurity by making her nameless. Also, since biblical history is written by court historians, it focuses on the male hierarchy surrounding the monarch. The local political participation of women becomes important only when, as in II Samuel 20, it impinges upon the historian's primary concern. In addition, until quite recently, biblical commentators, interpreters, and translators inhabited a world in which the actions and thoughts of men were central and women were significant only in relation to the men, hence only peripherally. Perceptions of women both in the present and in the past were distorted to conform to this expectation. Only through questioning its universal applicability do we notice women sufficiently to recover stories like that of the wise woman of Abel. But the capacity of these texts to sustain inter-rogation is an indication of their holiness, and our willingness to interrogate them is an intimation of ours.

What can we learn from this story? We learn that there were

epochs in ancient Israel during which some women were active in the public sphere, exercising authority and wielding power. We learn to surrender some gender stereotypes and idealizations: Not all stories about women revolve around family or sexual relations and not all heroines are tenderhearted. The wise woman of Abel is depicted as no less complex and morally ambiguous than the men in II Samuel. In a society in which the laws of hospitality are revered, she has a man killed after the city has sheltered him. At the same time she is a fierce and imposing figure. Even Joab seems a little awed by her rhetoric and her bearing. Parrying and conditioning with the most dangerous and unpredictable man in Israel, she seizes the initiative from him in one swift stroke. Not without cost to her city's independence and integrity, she snatches it out of the jaws of destruction.

Was her decision a just observance of a political covenant or an expedient solution to a public danger? What are the moral limits of expediency? The wise woman's act provides a precedent for such limits in rabbinic law. *Tosefta Terumot* 7:23 teaches that if a group of Jews is told to surrender one person to be killed on the threat that if they do not, all of them will be killed, they may comply only if the person has been singled out by name, as Sheba ben Bichri was. The distinction concerns who bears primary responsibility for the killing. Once the community selects who is to die, it has made itself the source of the death sentence, while the murderers who carry it out become the community's agents. This ancient moral issue and the biblical story to which it is attached take on new poignancy in Holocaust responsa, as well as in contemporary situations in which hostages negotiate with terrorists. Unhappily, weighing the lives and welfare of the many against the sanctity of the individual life has not become any less necessary or any easier to resolve in the intervening millennia.

The story also demonstrates vividly how the specificity of our gender distinguishes us as human beings. That the wise woman *is* a woman is inextricable from her characterization. Had she been a man, the outcome of the story may not have changed, but its shape and its balance would have. The wise woman's use of the protecting mother as an image for her city would ring differently if she did not mirror that image in her own person. If she had been a man, there would have been no electricity of gender opposition to highlight the other oppositions and parallels between these two redoubtable opponents. Both are politically astute and both are willing to break their promises and shed blood to attain their goals. But the wise woman has a moral vision, even if it is not one Kant would have approved. She upholds her city's tradition as a place in which difficult questions are resolved. With burning indignation she reminds the invader that Abel is the inheritance of YHWH. Indeed hers is the sole introduction of God into the world of betrayals and griefs chronicled in this chapter. Her willingness to invoke the divine name and to bear responsibility for her imperfect decision constitute perhaps her greatest acts of courage and faith.

Appendix: A Guide to Feminist Textual Study

As an appendix to this essay, I have reproduced the guide I use for students at all levels. My reading of II Samuel 20 responds to some of the questions raised in this guide.

TALKING OUR WAY IN
Types of Questions to Ask a Story

For what must be interpreted in a text is a *proposed world* which I could inhabit and wherein I could project my ownmost possibilities.[17]

1. Questions from within the World of the Story

A. Literary
What is the setting? What is the plot? Who are the characters? Which are central and which are peripheral? How is the story told? Are there comic or tragic elements, poetry, chronicles, or catalogs? What kinds of patterns (linguistic, thematic, or narrative) can be noted? Are there repetitions, contrasts, correspondences, conflicts, continuities, reversals, ironies, or outstanding words or images?

B. Literary-Psychological
What kind of people do the characters reveal themselves to

---

be during the course of the story? Do they grow or remain static? How do they interact with others? What fears or desires are evident? How would you describe their moral universe? What rules and constraints operate?

What is the impact of gender and social position upon the roundness of characterization and upon the insight offered into a character's internal world and motivations? Can psychological mechanisms such as omissions, projections, distortions, denials, rationalizations, or stereotypes provide a plausible explanation of character depictions or narrative emphases? Are there psychological theories or constructs (e.g., psychoanalytic theory or object-relations) that yield particularly persuasive readings of given narratives?

2. Questions about the Frame of the Story
(Historical, Anthropological, Sociological)

A. Context Questions
Where was the story written? When was it written? What historical or archaeological findings, external to this story, provide information about how people lived and thought at that time that might shed light on the story? Does anthropology or sociology offer data or theory that would help us categorize the social organization, the construction of gender, the distribution of power and authority implicit in the story?

B. Perspective Questions
Who is telling the story and why? Who edited the story? How and by whom was the story transmitted and for what purpose? Who was the intended audience?

3. Questions Comparing the Story to Other Stories
(Literary and Folkloric)

What relationships exist between this story and other stories surrounding it? What parallels, echoes, or analogies of form or content exist between this story and other stories from the same tradition? Are there parallels with literature from other civilizations?

Does the story draw upon folkloric motifs found in tales from all over the world? Which motifs? How are they used?

4. Questions about How Readers in the Past Responded to the Story

Are there *midrashim* on the story? If so, what prompted them—something missing or confusing in the story, dissonances between the story and the worldview of the midrashist, language or themes that are "overdetermined" in the midrashist's religious perspective?

Is there *halachah*, Jewish law, based upon this story? What is the relationship between the law and the story? Does the story ground the law or reinforce the law? Could the story potentially challenge or destabilize law?

What do commentaries (ancient and modern) focus upon? What interests them? What bothers them? What do they evade or ignore?

5. Questions from the Moral Universe We Bring to the Texts We Read
(Ethical, Theological, Philosophical)

Can we bring ourselves into this story's world? If not, how have we been shut out and why? Unlike other hermeneutics that work with what is overt and explicit in texts, feminist hermeneutics try to hear silences and see the invisible. What is absent? What is repressed or hidden?

Could we imagine the story progressing or ending differently? If the story were transposed into a contemporary moral universe, what elements would remain constant and what would change?

What is the story's philosophical or theological anthropology? What does being human mean in this story in terms of interdependency/autonomy, mortality, choice/constraint, suffering/pleasure, joy/grief, work/play, sexuality, violence, evil, capacity for change? How human are women in the story?

What is God telling us through the story? What are we telling God through the story? Having wrestled the story for a blessing, what meanings have we wrested from it? How does the story shape our collective memory as a people? What demands does it make upon us that we should integrate into the way we live our lives? How will we transmit the story?

Is it possible that the antonym of "forgetting" is not "remembering" but justice?[18]

Some of the ideas in this article appeared in *Sh'ma*, vol. 23/441 (November 13, 1992), pp. 5–6.

NOTES

1. All those who use the metaphor of conversation are ultimately indebted to Jurgen Habermas. For a lucid and accessible discussion of the relationship between conversation and interpretation, see David Tracy, *Plurality and Ambiguity: Hermeneutics, Religion and Hope* (San Francisco: Harper & Row, 1987), pp. 1–27.

2. The issue of confidence is also discussed by Franz Rosenzweig, "Towards a Renaissance of Jewish Learning," *On Jewish Learning*, ed. N. N. Glatzer (New York: Schocken, 1965).

3. See, for example, Michel Foucault, *Power/Knowledge: Selected Interviews and Other Writings, 1972–1977* (New York: Pantheon Books, 1980).

4. See, for example, Deuteronomy 33:4 or the petition "Grant us our share in Your Torah" in the middle blessing of the Shabbat or *yom tov tefilah* (*kedushat hayom*).

5. For a political analysis of the import of this group, see Deborah Butler, "Facing the Wall: The Politics of Women and Prayer," *New Outlook* (May/June, 1989), pp. 25–26. See also Deborah Brin, "Up Against the Wall: How We Answered Our Own Prayers," *Reconstructionist* (June 1989), pp. 13–15.

6. At the time of this writing, the Supreme Court had directed that a commission be formed to determine how women might pray at the Wall without offending the sensibilities of the ultra-Orthodox. The commission's deliberations were scheduled to conclude in November 1994.

7. Robert Cover, "The Supreme Court 1982 Term: Forward: *Nomos* and Narrative," *Harvard Law Review*, vol. 97, no. 4 (1983), pp. 11–19. See also my article

"Feminist Folktales of Justice: Robert Cover as a Resource for the Renewal of *Halakhah*," *Conservative Judaism*, vol. 45 (Spring 1993), pp. 40–55.

8. David Ellenson must be credited with introducing sociological deviance theory into the study of nineteenth-century Jewish thought. By labeling certain opinions or practices deviant, a group seeks to refine its identity in the face of new issues and maintain the integrity of its boundaries. David Ellenson, "The Role of Reform in Selected German-Jewish Responsa," *Tradition in Transition: Orthodoxy, Halakhah, and the Boundaries of Modern Jewish Identity* (Lanham, MD: University Press of America, 1989), pp. 33–57.

9. Susannah Heschel, "Introduction," *On Being a Jewish Feminist*, ed. Susannah Heschel (New York: Schocken, 1983), p. xxiii.

10. For a good brief analysis of these factors, see Jo Ann Hackett, "Samuel 1 and 2," *The Women's Bible Commentary*, eds. Carol A. Newman and Sharon H. Ringe (London and Louisville, Kentucky: SPCK and Westminster/John Knox Press, 1992), pp. 85–95.

11. Joab has a personal motive: Abner slew his brother in battle. But he defends his action as politically necessary, accusing Abner of being a spy. (II Samuel 3)

12. Joab's instructions and the messenger's interchange with the king in II Samuel 11: 18–24 anticipate David's awareness that the casualties were caused by poor tactics.

13. Claudia V. Camp, "The Wise Women of II Samuel: A Role Model for Women in Early Israel?" *Catholic Biblical Quarterly* 43 (1981), pp. 14–29.

14. My friend and study partner Professor Tamara Eskenazi suggests that the wise woman's later use of this more emphatic form of the first-person pronoun is meant to establish her as Joab's equal. See my discussion of the first-person pronoun on page 239.

15. Roland De Vaux, *Ancient Israel*, vol. 1, *Social Institutions* (New York: McGraw-Hill, 1965), pp. 68–72, 229–240.

16. My translation. For a summary of scholarship on this passage, see II Samuel, *The Anchor Bible*, vol. 9, a new translation with introduction, notes, and commentary by P. Kyle McCarter (Garden City, NY: Doubleday, 1984), pp. 425–432. McCarter emends *emunei*, "faithful" or "loyal," to *amunei*, "architects," and translates, "Let them inquire in Abel and Dan whether that which the architects of Israel ordained has been carried out."

17. Paul Ricoeur, "The Hermeneutical Function of Distanciation," *Hermeneutics and the Social Sciences* (Cambridge, 1981), p. 142.

18. Yosef Hayim Yerushalmi, "Postscript," *Zakhor: Jewish History, Jewish Memory* (New York: Schocken, 1989), p. 117.

Outreach is Reform Judaism's response to the problem of intermarriage. It is our collective effort to convert a crisis into an opportunity, to turn the threat of a serious drain on our numeric strength into a vital source for our enlargement.

This is not to say that we are encouraging intermarriage. Quite the contrary! We encourage Jewish romances to flourish among our young people. But the reality is that even our best efforts do not suffice, nor do the efforts of the other branches of Judaism. We live in an open society, and intermarriage is its inevitable concomitant. Unless we are willing to withdraw from the advantages of the American way of life, we cannot hypocritically beat our breasts about the social consequences of that way of life.

We have but one of two options: We can either exile our children or continue to embrace them. We can either do what our forebears did and sit *shivah* for them, or we can draw them even closer to our hearts, in the hope of eventually retaining or regaining them. We have resolved to take the latter course. We refuse to alienate our children. We will not banish them. Quite the contrary, we intend to reach out to them, to embrace them. In this manner, we fervently hope, our children will be able to overcome their ambivalences toward an active involvement in Jewish life. Their non-Jewish partners might then conceivably be inclined to initiate the process of conversion to Judaism. And, at the very least, we will dramatically increase the probability that the children of such marriages, our grandchildren, *will* be reared as Jews and share the destiny of the Jewish people.

My conception of outreach, however, goes beyond the non-Jewish partners of our children. My dream is to see our Judaism unleashed as a resource for a world in need: not as the exclusive inheritance of the few, but as a renewable resource for the many;

not as a religious stream too small to be seen on the map of the world, but as a deep flowing river, hidden by the overgrown confusion of modern times, that could nourish humanity's highest aspirations.

Let us, therefore, be champions of Judaism. Let us not be among those who in their pain and confusion respond to the fear of self-extinction by declaring casualties before the fact; who respond to the suffering of the past by living in the past; who react to the long-drawn isolation of our people with an isolationism of their own. Let us rather recall and act on those lofty passages from the *Tanach* and the *Chazal*, from Bible and Commentary that define Jewish "chosenness" not as exclusive but as exemplary, not as separatist but as representative, not as closed but as open, not as rejecting but as all-embracing and compassionate.

Rabbi Alexander M. Schindler
Address to the ULPS of Great Britain
London, England
February 13, 1995

THE OUTREACH MOVEMENT MAKING JUDAISM AN INCLUSIVE RELIGION

EGON MAYER

On December 2, 1978, Rabbi Alexander Schindler, president of the Union of American Hebrew Congregations—whose members comprise about one-third of organized American Jewry—proposed that Jews, or at least Reform Jews, begin to "reach out" to the religiously unaffiliated non-Jews and particularly those who have married Jews.

"I believe," he said in his address to the Board of Trustees of the UAHC, "that it is time for our movement to launch a carefully conceived outreach program aimed at all *Americans who are unchurched and who are seeking roots in religion....* My friends, we Jews possess the water that can slake the thirst, the bread that can sate the great hunger. Let us offer it freely, proudly—for *our* well-being and for the sake of those who earnestly seek what is ours to give."

Those were remarkable words for a religious leader of a community that has borne the reputation and practice, since the fall of the Roman Empire, of *not* seeking converts. Perhaps, even more remarkable is the fact that fifteen years after that dramatic clarion call the great majority of America's Jews are rapidly arriving at consensus over the issue that was virtually nonexistent for Jews just a generation ago: what to do about the non-Jews who are becoming an ever-increasing presence within the network of the modern Jewish family. Schindler's solution: Welcome them into the bosom of the Jewish community even as they've been welcomed into so many Jewish families. Foster their Jewish education, encourage them to raise their children as Jews, and create an inclusionary environment that invites conversion to Judaism.

To be sure, this bold message has not engendered anything resembling the Christian or the Muslim forms of spreading the faith. Nor was such ever intended. Rabbi Schindler's proposal, and the favorable response of other Jewish leaders to the idea of "outreach," has steadfastly focused on the "unchurched"—particularly on the spouses and children of intermarried Jews. No one has suggested that Jews emulate the model of Christian or Muslim evangelism, triumphantly proclaiming Judaism the only true faith.

In contrast to evangelistic faith communities that have sought dominion through universality, the Jewish outreach effort advocates religious pluralism and tolerance.

This climate of congeniality and inclusion has begun to transform the age-old attitude of Jews toward intermarriage from one of outrage to one of outreach.

This transformation in the *weltanschauung* of American Jews and the institutional and programmatic manifestations of that change will surely rank high among the historic achievements of Rabbi

Schindler, earning for him a rightful place in the annals of Jewish history among the visionaries of his people.

However, even as one reflects upon and rejoices in the formidable success of the Jewish outreach message, it is well to remember that Rabbi Schindler's words have not been welcome in a number of Jewish quarters. Traditional Jews, particularly those in the Orthodox camp, are outraged at the *chutzpah* of a Reform rabbi proposing to "make Jews" by standards that are contrary to the traditional Jewish law, the *halachah*.

Apart from its general hesitancy in welcoming converts, *halachah* requires that converts "accept the yoke of the Torah"; that is, they must obey the complex Jewish ritual system; undergo ritual immersion in a *mikveh*; and, in the case of males, be circumcised. Even as it pioneered "outreach," the Reform movement has not followed all of the traditional standards for conversion. For example, many Reform rabbis were and are quite ready to accept converts without requiring ritual immersion or circumcision for men.

The Conservative and Reconstructionist movements, which followed Reform's lead on "outreach," also take a less stringent attitude toward the acceptance of converts to Judaism. Although the rabbis of these two latter movements do require *mikveh* immersion and ritual circumcision for men, they are far more willing than their Orthodox counterparts to accept those converts to Judaism who may be motivated by a prospective marriage to a Jew but uncommitted to full practice of all the rituals required by the traditional religious system.

Indeed, more than a decade of battles in the Israeli Knesset over the "Law of Return"—which revolves around the question, Who is a Jew?—were largely stimulated by Rabbi Schindler's 1978 Houston manifesto and the programs of outreach that flowed from it.

One group of militant Orthodox rabbis, calling itself the Shofar Association, has periodically resorted to full-page advertisements in *The New York Times* and other newspapers, warning readers to "Beware of Counterfeit Conversions" to Judaism. The Association of Sephardic Rabbis, also a highly traditionalist group, has placed a complete ban on all conversions to Judaism.

Interestingly, liberal, secular American Jews were almost equally frightened that Rabbi Schindler's call for "outreach" might upset the détente in Jewish-Christian relations, in effect since Vatican II, according to which the Catholic church eschewed its traditional position on seeking to convert Jews. Some have feared that a "Jewish outreach" program would rekindle theological anti-Semitism and possibly even undermine American support for Israel.

Reflecting on Rabbi Schindler's famed Houston statement, Peter Berger observed in a May 1979 article in *Commentary*: "The mainline Christian churches are in a state of theological exhaustion and are most unlikely to be roused from it by a little Jewish proselytizing.... It seems unlikely that the conversion to Judaism of a few lapsed Presbyterians would provoke anti-Semitic reactions—except among those already so disposed. It is equally hard to imagine that irate Presbyterians [or anyone else] would launch a missionary counteroffensive."

The reaction from Protestant and Catholic quarters has remained to this day a resounding silence. But if the Christian denominations were not roused to "defend the faith" against the call for "Jewish outreach" neither were the various branches of Judaism moved to *actively* seek out America's "unchurched" and bring them to temple. Although Rabbi Schindler's own Reform movement created a Commission on Outreach in 1983, its principal function in the beginning was to create educational programs that would help intermarried families and their children feel more comfortable in the Jewish community—to *facilitate* rather than to *instigate* conversion.

Though professing philosophical support for the idea of "outreach," neither the Conservative nor the Reconstructionist branch of American Judaism made the least effort to seek out religiously unaffiliated non-Jews or even to aid those who are seeking entry into Judaism of their own volition.

All the while, the major secular Jewish organizations that each year collect hundreds of millions of dollars for Jewish philanthropies in Israel and in the United States and provide such services as local community centers for education, culture, and recreation and social services for troubled families and the like have remained totally aloof from the issue. Even long-established community relations agencies like the Anti-Defamation League of B'nai B'rith, the American Jewish Congress, and the American Jewish Committee, which have many decades of experience in interfaith dialogue and cooperation, had for a long time taken a position of "benign neglect" when it came to promoting "outreach." They studied it, earnestly discussed it at conferences, maybe even hoped for it. But, in fact, they did nothing to advance it.

How, then, did it happen that by the closing years of the twentieth century there are more than 200,000 "new Jews" or "Jews-by-choice"—up from only about a third as many as twenty-five years earlier? How did it happen that by 1992 the Jewish Outreach Institute, an independent think tank, could publish a national directory entitled *Jewish Connections for Interfaith Families*, listing over five hundred organized programs of outreach coast to coast for interfaith families?

After a hiatus of nearly two thousand years, Jews are openly and actively welcoming converts again, largely, if not entirely, as a result of Rabbi Schindler's call for outreach in 1978. If present trends continue, converts to Judaism—or Jews-by-choice, as many prefer to be called—will comprise a substantial and increasing proportion of the American Jewish population. From about 1 percent in the first few decades of this century, they have grown to about 3 percent in the seventies and eighties. With their numbers greatly increasing in the past two decades, it is entirely possible that Jews-by-choice will comprise between 7 to 10 percent of the American Jewish population by 2010.

The social force driving this transformation is the movement for Jewish outreach, consisting of a delicate blend of modest missionizing, marketing, and social work. Unlike Christian or Muslim missionizing, however, the objects of Jewish outreach are group survival and family harmony rather than soul saving or the propagation of the faith.

According to the 1990 National Jewish Population Study, about 120,000 American Jews have joined the fold by way of formal religious conversion. Another 65,000 identify themselves as Jewish even though they were not born Jewish and did not undergo formal conversion. These people are Jewish by self-definition. The two groups comprise 3.3 percent of the current American Jewish population of 5.5 million.

About a thousand non-Jews converted to Judaism per year prior to 1965. In that same era, more than twice as many Jews converted *out* of Judaism. Conversion into Judaism more than doubled between the mid-1960s and the early 1970s while apostasy declined. In the early 1980s the number hovered around 2,500 per year. Recently it has eased back to about 1,500 per year. The number of people who say they are Jewish although they were neither born nor raised as such nor have formally converted has increased from about 100 per year in the early 1960s to more than 500 per year since the mid-1970s and eighties.

Interestingly, the most dynamic force stimulating the entry of large numbers of Jews-by-choice into the Jewish folk is not to be found in the policies of any of the denominations or organizations. Rather, it is rooted in what might be called the *conditional embrace of the Jewish family*. One facet of this *conditional embrace*, its matrimonial dimension, is captured in a vignette by the late Paul Cowan, co-author of *Mixed Blessings: Marriage between Jews and Christians*, reflecting on his wife's conversion to Judaism.

> For years I had thought I was completely indifferent to Rachel's religious decisions. She was the wife I loved, no matter what she chose to call herself. But now I knew I felt stronger because Rachel was one of us.

Paul's elation that "Rachel was one of us" is a feeling reported by almost all Jews whose spouses convert to Judaism. With but rare exceptions, most Jews-by-choice will acknowledge that either in the courtship stage or after marriage they'd been made to feel, by spouse or in-laws, that they would be more enthusiastically loved and accepted by the Jewish family if they became Jewish themselves. Its impetus is the existential concern about the family's Jewish continuity. Perhaps this manner of psychological persuasion is as bold as Jewish "evangelism" gets.

For the first time since approximately the middle of the fourth century Jews are absorbing small but significant numbers of non-Jews without fear of persecution by their Christian or Muslim neighbors. Aside from their salutary impact on Jewish demography, Jews-by-choice are having a wide-ranging impact on the institutional programs and policies of the organized Jewish community, as well as upon its ideological mindscape.

Twenty-five or thirty years ago rabbis performed just a few conversions a year, privately in their study. Today there are formally organized Introduction to Judaism courses at such places as the 92nd Street Y in New York and the University of Judaism in Los

Angeles, and at centers of the Union of American Hebrew Congregations throughout the country, with some enrolling as many as several hundred students a year.

How did this change come about? And what does it mean?

Put more simply, a demographic revolution has broken out in the melting pot, striking at the heart of the Jewish family, that bulwark of continuity. Consequently, American Jewry finds itself struggling for survival of its cultural, ethnic, and religious distinctiveness. This time the struggle is not against any external enemy; rather, it is against a wide array of values and social forces that Jews themselves have embraced enthusiastically.

According to the findings of the 1990 NJPS, more than half of all Jews getting married since 1985 have married someone who was not born or raised Jewish. This figure contrasts sharply with the approximately 11 percent who chose non-Jewish partners prior to 1965. The first sign of change occurred among the Jewish marrying cohort between 1965 and 1974, of whom 31 percent chose a spouse who was not born or raised Jewish. Among Jews getting married between 1975 and 1984, about 51 percent chose a spouse who was not born or raised Jewish. Since the mid-1980s, that figure has risen to about 53 percent.

Synagogues, Jewish community centers, Jewish family service agencies, and even national service organizations like Hadassah and B'nai B'rith Women are rushing to create outreach programs to cope with the large-scale entry of non-Jews into the Jewish family. Though not all the programs have conversion as their main goal, all aim to help the intermarried family, particularly the non-Jewish spouse and the children, feel more "at home" in the Jewish community. Outreach, with muted elements of missionizing, is a newly forged strategy trying to cope with this revolution. How well it will serve the needs of the historical moment remains to be seen. The active attempt at spreading the faith does not come easily to Jews.

Historians disagree about whether Judaism was ever a vigorously proselytizing faith. Dio Cassius, a third-century Roman writer, asserts that when Jews flocked to Rome in great numbers in the first and second centuries of the common era, they converted many of the natives to their own ways. Seneca, a first-century Roman philosopher and tragedian, moaned, "The customs of this most accursed race have prevailed to such an extent that they are everywhere received. The conquered have imposed their laws on the conquerors." References can also be found in the writings of other ancient commentators, like Juvenal and Tacitus, about the apparently widespread acceptance of Judaism in the Graeco-Roman world. Philo, a first-century Alexandrian philosopher, wrote that "a great number of other nations imitate the Jewish way of living." He estimated that in his time there were as many as a million Jews in Egypt—a figure that would not have been possible without large-scale conversion among the native Egyptian population.

The late Professor Salo Baron of Columbia University estimated that perhaps as much as 10 percent of the population of the ancient Roman Empire was made up of Jews as a result of widespread conversions among the pagan populations who came under the influence of the exiles of ancient Judea.

Other scholars cite passages from the Talmud that suggest that the rabbis of ancient Israel accepted converts only reluctantly. "Converts are as troublesome to Israel as the plague of leprosy," says Rabbi Chelbo in the Talmud. (*Yevamot* 47b) Other rabbis worry that proselytes "delay the coming of the Messiah." It is not at all clear from the record of arcane ancient debates to what extent, if any, ordinary Jews extended themselves in their relations with the non-Jews of the ancient world to try to bring them "under the canopy of the Torah."

One fact about the history of Jewish evangelism does stand out quite clearly: As Christianity became the dominant religion in the waning Roman Empire, a succession of edicts made it increasingly more risky for Jews to accept, much less to seek out, converts. In 339, Emperor Constantine ordered the confiscation of property of anyone who abetted the conversion of a Christian to Judaism. Subsequent imperial edicts decreed imprisonment, expulsion, and, under some circumstances, even death for Jews who helped non-Jews convert.

The rise of Islam in the seventh century added yet another impediment to any Jewish inclination for evangelizing. In 624, Mohammed began a war of annihilation against the Jews of Arabia. After his victories in 628, he promulgated a series of laws that forbade any of the remaining Jews from accepting any Muslim convert on the pain of death. Any Muslim who converted on his own would face the loss of all his worldly possessions.

The historical record of the past 1,600 years gives ample evidence of the seriousness of these edicts in both the East and the West. As recently as in 1849, Warder Cresson, a well-to-do Quaker from Philadelphia, found himself declared insane by his family because he had converted to Judaism. Only after a protracted court battle was he able to establish his sanity. In 1749, Valentin Potocki, a Lithuanian nobleman, was burned at the stake in the center of the city of Vilnius because he chose to abandon his Christian faith and practice Judaism. Roughly at the same time in England, Lord George Gordon, a former president of the United Protestant League, was condemned to spend the rest of his life in prison on a concocted charge that thinly veiled his contemporaries' fury at his becoming Israel bar Abraham, a practicing Jew. In 1639, Don Lope de Vera, a Spanish nobleman, was arrested and jailed for five years because he had changed his name to Juda, renounced his Christian faith, and adopted Judaism; in 1644 he was burned at the stake.

Because of the seriousness with which Christian and Muslim authorities clamped down on any incidence of Jewish conversion, rabbis from the early Middle Ages on took a very restrictive attitude toward prospective proselytes. The *Shulchan Aruch*, the Code of Jewish Law, compiled in the late sixteenth century, informs the reader in its preface to the laws on conversion that its provisions apply "only where the civil authorities permit Jews to accept converts." It calls on Jews to try to discourage those seeking conversion. Only after the prospective convert refuses to be dissuaded are rabbis permitted to facilitate the Jewish education and ultimate conversion of the candidate.

In light of the long historical record of external constraints and internal restraints against seeking converts, Judaism has been regarded by both Jews and non-Jews as a nonproselytizing religion.

While Jewry throughout the world had long abandoned any programmatic effort to "missionize" to non-Jews, it never broke entirely with the creed of Isaiah, who believed that "Israel shall be a light unto the nations that My salvation may reach the end of the earth."

While Jews as a group never believed that the faith of Israel is a prerequisite for spiritual salvation (as, for example, Christians believe in the necessity of accepting Jesus as savior), most Jews have believed—and most probably continue to believe—in the world-perfecting efficacy of a life lived according to the social ethics of the Torah and the Talmud.

To be sure, American Jews are not likely anytime soon to knock on the doors of their Christian neighbors to try to bring them the "good news" of Moses or the Talmud. In that sense the Jewish outreach movement bears little resemblance to the more familiar Christian evangelism. Nor have American Jews experienced any theological change of heart. The Jewish belief system has always been fundamentally pluralistic, certain that all God's children have a place in the world to come, regardless of whether they believe in the Buddha, Christ, Allah, or *Elohim*. The emerging attitude is not about the salvation of the soul or even about the truth claims of a creed; rather, it is about the survival of Jewish family and, by extension, the Jewish community.

Rabbis are not mounting corner soapboxes anytime soon nor are Jewish philanthropists financing massive televangelistic campaigns to convince the world of the spiritual or moral supremacy of the Jewish faith. Jews don't preach salvation to others. Rather, Jewish outreach is emerging as a desperate effort on the part of American Jewish parents, whose children are increasingly choosing non-Jewish marriage partners, to insure that they will nevertheless have Jewish grandchildren. As Peter Berger stated in 1979, "It is reasonable to regard Rabbi Schindler's proposal as a sensible and low-risk measure of Jewish demographic self-defense."

The realization that intermarriage cannot be stopped has led American Jews in most cases to a fundamental philosophical change, which might be summed up, albeit somewhat glibly, in a twist on an old cliché: If we can't beat 'em, let them join us.

Thus, the Jewish outreach movement reflects the emerging reality of the 1980s and nineties that families are turning to their synagogues and communal institutions to help them deal with intermarriage after it has occurred, much as they had hoped those institutions would have helped prevent it in the first place.

Why should a movement that from its birth-hour insisted on the full equality of men and women in religious life unquestioningly accept the principle that Jewish lineage is valid through the maternal line alone—all the more so because there is substantial support in our tradition for the validity of Jewish lineage through the paternal line!

I am satisfied, indeed exceedingly pleased, therefore, that our Conference of Rabbis has resolved to eliminate the distinction between men and women, between fathers and mothers, and now insists that, insofar as genealogy is a factor in determining Jewishness, the maternal and the paternal lines should be given equal weight.

But the Reform resolution on Jewish identity does not limit itself to genealogy, and in this sense Reform is more stringent than is Orthodoxy. Tradition confers Jewishness automatically if the mother is Jewish. Reform Judaism does not. It sets added requirements. It insists that the Jewishness of children, whatever their lineage, be further confirmed by "acts of identification with the Jewish people" and "the performance of *mitzvot*." Jewishness cannot be transmitted merely through the genes. It must be expressed in some concrete way through an involvement in Jewish life and the willingness to share the fate of the Jewish people.

Moreover, how could we ignore the sensitivity of the many children of intermarriages—tens of thousands of them now, the preponderant majority among them the children of Jewish fathers and non-Jewish mothers! How do you think these children feel, though with the concurrence of both parents they were reared and now live as Jews, when they hear over and over again that only the child of a Jewish mother is Jewish? Barring the declaration on our part to the contrary, they are bound to feel that they are of a lesser state and worth.

It is high time that we say to them: By God, you are Jews. You are the sons and daughters of a Jewish parent. With the consent of both your parents, you were reared as Jews. You have resolved to share our fate. You are, therefore, flesh of our flesh, bone of our bone. You are in all truth what you consider yourself to be: Jews as worthy as any who were born Jewish!

Rabbi Alexander M. Schindler
Clal Conference on Jewish Unity
Princeton, New Jersey
March 16, 1986

PATRILINEAL DESCENT

BERNARD M. ZLOTOWITZ

From the beginning of Jewish history to the present time, the status of children in intermarried families has been of primary concern among communal authorities.

In the biblical period, "Jewishness" was determined patrilineally. However, beginning with Ezra the Scribe (5th century B.C.E.), that tradition was reversed; henceforth, the Jewishness of a child was determined by the mother's religion. If the mother was Jewish, the child was automatically Jewish. This became the *halachah* and remained in effect for Reform Judaism until 1983, when the Central Conference of American Rabbis voted a return to patrilineal descent.

At a board meeting of the Union of American Hebrew Congregations, Rabbi Alexander M. Schindler revived the concept of patrilineal descent, proposing a return to the biblical concept while simultaneously retaining matrilineal descent. That is, if either parent is Jewish, a child raised as a Jew is considered to be Jewish.

Rabbi Schindler's proposal was a means of preserving Jewish continuity in the face of escalating intermarriage rates between

Jews and non-Jews. Most Jews want their children and grand-children recognized as Jewish, regardless of the religious status of the mother.

Rabbi Schindler was certainly faithful to Jewish tradition when he made his proposal for a return to the patrilineal descent of the biblical period. There are in the Bible several famous examples of this concept of patrilineal descent.

The story of Joseph and Asenath, daughter of Poti-phera, priest of On, tells of their marriage and of the birth of their two sons, Manasseh and Ephraim.[1] Although Asenath, as the daughter of the priest of On, was certainly not a Jewess, no one denies the Jewish-ness of her sons. To this day, on Friday nights, Jewish parents bless their children with the prayer that they be like Ephraim and Manasseh.[2]

Zipporah, daughter of a priest of Midian, married Moses and bore him two sons, Gershom and Eliezer.[3] Again, Zipporah, as the daughter of a Midianite priest, is not Jewish, but her children and their descendants undoubtedly are.

Solomon married numerous non-Jewish women, among them daughters from the seven Canaanite nations, which the Bible expressly prohibited.[4] Are we to conclude that Solomon's children were not Jewish? In fact, Rehoboam, the son of Solomon and Na'amah, an Ammonite woman, ascends the throne of the southern kingdom of Judah, which his father, Solomon, and his grandfather, David, had occupied.[5]

To cite but one more example: Ahaziah, the son of Ahab and Jezebel, an idolatress, sat on the throne of the northern kingdom of Israel.[6]

The genealogical tables in the Bible bear witness to ample evidence of patrilineal descent.[7] And so it continued until Ezra and Nehemiah, upon the return of the Jewish exiles from Babylonia, changed the law from patrilineal to matrilineal, forbidding marriages not only with the seven Caananite nations but with Ammonites, Moabites, and Egyptians as well.[8] Not only were marriages with these people forbidden, but existing marriages were dissolved by casting out the non-Jewish wives and their children, who were no longer considered Jewish. Interestingly, non-Jewish husbands were not driven out by Ezra because Jewish women had had no choice in choosing their husbands; their mates were chosen for them.[9] The Jewish husband of a non-Jewish woman, on the other hand, was punished for choosing to intermarry.

Thus Ezra summarily swept away biblical law by instituting matrilineal descent, which officially stripped the children of Jewish husbands and non-Jewish wives of their Jewish identities. He did this under the authority of Persian Emperor Artaxerxes (465–425 B.C.E.). Ezra's edict met some opposition. In fact, the Bible states: "Only Jonathan the son of Asahel and Jahzeiah the son of Tikvah stood up against this matter [casting out the foreign wives]; and Meshullam and Shabbethai the Levite helped them."[10] Furthermore, the Book of Ruth probably was written as a polemic against Ezra's decree and was deliberatley predated to the period of the Judges to "prove" that if Ezra's edict had been in existence, there never would have been a King David, who is a descendant of Boaz (a Jew,) and Ruth (a Moabitess).

Ezra, it seems, had been influenced by the sociopolitical currents of his time. For example, the Athenian Law under Pericles (a contemporary of Ezra) opposed intermarriage in order to preserve racial purity[11] and avoid "contaminating their blood."[12]

Similarly, Ezra sought to safeguard Jewish purity, promote group self-preservation, and maintain exclusivity. This foreign concept, incorporated by Ezra into Jewish tradition, eventually found expression in the *Mishnah* and *Gemara*:

> If a woman's marriage with a particular [Jewish] man is invalid, and her marriage with other Jewish men is equally invalid, then the offspring follow her status. This is the case when the offspring is from a bond woman or a non-Jewish woman.[13]

The *Gemara* is equally explicit:

> Your son by an Israelite woman is called your son, but your son by a heathen woman is not called your son.[14]

Notwithstanding the authoritative position these new laws held, not all halachists accepted these rulings: Some rabbis like Jacob of Kefar Nibburaya (4th century) upheld the legitimacy of patrilineal descent. In a case brought before him, while he was on a visit to Tyre, he was asked if it were permissible to circumcise on the

Sabbath a boy whose mother was not Jewish but whose father was. He ruled that it was permissible on the basis of the biblical verse: "And they declared their pedigrees after their families, by their fathers' houses...."[15] Other rabbis countered by quoting different verses: "You shall not intermarry with them [the seven nations]: do not give your daughter to his son or take his daughter for your son. For he will turn away your son from following Me to worship other gods, and the anger of *Adonai* will blaze forth against you and *Adonai* will destroy you quickly."[16] Rabbi Jacob of Kefar Nibburaya recanted and was flogged for his unpopular ruling. But this did not still the debate.

Moses Isserles (16th century), one of the greatest authorities on Jewish law, similarly upheld the legitimacy of patrilineal descent:

> It appears to me that basically it is unlawful to have sexual relations with her. Some are of the opinion that the prohibition is biblical; namely, that the child follows the status of the slave or the non-Jewess, but on the basis of the rabbis, the child is to be regarded as *his, as the Jew's offspring.* [emphasis added] But in view of the doubt one must be rigorous from the outset.[17]

A case cited in Joseph Karo's *Shulchan Aruch* (1555) bears a similarity to the one brought before Rabbi Jacob of Kefar Nibburaya: Is a child born on the Sabbath to a non-Jewish mother and a Jewish father permitted to be circumcised on the Sabbath? Karo granted that the child may be circumcised but not on the Sabbath, implying that the child has some valid claim to membership in the Jewish people.[18]

The Talmud has never fully reconciled Ezra's decree of matrilineal descent with the long-held biblical concept of patrilineal descent. How could one conceive of the children of biblical Jewish heroic fathers and heathen mothers as not being Jewish! Could anyone say, for example, that the children of Joseph, Moses, or Solomon were not Jewish? To solve this dilemma, the talmudic sages introduced a grandfather clause: They reinterpreted the words *your son* in Deuteronomy 7:4 to be understood as *your grandson.*[19] Thus, through this legal fiction, the Talmud retained the Jewishness of the children of the great biblical heroes whose mothers were not Jewish.

Yet notwithstanding such attempts to eradicate patrilineal descent, vestiges of patrilinealism remained in the Talmud; for example, "The family of the father is considered family; the family of the mother is not considered family."[20] Thus, along with matrilineal descent, patrilineal descent was preserved, especially in the priesthood where "pure" genealogical lines were essential:

> If the betrothal was valid and no transgression befell [by reason of the marriage], the standing of the offspring follows that of the male [parent]. Such is the case when a woman is the daughter of a priest, a Levite, or an Israelite.[21]

The same holds true for naming children with the formula *son or daughter of the name of the father*. The mother's name is not included. And if the father is a *kohen* or a *Levi* or the mother is the daughter of a *kohen* or a *Levi*, no *pidyon haben* takes place, a further nod to patrilineal descent.

Patrilinealty is also reaffirmed when a man is called to the Torah for an *aliyah* by his name and his father's name. The traditional marriage contract, the *ketubah*, records the names of the groom and the bride and their fathers' names respectively. The witnesses to the *ketubah* sign their own names along with the names of their fathers. At no time is the mother's name mentioned in any of the examples cited above.

We also have evidence favoring patrilineal descent from later rabbinic decisions:

> Marry your children, O my sons and daughters, as soon as their age is ripe, to members of respectable families. Let no child of mine hunt after money by making a low match for that object; but if the family is undistinguished only on the mother's side, it does not matter, for all Israel counts descent from the father's side.[22]

At the 1983 convention of the Central Conference of American Rabbis, Rabbi Schindler's resolution on patrilineal descent was debated and decided. The conference voted to override the *halachah*, which recognizes matrilineal descent; that is, the child is automatically Jewish if born to a Jewish mother. Instead, the CCAR declared that in an intermarriage where either the father or the mother is Jewish, the child is "under presumption of Jewish descent." In other words, descent alone is not sufficient. Such a child will be considered Jewish only after identifying with the Jewish community by fulfilling the *mitzvot* and participating in Jewish life. Indeed, the CCAR's position is even more stringent than that of the *halachah*, which confers automatic Jewishness if the mother is Jewish, regardless of how the child is reared.

The changes enacted in the Reform movement fall within the traditional parameters of Judaism as a living faith. In times of necessity and for the welfare of the people, *halachah* was revised and traditions set aside in favor of more adaptive ones. I need only cite as examples Hillel's *prosbul*, Yochanan ben Zakkai's elimination of the law of the *sotah*, and Rabbenu Gershom's edict forbidding polygamy and husbands' arbitrary divorce of their wives against their will.

The Bible enjoined the cancellation of all debts in the Sabbatical year: "At the end of every seven years you shall make a release. And this is the manner of the release: Every creditor shall release that which he had lent his neighbor; he shall not exact it of his neighbor and his kinsfolk, for *Adonai*'s release has been proclaimed."[23] This created havoc with the economy because people refused to make loans prior to the advent of the Sabbatical year, fearing they would never collect their loan. Recognizing that the situation called for correction, Hillel introduced the *prosbul*, a declaration made in a rabbinic court before the loan was made that that particular loan was not to be affected by the release of debts in the Sabbatical year, thus allowing for the debt to be collected.[24] This institution protected both the rich and the poor. The rich knew that their loan would be protected and the poor could obtain loans.[25]

In another instance of altering biblical law, Rabbi Yochanan ben Zakkai eliminated the trial of ordeal enjoined in the Torah for the *sotah* (a woman suspected of unfaithfulness)[26] because adultery had become so rampant.[27]

Under the ban of excommunication, Rabbenu Gershom issued a decree that abolished polygamy and forbade a man from arbitrarily divorcing his wife, both of which were permitted by the Torah.[28]

These new laws were enacted to preserve and protect the integrity of the Jewish community.

Similarly, in our day, the conditions called forth for reexamining the question "Who is a Jew?" The Reform and Reconstructionist movements determined that the answer was to return to patrilineal descent. This solution responded to a desperate need of the Jewish people, which has been confirmed in a study conducted by Professor Egon Mayer, the senior research fellow of the Center for Jewish Studies and the executive director of the Jewish Outreach Institute. The survey found that a very high percentage of Jews, no matter what branch of Judaism they espouse, deeply desire their grandchildren to be Jewish, regardless of the daughter-in-law's religion.

Mayer concludes: "Though concerned about intermarriage, American Jews are more eager to see their children marry than to avoid intermarriage. When faced with the reality of an interfaith marriage where the mother is not Jewish but is committed to raise the children as Jews, they are almost most likely to consider their grandchildren as Jewish even if traditional Jewish law would dictate otherwise....

"The current survey also reveals a growing acceptance among the more traditional branches of American Judaism (Conservative and Orthodox) of the presumptive Jewishness of children born to non-Jewish mothers, provided that the children are raised Jewish."[29]

Of course, our goal should be to reach out to the non-Jewish spouses and encourage them to embrace Judaism, thus becoming an integral part of the Jewish people. In championing the Reform movement's Jewish Outreach initiative, Rabbi Schindler has been the prime mover in reaching out to such couples. In 1985, the great Orthodox Rabbi Joseph (Dov) Soloveitchik (z"l) sanctioned the Reform Outreach program by stating in an inteview: "The correct way is specifically the way of Reform."[30]

NOTES

1. Genesis 41:45,50–52.
2. Genesis 48:20. Though Manasseh is the firstborn, Ephraim's name precedes Manasseh's because of the wording of Jacob's blessing: "So he blessed them that day, saying: 'By you shall Israel bless, saying: God make you like Ephraim and Manasseh.' Thus he put Ephraim before Manasseh."
3. Exodus 2:21,22; 18:3,4; I Chronicles 23:15.

4. Deuteronomy 7:1–4; I Kings 11:1–6; Nehemiah 13:25,26.

5. I Kings 14:21.

6. I Kings 22:40.

7. Genesis 5:1ff.;10:1ff.;11:10ff.; I Chronicles 23:6ff. For a more detailed analysis of the Jewishness of children with Jewish fathers and non-Jewish mothers, see Philip Hiat and Bernard M. Zlotowitz, "Biblical and Rabbinic Sources on Patrilineal Descent," *Journal of Reform Judaism*, Winter 1983, pp. 43-48; also Bernard M. Zlotowitz, "A Perspective on Patrilineal Descent," *Judaism*, Winter 1985, pp. 129–135.

8. Ezra 9:1; see also Nehemiah 13:23–30. Shaye D. Cohen believes "the matrilineal principle is a legal innovation of the first or second century of our era." (*Judaism*, Winter 1985, pp. 10–11) I refute his thesis in the same issue of the magazine, pp. 129–135.

9. Ezra had declared specifically that the mother determined the status of the child. Since the mother was Jewish, the child was also Jewish; therefore, there was no reason to cast out the Jewish mother and her child.

10. Ezra 10:15.

11. For a detailed analysis of this subject, see Bernard M. Zlotowitz, "A Perspective on Patrilineal Descent," *Judaism*, Winter 1985, p. 130.

12. George Foot Moore, *Judaism*, vol. 1, Harvard University Press, 1904, p. 20.

13. *Mishnah Kiddushin* 3:12.

14. *Kiddushin* 68b.

15. Numbers 1:18; *Yerushalmi Kiddushin* 3:12; *Yerushalmi Yevamot* 42.

16. Deuteronomy 7:3–4.

17. Joseph Karo, *Shulchan Aruch, Even ha-Ezer* 15:10.

18. Ibid., *Yoreh Deah* 266:13.

19. *Kiddushin* 68 a,b; see also discussion in Hiat and Zlotowitz, "Biblical and Rabbinic Sources on Patrilineal Descent," pp. 46–48.

20. *Baba Batra* 109b.

21. *Kiddushin* 3:12 (Danby translation).

22. From the Testament of Eleazar of Mayence (d. 1357), quoted in *Hebrew Ethical Wills*, part II, selected and edited by Israel Abrahams, Jewish Publication Society, 1948, p. 210.

23. Deuteronomy 15:1-2.

24. *Shevi'it* 10:3,4.

25. *Gittin* 37a.

26. Numbers 5:11–31.

27. *Sotah* 9:9.

28. Deuteronomy 21:15;24:1–4.

29. *Summary Report on JOI* (Jewish Outreach Institute) *Readership Survey*, Center for Jewish Studies, September 21, 1993, pages unnumbered.

30. *The National Jewish Post and Opinion*, vol. 55, no. 15, January 4, 1989, 27 Tevet 5749.

For many Jews, the land of Israel has become the sole touchstone of their Jewish existence. They have for too long been plugged into Israel as if it were a dialysis machine, a scientific marvel that keeps them Jewishly alive. The state has become a synagogue and its prime minister their *rebbe*.

We do ourselves irreparable harm when we allow this to be, when we permit our Jewishness to consist almost entirely of a vicarious participation in the life of Israel. There is a greater Israel that sustained our Jewishness through the many centuries of our dispersion. It is not isomorphic with the political state. And it is this greater Israel that we must nurture if we—and it—are to endure.

Don't misunderstand me. I am not arguing that we should diminish our commitment to Israel. On the contrary, I want more involvement, not less. In other words, I argue primarily for a restoration of balance. We will not survive if all that we are about is Israel. And Israel will not survive if the Jews of the world become but pale peripheral extensions of its essence, mere solitary asteroids circling in space about a distant sun. Both are needed: a strong Israel and Jewishly strong communities throughout the world.

Somehow we must absorb two apparently contradictory lessons: We have a worth as Jews independent of Israel even while we must continue to love and support Israel. If we make too much of the first lesson, some will take it as an excuse to cut themselves off from Israel. And if we make too much of the second, we will never know who we are. We will continue to use Israel as a fig leaf to cover our own nakedness. We will have slipped into the sloppy equation that says that Judaism equals Zionism equals Israel.

Rabbi Alexander M. Schindler
Central Conference of American Rabbis
Sabbath Sermon, Jerusalem, Israel, 1973

ISRAEL AND THE DIASPORA
A RELATIONSHIP REEXAMINED

ARTHUR HERTZBERG

Historians keep telling each other the same story: On the sixth day of Creation, Adam fell into a deep sleep. When he awoke, his side was hurting and a human creature like himself, but of a different gender, was nearby. He turned to her and said, "We are living in an age of transition." From the moment that Zionism emerged as an organized movement more than a century ago, the Jewish people has been living in an age of transition. In the beginning the Zionists in the Diaspora set out to create a Jewish state in Palestine. When that state was established, it insisted that it ought to dominate the Diaspora.

The most recent turning in the tension between Israel and the Diaspora occurred on September 13, 1993, when Yitzhak Rabin and Yasir Arafat shook hands on the White House lawn. Shortly thereafter Yossi Beilin, the deputy foreign minister of Israel, suggested that Israel was now strong enough to dispense with the financial aid of the Diaspora. Although Beilin was immediately reprimanded by Prime Minister Yitzhak Rabin, his notion is not a new heresy. On the contrary, Theodor Herzl himself had been far more radical a century ago when he said that once the Jewish state came into being, he would encourage those who chose to remain among the gentiles to assimilate. Beilin is right when he says that peace with the Arab world will alter the relations between Israel and the Jewish Diaspora and create a new historical framework, but we cannot predict this new age. At the very least, before we embrace the idea that a new heaven and a new earth are about to be created, we must take a sober look at what took place during the last century.

In the very beginning the Zionist movement was split between those who "denied the Diaspora" and those who wanted to find a new way of keeping it alive. There is almost no trace of any loyalty to traditional Jewish culture in Theodor Herzl's writings or in his personal life. Herzl was not a revolutionary. He was too bourgeois— too eager to be accepted as a proper European gentleman—to be significantly influenced by a contemporary like Friedrich Nietzsche, although Nietzsche was a profound influence on the younger generation in Europe at the time. Some East European Jewish intellectuals like the writers Yosef Brenner and Micah Yosef Berdichevsky followed Herzl because they thought that Zionism offered the chance for a Nietzschean "transvaluation of values" within Jewry. The Zionist settlement in Palestine would create its own world, unencumbered by the culture of the Jewish ghetto. Brenner and Berdichevsky had not acquired their distaste for traditional Jewish culture solely from Nietzsche. They had also been influenced by the writers in the second half of the nineteenth century who had pleaded for the need for "enlightenment" in both Hebrew and Yiddish. The greatest of these writers like Mendele Mocher Sefarim and Yehudah Leib Gordon were testy about and even infuriated by the Jewish life in the ghetto. Although they deplored the suffering of the Jews during centuries of persecution, they insisted that suffering was no excuse. It was within the power of the Jews themselves to broaden their culture and become modern men. These writers felt that the windows of the ghetto should be opened to let in the general culture.

Nietzsche, the radical thinker, and Herzl, the political innovator, paved a path for the handful of young Jewish ideologues who went to Palestine after the turn of the century. They proposed creating a society that would be Jewish but very new. Many of these pioneers hoped that the Zionist community would achieve a just, socialist life that would be a model for all the progressive forces in the world and the antithesis of the ghetto in which they had been born.

Herzl's detachment from Jewish culture evoked the first major clash within the Zionist movement over the issue of values and tradition. The leading traditionalist among the Zionists was Asher Ginzberg, who wrote under the pen name Ahad Ha-Am. He attended the First Zionist Congress in Basel in 1897, at which he described himself as "a mourner at a wedding." Herzl and especially many of his new followers in Eastern Europe were dreaming of a modern Jewish state that would transcend the past and make it irrelevant. Ahad Ha-Am was a cultural nationalist who regarded all of the Jewish past as precious. He wanted a Hebraic Jewish community in Palestine that would radiate renewed spiritual energies of the Jewish tradition to the Diaspora. Ahad Ha-Am did not deny the Diaspora or hold it in contempt. On the contrary, he admired and even revered its creativity throughout the centuries.

Within a few years Ahad Ha-Am was engaged in a bitter battle with Berdichevsky and Brenner over the issue of continuity. The latter mounted one powerful argument against Ahad Ha-Am: They demanded to know how he defined the Jewish tradition. By what authority did Ahad Ha-Am impose limits on contemporary Jewish life? Having once been rabbinic scholars, both Brenner and Berdichevsky understood that an Orthodox believer could, and indeed had to, insist that the meaning of Judaism was clear and essentially unchanging. God had revealed God's will to man in the Torah. Those who disregarded God's teaching were not creators of new values. They were rebels against the will of God. But Ahad Ha-Am was, like them, an ex-believer, an agnostic. Ahad Ha-Am invoked "the spirit of the people" as a judge of what had to be preserved and which new ideas had to be excluded, but he seemed to be speaking only for himself. Brenner and Berdichevsky argued against him that the Jewish tradition was not to be found within the constraints proposed by Ahad Ha-Am. On the contrary, the revolts throughout the ages against the dominant religious and intellectual establishments played a key role in the true Jewish history. The first Christians, the Cabalists, the repeated messianic movements, and the Chasidim who emerged in the eighteenth century had been spiritual revolutionaries. Why was a contemporary revolt based on physical power and even the worship of the body any different?

The thirty thousand Jews who went to settle in Palestine in the early years of the twentieth century were not clear-cut followers of either of these views, but they thought of themselves in heroic terms. These pioneers could suffer hunger and malaria—and attacks by Arabs—as long as they believed that their life was morally superior to the life in the Diaspora. This belief was ail the more necessary because the overwhelming majority of their contemporaries were going westward to the United States. A. D. Gordon, the leading moral figure among the minority that chose to go to

Palestine, assured his followers that theirs was the greater destiny. They were creating a new Jew who was rooted in the land. Such healthy, primal Jews last existed in biblical times, when Jews had lived on their own land and worked it. To create these "new Jews" was the central task of the Jewish people in the modern age. All other Jewish purposes were secondary, and even irrelevant. The "new Jew" had the right to admire the Diaspora, which he was engaged in transcending. He could expect support without feeling demeaned as a supplicant. David Ben-Gurion often summarized the attitude of these "new Jews" by saying that Jewish history ended in the second century and began again in the middle of the nineteenth, when the first modern agricultural settlement was founded in Palestine.

Even the conservative Ahad Ha-Am downgraded the Diaspora of his time. Although he believed the Diaspora would continue to exist and he wanted to help it, Ahad Ha-Am felt that the new Zionist center in Palestine would be a sun that would give light and warmth to its periphery, the Diaspora communities, which would be passive moons. He did not believe that the Diaspora could continue to create a substantial culture from its own energies. Ahad Ha-Am was well read in a half dozen languages. He certainly knew that in his time, at the turn of the century, Jews were playing a significant role in all fields of European culture, but that was not what Ahad Ha-Am meant by Jewish cultural creativity. For him Jewish culture was Hebraic literature.

Ahad Ha-Am's most famous disciple, the Hebrew poet Chaim Nachman Bialik, held this view even more strongly. Bialik maintained that the great spiritual creations during the centuries since the end of the writing of the Talmud, that is, from the sixth to the nineteenth centuries, needed to be collected. He felt that the best of these works should be edited into a new canon that would stand beside the Bible and the Talmud. This survey of the culture of the past was to be studied and remembered. It would be the springboard for the new Zionist stage of Jewish creativity. When Bialik spoke in 1925 at the dedication of the Hebrew University in Jerusalem, he proclaimed that its lecture halls and laboratories would be the crucibles in which the national spirit would fashion itself in this age, as it had once defined itself in the academies for the study of Talmud. Bialik more than implied that those who chose not to participate in this enterprise were only serving their own careers or were contributing, often mightily, to other national cultures, but they were not expressing the Jewish national spirit.

This conviction that the Zionist settlement and the state that resulted from it were superior to the Diaspora very early became central to the Zionist narrative of Jewish history. Ben Zion Dinur, who was professor of Jewish History at the Hebrew University and the minister of culture in Israel's first cabinet, constructed a Zionist explanation of the whole of Jewish history in nationalist terms. The Jewish people had gone through three great stages. The first was the creation of their national existence on their own land in biblical times; the second was their survival in the Diaspora, not primarily because of their religion but because they always thought of themselves as a people in exile; the third and final stage was the present, the return of this exiled people to their own land. The Dinur thesis was contested even in Israel, but it dominated the teaching of history in the schools. It clearly implied that those who chose not to go to the land of Israel, now that Jewish history had reached its climactic stage, were shirking their duty. David Ben-Gurion reiterated this thesis immediately after the State of Israel was declared. He insisted that the term *Zionist* could be applied only to those Jews who were in Israel or on their way. All others, no matter how deeply concerned about and helpful they might be to the Jewish state, were "Friends of Israel." They were of lower status in the hierarchy of Jewish values.

This negative view of the Diaspora was the doctrine of the elite that created the Jewish state. It was a necessary doctrine. It made removing rocks by hand from bad soil or draining marshes while suffering malaria mythic tasks. The battles with the Arabs and with the British were the birth pangs of a new age for the new Jew. This was the central story of contemporary Jewish history. All the rest was offstage noise. Whenever the Diaspora helped Israel in crucial ways, its efforts were largely ignored. Thus the Israeli historians who have written about their country's War of Independence in 1948 all tell of the ways in which arms were procured by agents of the new government, but they hardly mention that American Jews paid for the purchases. According to these historians, if the creation of the Zionist state is the central mandate of Jewish history, only those who fought the battle on the ground are of essence in this drama. All the rest is of little consequence.

These attitudes have inevitably been qualified during the last forty years. Those who founded the Zionist settlement in the early decades of the century have died, and many of their children are in their seventies. The Sabra generation of today is socialist in name only, for Israel has now become a bourgeois society that measures itself against contemporary Western standards of consumerism. Nonetheless, enough remains of the old idealism, and even more of its rhetoric, to help sustain Israel's sense of superiority over the Diaspora. The majority of Israelis, men and women alike, serve in the army. There is hardly a family in Israel that has not lost a loved one in the country's many wars or in the continuing attacks by terrorists. Precisely because Israel's army is based on national service, the losses of war are felt by every social class. During a term that I spent at the Hebrew University in 1982, I attended the memorial meeting that is held each year on campus to remember students and professors who fell in Israel's wars. The number in 1982 was already nearly six hundred. I stood there in tears, holding on to friends that included some of Israel's most famous scholars who were there mourning their children. From the right to the left and throughout the social structure, Israelis feel that they are paying with their safety and their lives for the future of the Jewish people.

This feeling has been reinforced by two recent phenomena. One is the number of *yordim*, the hundreds of thousands of Israelis who have left the country to live permanently abroad, mostly in the United States. This immigration is often cited in the Diaspora as proof that the demand on Jews in New York and Los Angeles to move to Israel is misplaced. After all, aren't many Israelis opting for the better life in America? However, this is not the perception of the *yordim* that is generally held in Israel. To be sure, those who have become very successful are called upon to help Israel. Essentially, however, the *yordim* are deplored because of the near certainty that their children or grandchildren will disappear by intermarriage into American society. This conviction has been reinforced by repeated and increasingly worried accounts from communities in the United States and other Diaspora countries that intermarriage and assimilation are eroding the numbers of committed Jews. Israeli demographers are predicting, with a mixture of concern and "I told you so,"

that by the year 2025, the majority of those who identify themselves as Jews will be living in Israel because the number of Jews in
the Diaspora will have shrunk to less than four million. Theodor
Herzl suggested a century ago that a Jewish state was necessary in
order to provide a refuge for those who would ultimately be endangered throughout the world by anti-Semitism. Ahad Ha-Am argued
that the real problem was not anti-Semitism but the danger of
assimilation. It is this second danger that now provides Israel with
the sense that it is the last chance for the Jews.

It must be noted that the Zionist conceptions of the meaning of
Jewish existence are challenged by two other accounts of Jewish
existence. Both liberal and Orthodox religious believers continue to
insist that the Jewish people have survived because they bear divine
teaching and that teaching is valid everywhere. The many secular
movements among Jews in the modern era repeat names like
Spinoza, Marx, and Freud—separately or together—as a kind of
incantation to suggest that the true destiny of Jews is to be in the
vanguard of universal human culture. But even these two camps
were touched by Zionism. Many among the Orthodox believers
think that we are living in the days of the Messiah and that all Jews
must strive toward being ingathered in the Holy Land. Although
many secularists in Israel and even some in the Diaspora prefer
Spinoza, Marx, and Freud to the Gaon Elijah of Vilna and Rabbi
Abraham Isaac Kook, they, too, insist that a life that is lasting and
Jewish can only be lived by those speaking Hebrew in the land of
Israel. Thus, the dominant belief in most of Israel and much of the
Diaspora that the future of Jewish life, whatever form it might
ultimately take, is best secured in Israel. This estimate is not true of
those Jews who care little or nothing about the discrete survival of
the Jews as a people. But the majority of the Jews who do care
believe that a Jewish life in Israel is superior to the life in the
Diaspora.

One other element must be added to this discussion about the
relationship between Israel and the Diaspora. It is the matter of
giving charity. We know that in ancient times, during the last two
centuries of the existence of the Second Temple in Jerusalem, there
were many more Jews in the Diaspora than in the Holy Land. With
some sectarian exceptions, the communities in the Diaspora
accepted their responsibility to transmit large donations for the

upkeep of the Temple and to leave it to the discretion of the priests to use the money without accounting to the donors. Throughout the centuries many, and in some generations most, of the Jews who lived in the Holy Land were supported by money donated by the pious abroad. In recent times, especially from the seventeenth to the nineteenth centuries, fights broke out repeatedly between the donors and the recipients. Often the donors suspected that much of the money they had given was not even reaching the causes for which it had been collected or was being spent in the Holy Land by friends of those who distributed the alms. Indeed, many sought to be in charge of the money collected abroad and those who attained such power were usually feared and often reviled. Those functionaries who died with clean hands were remembered, and their saintliness became the stuff of legend.

The recipients of funds had power not only over those to whom they distributed the money but even over the donors. Usually in any relationship between those who give and those who collect, it is presumed that the dominant power is in the hands of the donors, but this was almost never true among Jews. The Diaspora that contributed to the upkeep of the Second Temple had been taught by the Bible itself that the priests were in charge of spending the money and that nobody was to check on them. In the Middle Ages few Jews survived the wars between the Crusaders and the Muslims. Those Jews who remained in the Holy Land were regarded as representatives of all the Jewish people. They represented all who remained in mourning for Zion. How could one question these candidates for martyrdom? In more recent centuries the justification given for the Jewish presence in the Holy Land was often overtly messianic. Since every version of Jewish theology called for some foothold in the Holy Land, the presence of Jews there was required in order to serve as the vanguard for receiving the Messiah. Even if one disapproved of how some Jews in the Holy Land were behaving, how could one treat people who were, by definition, a consecrated elite as if they were poor country cousins living off alms?

Modern Zionism inherited this view of the Israel-Diaspora relationship with great eagerness. The founders of the *kibbutzim* were depicted—and they viewed themselves—as the priesthood of the new Jew. In 1921 a bitter and complicated dispute erupted between

Chaim Weizmann and Louis D. Brandeis over the leadership and policy of the World Zionist Organization. The most tangible issue was the control of money. The American Brandeis insisted on absolute accountability; the European Weizmann, who was one of the principal architects of the *Yishuv* in Palestine, fought for the right of the Zionist organization to spend its funds as it wished and to move funds for its various purposes without public explanation. Weizmann's rationale was that a movement engaged in acquiring land for settlement amidst unrelenting battles with the British and the Arabs needed both secrecy and flexibility, but this rationale was not the essence of the matter. A larger issue was at stake. It concerned who would decide Zionist policy. Weizmann came to America and waged and won a bitter campaign against Brandeis. The majority of the American Zionists agreed that those who were in Palestine, or most closely linked to the scene, had the right to decide what to do with Jewish charity funds. Important forces among the Zionists in the Diaspora—and even more among the non-Zionists—refused to accept the dominance of the leaders of the *Yishuv* in the 1930s and 1940s, but theirs was a losing battle. By the time the state was declared and immediately thereafter, David Ben-Gurion was the undisputed leader of world Jewry. He played without hesitancy on the ancient guilt of Jews who did not live in the land of Israel. This total secularist wrapped himself in the mantle of an ancient high priest and decided what was pure and what was impure among Jews.

In the Western Diaspora and especially in the United States, the Zionists produced their own version of the relationship between the Jews in their own land and those who persisted in living on foreign shores. The overwhelming majority of Zionists in America have always refused to accept the notion that America is exile or that American Jews could also become possible candidates for expulsion by anti-Semites. The American Zionists wanted to help the millions of Jews in Europe who were the targets of attack. But what was the difference between Zionists in America and other American Jews who just wanted to rescue their endangered brethren abroad? In the middle years of the century, when the issue of "dual loyalty" was often raised with much bitterness, the following answer was usually given: The Zionists insisted that they were not merely saving refugees. They were helping create a Jewish national state, and they did not view their efforts on behalf of this cause as traducing their Americanism. The deeper truth was that Zionist endeavors became the tool that many American Jews used to preserve their Jewish identity.

This notion was first defined in the 1930s by Mordecai M. Kaplan. At that time it did not appear likely that the British government, which ruled Palestine, would permit the *Yishuv* to create a Jewish state. During those discouraging years Kaplan argued that it did not matter whether the Zionists' purpose would ever be achieved. The very task of working for the creation of the Jewish state would bind American Jews together and preserve their Jewish loyalties. This elegant formulation by an intellectual is really not far removed from a remark I heard many years later from an avowed anti-intellectual among the leading fund-raisers. He said that he did not want to know what Israel was doing with his money. He gave a substantial check every year to assuage his guilt for not being a better Jew in his personal life and in the hope that his giving would be a model for his children, inducing them to make some Jewish commitment.

Israel and the Diaspora are actually divided—and not united—by the central formula of post-state Zionism, which is enshrined in the platform of the World Zionist Organization. Both Israel and the Diaspora assent to the proposition of "the centrality of Israel to Jewish life." Israel interprets this formula to mean that its purposes and needs must predominate in all Jewish agendas everywhere. The Diaspora interprets the Zionist formula to mean that the effort on behalf of Israel is the prime tool for preserving the Diaspora. For Israel, asserting its centrality in Jewish life is a way of reminding the Diaspora that the latter is less than legitimate. In the American Diaspora those people who work on behalf of Israel are the leaders of the organized Jewish community. Their effort is the surest ticket to receptions and dinners at the State Department and the White House.

Pro-Israel endeavor, as seen through Diaspora lenses, seemed to be the way to preserve Jewishness and to increase the dignity of Jews in America. Thus, the cozy marriage between the two communities was based on illusions that each had about the other. Israel believed that American Jews would always accept its authority and follow its lead. American Jews believed that Israel would solve their deepest problem, which was their fear of disappearing. It has become harder to believe in both these illusions in recent years. Israel has been finding out that it no longer commands the Jewish world, as it did in the first twenty-five years of its existence. The Diaspora knows that Israel is not the magic pill that it can use to solve its own internal problems.

Israel's disillusionment with the leaders of the Diaspora, and especially with the Americans, began in the early 1970s. The two parts of the Jewish world clashed over Russian Jewry. The exodus had begun, and the Israeli representatives at all international Jewish forums insisted, with considerable vehemence, that Jewish support should be given only to those Russian Jews who were headed for Israel. The Israelis further argued that the work being done on behalf of Russian Jews inside the Soviet Union should be directed toward preparing them for *aliyah* and that any attempts to help create institutions that would sustain Jewish life in the Soviet Union were futile. In this battle, the Israelis lost. The proportion of immigrants from the Soviet Union who wanted to go to the United States kept increasing, and the American Jewish fund-raising establishment insisted on helping these Soviet Jews find their way to America. The arguments by the leaders of the Diaspora ranged from the assertion that Jews who had chosen to live in America had no right to tell other Jews that they must go to Israel to the reluctant admission that American Jewish organizations, which had long been dealing with refugees, would not now go out of business at the behest of the Israelis.

The next open battle took place in the mid-1980s over the issue of "Who is a Jew?" and that fight still continues today. Israel's religious establishment wanted to amend the law of personal status and to define a Jew as someone who was born of a Jewish mother or is "converted according to the *halachah*." In the Israeli context, this would have meant that the only acceptable conversions would be those performed by Orthodox rabbinic authorities. If this amendment had passed, tens of thousands of converts in the Diaspora who had been admitted to Judaism by Conservative and Reform rabbis would have been declared to be still gentile by the law of Israel's parliament. This proposal aroused open rebellion in American Jewry. More than four-fifths of American Jews are not Orthodox, and the representatives of the Orthodox minority are dominant only in their own national organizations. The non-Orthodox and especially their leaders were not moved by pleas issued from Israel that the religious parties needed to be indulged in order to keep the governing coalition intact. When this battle was joined in the mid-1980s, the rate of intermarriage was sufficiently high—it was already more than one in three—that most families in American Jewry had a close relative who was married to a convert. The leaders of the fund-raising organizations, of the political bodies, and even of the synagogue bodies counted converts among the spouses of their children or of their nephews and nieces who had been admitted by Conservative and Reform rabbis. They could not allow Israel to delegitimize their Conservative and Reform rabbis. The outcry in America, including the overt threat to withhold contributions, was sufficiently loud that the amendment did not pass.

During the 1980s a quiet process that was hardly noticed publicly became at least as important as the overt battles over Russian Jews and "Who is a Jew?" were. The percentage of money going to Israel from central Jewish fund-raising kept dropping. In 1970, at the high point of Israel's reputation in America soon after the Six Day War, nearly two-thirds of these fund-raising dollars were being allocated to Israel; by 1990, the proportion had fallen to not much more than one-third. This change did not represent a conscious decision made by American Jews that Israel was any less important to them. It was more that each community had considerations other than Israel. The local organizations were pushing for more money; local institutions wanted new, more elaborate and elegant buildings; and Israel was getting more and more direct support from Washington. As a result, those who were in charge of dispensing charity funds felt freer to use more of the money at home. Occasionally Israeli representatives would explode in private meetings, maintaining that those who gave to combined fund-raising appeals were moved by concern for Israel and not by local causes, but these people were soon proved wrong. In every American Jewish community, people felt that they needed a retirement home for their aging parents or a Jewish community center for themselves and their children, and they were not reluctant to use substantial proportions of charity funds to help support such institutions.

The most important factor in changing the attitude of the American Diaspora toward Israel was almost never discussed. After 1948,

Jews in the Diaspora thought that the State of Israel had promised them that the children and grandchildren of those who were activists on its behalf would remain Jewish in Topeka, Los Angeles, or Seattle. By the 1980s this had clearly not happened. The rate of intermarriage between Jews and non-Jews in 1948 was less than one out of ten; by 1990, it was approaching six out of ten. This occurred during the four decades in which the American Jewish community performed heroic tasks both in politics and fund-raising in support of Israel. The politics of Israel was also becoming increasingly problematic to the Diaspora. The Likud party was voted into office in 1977 and dominated Israel's politics for the next fifteen years. American Jews, and especially their organizations, tried hard to support Israel's government, but the hearts of the majority of American Jews were not engaged. In every poll that was taken in those years, the majority of the American Jewish community opposed the permanent control of the West Bank by Israel and supported some version of "territorial compromise." This rift was largely kept quiet, but it did surface on occasion, especially when American presidents put pressure on Israel to be more moderate. In 1982, when Ronald Reagan briefly proposed territorial concessions, and again in 1991, when George Bush arranged a conference between Israel and the Arabs in Madrid, some American Jewish leaders and organizations publicly sided with Washington against the foot-dragging by Jerusalem.

The deepest issue between Israel and the Diaspora is generational. In 1948, when the State of Israel was declared, the language of international Jewish gatherings was still Yiddish. Both the leaders of the state and the leaders of the Diaspora had all, almost without exception, been born in East Central or Eastern Europe, and they shared the common culture of their youth. Although Ben-Gurion insisted on speaking only Hebrew and Abba Hillel Silver, an important Zionist leader and a Reform rabbi in Cleveland, was a peerless orator in English, both had spoken Yiddish until they were teenagers and each had received an early education in the classic religious texts. Now, nearly a half century later, Jews have no common language and very little shared Jewish culture. Few American Jews speak and read enough Hebrew to comprehend the culture of contemporary Israel. Many have argued that the lack of Hebrew is unimportant because even semieducated Israelis speak English. This is not true. I am not the only one who has taken part in conversations in Israeli homes that assumed a totally different tone after the last American who spoke only English left. Whatever may be the meaning of the slogan so much favored by activists in the Diaspora that "we are one," it does not include culture.

The dominant cliché since the famous handshake on the White House lawn on September 13, 1993, is that the making of peace between Israel and the Arabs will create a new relationship between Israel and the Diaspora. What this "new relationship" will be no one seems to know, even though some American Jews have already cast themselves in the role of being the catalyst for Israeli-Arab economic connections and transforming Jews and Arabs into friendly neighbors. Although such endeavors will continue and increase, the basic efforts—even the economic ones—will have to be made by the people in the Middle East. American Jewish participation in joint Israeli-Arab investments in Gaza will not transform Diaspora Jewry. What will continue in the next decade or so as Israel works out its new relationship to the Arab world is the usual business of marshaling political support in the United States and of raising money. Israeli leaders of several political persuasions, from Menachem Begin to Yitzhak Rabin, have wanted to believe that Israel's strength in America is based on its importance to American policy and strategic interests and that the American Jewish lobby is not important. The truth that even these leaders have recognized—at least when they were alone—is that Israel is a special case because the American Jewish community has made it so. The political connection between Israel and the Diaspora will continue because it will be necessary to Israel in difficult and changing times.

That charity dollars will continue to be raised by Jews in America for various causes in Israel is equally beyond doubt. In his angry put-down of Yossi Beilin, Prime Minister Rabin insisted that absorbing Russian and Ethiopian Jews and all the other humanitarian tasks that Israel has accepted are not Israel's responsibility alone. He could have added that the Diaspora shares with Israel the concern that its universities, research institutions, and hospitals—as well as its museums and symphony orchestras—remain in the front rank of contemporary culture, thus bringing honor to all Jews as a "wise and perceptive people." But the most important reason to continue American Jewish fund-raising for Israel has not been stated publicly: If the Jews of America stopped giving money to Israel, Congress may have second thoughts about the much larger sums that it is appropriating. As long as Jewish fund-raising is perceived to be centered on Israel and to be strikingly successful, American Jews will be viewed as caring. That caring will exert power in Washington.

Thus, although politics and fund-raising will continue, the fundamental relationship has changed. Israel and the Diaspora had initially thought that each was the solution to the other's problems. Israel expected that the support and man power that it may need would come from the Diaspora. The Diaspora thought the work that it did for Israel would sustain Jewish life in all countries. In the last ten years both sides have been disappointed. The Diaspora knows that Israel cannot solve the problems of Jewish survival, and Jews all over the world and especially in America are no longer united in their uncritical admiration of Israel. Opinions are divided over the difficult political decisions that Israel will have to make about the future nature of the state. For many Jews these embittered quarrels are an embarrassment. The clustering of the Diaspora around Israel no longer resembles the bustle of the heady years after the Six Day War in 1967. Then it was like a family gathering held to admire a close cousin who had just received a Nobel Prize. Now Israel has become a problem that all the relatives must help solve.

On the Israeli side there is now little illusion that the Jews of the Western Diaspora, the richest and best educated, will ever come en masse to Israel. At the very height of its prestige, in the late 1960s and early 1970s, between the Six Day War of 1967 and the Yom Kippur War of 1973, a few thousand people, no more, annually went to Israel from America. A large proportion of those who did go were from that small minority of American Jews who were zealots on behalf of the cause of the "undivided land of Israel." Regrets were being expressed more than twenty years ago when Rabbi Meir Kahane first moved to Israel that this immigration was not the one for which the country longed. Israel was disappointed with American Jews. The latter had always been regarded as deficient in their attachment to true Zionist ideology. What disappointed Israel more was that well-off and well-educated Western Jews from South Africa who were on the run from social disturbance and were fearful of anti-Semitism were not going to Israel. As the racial turmoil in South Africa increased in the 1980s and the end of white rule became more certain, South African Jews began to leave the country. This community had always been very Zionist, with a pronounced tendency toward the right-wing ideology of the Likud. Nonetheless, few of the South Africans who left went to Israel. The large majority preferred to immigrate to the United States, Canada, and Australia. Anger has been rising in Israel in recent years that the Diaspora sends hard cases—those who are the most difficult to absorb, like Kahane followers from Brooklyn or premodern Ethiopian Jews—to Israel, but those who can navigate in the twentieth century go elsewhere. Because Israel's deepest fear is that a population of four or five million Jews will become isolated among many tens of millions of Arabs, it feels that the Diaspora has let it down.

These problems of Israel are not the central concern of the American Diaspora. Its internal agenda is headed by a new buzz-word, "Jewish continuity." Some observers knew many years ago that the tide of assimilation was rising. In an essay that was published in 1963 when the rate of intermarriage was less than one out of ten, I predicted on the basis of evidence that was already available that intermarriage would rise to at least one out of three within the next twenty years. The sociologist and historian Charles Liebman soon came to the same conclusion. Nonetheless, the American Jewish community persisted in ignoring such Cassandras. It preferred to believe the sociologist Charles Goldscheider and the writer Charles Silverman who stated that a stable unprecedented American Judaism had evolved. This American Judaism had a secure future and thus "all was for the best in the best of all possible worlds." The shock came with the publication of the results of a major population study conducted in 1990 on behalf of the Conference of Jewish Welfare Funds. The greatest single shock produced by that study was that intermarriage had risen to one out of two. Almost equally upsetting was the discovery that there were only four and one-half million fully identified Jews in America, and that there was a large penumbra of at least three and one-half million who had some Jewish memories or biological connections but were in various stages of leaving the community.

Since the study had been commissioned by the most central

agency of the Jewish community, it could not be ignored. Every national convention that has been held in the last several years has given the question of "Jewish continuity" a prominent place in its deliberations. Many suggestions have been debated. The consensus seems to be that more Jewish education and more exposure of the young to Israel through a year abroad during high school or college will raise the level of Jewish commitment. Others are talking of an expanded network of Jewish day schools and, more nebulously, of a national effort to "strengthen the Jewishness of the Jewish family." No one has suggested the one answer that Israel continues to give unhesitatingly: If American Jews want to preserve their Jewishness, they should move to Israel.

The attention of American Jews is shifting toward themselves in the political realm as well. More anxiously than at any other time in the last generation, they are thinking of their future in the United States. American society has passed a watershed. Early in the next century white Europeans will cease to be the majority and will become one of many minorities in this, the most multiethnic of countries. Jews will have to work out their relationship not, as before, to a majority consisting of white Christians and a deprived minority of African Americans but to Hispanics and a number of Asian communities. This will not be an easy process because Jews have no important ancient connections with any of these newer immigrant groups. The American Jewish community of the next century will make up an ever smaller percentage of the population of the whole—it is now a little more than 2 percent—and will have to come to terms with the new arrivals and especially their children, who will demand greater roles in the economy and the society as a whole. The immediate battles today with a few white and black anti-Semites are much less important than the greater problems of living in the future with the many new American groups. No one has suggested that American Jews ought to choose to put their future troubles into one basket and join the Israelis, whose only problem is the Arabs.

Although both Israel and the American Diaspora will increasingly focus on themselves in the years ahead, their drifting apart will be checked, at least to some degree, by several countertendencies. Despite the fact that the dreams of vast new cooperative economic enterprises after peace comes are too rosy, American Jewish investment in Israel will increase. A larger economic involvement will require investors to make frequent visits to Israel. American executives and experts who will most likely be Jews will be stationed in the offices of the new enterprises in Israel. New concern for the Jewishness of the Diaspora will provide another connection. Increasingly discussions are evoking the conviction that Jewish culture in any formulation is inconceivable without the knowledge of Hebrew and classic Jewish texts. Such ideas will persuade some people in the Diaspora that the best way to learn Hebrew and texts in the Hebrew language is to spend some time in Israel, for it is the only country in the world in which Hebrew is the language of everyday life.

Cultural and religious connections between Israel and the American Diaspora will undoubtedly increase precisely because culture and religion are the main elements of the two communities' shared Jewishness. But deep political and societal tides will continue to push the two apart. The generational clock keeps ticking as Israelis and American Jews become evermore distant cousins. In the years ahead Israel will work to integrate itself into the Middle East, while American Jews will look for ways to live in the new America. In the past Jewish unity has been sustained by religion and culture, but that happened only in times of belief. We do not know if Jewish unity can be achieved in a secular age. However, we do know that Israel and the Diaspora will not willingly let go of each other and that most Jews everywhere want to continue somehow to be Jewish.

· V ·

CHESHBON
HANEFESH

Reform:
A Critical
Self-Examination

The Union of American Hebrew Congregations was founded in 1873. It has now reached the age limit, 120 years, our Torah sets as a life span for human beings. It is the age at which Moses, "his eyes undimmed and his vigor unabated," died in the land of Moab. We begin a new cycle of life, and I deem it altogether fitting and proper that we mark this birth-hour of the renewed life by choosing a new name.

But what's wrong with our present name? It has served us so well for so many years. So why discard it?

To begin with, the name Union of American Hebrew Congregations is nonreferential: It does not describe who we are and what we are about. And so in our publications and releases and even on our letterheads, we always have to add all sorts of qualifying phrases to identify ourselves and what we do.

Furthermore, elements of our present name are anachronistic. The word *Hebrew* was imposed on us from the outside by anti-Semitic Church Fathers who were eager to proclaim their religious roots in the spiritual legacy of the Hebrew prophets, even while they distanced themselves from the much reviled Jews who lived around them.

Alas, most of our co-religionists of the nineteenth century accepted this invidious distinction and adorned their institutions with the name *Hebrew*, while the word *Jew* was cautiously avoided.

Last, and this is most important to me, the word *Reform* does not appear in our institutional name, and yet it is precisely this adjective that defines our essence and has made us the religion of choice for American Jewry.

Let us, therefore, go about the task of choosing a new name. We should no longer allow our prophets to be separated from our people; we should no longer accept a name rooted in nonacceptance.

We are Jews whose community is a *union* of *Jewish* congregations committed to reform. That new name should ring out with a clarity of purpose. Let us henceforth be known for what we are and what we intend to be.

Rabbi Alexander M. Schindler
State of the Union Message
San Francisco, California
October 23, 1995

INTERTWINING YESTERDAY, TODAY, AND TOMORROW THE UNION OF AMERICAN HEBREW CONGREGATIONS

JANE EVANS

The first General Convention of the Union of American Hebrew Congregations (UAHC), held on July 8–10, 1873, in Cincinnati, Ohio, included representatives from twenty-eight temples. The smallest of these had fourteen members; the three largest were Bene Israel of Cincinnati with 185, Bene Yeshurun of Cincinnati with 200, and Adas Israel of Louisville, Kentucky, also with 200. There were delegates from congregations in Arkansas, Illinois, Indiana, Kentucky, Louisiana, Mississippi, Ohio, Tennessee, Texas, and West Virginia. The delegates who attended were encouraged by the fact that a few congregations who could not send representatives expressed their eagerness to be included in the convention.

An important resolution adopted at this first convention called for all Hebrew congregations in every part of the United States and its territories to be invited to join the "Union of American Hebrew Congregations." That name was chosen by Rabbi Isaac Mayer Wise, who strongly desired and believed that all of American Jewry might ultimately join under such a title. Some have claimed that Wise used the word *Hebrew* because the word *Jewish* might arouse anti-Semitism.

Another resolution stated that whenever a law is drawn up for the establishment and government of the Hebrew Theological College under this Union, "it shall give the right of membership and participation in its government to Israelites or Hebrew societies [laypeople] as such who are desirous of contributing under the rules and regulations of the Council." Although these proceedings seemingly were handled entirely by laypersons, including Mr. Julius Freiberg and Mr. Moritz Loth of Cincinnati, Rabbi Isaac Mayer Wise of Bene Yeshurun was the moving spirit and the founder who gave birth to the Union and, in 1875, to the Hebrew Union College (HUC).

One hundred years later, in April 1973, the American Jewish Archives published a centennial portrait of the UAHC, stressing that the East Coast Jews, most of whom were members of the Board of Delegates of American Israelites, at first had nothing to do with Rabbi Wise and his Union. The Board of Delegates of American Israelites, patterned on a similar organization of British Jewry, was a coordinating voice for national and international concerns of both secular and religious Jewry. Through Rabbi Wise's perseverance, the Board amalgamated with the Union, thus making the UAHC fully national. As a result, the concerns of the Board of Delegates in civil libertarian and political defense activities in the United States and abroad added to issues that interested the Union.

In 1903, three years after Wise's death, the Union's first full-time executive was chosen to head its Department of Synagogue and School Extension: Rabbi George Zepin, who would become a master craftsman in building the UAHC.

He was mild in manner, brilliant in organizational concepts, and convinced that while the laity should take full credit, most speeches and reports should be written for them by the staff. Eventually, Zepin became the top executive of the Union and added a handful of gifted rabbis and laypersons to the Union's small professional staff. One of these, who became Zepin's close confidant, was

Rabbi Louis I. Egelson, a graduate of the Jewish Theological Seminary in New York.

It was Zepin who conceived the idea of organizing the women in congregations into the first major agency of the Union. For that purpose he asked Carrie Simon, the wife of Rabbi Abram Simon of Washington, D.C., to organize the National Federation of Temple Sisterhoods (NFTS), and she was elected to serve as its first president. (In 1993, its name was changed to Women of Reform Judaism, the Federation of Temple Sisterhoods.) However, at its organizing convention in 1913, all the major addresses were given by men. The influence of Zepin remained significant in NFTS's early years during which he was its chief executive, in addition to his other duties.

This first agency of the Union was followed in a decade by the National Federation of Temple Brotherhoods (NFTB) and, in ensuing years, by other Union affiliates, which have added to the strength and influence of the Reform movement. In 1926, with the establishment of the World Union for Progressive Judaism (WUPJ), which included the UAHC, the Reform movement became truly international, with WUPJ headquarters first in England, later in the United States, and now in Jerusalem.

Immediately after its organization, NFTS dedicated itself to serving the Hebrew Union College through student scholarships. The difficulty presented by students who had to board with families in the community troubled the NFTS. Therefore, at a cost of $345,000, it built and furnished the first dormitory on the campus in Cincinnati.

It should be noted also that in 1931 NFTS helped bring into being the Jewish Braille Institute of America. The total budget of the Jewish Braille Institute, modest as it was in the beginning, was included in the NFTS budget just as the total budget of Hebrew Union College, in its early years, was included in that of the UAHC. Today NFTS richly contributes to the Jewish Braille Institute, and half the Union Maintenance of Membership (MUM) dues from congregations are forwarded to the College-Institute.

Classical Reform passionately felt itself centered in the United States although its preliminary steps had been taken in Germany. It tended to separate itself from those who longed for a physical return to Zion. While some might argue that the anti-Zionist stance limited the growth of the Reform movement, a number of its rabbis, notably Rabbi Stephen S. Wise, championed Zionism. In 1922 Stephen Wise, troubled by Reform's anti-Zionism and what he interpreted as the conservatism of Hebrew Union College, founded the Jewish Institute of Religion (JIR). (In 1950 the Jewish Institute of Religion merged with the Hebrew Union College [HUC-JIR].) The birth of the State of Israel saw Reform's anti-Zionist position undergo marked change and reversal. The American Council for Judaism, the controversial anti-Zionist adherent of classical Reform Judaism, faded into near oblivion.

In building the professional staff of the UAHC, George Zepin asked Dr. Emanuel Gamoran to leave New York to become the Union's director of the Department of Education. Still at Columbia University and planning to marry and take his bride for a year of further study and travel in Europe and Palestine, Gamoran at first refused. An additional consideration was Gamoran's conviction that enhancing the Reform Sunday schools would be inadequate to educate a Jewish child properly. However, Gamoran eventually accepted the position and built for the Union a truly strong education department, which under his successors played a role in the development of after-school classes on weekdays and Reform Jewish day schools.

Another development under Zepin was the appointment of regional rabbis and more importantly what might be called "circuit-riding rabbis." These rabbis went from Cincinnati into isolated and distant Jewish communities that lacked Jewish congregations and religious schools. Walking along the main street looking for Jewish names on stores, they introduced themselves, drew Jewish people to meetings, and started Jewish schools in private homes, often leading to the founding of congregations.

Beginning in the thirties there were times when, as director of NFTS, I personally followed this recruitment pattern. As a result, there was a period when there were more sisterhoods in the National Federation of Temple Sisterhoods than there were congregations in the Union. Today there are a couple of hundred more congregations than sisterhoods. This change has occurred in part because many rabbis wanted their congregations to operate as a community of men, women, and young people rather than as a coalition of groups separated by gender, age, or financial obligations to a distant center. There may be a new attitude today as the women's movement has reestablished the need for "sister" relationships.

It would be unfair to speak of George Zepin without reference to the loyalty he displayed to each member of his professional staff. One day an important constituent unexpectedly walked into the office of an unmarried Union staff rabbi and, finding him embracing, by mutual consent, a non-Jewish secretary, demanded the rabbi's immediate dismissal. Despite Zepin's very strong objections, the punitive action was carried out. However, Rabbi Zepin continued to insist on a reversal of the decision and, although it took more than a year, finally won the reinstatement.

Having mentioned this incident, I must add a personal note. After joining the staff, Rabbi Zepin consistently offered me the most courteous assistance, warmth, and friendship. However, I knew that prior to my acceptance when he interviewed me in the home of the then NFTS president, the late Martha Steinfeld of St. Louis, he warned her against employing me on the grounds that he thought I had too strong a personality and might be more in the forefront than quietly behind the leaders.

At the 1941 UAHC General Assembly George Zepin's career plummeted. In a speech, "While the Union Slept," Rabbi Louis Mann of Chicago's Sinai Temple denounced the program of the Union, charging that other agencies had appropriated many activities once solely under UAHC auspices. Zepin sat quietly in a front row of the conference hall. Many of us who loved and respected him felt heartsick. Much later, when one read the text of Rabbi Mann's speech, it seemed less harsh; it had probably been "toned down." Following that assembly George Zepin retired, but he maintained an office in the headquarters in the Merchants Building in downtown Cincinnati and, as a volunteer, continued to serve unselfishly and with dedication. For several years after his retirement he continued his work on the development of a pension plan for all UAHC employees.

After Zepin, the Union briefly had two other dynamic rabbis as leaders: Dr. Nelson Glueck, who would become president of the Hebrew Union College, and Rabbi Edward Israel of Baltimore, Maryland. During World War II, Dr. Glueck served in various strategic services for the United States government in the Near East.

Because his government duties interfered with his ability to direct the Union, Dr. Glueck resigned the Union position, but he later served for many years as the greatly admired president of the College-Institute. He was succeeded at the Union by Rabbi Israel, who tragically suffered a fatal heart attack as he stood up to speak at his very first meeting with the Union Board in Cincinnati.

The new chief executive of the Union was Rabbi Maurice N. Eisendrath, the rabbi at Holy Blossom Temple in Toronto and the leader of Canadian Jewry. When he first came to the Union his title was executive director, but he chafed under it. He believed that since the title of the professional head of the College was "president," his title should also be president to give his position equal status. This was granted by the Union's Board of Trustees. The lay president, Adolph Rosenberg, then assumed the title of chairman of the Board of Trustees.

The title of a recent biography of Maurice Eisendrath by Rabbi Avi M. Schulman, *Like a Raging Fire* (New York: UAHC Press, 1993), correctly describes a man who was indeed one of the most influential rabbis of this century and a totally committed leader of the Reform congregational movement. Eisendrath was a brilliant orator and political analyst and theorist, as well as a vociferous commentator on Jewish, national, and international issues. His fearless and sometimes pugnacious stands on controversial issues antagonized a number of congregational members, but in the end, his opponents either accepted his views or tolerated them.

To the strong foundations of the Union that Zepin had laid in many departments of service to congregations, Eisendrath not only added new ones but also recruited a larger professional staff to head them. Eisendrath, who was particularly concerned with social justice, steadfastly supported the UAHC Religious Action Center (RAC), developed in Washington, D.C., during his tenure. He stood firm and unafraid when some large congregations threatened to sever their membership, while others temporarily did, in protest against the Union's stance on national or international issues that they considered controversial and beyond the Union's responsibility. Today the Religious Action Center and the Commission on Social Action of Reform Judaism, which involve the Union, many of its affiliates, the Central Conference of American Rabbis (CCAR), and HUC-JIR, are among the Reform movement's most respected instruments for translating Judaic ethics into social action.

Eisendrath faced the issues of his time, including the Holocaust, the Vietnam War, nuclear disarmament, and civil rights, with courage and determination. He accepted on behalf of Reform Jewry a position of leadership in the American Jewish Conference, despite the opposition of a number of influential Reform congregational leaders who regarded the Conference as largely Zionist. He saw the need for a Jewish homeland for those who deeply desired it and too often had no other place to rest their hope. Although not in a full sense a pacifist, Eisendrath recognized early the need for the United States to extricate itself from the war in southeast Asia.

As early as 1960 he thought an organization was needed to raise the voice of all religions toward solutions on critical issues of international relations. A liberal Christian minister in New England, Dana McLean Greeley, came to a similar conclusion and in January 1969, in Istanbul, under the impetus of Dr. Homer Jack, fifteen persons gathered from Japan, India, and the United States to form a new interreligious body. At its first assembly in Kyoto, Japan, in 1970, Greeley and Eisendrath became presidents of the World Conference on Religion and Peace (WCRP). Through the years WCRP has continued to grow, seeking sanity and conflict resolution in the midst of the turbulences of this century.

The Union of American Hebrew Congregations had expanded its youth movement through the development of camps. While the movement for young people had begun years before, in part stimulated by Jean Wise May, a daughter of Isaac Mayer Wise, its growth intensified under Eisendrath. Today the Union supports nine Camp Institutes throughout the United States, serving not only youth but congregational members as well.

In 1973 Maurice Eisendrath died of a sudden heart attack in New York City at the UAHC General Assembly. He collapsed in his hotel room before he was to deliver his presidential address at his last Shabbat service before retirement. His chosen successor, Rabbi Alexander Schindler, read Eisendrath's message to the shocked thousands waiting to hear their leader's farewell message.

Rabbi Schindler was one of the gifted rabbis that Eisendrath over the years had added to the Union's staff, first as a regional rabbi in New England and then as the director of the Department of Jewish

Education in the New York headquarters. The son of a distinguished Yiddish poet and a remarkable businesswoman, Schindler was born in Germany from where the family escaped during the Nazi years. In World War II he was a decorated ski trooper in the United States Army. Having been ordained in 1953 in Cincinnati by the Hebrew Union College-Jewish Institute of Religion, he fulfilled his first rabbinic position at Temple Emanu-El in Worcester, Massachusetts.

Schindler combined Judaic scholarship and sensitivity with organizational skills and broad vision. Whereas often there had been a love-hate relationship between UAHC President Eisendrath and HUC-JIR President Nelson Glueck, there was now to be a period of calm and cooperation between Schindler and his HUC-JIR counterpart, Rabbi Dr. Alfred Gottschalk, a fellow German survivor of the Holocaust. Whereas Eisendrath developed a relationship with some of his staff that led, on his part, to a feeling of betrayal if they chose to leave the Union for another post—especially if they went to the College-Institute—Schindler was more gracious in seeing personnel advancement, even if the Union lost a staff member.

Rabbi Schindler not only continued to foster the necessary development of the ever-expanding Union of American Hebrew Congregations but also raised to a far greater degree than did his predecessors the voice of the Reform movement in Israeli affairs. Perhaps out of his broad background and the years of earlier service in the Reform movement, Schindler brought to the movement a broad vision. Furthermore, he became chairman of the Conference of Presidents of Major Jewish Organizations and a deservedly respected advisor to prime ministers and other leaders of Israel, whether or not he and they were in agreement. *Time* magazine has called Alexander Schindler "the most prominent spokesman for America's disparate Jewish groups." Certainly under his dynamic and creative leadership Reform Judaism has indeed become one of the fastest growing and most influential forces in American religious life.

Sensitive to the need of the World Union for Progresive Judaism to expand its programs despite urgent financial limitations, he was consistent in giving the World Union monetary support and welcomed its recent advances through its North American Board and the presidency of Donald S. Day, a former chairman of the Union's Board of Trustees.

One of Schindler's significant contributions has been the Outreach program, calling on religiously nonidentified Americans to choose Judaism. In doing so he reversed a 500-year-old tradition that discouraged converts to Judaism. He believes that Reform should welcome non-Jewish spouses into the Jewish community and that a child born of a Jewish father and non-Jewish mother, when reared as a Jew, should have equal status with and acceptance as any child born of a Jewish mother. In other words, he has proposed equating patrilineal descent with matrilineal descent. Eisendrath, without using the term *outreach* or recognizing patrilineal descent, had also called for approaching non-Jews for possible conversion, but it was Schindler who championed the outreach idea and created the institutional apparatus to implement it across the continent.

While Reform from the days of Isaac Mayer Wise advocated equal status for men and women in Jewish religious life, this idea had not been actualized. Major progress was not achieved until the early 1970s when the Hebrew Union College-Jewish Institute of Religion began ordaining women as rabbis and investing women as cantors. Obviously, Dr. Gottschalk, the College-Institute, and the Central Conference of American Rabbis deserve much credit in this advancement of women. Furthermore, ever-increasing numbers of women have been elected as presidents and other officers of congregations, as well as to the boards of the Union and its affiliates. Schindler has consistently sought to overcome inequality based on gender.

For his services to the Jewish people, Rabbi Schindler was awarded the Bublik Prize of the Hebrew University in Jerusalem, an honor he shares with David Ben-Gurion, Harry S. Truman, and a limited number of other prominent world leaders.

Alex Schindler is an officer of many of the major world Jewish organizations: a vice president of the World Jewish Congress, a member of the Governing Board of the Jewish Agency, secretary of the Joint Distribution Committee, a vice president of the Memorial Foundation for Jewish Culture, and a former president of the Federation of Polish Jews. He also is the recipient of honorary degrees from several American colleges and universities, and in Israel half a million trees have been planted in the Schindler Forest of the Jewish National Fund.

Under Schindler, the Reform movement expanded its departments and affiliates, including the Association of Reform Zionists of America (ARZA) and, more recently, the Progressive Association of Reform Day Schools (PARDeS).

However, with this growth comes possible dangers. In the early days, the executive staff of the Union met once a week around a lunch table for eight or ten in a downtown Cincinnati restaurant. Understandably, today the executive staff of the Union, which includes many more professionals—generally acknowledged to be among the finest in agencies of the Jewish and non-Jewish communities—takes a large conference room, not one table in a restaurant. With so many departments and affiliates of the Union, there is bound to be some overlapping of activity—however much the different boards seek to avoid it—and a sensitivity to what might be called their turf by the professionals. Years ago the Union organized the United States and its Canadian Council into regions to draw members and congregations closer together and, in turn, closer to the Union. There is, however, the danger that constantly growing regions, with their individual concerns, may be in competition with the national office in developing their own interpretations and emphases on programs. Recently the Union's North American Federation of Temple Youth has undertaken a major conceptual shift that, while possibly negative in the short term, has set the stage for new growth and vitality. This shift does away with regional acronyms for different branches because the youth board recognizes that emphasis on the regional name has kept the vast majority of its members from understanding or appreciating the larger true nature of the national organization of which they are a part. One wonders if the young people of the movement have more quickly than the Union seen a danger and moved to overcome it.

In the early days of the American rabbinate, there was little, if any, freedom of the pulpit. Rabbis were considered employees of a congregation, expected to have their sermons limited either to the portion of the week or a similarly appropriate "religious" subject sans any emphasis on current political or social events. Isaac Mayer Wise during the agony of the Civil War never once spoke from the pulpit on that subject. Fortunately, today in Reform congregations there is total freedom of the pulpit. But in an age in which many of our members are seeking answers to the loneliness, the perplexity, and personal and societal crises that face them, there may be those who wish the pulpit, while free, to be more concerned with theology and spiritual matters. It is true that Jewish theology has not been as dominant a factor in Jewish thought as theology has been in the thought of its daughter religion, Christianity. Yet in the future, there is a need for balance between the current and the eternal. And Rabbi Schindler's insistence that spirituality be a part not only of UAHC concern but also a necessity of action and study among the members, leadership, and congregations adds another deep dimension to the Reform movement.

The statistics of intermarriage, the low number of Jewish children being educated Jewishly, and the attitudes of college students are issues that both challenge and depress. However, one dares to believe that more intensive emphasis on a well-rounded educational program from earliest childhood through every stage of life, a plan to which the Union and Rabbi Schindler are dedicated, should increasingly prove of value. The history of the Jewish people, through its thousands of years of existence, has known periods of abject misery and experiences that could lead seemingly to total loss. But God, Israel, and Torah always survive. A strongly growing Reform movement, willing to recognize and face dangers, will surely advance to overcome them and to strengthen hope, the eternal perspective of the Jewish people.

We Jews, whatever the label that defines us, are profoundly aware of our essential unity as a people. We share a common faith and fate. When one Jew is hurt, we all are hurt. When one Jew bleeds, all Jews bleed.

And when this happens, there is precious little that we can say to offer comfort. But there is something we can do, and that is to resolve to act as members of one family should.

As we are kindred in death, so must we be kindred in life. Wherever there is a Jewish community that is embattled, our help will be forthcoming. Wherever there is a single Jew in danger, in whatever country or continent or the remotest corner of our far-flung world, there will we find him, there will we reach out to him, offering our hand, our heart, our life. Never more will it be said that we had eyes but did not see, that we had ears but did not hear, that we had mouths but failed to speak.

Aye, we are one and indivisible. Our life forever demands involvement with a larger fate—the fate of this people Israel.

We may have words that designate us in our divergence—a geographic divergence: Latin American Jews, North American Jews, Australian Jews, European Jews....There is also an ideological divergence: Orthodox, Conservative, Reform, Zionist, nationalist, Yiddishist....But all of these words are only adjectives. They are not nouns. The noun is Jew: *Vos mir zenen zenen mir ober Yiden zenen mir,* "Whatever we may be, we may be, but this above all, we are Jews!"

Rabbi Alexander M. Schindler
Address to the Conference of Latin
American Jews
Mexico City, Mexico
November 8, 1994

FROM CINCINNATI
TO NEW YORK
A SYMBOLIC MOVE

MICHAEL A. MEYER

When Rabbi Alexander Schindler left the directorship of the New England Council of the Union of American Hebrew Congregations (UAHC) in 1963 to assume his new position as director of the Department of Education, he came to New York, where the headquarters of the Union had already been located for more than a decade. The expansive character of his presidency of the UAHC and his major role in Jewish affairs nationally and worldwide would scarcely have been conceivable had he moved instead to Cincinnati. Yet whether the spirit of Reform and the spirit of New York could ever mix was once a deeply disputed matter, and the final decision to move from the midwestern cradle of the movement to the teeming eastern metropolis was not easily made. It provoked a crisis without parallel in the history of Reform, whose full story remains to be told.

That the Union of American Hebrew Congregations should be headquartered in Cincinnati was never in doubt during its earliest days. Moritz Loth, the president of Cincinnati's Bene Yeshurun Congregation, in conjunction with other Cincinnati congregations, had convened the initial conference in Cincinnati in 1873, largely upon the prompting of the rabbi of that synagogue, Isaac Mayer Wise. Moreover, since the Union's chief task was to support the Hebrew Union College, which it had established in 1875 and was headed by Wise, it seemed obvious that the Union should be in the same city with the College. For its limited purposes the Union required only rented office space downtown. By the 1940s the Union still was lodged on a floor and a half of the Merchants Building on Sixth Street, its staff ensconced in cubbyhole-like offices that were described by contemporaries as most closely resembling rabbits' warrens. Although its activities expanded over the decades, especially in the area of education, the UAHC during World War II was still very much in the shadow of its creation, the Hebrew Union College, which enjoyed a stately campus to the north, near the University of Cincinnati.

In the 1850s Cincinnati had truly been the "Queen City of the West," the largest metropolis west of the Alleghenies. Riverboat traffic along the Ohio made it a bustling commercial center. The Jewish community was growing rapidly. Bene Yeshurun around 1860 was the second largest Jewish congregation in the United States.[1] From Cincinnati, Wise issued his weekly Jewish newspaper, *The Israelite* (later known as the *American Israelite*), which served to unite scattered Jewish communities large and small. But with the massive influx of Eastern European Jews beginning in the 1880s, the Jewish community in New York, already the largest in the United States, became even more significant. By World War II it was clearly dominant, harboring more Jews than all the rest of the United States combined and also serving as the home of nearly all major national Jewish organizations. Cincinnati, once at the center, began to look peripheral.

As early as the first years of the twentieth century, the prominent German Jewish financier Jacob Schiff, a member of New York's Congregation Emanu-El and of the Executive Board of the UAHC from 1899 until his death in 1920, had proposed that both the College and the Union move to New York City. Later the New York metal magnate Ludwig Vogelstein, who headed the Executive Board from 1925 to 1934, had likewise toyed with the idea of moving the Union eastward. But nothing came of these early proposals.[2] Then, in 1941, Rabbi Edward Israel replaced Rabbi George Zepin as the top staff member of the UAHC. At his first Executive Board meeting, on October 19, a specially appointed committee, chaired by Robert P. Goldman of Cincinnati, presented its recommendation that the executive director be authorized to open an office in Washington, D.C. The minutes then record: "In the discussion that followed, Rabbi Israel, who was speaking to the recommendation, suffered a heart attack and passed away immediately."[3] However, this event did not reduce the pressure for moving, gradually or swiftly, to an eastern city. Rabbi Israel, who had occupied a pulpit in Baltimore, had preferred Washington. His successor (after a brief interim during which the biblical archaeologist and HUC professor Nelson Glueck was at least in name the director), Rabbi Maurice Eisendrath, would use his influence to bring the Union to New York.[4]

When Maurice Eisendrath gave up his pulpit in Toronto and traveled to Cincinnati to take over as chief executive of the UAHC in 1943, a major expansion plan was already underway. The National Federation of Temple Sisterhoods (NFTS), which had built the dormitory on the Hebrew Union College campus in the 1930s, was determined now to do its share for the UAHC. In 1941 it launched its "Victory Project," a major money-raising effort that invested its funds in Liberty Bonds with the intention of cashing them for a beneficial purpose after the Allied victory. Conceived by Jane Evans, the executive director of NFTS, and officially proposed by its president, Gertrude Waters, at the Biennial that year in Detroit, this project originally bore the title "Book of Living Judaism." Donors would have the names of loved ones duly inscribed in such a book. At a future time the funds would be used to erect a building. No one assumed it would be located anywhere but in Cincinnati.

Once the war was over, the revitalized project assumed a new name, proposed by then NFTS president Frieda Rosett. No longer was the stated object a book but it was a *"House* of Living Judaism." Sisterhood members all over the country were urged to contribute at least ten dollars for the "erection on the campus of the Hebrew Union College" of this "House" and also for "the provision of suitable metropolitan quarters in New York City."[5] Not until 1947, after about $75,000 had already been collected, did NFTS change the plan to specify that the House of Living Judaism would be built in New York.

For a time it seemed that it would be relatively easy to bring the Union uptown from its unpleasant quarters among diamond merchants and similar commercial enterprises on Sixth Street in Cincinnati. The Bernheim Library building, the first library of the Hebrew Union College, stood vacant after a second one had been built in 1931. As late as 1944 it was envisioned that, at slight expense, the Bernheim Library could be refurbished and serve as the headquarters of the UAHC, right on the HUC campus. But three years later that option was abandoned as the same building had by then become the home of the newly established American Jewish Archives.

Meanwhile, Maurice Eisendrath, who later claimed initial ambivalence regarding a move to what he then considered "the somewhat too tempestuous maelstrom of New York,"[6] had come out firmly in favor of not merely expanding the regional office that had earlier been established in New York but of moving himself and his staff there, leaving Cincinnati with only a regional office. And by 1946 he was in a much better position to push for his proposal. With the death of the UAHC president, Cincinnatian Adolph Rosenberg, late in 1946, Eisendrath immediately had himself elected the new president, the first time that either a paid employee or a rabbi held that position. The top lay leader was now Jacob Aronson of New York, who served as "Chairman of the Board." Eisendrath had also begun to expand the Union, taking advantage of the favorable circumstances that the postwar years afforded to organized religion. His dynamic style of leadership, a novum within the Union's top leadership, was beginning to pay dividends and to strengthen his hand.

A "Committee for the Removal of Headquarters of the Union" (later called the "Committee on Future Headquarters of the UAHC"), chaired in succession by two prominent and amenable Cincinnatians, Jacob W. Mack and Philip Meyers, now came into existence. On April 26, 1947, Mack reported the committee's favorable recommendation to the Executive Board. The Board at that time had fourteen members from Cincinnati, all of whom were present at the meeting, along with about twenty-five non-Cincinnatians. What exactly transpired at that meeting, held in Cincinnati, is not recorded. We know, however, that Rabbi James Heller of Isaac Mayer Wise Temple expressed serious reservations. It seems also that at least seven other members of the Executive Board were likewise opposed, although they did not express their opinions. It is not clear whether an initial vote was taken. It was widely reported that the vote was unanimous, but this vote was apparently only on a motion to make the recommendation unanimous in view of the fact that the final decision would be made, not by the Board, but by the forthcoming Union Biennial Assembly.

What the Board decided was to "recommend to the next General Assembly that the executive headquarters of the Union be removed to New York, retaining in Cincinnati, either permanently or at least for the immediate future, such departments of the Union as may more efficiently and economically be operated there, including a regional office in Cincinnati."[7]

In the eyes of some leading Cincinnati Jews—but not Cincinnati Jews alone—this recommendation was a declaration of war. In the succeeding months up until the final vote was cast at the Biennial on November 16, 1948, opposing camps gradually emerged, and verbal missiles were soon fired from both sides. The tension escalated to its highest level in October and early November. Rabbi Solomon Freehof of Pittsburgh spoke of a tempest that had turned into an "emotional tornado"; Cleveland's Rabbi Barnett Brickner of "six months nearly verging on hysteria"; NFTS's Jane Evans of "passion of almost unbelievable proportions."[8]

Maurice Eisendrath led the charge for his side in the dispute, repeatedly using the pages of the Union's periodical, *Liberal Judaism*, as his sounding board. With great skill he combined practical and ideological arguments. Reform Judaism, he noted, had fallen behind on the East Coast. Already in 1944 he had called attention to the fact that less than a fifth of the Reform constituency was located in New York, only 12,000 UAHC membership units in a city of two and a half million Jews. The Union was not deriving nearly the revenue that it should from the great metropolis. As a result, he was spending more and more of his time there, in part to expand the movement where its weakness was most evident. If he and his staff were domiciled in New York, he was sure, the efforts would more easily be crowned with success.

Eisendrath offered Cincinnati Jewry a double consolation: a regional office, which would always remain there, and the assurance that "the Hebrew Union College will continue to grace that fair city with its stately buildings and gracious campus, with its erudite faculty—now headed by our eminent colleague and cherished friend, Dr. Nelson Glueck."[9] There was some dissembling in both statements: Eisendrath did not keep the first promise, soon moving the regional office to Cleveland; and Glueck was more his respected rival than his cherished friend. The archaeologist's selection as president of HUC in 1947 was, nonetheless, quite relevant. Like

Eisendrath, Glueck represented a new expansionist style of leadership. He was determined that the College would grow, initially by merger with the Jewish Institute of Religion in New York, then through the construction of new buildings in Cincinnati. It was apparent that the two men would soon be at each other's throats over financial support from the Reform constituency. In the Queen City, the College, and therefore native son Nelson Glueck, would enjoy primacy. In New York, Eisendrath would be in no one's shadow as the spokesman of Reform Judaism to the Jewish and non-Jewish worlds. Cincinnati was not big enough for both of them.

But beyond these practical and personal considerations lay an ideological argument. Eisendrath wanted to bring the Reform movement into what he considered the mainstream of American Judaism. The major national Jewish organizations were headquartered in New York, as were a number of Protestant denominations. In the years between the Holocaust and the creation of the State of Israel, New York was indisputably the capital of world Jewry. Eisendrath was determined to break what he called the "isolationism" of the Reform movement. He did this initially by getting the UAHC to participate in the American Jewish Conference, a representative assembly organized to deal with the problems of European Jewry and Palestine in 1943. The move to New York was to be another step in the direction of association with *K'lal Yisrael*, the "totality of the Jewish people." It was, Eisendrath said later, "make or break" for the Reform movement.[10]

Once the Board had made its recommendation, Eisendrath would brook no opposition from within. When the executive director of the National Federation of Temple Brotherhoods (NFTB) dared to make propaganda for the other side, Eisendrath flew into a rage and refused to rest until NFTB agreed to his immediate dismissal. But the real opposition came from outside the bureaucracy. As the proponents had their vehicle in *Liberal Judaism*, the opponents had theirs in the newspaper Isaac Mayer Wise himself had founded, the *American Israelite*, now edited by Henry C. Segal.

Even before the Board's decision, Segal had written editorials against the move. Like Eisendrath, he stressed practical considerations: "Why must scores of families of the Union's staff be uprooted for a hegira whose benefits are highly debatable?"[11] Fearing (correctly) that the Executive Board was in Eisendrath's pocket, he urged that the final decision be postponed until the next Union Biennial in 1948 when a larger body could vote on the proposal. He also noted that overhead would run 20–25 percent higher in New York than in Cincinnati, an estimate that proved to be conservative, even if some Union expenses remained unchanged. In New York, too, the UAHC would be forced to accept the unionization of its work staff.

Segal soon realized that he had made a tactical error in recommending that the next Biennial make the final decision. That conference was scheduled for Boston, and it soon became apparent that the attending delegates would come disproportionately from the eastern states. He, therefore, reversed his course. He now held that democracy demanded either a mail vote by all congregations or a proxy voting system whereby a midwestern or western congregation that could not send its full complement of delegates could, nonetheless, cast the full number of votes to which it was entitled.

Under the co-chairmanship of the presidents of the two Reform congregations of Cincinnati, Leon Saks of Rockdale Avenue Temple and Sidney Meyers (brother of the aforementioned Philip Meyers) of Isaac Mayer Wise Temple, a "National Committee to Retain UAHC Headquarters in Cincinnati" was formed and began to send literature to the leadership of Reform congregations around the country. The addressees were asked to sign their names on a card to be sent to the Cincinnati committee. In turn, the *American Israelite* printed the growing list of support, along with the geographically skewed list of prospective delegates. By the time of the Biennial about 800 signatures had been obtained representing members in thirty-nine of the forty-one states that had UAHC congregations. Opposition was especially strong in the Bible Belt and the Far West. Proudly, the *American Israelite* reported that Mrs. J. Walter Freiberg, a former president of NFTS and honorary chairman of the campaign for the House of Living Judaism, had joined the committee, as had the founder of NFTS, Carrie Simon, and the prominent Rabbis David Philipson of Cincinnati and Edgar Magnin of Los Angeles. On Monday, November 15, 1948, the *American Israelite* distributed to the Biennial delegates a special edition on glossy paper devoted solely to pressing its case.

The pro-Cincinnati committee had its own answer for exactly

where the House of Living Judaism should be located. It had found that the Hanselmann Masonic Lodge, immediately adjacent to the campus of the Hebrew Union College, was for sale for only $140,000. The committee sent out a photograph of it and sang its praises. "Compare this with the cost of a new building or its equivalent in rented space in New York City!" they wrote in a small, widely circulated brochure. "Money is easy to spend... but harder and harder to raise."[12]

The committee chairmen noted that their temple boards had each voted unanimously in favor of having the Union remain in Cincinnati and that the Ohio Valley Region had overwhelmingly voted to support the proxy amendment to the UAHC constitution and to keep the Union in Cincinnati. Similarly, the Ohio Federation of Temple Sisterhoods had voted against the proposal to move and received endorsements for their position from fifty-six individual sisterhoods from California to New York City. Clearly opposition was mounting.

On Tuesday morning, November 16, 1948, the assembled group of more than a thousand delegates and alternates overflowed the Imperial Ballroom of Boston's Statler Hotel. Although most delegates had already made up their minds, the atmosphere was tense. Robert P. Goldman of Cincinnati, who would later severely criticize Eisendrath on other matters but was a supporter of the move, was in the chair; a stenographer made a careful transcript of the proceedings. Philip Meyers, introduced as a "distinguished citizen of Cincinnati" and chairman of the UAHC committee that had made the recommendation, led off the discussion. Thereafter, proponents and opponents spoke in alternation. Both sides tried to link their cause with the founder, Isaac Mayer Wise. Jonah B. Wise, his son and rabbi of New York's Central Synagogue, spoke in favor; Jonah's niece, Isaac's granddaughter, Iphigene Ochs Sulzberger, who had lived in New York since the age of four, spoke against the move. Eisendrath, who had made his pitch during his "State of Our Union" address, remained silent. In fact, he no longer needed to speak. The relative lack of strength of the opponents had become apparent a day earlier when their amendment to the constitution to allow proxy votes failed to win sufficient support. Now a substitute motion calling for a mail vote on the issue likewise lost. After about three hours of oratory and some parliamentary wrangling,

Goldman took the vote. It was neither secret nor was it tallied. Proponents claimed it showed a large majority in favor; opponents admitted to a proportion of about three to two but insisted the proposal would never have passed if the Biennial had not been held on the eastern seaboard.

The significance of the vote lay not only in its practical consequences that the House of Living Judaism would be built in New York; it lay no less in its symbolic significance. In the course of the extended debate, both before the Biennial and in Boston, it became apparent that deeper issues separated the two sides. They represented two competing philosophies of Reform Judaism, the one symbolized by Cincinnati and the other by New York. In the words of a particularly strident opposition flier: "This is more than a fight over a city or a building. It is a determination *not* to allow our American Reform Jewish movement to change its character and purpose."[13]

Cincinnati, the center of the American movement for seventy-five years, had come to represent what the movement stood for in its classical phase: integration into an optimistic, forward-looking America, untroubled by ethnic strife and industrial conflict. The UAHC "must have an American outlook rather than a New York outlook," Iphigene Sulzberger maintained.[14] "Cincinnati breathes the spirit of America's 'grass roots' with its objective viewpoint," wrote the committee opposing the move in its literature.[15] One of the delegates to Boston from San Antonio, Texas, Sylvan Lang, put it most baldly: "New York has great extremes of wealth and poverty, of standpat conservatism and of left-wing radicalism.... Keep the headquarters where the background will be genuinely representative of the United States. Reform Judaism is the spearhead; do not submerge it in the crosscurrents of conflicting Jewish problems with which New York Jewry is peculiarly faced. We regard Reform Judaism primarily as a religion. Move the headquarters to New York and whether it be the State of Israel or the Taft-Hartley Act, our Union will inevitably become embroiled in politics."[16]

Called by its supporters both the "fountainhead" and the "capital" of Reform Judaism, Cincinnati, because of its isolation from the East, had been able to preserve Reform Judaism in its pure state. In New York it would lose its identity; it would become "contaminated" both by a fractious and often radical Jewry and by the social cleavages that were all too apparent there. More traditional congregations in the New York area might seek to enter the Union. To the opponents of the move, Cincinnati represented both the past that they wanted to preserve and the future as they wished it to be.

The other side had its own symbolism. For Eisendrath, New York was vibrant and alive while Cincinnati was static if not fossilized. When he spoke of New York, his biological metaphor was invariably the human heart. New York, he said repeatedly, "pulsated," or it "throbbed." Unlike the opponents of the move, he welcomed the social challenges that New York offered. There he could thrust social justice more forcefully into the program of the UAHC than would have been possible in politically conservative Cincinnati. He had his own metaphor for Cincinnati as well. He called it the "shrine" of Reform Judaism. Thereby he recognized the historical centrality of the city while at the same time assigning it clearly to the past. Reform Jews would pilgrimage to the city of Reform origins; there they would visit the Hebrew Union College, which would ever remain in Cincinnati.[17] But if they were concerned for the future, they would come to the House of Living Judaism in the Jewish metropolis of New York, which, in any case, drew more Reform visitors from all over the country than did Cincinnati.

It took nearly another three years from the Boston Biennial until the opening of the House of Living Judaism on 65th Street and Fifth Avenue in September 1951. NFTS paid for a large share of it, but close to half came from the single donation of more than $400,000 given in memory of his parents by a New York physician and member of Congregation Emanu-El, Albert A. Berg. Of course, it ended up costing more than anticipated, and there were problems with its location not being zoned for "offices." But the House itself soon became a symbol: The Reform movement was now "in the thick of things," Jewishly and generally. Maurice Eisendrath regarded the move as a "high point" of his career. No doubt it was also the presence in New York that served as a springboard for Eisendrath's second controversial proposal a decade later: the establishment of a social action center in Washington, D.C. Once again, it was the realization that the Reform movement can be effective only when it is on the scene most relevant to its activity that prompted the creation of a Reform presence in the city where legislation affecting the moral character of the nation was being formulated.

When, upon the death of Maurice Eisendrath, Alexander Schindler took over the reins of the Union, he could build upon his predecessor's accomplishments and further expand the influence of the Reform movement within Jewish circles and beyond them. During the last twenty years the UAHC has not only maintained its position as a union of Reform congregations but enlarged it as a constituent within the bodies that determine policy for the Jewish people as a whole. Through ARZA it has been able to play an active and independent role in the world Zionist movement. When Rabbi Schindler assumed the chairmanship of the Conference of Presidents of Major American Jewish Organizations, a Reform rabbi became the principal spokesman for American Jewry at a crucial time in Israel-Diaspora relations.

As the Reform movement approaches the end of the twentieth century, it will continue to face the problems brought about by social changes within the American Jewish community and, if it is to remain loyal to its liberal stance, will need to advocate and implement solutions that set it apart from the more traditional forms of Judaism. To some extent we have already seen this happen, with outreach to mixed couples and the acceptance of patrilineal Jewish descent, for example. But on account of the decision to be in the midst of the Jewish people, first indicated by the move to New York, new solutions will not be arrived at from the periphery. They will arise out of a Reform movement anchored in *K'lal Yisrael,* the "totality of the Jewish people," even as they respond to contemporary concerns in the spirit of Reform Judaism.

NOTES

1. For the history of Cincinnati Jewry, see Jonathan D. Sarna and Nancy H. Klein, *The Jews of Cincinnati* (Cincinnati: Center for the Study of the American Jewish Experience, 1989).

2. *Liberal Judaism (LJ),* April–May 1948, p. 9.

3. *Proceedings of the Union of American Hebrew Congregations (PUAHC), 68th–70th Annual Reports* (1943), p. 19.

4. On Eisendrath's life, see Avi M. Schulman, *Like a Raging Fire: A Biography of Maurice N. Eisendrath* (New York: UAHC Press, 1993).

5. *LJ*, August 1946, p. 46.

6. *PUAHC, 71st–73d Annual Reports* (1947), p. 163.

7. Ibid., *74th–76th Annual Reports* (1950), pp. 26–27.

8. Transcript of Joint Session, UAHC and NFTS, Morton M. Berman Papers, American Jewish Archives (AJA) Collection 314, File 1/4; transcript of interview with Jane Evans concerning UAHC, August 2, 1985, AJA Small Collections, SC-3291. My thanks to Mr. Kevin Proffitt and the Archives staff for their assistance in locating archival material for this study.

9. *LJ*, June–July 1947, p. 29.

10. Daniel B. Syme interview with Maurice Eisendrath, May 10, 1972, AJA, Tape 1159.

11. *American Israelite (AI)*, January 23, 1947, p. 4.

12. Robert P. Goldman Papers, AJA, Ms. 31, Box 14, Folder 2.

13. Ibid., "To All Member Congregations."

14. Transcript of Joint Session, p. 18.

15. Open Letter of Saks and S. Meyers, Goldman Papers.

16. Transcript of Joint Session, pp. 40–41.

17. However, Rabbi Joseph Rauch of Louisville wrote to *Liberal Judaism* (October 1948, p. 42): "I have even heard whispers that in the not distant future it is contemplated to move the College there [to New York] also."

I am confident of our future as a movement within Judaism. That message whose bearers we are has certainly not outlived its usefulness. And the institution that we primarily serve, the synagogue, is still capable of the change that will secure its viability as an effective vehicle for the preservation and transmission of Judaism.

My confidence is given substance by the knowledge that we have in our constituency, in our congregations, people who care, who are earnestly concerned about the synagogue and its future, men and women of high motive and of serious purpose, who are determined to bring about a veritable "revolution of rising Judaic aspirations."

These people long for leaders who share their hopes. Let no one tell you otherwise! They are prepared to respond to such leaders, giving their best when the best is sought. True enough, the rabbi's role is changing, has changed. No longer is the rabbi *in* authority, as it were, given allegiance by virtue of his office. But the rabbi is freely offered such allegiance when he (or she) becomes *an* authority, when rabbis teach and exemplify those ideas and ideals their office presumably enshrines.

The modern mood calls for a rabbi who is also something of a "rebbe" in the more ideal conception of that word, not just a teacher of Judaism but also a fervent Jew who loves his people with an abounding love and who has the conviction and the courage to be a witness to God in a secular, post-Auschwitz, post-Hiroshima world. *This* is the kind of leadership to which our people respond. *This* is the kind of leadership for which they thirst, much like parched earth thirsts for the dew of heaven.

Rabbi Alexander M. Schindler
Founders' Day Address
Cincinnati, Ohio
March 28, 1973

THE EVOLVING ROLE
OF THE REFORM RABBI

ROLAND B. GITTELSOHN

Never in nearly six decades since my ordination—not even in my moments of deepest discouragement or despair—did I regret my choice of vocation. Yet if I were a college undergraduate today, I am not sure I would follow the same path. This, I firmly believe, is less a reflection of ennui or burnout than of the substantial change in the role of the rabbi since 1936. At the very outset, let me confess to an uncomfortable sense of imbalance as I undertake this comparison. The functions and responsibilities of the Reform rabbinate during my active years are still very clear to me. As these words are being published, however, I am in the nineteenth year of my retirement; I cannot pretend to exact or precise personal knowledge, therefore, of the rabbinic role today. What follows, then, is a comparison between one side of the scale, which I know from visceral personal experience, and the other side, which I "know" only through indirect observation.

It shouldn't surprise us that our rabbinic role has changed significantly in a world that has changed so dramatically during these decades. Since the day Julian Morgenstern held his hands on my head and pronounced *Yoreh, yoreh; yadin, yadin*, the human adventure on this planet has been transformed beyond any boundaries that even the wisest of his contemporaries could have anticipated. We have learned to sail the seas of space and explore the moon. We have created computers that not only duplicate but in some respects exceed human intelligence. We have probed the arcane mysteries of outer space and of our inner psyches. By way of more mundane, less profound illustration, I am incredibly (and unforgivably?) old-fashioned in producing these paragraphs on a typewriter, not a word processor. How foolishly naive it would be to expect that with such sensational expansion of our knowledge and power, the role of the rabbi would remain unchanged!

It never has been static—not even before the advent of Reform Judaism. In every age religious doctrine and leadership have reflected current knowledge of the cosmos and the human condition. Why should our time be different? The rabbinic responsibilities of Akiba and Maimonides and Joseph Soloveitchik were by no means identical, despite their having been equally "Orthodox." Because the world has changed more drastically in this century than ever before, and because our movement has always welcomed, even encouraged, development and adaptation, we must commence by assuming that the tasks confronting this year's ordinees will differ considerably from those faced by my classmates and myself. There will be neither logic nor priority in the paragraphs to follow as I attempt to catalogue these differences.

The Preaching Rabbi

The first and perhaps most obvious difference is the decreased role of preaching. Abba Hillel Silver preached at both my graduation from Western Reserve University and my ordination five years later at the Hebrew Union College (delivering exactly the same address on both occasions). I doubt that anyone would dispute the assertion that there is no Abba Hillel Silver in the American rabbinate today—nor a Stephen Samuel Wise. The reasons for this decline of preaching are in large part obvious. The rabbi is no longer the most highly educated or intellectually sophisticated person in the congregation. Nor is he or she the sole source of reliable information on spiritual matters; on almost any night of the week the average congregant can "commune" with a variety of experts on ethics and spirituality just by activating a television switch at home.

The reduced role of preaching had, in fact, begun to manifest itself even before my matriculation at Hebrew Union College. More than once during my high school and college years in Cleveland, I had to join a long line outside Rabbi Silver's synagogue to be sure of a seat at his Sunday morning service. Near the end of his career, his preaching skills had by no means diminished; if anything, they had been honed to a sharper edge. Yet his average Sunday morning attendance had been reduced to perhaps five or six hundred.

This brings us to the old chicken-and-egg dilemma. I was far from the exception in devoting an average of ten to twelve hours (not counting preliminary reading, studying, and filing) to the preparation of each Friday night sermon. Rabbis today would call this a cost-ineffective use of their time. There are not nearly enough congregants present for their sermons, they say, to justify such expenditure of energy. Are they correct? Or have they confused cause and effect?

Whichever the answer, we ought to think more than twice before dismissing too hastily the possible importance of preaching. I am repeatedly amazed at the accuracy with which an individual will remember something I said years ago in a sermon, insisting that my words had substantially influenced his or her life: helped in a vocational choice, consoled at a time of great grief, inspired to a high degree of courage. There have even been occasions when I went back to my files to confirm that I had been quoted accurately. Conversations with more than a few colleagues convince me that I am by no means unique in this respect.

The Community Rabbi

Closely related to the foregoing is the diminished (if not vanished) role of the rabbi as communal power broker, social activist, or ambassador to non-Jews. It is scarcely conceivable that a rabbi today would be principal spokesperson advocating establishment of a Jewish state before the United Nations, or even in combating anti-Semitism. A host of organizations, led mostly by laypeople, serve in our stead. The individual rabbi who speaks for the Jewish community in public forums or before congressional committees is now more often an exception than the rule.

I have in my files two revealing photographs. One, taken in 1938, shows the three men who signed the original agreement establishing the United Jewish Appeal; two of them are rabbis. The second photograph, snapped in 1984, portrays fourteen individuals who signed the agreement of renewal between the United Israel Appeal and the Joint Distribution Committee; not a single rabbi is among them! I was one of only two rabbis attending a luncheon of approximately eighty individuals later that day to mark this renewal.

Much of the same kind of change has occurred in social action. I recall from my earliest years in the Central Conference of American Rabbis being stirred to the very pit of my conscience and soul by the social challenges so regularly and eloquently emanating from Jacob Weinstein, Edward Israel, Barnett Brickner, and Maurice Eisendrath. They were twentieth-century clones of Isaiah and Amos.

Here we touch again on the good news/bad news syndrome. Bad news: Even when today's Reform rabbi espouses social causes, he or she is more often urging social *welfare* than social *action*, more frequently striving to feed the hungry and house the homeless— altogether necessary and praiseworthy endeavors, to be sure—than advocating correction of those flaws in our social structure that cause impoverishment and homelessness in the first place. Good news: The Commission on Social Action, probably inspired and directed today more by laypeople than by rabbis, has replaced the CCAR Committee on Justice and Peace as our movement's most effective agency for social change. This is, properly evaluated, a compliment to those rabbis who taught and encouraged them.

There is another positive aspect to this phenomenon: We know now that individuals choose to become rabbis for neurotic as well as wholesome reasons. This is probably truer of medicine and the clergy than of other vocations. Some of us in my generation may have become rabbis precisely to compensate for unconscious suspicion of personal inadequacy. Standing in the public eye so dominantly, speaking to the public ear so authoritatively may have camouflaged our gnawing sense of inner weakness. My guess—only a guess, but I hope an educated, informed one—is that the quieter, less conspicuous spheres of rabbinic activity today—relating to congregants in smaller, less formal settings, influencing their lives in quieter, less conspicuous relationships—may serve to increase the proportion of colleagues who choose to be rabbis for healthy, constructive reasons.

The Rabbi as Theologian

There is probably more "spirituality" among today's Reform rabbis than existed a generation or two ago. I enclose "spirituality" in quotation marks because the word is of such imprecise meaning, often signifying a flight from harsh fact to comforting illusion, from science and reason to mysticism and meditation, from challenge to bromide. Harold Schulweis expresses my apprehensions cogently: "'Spirituality' in our time is often biased towards the transcendence of our mundane world. 'Spirituality' would favor withdrawing from the battle, from confrontation. But in biblical *kedushah* there is little to suggest muteness before the mystery of God.... Silence is not always harmless meditation. It is not infrequently used to disguise a passive acquiescence to evil....

"[T]he new longing for spirituality in our era tends towards self-absorption, an interiority oblivious to the mundane external world."[1]

Admittedly, earlier generations of Reform rabbis may have invested too much faith in the curative power of logic and fact. Does that give their successors the right to reject reason and science totally? They do so, I firmly believe, only at risk of adopting the all-or-nothing fallacy. Either reason and fact solve all our problems completely, or they are assumed to have no validity. Neither extreme, I suggest, can suffice of itself. The absolute certainty and security for which we understandably yearn in the face of change so threatening and vast is, plainly and simply, even if uncomfortably, beyond human attainment. Tomorrow's responsible Reform rabbi must eschew both the severely astringent rationalism of yesterday and the escapist flight to pseudocertainty of today. He or she must adopt a comprehensive search for truth and faith based on the best of both.

I remember participating some years ago in a rabbinic camp retreat. One delightful morning, we stood in a circle under the trees for *Shacharit*. Our service was led by a colleague renowned as a leading mystic. By way of inviting us to join in a unison reading, he said, "Join me now in reading this paragraph, even if you don't believe it; in fact, join me with extra fervor *especially* if you don't believe it!" I hope I don't do my colleagues an injustice in suspecting that too many of them might conceive their changing professional role as a stamp of approval on this kind of obfuscation.

Even among those who successfully avoid this extreme, however, there is, it seems to me, much less theological creativity in our ranks than there should be. Come to think of it, we Reform rabbis never did match our Conservative colleagues as theological innovators. Who were the rabbis expanding our horizons of theological speculation a half century ago, striving most zealously to combine the insights of science, reason, and faith in a creative synthesis? Mordecai Kaplan, of course. Followed and abetted by Ira Eisenstein, Milton Steinberg, and Jack Cohen—all Conservative rabbis! A strange paradox here: While we in the Reform movement were experimenting with modern approaches to ritual, an area where our Conservative colleagues lagged, they exceeded us by far in stretching the boundaries of theology. Now that we have eschewed our radical rejection of ritual, perhaps it is time for us to become bolder and more creative theologically.

The Rabbi as Ethicist

Has our role as ethical guides to the congregation changed? No— and yes. No, in the sense that we remain franchised to applying the ethical values of Jewish tradition to the personal and communal problems of our people. Yes, because it is far more difficult to accomplish this imperative task today than it was in the past. Life is far more complicated now; ethical guidelines of equal importance more often conflict now; there are more gray than distinctively black and white areas now.

To illustrate: A half century ago few of us experienced serious qualms in defending the proposition that government should fill the gap when private enterprisers could not provide needed levels of housing and feeding the disadvantaged. We have since learned, to our dismay, that welfare benefits can be shamelessly exploited, that public housing can be contaminated by bribery and fraud. How do we now correct these abuses without forsaking the needy, without turning them over to those whose only guide is greed?

To illustrate on an even more complicated level: In order to protect our environment against destructive contamination and reduce our dependence on foreign oil, we are urged to increase the development of nuclear energy; yet we know the grave danger to both the environment and human health resulting from additional nuclear experiments. How do we resolve dilemmas such as these? What do we advise our congregants and political leaders when ethical values of equal validity and urgency conflict so irreconcilably? The ancient prophet faced a much simpler task as ethical guide than does today's Reform rabbi. Yet this in no manner exonerates us from our responsibility as ethical guides.

However we may disagree in our responses to the difficult, complicated social problems of our day, on one thing we must be unanimous: In our personal conduct we rabbis must always teach best by example. Rachel Adler, Jeffrey Salkin, and Julie Spitzer, in their remarkable symposium on the sexual misdemeanors of some rabbis (*CCAR Journal*, Spring 1993), have skillfully exposed a problem that was previously discussed only through innuendo and gossip.

It is easy but woefully inadequate to hide behind the undeniable truth that rabbis are guilty on this count far less than members of other clergy, or to claim as a defense that we are, after all, only human. At the very least, our behavior must illustrate sexuality that is truly and Jewishly human, not basically animalistic. In this, as in other spheres of ethical value, what we teach by example is far more impressive and important than what we preach by word. In this, we can tolerate no change in the Reform rabbi's role.

Another dimension of our responsibility as ethical guides concerns remuneration. Though the average income of Reform rabbis is still much lower than it should be, we have reached a point where rabbis in larger, more prestigious pulpits receive sums that are beginning to compare with those of other professionals in the congregation. Too often, in making this kind of comparison, we fail to consider that rabbis are free from the considerable expenses faced by others: rent, secretarial salaries, expensive equipment, and so on. As our incomes advance, does our stake in the status quo also increase? Does our inclination to criticize the inequities and iniquities of the social structure decline accordingly? At the very least, red lights warn us at this intersection. We must carefully heed them.

The Rabbi as Teacher and Judge

How has our role changed regarding the two specific mandates voiced in the traditional ordination formula, *Yoreh, yoreh; yadin, yadin*, "You shall surely teach; you shall certainly judge"? On the first count, we have learned in the last half century what we really should have known long before: In this modern day, rabbinic ordination by itself in no way qualifies the rabbi as an educator.

During our Cincinnati student days, Samuel Glasner and I fully intended to concentrate our careers on education. (He, in fact, substantially did; I did not.) Because of this intention, we spent many more than the required curricular hours studying education under the expert guidance of Abraham Franzblau. It would not be too great an exaggeration to say that during our final year at HUC we practically ran the education department, while Abe was in his first year of medical studies. Yet on graduation, neither Sam nor I felt competent as educators, not even to supervise a congregational religious school; we both enrolled for further postgraduate studies in pedagogy.

Today, largely through the endeavors of NATE (National Association of Temple Educators) and the Commission for Jewish Education, a considerable cadre of nonrabbinical professional Jewish educators has been created. Those rabbis who still wish to concentrate primarily on education know that in addition to *Semichah*, they must earn the "degree" of RJE (Reform Jewish Educator).

The change in our rabbinic role has been even greater with reference to *yadin*. Seldom do congregants come to us for judgment on matters of traditional Jewish law. Most of us would scarcely be able to respond adequately if they did. Yet we Reform rabbis think and speak much more today than before about *halachah*, traditional rabbinic law. Where our predecessors tended to reject or ignore *halachah* entirely, most of us approach it today selectively and with great respect. This does not mean, as some among our congregants have suspected, that we have become more Orthodox, less Reform. It reflects, rather, our conviction that no part of Jewish tradition should be either accepted or rejected unless it and its intent be fully understood.

This means, obviously, that today's Reform rabbis need greater knowledge of *halachah* than most of their immediate predecessors possessed. We must also be tolerant of diversity among our colleagues. Our new stance on paternal descent is as good an example as any. It is of enormous significance that Rabbi Alexander Schindler, who first proposed this innovation at a UAHC Biennial Convention, then pursued it toward adoption by the CCAR. He and those colleagues who disagree with him have great respect for the tradition we have thus amended. They understand and respect the reasons for insisting on only maternal descent at a previous point in Jewish history. The Conference majority, despite this respect, however, is convinced that historic circumstance now demands a substantial change. This, I submit, is probably the best available example of both the essential nature of Reform Judaism and the changed role of its rabbis.

The Helping Rabbi

Not even so brief a survey as this can be concluded in good conscience without reference to the Reform rabbi's role in counseling. As a group we are certainly better prepared here today than we were in the past. During my student years, the College-Institute offered not a single course in human relations or pastoral psychology. This deficiency has long since been corrected. The danger we confront now is quite the opposite: We rabbis, having acquired some knowledge of psychodynamics, may precisely for that reason confuse our role with that of the psychiatrist. I have heard colleagues recount instances of counseling so far beyond rabbinic competence or skill that their stories chilled my blood. They might as well have undertaken to remove a patient's appendix with a rusty knife!

In our changed role as counselors, we rabbis must recognize our limitations. We must know when to assume sole responsibility, when to make referrals, when to continue seeing our congregants to supplement their depth therapy. We must never overlook the very unique aspect of the help we can offer, above and beyond that of other professionals. Without ever ignoring the psychological principles undergirding mental health, we must remember the special spiritual quality that should infuse our kind of counseling.

If my experience here is at all typical, I would suggest that most individuals suffering emotional distress above all lack a sense of belonging. They don't need us to help restore the sense of belonging to their parents, to their siblings, their mates, their friends. They may very well need us for what I like to call a cosmic address, a sense of belonging to the entire human family, to the human adventure on this planet and in the universe. We need to see pervasive purpose and meaning in the entire scheme of things and to perceive that we play an important part in the fulfillment of that purpose. In theological terminology, we are, in truth, partners of the Divine. Unless the universe that spawned me possesses purpose, how can any segment or aspect of my life have meaning? This is the one indispensable ingredient of mental health that we rabbis are uniquely qualified to offer our counselees.

We can't succeed at that by preaching sermons to them in the privacy of our studies. I'm not even sure I can recommend precise methods or techniques aimed at this target. Perhaps the best we can do, while our congregants are receiving the proper treatment from others far more expert in this field than ourselves, is to share with them in quiet conversation our own pervasive sense of cosmic belonging.

The Rabbi's Rabbi

In writing each of the preceding sections of this essay, my mind kept reverting to the rabbi in whose honor this entire volume has been prepared. In a unique and challenging way, Alexander Schindler exemplifies both the old and the new rabbinic roles at their best. He is among the few remaining preachers who prepare scrupulously, speak eloquently, even poetically; he can move congregations to elevate both sentiment and deed; yet he is equally effective in one-on-one relationships. He has effectively led not only the Union of American Hebrew Congregations but even larger bodies of Jews, nationally and internationally, without ignoring the rabbi's role in quiet moments of painful need. He has been among Israel's chief interpreters and defenders in the public domain; yet he has also been among its most lovingly prophetic critics. He embraces a richly poetic mysticism without denying the demands of reason and fact. He urges his colleagues toward the highest levels of ethical behavior without condemning them judgmentally for their failings. He has elevated our movement's pedagogic programs to a new standard of excellence. As already observed, he combines reverent respect for tradition with bold understanding of how it must be modified or amended.

Note, in this connection, how often in preceding paragraphs I have said "he or she" in referring to my colleagues. This is another area in which Alex has excelled: welcoming our women rabbis not only as a matter of gender justice but even more for the unique talents they add to the religious leadership of our movement. He is, in truth, in more ways than I could even hope to describe, the rabbis' rabbi of Reform Judaism.

Some thirty years ago, in a volume commemorating the seventy-fifth anniversary of the Central Conference of American Rabbis, Rabbi Jacob Shankman wrote words that more aptly conclude this essay than any phrases of mine. Were he writing this today, Jake would be the first to change the gender references still accurate and appropriate then.

> [The rabbi's] tasks are endless....A catalogue of what is expected from him is varied and exhausting: He must be a philosopher who can answer the ultimate questions about life and the universe; a theologian who can respond to the "show me God" demands of a confirmand, who can justify the mystery and anguish of death to grief-crushed parents who have just lost a child; a teacher who can reveal and illumine the drama of Jewish history and the glory of Jewish literature and relate them to contemporary Jewish living; ... who can interweave faith and worship with reverence and moral fervor; a pastor who knows his people and is their listening ear and friend, who participates in every significant personal and family occasion from infancy to death....
>
> These are by no means all the tasks that he is expected to undertake. To discharge them he must possess not only high-mindedness, dedication, and superlative gifts of mind and heart but also the physical energies that would tax a perfectly conditioned athlete and the psychic equilibrium of a saint.[2]

This has not changed.

NOTES

1. Harold Schulweis, *In God's Mirror* (New York: Ktav, 1990), pp. 292 ff.
2. Bertram Korn, ed., *Retrospect and Prospect* (New York: CCAR, 1965).

Those resolutions we pass at our biennials express our resolve to act. There is one realm, however, in which our resolutions have been forthright but our actions considerably less so. I speak now of the plea of gay and lesbian Jews for fuller acceptance in our midst.

I know that I raise a subject that will make many here feel uncomfortable, but this is precisely why I must raise it. Our discomfort is a measure of our continuing prejudice. I do not exclude myself from this harsh decree for, in thinking about what I would say today, I had to wrestle with demons in the depths of my own being, demons I never acknowledged were there.

Let us admit, then, that in spite of past declaration urging the contrary, the singling out of homosexuality from the whole human constellation as a loathsome affliction remains a widespread sentiment in our midst.

In most mainstream congregations, we have not extended our embrace to include gay and lesbian Jews. We have not acknowledged their presence in the midst of our synagogues. We have not dispelled the myth of the "corrupting" homosexual, of the counselor or teacher who would fashion children in his or her sexual image. And we have not consciously included gay and lesbian parents as part of the Jewish family circle.

To be sure, many of us feel pity for gays and lesbians, and we agree intellectually that it is a grievous wrong to stigmatize them, to ostracize them, to hold them in moral disdain. But something more than a grasp of the mind is required; there is a need for a grasp of the heart. Something different from pity is called for; we need, as a community, to cross those boundaries of Otherness, where compassion gives way to identification. Indeed, we have not affirmed that we *all* are family. We speak of "them" and "us" as though gay men and women were descended from a distant planet.

326

But they are not! They are our fellow congregants, our friends, and committee members—and yes, our leaders both professional and lay. Whether we know it or not, whether we acknowledge it or not, some of them are our sisters and brothers, our daughters and our sons. In our denial, in our failure to see one another as one family—indeed, as one holy body—we forget Jewish history; we opt for amnesia. We who were beaten in the streets of Berlin cannot turn away from the plague of gay-bashing. We who were Marranos in Madrid, who clung to the closet of assimilation and conversion in order to live without molestation, cannot deny the demand for gay and lesbian visibility!

Rabbi Alexander M. Schindler
State of the Union Message
New Orleans, Louisiana
November 4, 1989

TRULY WELCOMING LESBIAN AND GAY JEWS

MARGARET MOERS WENIG

I declare myself the compassionate ally of every person, heterosexual and homosexual, Jew and non-Jew, who is wrestling with the shame, the confusion, the fear, the endless torment involved in the inner struggle for sexual identity. It is a struggle that includes, but also goes beyond, civil liberties. It is, when all is said and done, a struggle for the integrity of selfhood.[1]

Note: This essay does not argue for the acceptance of openly gay and lesbian Jews as members of our community. Such arguments have been forcefully made elsewhere.[2] This essay takes such acceptance as a starting point for that is where the American non-Orthodox community now stands—at least in principle. Instead, this paper raises some of the issues the Jewish community will have to address in the next century, having opened its doors to lesbian and gay Jews in this one.

The Road We Have Traveled

Until 1965 the only official Jewish position on homosexuality was that it was an abomination.[3] Sexual relations between men were strictly forbidden, and lesbianism, though a lesser offense, was prohibited as well. While this official position was reiterated, year after year, in the list of prohibited sexual relations read on Yom Kippur afternoon in Orthodox and Conservative congregations,[4] homosexuality received relatively little explicit attention in responsa literature or in the Jewish press and periodicals. Nonetheless, the supreme value placed by the tradition and the community on heterosexual marriage and procreation must have communicated implicit disapproval to anyone who thought he or she might be gay or lesbian and probably exerted pressure on many gay and lesbian Jews to enter heterosexual marriages. This Jewish pressure, combined with criminal penalties in most states for sodomy, solicitation, and cross-dressing, taught Jews that being gay was unacceptable.

How gay Jews responded to or were affected by the Jewish prohibition against homosexuality and the pressure to marry we do not know. This history has yet to be written. The classic histories of gay men and lesbians in America tell us little about Jews,[5] and the anthologies of Jewish gay and lesbian autobiographical and historical essays contain few accounts of gay Jewish life before the seventies.[6]

We can say with some certainty, however, that fifty years ago a gay or lesbian Jew could avoid criminal charges, remain employed, and be an active member of a synagogue only by concealing his or her sexual orientation. We do not know, however, how many gay or lesbian Jews married, how many maintained extramarital homosexual or lesbian relationships, how many divorced. We do not know how many bachelor brothers or maiden aunts were in fact gay or lesbian. We do not know how many lesbian or gay Jews committed suicide.

Some of the few portraits of gay Jewish life we have come,

ironically, from gay rabbis, whose anonymous testimonies were solicited in 1987 by the CCAR Ad Hoc Committee on Homosexuality and the Rabbinate. One man, in his fifties, wrote:

Through all the years I was a student at HUC and for years beyond when I occupied a pulpit, I was simultaneously in therapy. I believed that I must be sick in some deep and profound way and assumed that I must work toward some "cure." I had the terrible misfortune of working with two professionals, one more adamant than the next, who claimed that they could indeed cure me; that homosexuality was, in fact, an aberration; and that, in time, I would reverse my sexual orientation altogether. I was hapless enough to believe these groundless (and, therefore, fraudulent) claims because I wanted to. I strove to do everything they urged me to: dreams, screams, drugs, and women. The years wore on while the contradictions compounded. I discontinued the torture when my doctor urged me with some glee to prepare myself for a new and promising approach: aversion therapy featuring electroshock behavior modification.

This entire personal struggle, my sexual activities and the endless consuming therapies, I managed to keep invisible and altogether separate from my life at HUC, among my colleagues there and later from the life I lived in the synagogue community. This capacity to live in separate realities is a dubious skill developed by gay people everywhere. It will assure survival for a while at a very high price to the soul....

In retrospect, it is easy to see that the whole charade was absurd. I have since learned that a good number of gay people were associated with the synagogue, but there was simply no model then for open and honest living.... Life in the closet was morally repugnant and personally destructive, but life out of the closet promised only rejection and banishment....

Consider the colossal waste of the vibrant life God gave us and the enormous energy squandered in decades of self-denial and social deception. Clearly, we all lose—parents, children, and certainly the whole Jewish community. I spent more than thirty-five years of my life buried away and struggling to come out and in the process had to leave the Jewish community to find respite, solace, and healing elsewhere....

The fact is that I remained unhappily celibate for years at a time. I would estimate that more than half of my tenure in the congregational rabbinate was spent that way. I understand now that whether I was practicing continence or not, I was only collecting kindling for my own burnout.... It grew more and more painful to return home late at night after endless board or committee meetings, projects, or classes to an empty house and an empty bed....

Judaism had held a great promise for me. I was drawn to it and grew more enamored of it the more I heard its message of honest living, the more I perceived its emphasis on the sanctity of human life and relationship and its devotion to authenticity in human affairs. These values are what I strove for in my own life, and they are what I preached about.... I hoped to find ...courage and integrity imbedded in the deliberate Jewish life of the temple community. Yet I lived in a closet, trembling with denial. The more I suffocated in the closet, the more desperate I became for the fresh air of authenticity. But everywhere I turned, authenticity seemed to be defined as heterosexuality: Reb Zusya notwithstanding.... My soul yearned for authenticity and integrity, but the reality of my life was denial and deception.... The anguish this caused me ironically drove me from the *shul*.[7]

The organized Jewish community did not rush to rescue gay and lesbian Jews. In the 1950s gay people were linked to Communists, purged from government jobs, and hounded out of the military. The Jewish community was silent. In the 1960s gay people faced discrimination in employment, housing, and professional licensing and mass arrests in police raids on gay bars. The Jewish community was silent. Following the passage of the Civil Rights Bill (1964), when gay men and lesbians began public protests, only one national Jewish organization spoke out against the harassment of homosexuals, in favor of the decriminalization of sodomy between consenting adults, and in support of [Christian] clergy who were beginning to come to their defense.[8] That was the National Federation of Temple Sisterhoods.[9] Its own parent body, the Union of American Hebrew Congregations, did not follow suit for another twelve years.

Only when singer and evangelist Anita Bryant successfully led a grass-roots campaign to repeal a gay rights ordinance in Dade County, Florida, which gained steam and inspired other successful gay rights repeal campaigns across the country, only after gay people held large-scale public demonstrations,[10] only after several Christian denominations went on record in support of gay civil rights—only then in 1977 did two national Jewish bodies respond with resolutions calling for decriminalization of sodomy and an end to civil discrimination against homosexuals.[11] It was at least another ten years until national Jewish organizations became *active* in the struggle for gay and lesbian civil rights. Though Rabbis Maurice Eisendrath and Abraham Joshua Heschel had marched on Washington with Dr. Martin Luther King, Jr., no leader of or official delegation from a national Jewish body marched on Washington for gay and lesbian rights until 1993 (ignoring previous marches in 1979[12] and 1987).[13]

Out of the mainstream of organized Jewish life, however, and partly in response to anti-Semitism in the feminist and civil rights movements of which they were a part, Jewish gay men and lesbians began to gather as Jews for Passover seders and eventually to form synagogues of their own. Inspired by the Metropolitan Community Church, a Christian fellowship for gay men and lesbians (founded in 1968)—which some Jews attended—a group of gay Jews in Los Angeles decided to form a gay synagogue. The 1973 application for membership in the UAHC by the Metropolitan Community Temple, later BCC (Beit Chayim Chadashim), was the first time in Jewish history that gay and lesbian Jews had asked the organized Jewish community to recognize their existence and grant them some measure of acceptance.[14]

Although the Responsa Committee of the Central Conference of American Rabbis, to whom the UAHC turned for guidance, denied BCC the acceptance they sought, the UAHC admitted them. The presence of BCC and the lobbying of their delegates at the 54th UAHC Biennial Convention in 1977 are directly responsible for the passage of the Reform movement's first resolution in support of gay civil rights.[15]

In 1985 the workshop presented by delegates of the then four gay outreach synagogues, "Towards a Better Understanding of Our Gay and Lesbian Brothers and Sisters," was the first workshop on homosexuality ever offered at a UAHC national biennial. It attracted a standing-room-only crowd.[16]

AIDS accelerated the rate at which the mainstream Jewish community came to acknowledge the existence of gay Jews (and came to terms with some of their needs). Heterosexual Jews, members of mainstream congregations, were losing sons and brothers, many of whom they learned were gay only when they were informed of their loved ones' illness. The rise in violence against homosexuals, attempts to discriminate against people with AIDS (more public than the earlier discrimination against gay men), and calls for the confinement in camps of those with AIDS were reminders to Jews of their own experiences in Germany. In Rabbi Schindler's words:

> We who were beaten in the streets of Berlin cannot turn away from the plague of gay-bashing. We who were Marranos in Madrid, who clung to the closet of assimilation and conversion in order to live without molestation, cannot deny the demand for gay and lesbian visibility![17]

In 1985 the UAHC established its Committee on AIDS. Two years later it called upon all UAHC congregations to "welcome gay and lesbian Jews to membership as singles, couples, and families."[18] Two years after that, Rabbi Alexander Schindler proclaimed, "I declare myself a rabbi for *all* Jews at every moment of life, not only for heterosexual Jews or for gay Jews only at their funerals."[19] He included, for the first time as part of the agenda of his presidential address, outreach to lesbian and gay Jews.[20] Ten years after demonstrating its support of lesbian and gay *civil* rights, the UAHC acknowledged that the logical consequence was granting to gay and lesbian Jews the same rights *within* the Jewish community.

This incremental change in Jewish attitude towards homosexuality should not obscure the fact that in only twenty years the 2,000-year-old traditional abhorrence of homosexuality was overturned.

Where Do We Go from Here? Following the Path of the Pioneers The Visibility of Lesbian and Gay Jews

Officially, all three non-Orthodox movements now welcome lesbian and gay Jews as equal members of mainstream congregations,[21] but some members of these synagogues want to "welcome" gay and lesbian members only if they remain invisible. A mother speaking at a Conservative synagogue in suburban Philadelphia commented in spring 1994:

> I don't mind if our rabbi officiates at commitment ceremonies as long as my children don't know [that the rabbi is gay]. I don't want them to think that being gay is okay. I want to do everything I can to stack the deck in favor of their growing up straight—like me.[22]

> If our synagogue advertises that we welcome gay/lesbian Jews, then we will be inundated with them and the straight members will no longer feel comfortable and will leave.
> Our synagogue is open to everyone. I don't care what someone does in bed as long as I don't have my nose rubbed in it.[23]

The presence of openly gay and lesbian Jews challenges the congregation to confront the questions: How far do we want to go in condoning homosexuality? What do we want to teach our children about homosexuality?

Some parents do not want to discuss homosexuality with their young children. They don't want their six-year-old coming home from religious school asking, "Why does Joshua have two mommies?"

If a synagogue admits to family membership a lesbian or gay couple, if a synagogue calls a gay couple up to the Torah on the Shabbat before they are to stand under the *chupah*, if the rabbi officiates at their ceremony of *kiddushin*, if their baby is given the Hebrew name *Sarah bat Yaakov ve-Chayim*, if the youth group adviser is openly gay, if the rabbi marches in a gay/lesbian pride parade, then the children of that synagogue will surely grow up understanding that being gay or lesbian is okay—at least within their own Jewish community.

Some parents are afraid that a gay teacher or rabbi will seduce their children or "recruit" them to be gay. Some parents believe that an environment that accepts homosexuality will influence their children to be gay.[24] Other parents worry that if their children are bisexual, a gay-friendly environment will decrease the likelihood that those children will choose heterosexuality. And so the parents would like to insist that the gay and lesbian members of their synagogues either remain invisible or accept inferior status and community disapproval (no family membership for gay couples, no *aliyot* for gay couples, no *kiddushin* for gay couples, no lesbian or gay Jews as educators, rabbis, or cantors).

Synagogues that "accept" but refuse to "sanction" homosexuality will not become synagogues of choice in cities where lesbian and gay Jews have a choice.

Rabbi Schindler understood this, stating:

> Ultimately, there must be a policy enunciated by which the many gay and lesbian Jews of our community can know that they are accepted on terms of visibility, not invisibility. Ultimately, they must know that we place no limits on their communal or spiritual aspirations.[25]

The Question of Choice

With or without the benefit of definitive scientific research on the etiology of sexual orientation and its diverse manifestations, the Jewish community in the coming decades will have to come to terms with the fundamental question: As long as some people claim to have a choice, is it okay to be gay?

A *New York Times*/CBS Poll found that those who think sexual identity cannot be changed are more sympathetic to gay rights.[26] Within the Jewish community as well, it is partly sympathy for women and men who *can't help but be lesbian or gay* that has garnered the support of heterosexuals.[27]

If gay men and lesbians have no choice but to be attracted to members of their own sex, then the halachic principle of *ones*, "duress," can be applied. In the words of a gay Orthodox rabbi who wrote under the pseudonym Yaakov Levado:

> One of the mitigating factors in halachic discourse is the presence of free will in matters of law. A command is only meaningful in the context of our freedom to obey or disobey. Thus the degree of choice involved in homosexuality is central to the shaping of a halachic response. There is, indeed, a certain percentage of gay

people who claim to exercise some volition in their sexual choices. But for the vast majority of gay people, there is no "choice" in the ordinary sense of the word. Gay feelings are hardwired into our bodies, minds, and hearts. The strangeness and mystery of sexuality are universal. What we share, gay or straight, is the surprising "queerness" of all sexual desire. The experience of heterosexuals may seem less outlandish for its being more common, but all sexual feeling is deeply mysterious, beyond explanation or a simple notion of choice.[28]

In response to the argument that sexual orientation is not a matter of choice, Rabbi Joel Roth countered that even if a gay Jew cannot control his attractions, he can control his behavior. If a gay Jew cannot marry a woman, he should remain celibate.[29]

Celibacy, however, is, for many, not a viable option nor one that feels authentically Jewish. Quoting Rabbi Yaakov Levado:

> Always sleeping alone, in a cold bed, without touch, without the daily physical interplay of lives morning and night—this celibate scenario is life-denying and, for me, has always led to a shrinking of spirit. What sort of Torah, what voice of God would demand celibacy from all gay people? Such a reading of divine intent is nothing short of cruel.[30]

Other lesbian and gay Jews reject altogether the use of the argument "We have no choice" as ultimately harmful to lesbians and gay men and as a distortion of experience. Theologian Judith Plaskow argues that though compassion towards and acceptance of gay people by religious communities and society at large is greater when people believe that homosexuality is not chosen, nonetheless, it "is not in the interest of lesbians, gays, or our allies to stake our claims for equal rights on these grounds." She argues further:

> Though skin color is not chosen, racism has not ended. And as soon as a gene for homosexuality is purportedly found, homophobic people will call for genetic engineering or prenatal testing to prevent or eliminate homosexuality.
>
> Our definitions of gay and straight are socially constructed... and do not make room for the wide range of sexualities:

exclusively gay, primarily gay, bisexual, asexual, primarily heterosexual, exclusively heterosexual.[31]

The notion that a Jew who has choice might choose a partner of the same sex was so objectionable to some members of the CCAR Ad Hoc Committee on Homosexuality and the Rabbinate that they agreed to endorse the report [urging that "all rabbis, regardless of sexual orientation, be accorded the opportunity to fulfill the sacred vocation they have chosen"] only on condition that it include a stated preference for heterosexuality:

> To the extent that sexual orientation is a matter of choice, the majority of the committee affirms that heterosexuality is the only appropriate Jewish choice for fulfilling one's covenantal obligations.[32]

This question of choice is now exacerbated by the growing visibility of and call for acceptance by people who identify themselves as bisexuals. Will the non-Orthodox movements actively discourage self-proclaimed bisexuals from entering homosexual/lesbian relationships? Will a Reform or Reconstructionist rabbi refuse to officiate at a ceremony of *kiddushin* for a bisexual woman who wants to stand under the *chupah* with another woman? Will a Reform or Reconstructionist congregation agree to hire a single bisexual male rabbi on the condition that he date only women? Truly welcoming lesbian and gay Jews into the Jewish community may mean giving up on the distinction between "those who have choice" and "those who don't have choice."

Truly Welcoming Lesbian and Gay Jews into Our Synagogues

Some synagogue trustees argue: "We welcome *everyone*. Why do we have to make special mention of lesbian and gay Jews?" Most lesbian and gay Jews are accustomed to rejection and will assume that they are not wanted by a mainstream synagogue unless that synagogue is explicit in its welcome. Being explicit means using the words *lesbian* and *gay* in the synagogue's publicity (newsletter, brochure, flyers, press releases, and High Holy Day advertisements), as well as advertising in publications read by lesbians and gay men (e.g., the local gay newspaper).

Welcoming lesbian and gay Jews into the synagogue means revising membership applications to include the word *partner* beside *spouse*; expanding the marital status options beyond single, widowed, or divorced; offering family membership to lesbian and gay couples; and listing them together in the membership directory.

Welcoming lesbian and gay Jews means calling lesbian and gay couples up for *aliyot* in honor of their upcoming *kiddushin* or anniversary, naming their children in the synagogue, and arranging a *minyan* for *shivah* when the lover of a gay or lesbian member has died.

Welcoming lesbian and gay Jews means offering support to their parents and children, who may be afraid of or actually experiencing prejudice. Truly welcoming lesbian and gay Jews means not discriminating against lesbian and gay applicants in the hiring of synagogue professional and nonprofessional staff,[33] providing spousal benefits for the partners of lesbian and gay employees,[34] and not discriminating against gay and lesbian members in the appointment of volunteers to such positions of synagogue leadership as trustees, officers, committee chairs, and leaders of prayer.

Congregations that wish to welcome lesbian and gay Jews can ask themselves, "Would a lesbian/gay couple or single lesbian/gay member feel welcome at synagogue social events? Could same-sex couples dance together? Could a teenager bring a same-sex date to a youth group social event? Could the synagogue offer to rent or lend space to a local lesbian/gay organization for social or educational events (as it offers space to AA and to scouts)?"

In a welcoming synagogue, the rabbi's sermons would not presume that all Jews are heterosexual, married, and the biological parents of children. Sermons would address events[35] and issues of concern to lesbians and gay men.[36] Lesbian and gay concerns would be reflected in the advocacy, direct service, and educational work of the Social Action committee and the congregation as a whole. The congregation's liturgy would reflect the hopes and fears of lesbians and gay men and would include poems, prayers, and music written by lesbian and gay Jews. If secular holidays such as the birthday of Martin Luther King, Jr., are included in the congregation's ritual calendar, then Lesbian/Gay Pride Day would be observed as well.

The Future of Gay Synagogues

The question is often asked, "Why do gay and lesbian Jews need their own synagogues?" In the late seventies a high school student noticed the tiny *New York Times* ad for Shabbat services at Congregation Beth Simchat Torah, New York's gay and lesbian synagogue, and mustered the courage to go on a Friday night. His first kiss from another gay man, though completely innocent, was a greeting of *Shabbat Shalom*....His first public act as a gay man was going to a synagogue....

> Most gay people do not "come out" in a synagogue or church. Gay men, in particular, often find bars and baths more typical places for coming out. These places ... often lead to casual and sometimes unsafe relationships. Coming out in a synagogue doesn't mean that one will not enter into such relationships. However, coming out in a religious context ... has a profound effect on a person. It is difficult to like yourself, to have a positive self-image when much of society would tell you that what you are is abnormal or that you are a sinner [and] would seek to deny your civil rights [...and] make your expressions of love against the law. Coming out in a religious context challenges all that. We can learn, in synagogues that welcome us, that what we are is good; that we can love and be loved; that we are created, like everyone else, in God's image; and that...God loves us with an unqualified love.
>
> Gay people who come to believe these things about themselves love and care for themselves. I believe such people are more likely to attempt to establish healthy relationships and less likely to flirt with the dangers of promiscuity or unsafe behavior [or to attempt suicide]. Religion and spirituality have the ability to transform us. With people not only hating us but trying to make us hate ourselves, we desperately need places where we can learn to love ourselves.[37]

The synagogue of choice for most gay Jews in Los Angeles, San Francisco, Chicago, Miami, Philadelphia, Atlanta, New York, and Washington, D.C., is a lesbian and gay synagogue. These synagogues have provided a safe haven for over twenty years for gay/lesbian Jews looking for community, for partners, for reminders of their grandparents' *shul*, for a synagogue open to feminism, for Jews who will comfort them when they are mourning and care for them when they are dying, for a place to be themselves where they would suffer no loss of job or family[38]—a place in which they can create a liturgy that reflects their fears and hopes[39] and a place from which to launch political struggles for their acceptance into the wider Jewish community.

As long as the acceptance of lesbian and gay Jews into mainstream synagogues remains partial, there will be a need for predominantly gay and lesbian synagogues. Moreover, mainstream synagogues may never draw the critical mass of lesbian and gay Jews that will enable those synagogues to serve lesbian and gay *social* needs. In New York, for example, a gay Jew is more likely to find a partner at the gay synagogue, where 300 gay Jews gather every Shabbat, than at one of the half-dozen mainstream synagogues with ten to fifty gay and lesbian Jews at a given service.

Furthermore, because gay and lesbian members will never be more than a minority in mainstream synagogues, their concerns will never dominate the agenda of those synagogues. While gay and straight Jews care about many of the same things, gay and lesbian Jews have issues in which they are more heavily invested than are heterosexual Jews. Only in a gay synagogue can gay Jews be assured that their top priorities will also be the top priorities of the rabbi and the board.[40]

The same gay rabbi whose anonymous testimony to the CCAR documented his flight from Judaism years ago concludes his testimony:

> I recently affiliated with ... [a] gay temple and am happy to have found brothers and sisters who share my experience. I am delighted with the rabbi who is gay and proud and knowledgeable and who can speak to my heart. For the first time in my life, I am faced with the possibility of being openly and proudly gay and Jewish at the same time and in the same place. I genuinely look forward to contributing again to a Jewish community that can nurture me in return.[41]

Lesbian and Gay Marriage

The Reconstructionist Rabbinical Association (RRA) is to date the only national Jewish body to go on record supporting commitment ceremonies for lesbian and gay couples.[42] While the Reform movement did call for civil legislation that would afford lesbian and gay couples spousal benefits and "the means of legally acknowledging" their relationships, it stopped short of supporting "marriage" for lesbian and gay couples, and it refrained from supporting *kiddushin* for Jewish gay and lesbian couples.[43]

In the twenty-first century the legalization of gay and lesbian marriage will be among the most heated political battles.[44]

The need for legalized lesbian and gay marriage and especially for greater ease in co-parent adoption becomes increasingly pressing as more and more gay and lesbian couples become parents of children. No one knows how many gay and lesbian couples have adopted children or have conceived children through alternative insemination. It is commonly said, however, that a "baby boom" is taking place within the lesbian community. And as more and more states permit adoptions by gay men, gay parent families are growing in number as well. Though many of these children are being raised by two parents, legally most of them have only one.[45]

As a result, most children of lesbian and gay parents are not entitled to financial support from their nonbiological or nonadoptive parent, not entitled to inherit from that parent, not entitled to Social Security benefits in the event of that parent's disability or death, not entitled to participate in medical and educational benefits provided by that parent's employer. In addition, that parent is not entitled to visitation rights or custody should the relationship with the biological or adoptive parent end. And even if the nonbiological or nonadoptive parent is named as the child's guardian in the biological/adoptive parent's will, he or she can be separated from the child if guardianship is contested by the parents or siblings of the deceased biological/adoptive parent.

Lesbian and gay marriage and co-parent adoption would provide children raised by gay and lesbian couples the legal benefits of two parents rather than one.

For lesbian and gay couples, legal marriage would offer much more than the opportunity of joint income tax filing: health care benefits, rights of inheritance (nontaxed passage of property from the dead spouse to the surviving spouse), Social Security and pension benefits, immigration privileges, and the authority to make health care decisions for each other. And in the event of a breakup, a once-"married" lesbian or gay partner might be entitled to half of the marital property, to alimony, or to child support payments.

Moreover, as high as the divorce rate is among heterosexual couples, it may even be higher among lesbian and gay couples. Lesbian and gay couples receive little societal support for their relationships; in fact, they usually encounter antagonism. It is not uncommon for the parents of an adult gay man or lesbian to refuse to acknowledge even the existence of their child's partner or to refuse to allow the partner to visit their home or to participate in family seders or celebrations. Having to choose between their parents and their lover places a great deal of stress on lesbian and gay relationships. Legalizing gay marriage and *kiddushin* ceremonies for gay couples would provide some needed support for lesbian and gay couples attempting to maintain long-term committed relationships.

The Jewish community has an investment in the legalization of lesbian and gay marriage: to protect the children of those relationships, to give their lesbian and gay parents as much support as they need to provide and maintain stable, loving homes for them, to protect lesbian and gay widows and widowers, to protect the economically less powerful partner in the case of a breakup.

Moreover, if the Jewish community wants to see its lesbian and gay children stand beneath a *chupah*, if we want to dance at their wedding, then we need to support legal gay marriage. Even though *kiddushin* is now available for lesbian and gay couples, many, perhaps most, still refuse this option until *kiddushin* affords us the same legal and economic benefits that it affords heterosexual couples. Even without legal benefits some lesbian and gay couples will, nonetheless, welcome the opportunity to have a Jewish wedding, which was more than we ever dared to hope for. Others, however, will continue to resent all weddings (even lesbian or gay weddings) as a reminder of legal and economic privileges still denied us.

Issues in Lesbian and Gay Parenting

Questions arise when biological and social parenting are separated. These questions exist in heterosexual parent families where there are stepparents, but they are universal in lesbian and gay parent families. Whether the children are the product of a former heterosexual marriage, of adoption, or of alternative insemination, only one of the two social parents is also a biological parent. In the coming century, the Jewish community will be faced with questions like these: What does Judaism have to say when a man who donated sperm to a lesbian couple returns some years later and demands parental rights although he forswore them at the time of insemination? What does Judaism have to say when a lesbian couple breaks up, ten years after one of them bore a child through alternative insemination, and the biological mother refuses the nonbiological mother joint custody? Complicate the scenario by imagining that the biological mother is not Jewish, but the co-parent is. Before the mothers split up, their child was named in the synagogue, attended Hebrew school for several years, and was preparing for bar/bat mitzvah. According to the Reform understanding of patrilineal descent (inappropriately titled in this case), is this ten-year-old child Jewish? Did the rabbi who named the baby ask the non-Jew if she would commit to raising this child as a Jew even if she and her Jewish lover broke up?

Questions like custody will ultimately be decided in the courts. Nonetheless, rabbis who meet with gay and lesbian couples before they stand beneath the *chupah* or with prospective or new gay and lesbian parents should be familiar with such issues and ought to raise them in their pastoral counseling.

Conclusion

Lesbian and gay visibility, the question of choice, lesbian and gay marriage, and lesbian and gay parenting are just some of the issues the Jewish community will have to face in the twenty-first century, having now opened its doors to lesbian and gay Jews in this one. The welcoming of lesbian and gay Jews reflects profound social change. It will be remembered as one of those times in Jewish history when the *Torat chayim* (Torah of life) spoke to us more loudly than the *Torah Shebichetav* (Written Torah). As Rabbi Alexander Schindler said in his presidential address to the 60th General Assembly of the Union of American Hebrew Congregations, November 1989, in New Orleans:

> I know full well what our literal tradition has to say on the subject. Yet built within it is the possibility of change, once advancing knowledge enlarges our understanding....
>
> Why are *we*, and especially we Reform Jews, not willing to set aside the halachic despisals of homosexuality in order to reflect *our* newer knowledge?
>
> I am working to make the Reform Jewish community a home: a place where loneliness and suffering and exile end; a place that leaves it to God to validate relationships and demands of us only that these relationships be worthy in God's eyes; a place where we can search together, through the Written Torah and the Torah of life, to find those affirmations for which we yearn.

NOTES

1. Alexander M. Schindler, in an address at the Jewish Community Service in Support of People with AIDS, Los Angeles, California, March 12, 1989.

2. Hershel Matt, "Sin, Crime, Sickness, or Alternative Lifestyle?: A Jewish Approach to Homosexuality," *Judaism*, vol. 27, no. 1 (Winter 1978), pp. 13–24; "A Call for Compassion," *Judaism*, vol. 32 (Fall 1983), pp. 432–436; and "Homosexual Rabbis?" *Conservative Judaism*, vol. 39, no. 3 (Spring 1987).

Janet Marder, "Getting to Know the Gay and Lesbian Shul," *Reconstructionist*, vol. 51, no. 2 (October–November 1985).

Yoel Kahn, "The Kedusha of Homosexual Relationships," *CCAR Yearbook*, vol. 99 (New York: CCAR, 1989), pp. 136–141.

Bradley Artson, "Gay and Lesbian Jews: An Innovative Jewish Legal Position," *Jewish Spectator*, vol. 53, no. 3 (Winter 1990), pp. 6–14.

Alexander Schindler, "A Time to Reach Out," *Reform Judaism*, vol. 18, no. 3 (Spring 1990).

Harold Schulweis, "Morality, Legality, and Homosexuality," *Jewish Spectator* (Winter 1992-1993), pp. 23–27.

Rabbi Yaakov Levado [a pseudonym], "Gayness and God: Wrestlings of an Orthodox Rabbi," *Tikkun*, vol. 8, no. 5 (September/October 1993).

3. Leviticus prohibits sex between men and declares it to be a *toevah*, "abhorrence," punishable by death. *Sifra* understood the prohibition to include marriage

between men as well as sex and marriage between women. Maimonides deemed the latter a lesser offense but expanded the prohibition to include nongenital intercourse, even lustful hugs and kisses. Codes and responsa, what little they had to say about the subject, debated only whether or not the prohibition extended to *yichud*, two men alone in a room together. Two responsa acknowledged that *teshuvah*, "repentance," is possible for a man who has had sex with another man.

4. The *machzor* of the Reform movement substituted Leviticus 19 for the traditional reading of the sexual prohibitions in Leviticus 18.

5. Eric Marcus, *Making History: The Struggle for Gay and Lesbian Equal Rights, 1945–1990: An Oral History* (New York: HarperPerennial, 1993); Jonathan Ned Katz, *Gay American History: Lesbians and Gay Men in the U.S.A.*, rev. ed. (New York: Meridian Books, 1976, 1992).

6. *Nice Jewish Girls: A Lesbian Anthology*, ed. Evelyn Torton Beck (Watertown, MA: Persephone Press, 1982); *Twice Blessed: On Being Lesbian, Gay, and Jewish*, eds. Christie Balka and Andy Rose (Boston: Beacon Press, 1989).

7. Anonymous testimony, "A Summary of My Rabbinate," CCAR Ad Hoc Committee on Homosexuality and the Rabbinate, 1987, pp. 4–10. Used for this essay with permission of the author.

8. In 1964 the Council on Religion and the Homosexual (CRH) was formed in San Francisco. There were representatives from the Episcopalians, the Quakers, and the Baptists. On New Year's Day, 1965, the CRH sponsored a costume ball to raise funds for an organization that would welcome gay people back to the church. The ball was raided by the police. Tremendous publicity followed. (Marcus, *Making History*, pp. 140–146)

9. Resolution of the National Federation of Temple Sisterhoods (NFTS), San Francisco, November 1965: "The Bible treats homosexuality as an abomination ... and penalties for its practice were severe. Today, however, enlightened men understand that homosexuality may be a symptom of psychiatric disturbance, which requires sympathetic understanding and psychiatric evaluation.

"We, therefore, deplore the tendency on the part of community authorities to harass homosexuals. We associate ourselves with those religious leaders and legal experts who urge revisions in the criminal code as it relates to homosexuality, especially when it exists between consenting adults. While the young or nonconsenting person must be protected from the advances of disturbed individuals, the aberrations of such individuals must be considered as expressions of possible illness rather than of criminality. We further urge that all available resources of society be brought to bear on the alleviation of this problem."

10. San Francisco's 1977 Gay Pride Parade attracted more than 200,000 marchers. (Marcus, *Making History*, p. 259)

11. The CCAR and the UAHC went on record opposing civil discrimination against homosexuals in 1977; in the same year, NFTS called for "civil, legal, social, and political rights and guarantees for education, housing, employment, pursuit of self-fulfillment, the expression of cultural and ethnic identity, and the absence of coercion or invasion of privacy ... for all persons regardless of color, sex, sexual preference of consenting adults, national origin, religion, and political point of view." The American Jewish Congress and the American Jewish Committee passed resolutions opposing discrimination against homosexuals in 1980 and 1986,

respectively. In 1990 the Rabbinical Assembly and the United Synagogue called for "full civil equality for gays and lesbians in our national life."

12. There was a national march on Washington in 1979 by 75,000 to 100,000 in support of passage of national gay rights legislation and an end to the discrimination by the Department of Defense. (Marcus, *Making History*, p. 258)

13. A group of gay and lesbian students and alumni of the Hebrew Union College-Jewish Institute of Religion (HUC-JIR) wrote to the CCAR Ad Hoc Committee on Homosexuality and the Rabbinate, December 1, 1987:

> During the last ten years, the Gay Rights movement has made tremendous progress. At the recent National March on Washington for Gay and Lesbian Rights, 500,000 people, including clergy from many organized religious bodies, demonstrated their solidarity. The Reform movement's absence was keenly felt.
>
> The Reform movement has long stood for putting the vision of the prophets into action. Standing in the face of bigotry and opposition, our movement marched in Selma, marched to protest the involvement in Vietnam, and marched to give voices to our silent brothers and sisters who are prisoners of Zion. As you marched with them, march with us!
>
> May the God of our ancestors grant you the strength and the courage to embrace us as *am echad.*

14. 1973 was also the year that the American Psychiatric Association removed homosexuality as a mental disorder from its *Diagnostic and Statistical Manual.* "Between 1972 and 1975 at least ten lesbian and gay Jewish groups were established in the United States and abroad." (Aaron Cooper, "No Longer Invisible: Gay and Lesbian Jews Build a Movement," *Homosexuality and Religion* [New York/London: The Haworth Press, 1989], pp. 85–86)

15. In 1977 the presence of Beit Chayim Chadashim (BCC) as a member of the UAHC made a significant difference. On the agenda for the 54th General Assembly was a gay rights resolution entitled "The Human Rights of Homosexuals"; the resolution was not expected to be controversial by its authors and supporters. One of those, Rabbi Irv Herman, then UAHC regional director in Los Angeles, saw in the national landscape the rising tide of antigay bigotry in the form of Anita Bryant, California's Briggs Initiative, and voter referenda seeking to overturn existing gay rights ordinances in several cities. Rabbi Herman hoped that a UAHC resolution would lend support to the progressive, antiprejudicial position in the national debate. Yet when the resolution came before the UAHC delegates, it received a mere 20 percent vote of support and was returned to committee for rewriting.... As a result of a heroic twenty-four-hour effort by BCC delegates and several speakers who addressed the Assembly about the substantial role that BCC played within the Los Angeles Jewish community, ... a resolution passed with a nearly 80 percent vote of support. (Ibid., p. 87)

16. Ibid., pp. 93,94. As at the UAHC biennial, gay and lesbian Jews around the

country began to tell their stories and make their case for acceptance before the mainstream Jewish community. In 1981 San Francisco's Congregation Sha'ar Zahav, the Board of Jewish Education, and the Jewish Family and Children's Service co-sponsored a conference on "Judaism and Homosexuality" for professionals working in the Jewish community; a similar conference was sponsored in Seattle in 1985; in 1983 two members of *Yetziah* led a workshop for Boston-area Hillel rabbis; in 1986 Stephen Wise Free Synagogue, along with the New York chapter of the American Jewish Committee, NFTS District 3, the Federation of Reconstructionist Congregations and Chavurot, New Jewish Agenda, and several New York synagogues held a conference entitled "Lesbian and Gay Jews in the Jewish Community"; that same year, the New York chapter of the National Council of Jewish Women formed a support group for Jewish lesbians.

17. Alexander M. Schindler, in a speech in support of lesbian and gay Jews delivered at the Jewish Community Service in Support of People with AIDS, sponsored by the AIDS Committee of the UAHC, Pacific Southwest Council, Leo Baeck Temple, Los Angeles, March 12, 1989.

18. Prior to the 1987 UAHC resolution, a few mainstream synagogues had already opened their doors to openly lesbian and gay Jews. Stephen Wise Free Synagogue and Beth Am, The People's Temple, both in New York City, were among the first.

19. Alexander M. Schindler, in an address at the Jewish Community Service in Support of People with AIDS, Los Angeles, March 12, 1989.

20. 60th General Assembly of the UAHC, New Orleans, November 1989.

21. Reconstructionist Rabbinical Association (RRA), 1990; Rabbinical Assembly (RA), 1990; United Synagogue (US), 1991.

22. A mother speaking at a Conservative synagogue in suburban Philadelphia, spring 1994.

23. Comments made in 1987 at the first celebration of Lesbian and Gay Pride Shabbat held at Beth Am, The People's Temple, New York City.

24. It is as naive to think that an environment that accepts gay people will influence children to become gay as it is to think that an environment that rejects gay people will discourage children from becoming gay. Most gay men and lesbians currently over the age of thirty were raised in families, communities, religious traditions, and states hostile to homosexuality—and yet they grew up to be gay nonetheless.

25. Rabbi Alexander M. Schindler, in his presidential address, 60th General Assembly of the UAHC, New Orleans, November 1989.

26. *The New York Times*, Friday, March 5, 1993.

27. "In an unpublished, privately circulated responsum concerning the establishment of synagogues for homosexuals, Eugene Mihaly characterizes homosexuality as a category of duress, *ones*, that 'merits all the sympathy, consideration, and kindness that the *halachah* extends to the victim.'" (Robert Kirschner, "Halakhah and Homosexuality: A Reappraisal," *Judaism: A Quarterly Journal of Jewish Life and Thought*, vol. 37, no. 4 [Fall 1988], p. 451, note 3)

28. Levado, "Gayness and God," p. 55.

29. Rabbi Joel Roth, "Homosexuality," in the Conservative movement's *Teshuvot on Gay and Lesbian Issues*.

30. Levado, "Gayness and God," p. 57.

31. Judith Plaskow, "Lesbian and Gay Rights: Asking the Right Questions," *Tikkun,* vol. 9, no. 2 (March/April 1994), pp. 31–32.

32. Report of the CCAR Ad Hoc Committee on Homosexuality and the Rabbinate, adopted at the CCAR convention, June 1990. "A minority of the committee dissents, affirming the equal possibility of covenantal fulfillment in homosexual and heterosexual relationships. The relationship, not the gender, should determine its Jewish value—*kiddushin.*"

33. The C.S.A. passed a nondiscrimination-in-employment resolution on April 10, 1991.

34. The UAHC endorsed spousal benefits in 1993.

35. Events for discussion in rabbinic sermons might include milestone anniversaries of the Stonewall rebellion, the passage of a local gay civil rights ordinance, or the defeat of an antigay ballot initiative.

36. Issues addressed in rabbinic sermons might include rejection by one's parents, coming out to one's children, choosing a donor known or unknown for insemination, the spirituality of the stranger, the connection between sexuality and spirituality, hiding vs. honesty, and the role of lesbians and gay men in God's universe.

37. Victor Appell in his sermon at the seventh annual Lesbian/Gay Pride Shabbat Service at Beth Am, The People's Temple, New York City, June 18, 1993.

38. In the 1970s most members of gay synagogues used aliases or only first names, fearing that a newsletter might fall into the hands of an employer or parent.

39. See Yoel H. Kahn, "The Liturgy of Gay and Lesbian Jews," *Twice Blessed,* pp. 182 ff.

40. The celebration of Lesbian/Gay Pride Day, for example, is an annual event of great significance to most gay men and lesbians. Celebrating lesbian/gay pride in a Jewish way (e.g., with *Shehecheyanu, Hallel,* etc.) brings together two of the identities that matter most to a gay Jew. Outside of gay/lesbian synagogues, few mainstream synagogues place Shabbat Pride on their ritual calendars.

41. Anonymous testimony, CCAR Ad Hoc Committee on Homosexuality and the Rabbinate, 1987, pp. 11–12.

42. Resolution, RRA convention, March 1993, Federation of Reconstructionist Congregations and Havurot (FRCH) board, June 1993.

43. In 1991 a state clerk in Hawaii refused to issue marriage licenses for two lesbian couples and one gay couple. Since then several state legislatures have moved to ban same-sex marriages. The constitutionality of those bans is being challenged in the courts.

44. At the 1993 UAHC Biennial Convention in San Francisco, the President's Message Committee drafted and the delegates passed a resolution entitled "Recognition for Lesbian and Gay Partnerships":

...The UAHC resolves to:

1. call upon our federal, provincial, state, and local governments to adopt legislation that will (a) afford partners in committed lesbian and gay partnerships spousal benefits that include participation in health care plans and survivor benefits; (b) ensure that lesbians and gay men are not adjudged unfit to raise

children because of their sexual orientation; and (c) afford partners in committed lesbian and gay relationships the means of legally acknowledging such relationships and

2. call upon our congregations, the CCAR, and HUC-JIR to join with us in seeking to extend the same benefits that are extended to the spouses of married staff members and employees to the partners of all staff members living in committed lesbian and gay partnerships.

45. Co-parent adoption became possible in New York only in January 1992 with Judge Preminger's decision "In the Matter of the Adoption of a Child Whose First Name Is Evan." In April 1995, however, a panel of judges in a New York appellate court ruled *against* the co-parent adoption by the lesbian partner of the biological mother of "Dana" on the grounds that her mothers are not legally married. (*The New York Times*, April 6, 1995, p. B3)

R eform recasts tradition deliberately and openly. We conceive of Judaism as a dynamic and not a static faith, one that is never in a state of "being" but is always in a state of "becoming," a relentless flowing on. We insist that religious law is not frozen like ice but is a soluble substance to be mixed with human tears.

Rabbi Eleazar taught:

> A person should be as soft as a reed and not as hard as a cedar.
> Because of this quality, reeds have been privileged to be selected
> as pens with which Torahs, *tefilin,* and *mezuzot* are written.

So are we selected, in our flexibility, to write the Torahs and *tefilin* and *mezuzot* for this most dramatic period of Jewish history, this era of near-total destruction and epic reconstruction.

This very flexibility, however, directs our attention to another problem confronting Reform...the need to achieve ideological coherence. The elasticity of our Judaism has undoubtedly produced the elasticity of our numbers, but stretched too far it can rip us apart. Reform allows for a wide spectrum of belief, a ranging gamut of theological stances. Nonetheless, some common understanding *is* necessary to give us the kind of ideological cohesion a religious movement, or any movement for that matter, requires to retain its distinctiveness and to secure its continuity.

The parameters of Reform are especially difficult to draw. Which beliefs have a valid place in Reform Judaism and which do not? Is there *any* ideology that is beyond the pale of Reform? Can we accommodate all theological stances, just so long as they do not claim authoritative revelation or seek to impose their perceptions or practices on all of us? Just what *is* essential to a Reform outlook, what is optional, and what—if anything—is forbidden?

Rabbi Alexander M. Schindler
State of the Union Message
Baltimore, Maryland
November 1991

REFORM AS AN ADJECTIVE
WHAT ARE THE LIMITS?

W. GUNTHER PLAUT

Some years ago, Leonard Fein suggested that the best way to understand "Reform" was to treat it primarily as a verb.[1] He did so in order to underscore the dynamic quality of our movement, and his emphasis was eagerly taken up in our subsequent practice.

But times have changed, and the needs of our movement have changed with them. The challenge of our day is to remind ourselves that viewed from another angle, Reform must be treated as an *adjective*. When we say "Reform Judaism," the weight must be on "Judaism" as a noun with "Reform" as an adjective, describing a specific type of Jewish existence and hope.

I say this because I fear that a new spirit has gripped many of our people and leaders. There is a danger that Reform Judaism may cut itself off from its moorings.

We in North America are so eager for adjustment to the environment that we are stressing our ethnicity above all and, at the same time, diminishing our specific religious tradition more and more. We are constantly widening the borders of Judaism in the name of tolerance and openness so that today we have reached a point where "Reform" is becoming a determinative noun and "Judaism" a descriptive adjective; that is to say, we are stressing "Reform" at the expense of "Judaism."

But by making Reform Judaism a Jewish type of reform, we are standing our movement on its head and doing so in the name of progress. I call to mind the caution of the late Rabbi Julius Gordon who reminded the UAHC at a convention a generation ago: "Going forever forward is a noble slogan, but when you stand at a precipice, going forward is the opposite of progress."

✦   ✦   ✦

It is time to take a good look at ourselves and see if history can be our guide.

Reform began in Germany 180 years ago when a rabbi-business-man, Israel Jacobson, introduced a few innovations into the traditional prayer service. In the course of the next generation, additional reforms, which were bitterly opposed by the traditional-ists, initiated a new movement. However, its leaders were constantly on the watch not to let the movement innovate recklessly. They wanted to reform Jewish practice while at the same time maintaining their close identification with the essentials of Judaism. They did not want to become a Jewish sect like the Karaites a thousand years before, and each change they proposed or introduced was, therefore, solidly founded on precedent and prin-ciple. "Judaism" was always the noun and "Reform," "Liberal," or "Progressive" the modifying adjective.

The founders took it for granted that in all their innovations there were limits that had to be preserved—the principle of *yesh gevul*—limits that should not be transgressed, and they constantly reminded themselves and their constituents of this. Thus, when one of their leading scholars, Abraham Geiger, suggested that the time had come to abandon what he called the "barbaric" custom of circumcision, he was firmly rebuffed. So, too, was one of the most brilliant and learned of his colleagues, the redoubtable Samuel Holdheim, who made light of the principle *yesh gevul* by pushing the limits farther and farther, proposing all sorts of innovations that also failed to find resonance among the liberals of German Jewry.

But while the liberalism of the European founders of our move-ment remained orderly, no such measured progress prevailed once the reformers reached North America. Here, the frontiers of life were blurred, and so were the limits the founders of Reform had observed. In the New World there were no limits as to what could be changed. "Reform means change," our Reform rabbis proclaimed, and they did so without specifying whether any or all changes could fit the bill or where the limits of permissible change might be.

Of course, they did this in the spirit of high ideals and thought they were doing the right thing. The Pittsburgh Platform, formulated by nineteen rabbis, proclaimed what was later called "classical Reform." In retrospect, it was nothing of the sort. It was pure and simple radical, revolutionary reform for it abandoned with one fell stroke all *halachah*, which had been the unifying basis of the Judaism known until then. Jews had lived by a system of *mitzvot* that defined their relationship to the God of the covenant and to their fellow human beings. Without using the term, the new Reform proclaimed that *yesh gevul* no longer applied, and, therefore, the limits were all but abolished.

No wonder, then, that in the generation to follow everything was up for grabs: Sunday services replaced Shabbat, which as a twenty-four-hour observance completely disappeared; Hebrew vanished almost entirely from our services and from our religious schools; pork and shellfish became acceptable delicacies; we threw out the Talmud along with the *yarmulke*, the nonwearing of which became a symbol of true Reform, which considered the head covering offensive to civic behavior. The new Zionist movement was declared a nationalist aberration and ritual a hindrance to true religiosity.

We still asserted that Torah was our guide but proceeded to say that most of its laws were no longer relevant and, besides, Torah was a human reaction with dubious divine input. One of our movement's greatest stars, Rabbi Emil G. Hirsch of Chicago (brother-in-law of the HUC president Kaufmann Kohler and son-in-law of David Einhorn, creator of the old *Union Prayer Book*), took the logical step and removed the Torah scrolls from the sanctuary.

In plain fact, we replaced much, if not most, of Jewish tradition with elements of the new North American civic religion. We stressed social justice and ethical conduct, broad-mindedness and scientific pragmatism. If it worked, it was good; if it didn't, it was cast off. In effect, the old Judaism was considered obsolete.

Orthodox Jews were looked down upon, and their continued use of Yiddish and stubborn adherence to ritual, *kashrut,* and similar vestiges of the past were regarded as archaic and almost un-American. A number of our people perceived little difference between Reform Judaism and Unitarianism or Ethical Culture and crossed the line. The limits were disappearing.

With this new Reform radicalism, however, came also a surge of great idealism. The Reformers believed that the brotherhood of man was about to be realized and the new Judaism was to be one of its standard-bearers. Our movement engaged some of the finest people; they were generous and high-minded, believed in social reform, and, above all, were proud to be American.

✦ ✦ ✦

A profound change developed in the next generation, which experienced the advent of virulent anti-Semitism, the Holocaust, and the establishment of Israel. We had flirted with becoming a Jewish sect but were now thrust back into Jewish history. In honor of our movement, let it be said, we embraced the new opportunity with unbounded enthusiasm. We reformed ourselves and returned to the ideals of our founders.

We rediscovered a measure of tradition that we had needlessly discarded. The *yarmulke* did not reenter our sanctuaries as a returning hero, but its rejection ceased to be a signpost of true Reform. We established camps to inspire our young; we created opportunities for adults and considered their education an essential aspect of our endeavors. We reached out to the non-Jewish spouses in our midst and tried to have them become partners in our exciting search for meaning. We continued to make social action and ethical pursuits honored hallmarks of our movement, but we now made them part of a larger battle for the Jewish soul. Above all, we rediscovered the need for *mitzvah* as a vital cornerstone of our Judaism; Shabbat and holy days were given new meanings; and books like *Gates of Mitzvah* became textbooks for our confirmands. We are still short of making our homes once again the true bulwarks of Reform, but at least we know what needs to be done and are making a serious start.

There are those who think that this marks a headlong return to Orthodoxy or Conservatism. The fear is unfounded. When our members build a *sukah* at home rather than merely visit one in the temple, they are bringing a synagogue-oriented religion back to where it belongs first and foremost: the home. What we are doing is rediscovering the sources that have nourished us and from which we have been separated too long. Reform Judaism must not be a haven for convenience, although for some it has been just that. Reform is not the same as doing less or even doing nothing.

We hope to remain innovators, but at the same time we are determined to remain Jews in the religious and not merely the ethnic sense. If the survival of Judaism is primarily a matter of ethnicity, we are in deep trouble. Mixed-marriage statistics indicate that in the generation to come there will be fewer Jews in the Diaspora. Our percentage in the world's population, already very low, will shrink even more rapidly. We Jews, instead of being countless like the sand by the sea, as the blessing of Abraham holds out, are a dwindling part of an exploding humanity. If we obliterate or remove the landmarks that distinguish the territory of Judaism, we are in effect counseling religious suicide.

To put it bluntly, we cannot be all things to all people. We are not a secular movement. We must once again remind ourselves that, ultimately, we are here in an attempt to respond to the voice of God. That's what Judaism and, therefore, Reform Judaism is all about. We are part of a historic, religious people in a historic, religious context.

◆   ◆   ◆

Perhaps no other arm of our movement symbolizes this conviction as clearly as does the Responsa Committee of the Central Conference of American Rabbis, a group of eight rabbis appointed to answer questions that come to them from rabbis and laypeople alike, from men and women, and recently children as well, who are wondering what the proper response is to a variety of vexing problems. These questions run the gamut of life, and they always end with the question: "What does Reform Judaism have to say about this?"

For example, they ask about the religious permissibility of nuclear war. They want to know about the status of a congregation that does not believe in God and prayer but nonetheless wants to join the Union. They want to know if there is a need to circumcise a convert or how to treat a transsexual who applies for marriage—

that is to say, about everything from moral issues to ritual matters. Of course, the committee does not legislate; it merely renders an opinion, and those who ask the question are free to accept or disregard that opinion. This is the traditional way of responsa, of *she'elot* and *teshuvot*, and some of the leaders of our movement, from Kaufmann Kohler to Solomon Freehof and Walter Jacob, have been our sterling guides.

We always start by asking: "How would traditional Judaism respond to the question at hand?" While that in itself is not always clear, there is a general line of understanding that we can usually discern. In other words, we start with our past; we do not start *de novo*. And then we proceed to ask: "Given the traditional answer, are there commanding principles that have been expressed during the 180 years of Reform Judaism that would cause us to override this tradition and set it aside?" Thus, we have overridden traditional *halachah* in the area of the religious equality of the sexes, which Reform affirms as a principle and traditional Judaism denies. In following this process, we are creating a Liberal *halachah*.

I have considered the function of the Responsa Committee at some length because I see it as a paradigm of our movement. We are, so to speak, the Reform movement in miniature. We study the question at hand; we debate it; we prepare written analyses; and in the end we vote. Often we agree, and often we do not. The same set of facts is accorded different weight by different members. In a given instance some will stress tradition; others will cite the needs of society—or whatever the cause for difference may be. We render considered advice to the questioner—no more but also no less. And when in the end we choose to publish our responses in the *Journal of Reform Judaism*, in the *Yearbook* of the Central Conference of American Rabbis, or in a special volume of collected responses, we publish the dissents along with the majority opinions. Thus, everyone who asks questions of our committee becomes part of this process and helps to shape the values and limits of Reform. (Two sample responsa are appended to this essay.)

◆　◆　◆

Taking tradition seriously is, of course, only the starting point of true Reform. There are added considerations that determine what we should do and what we should not do.

1. *We must never forget that we are part of our people*. What we call *K'lal Yisrael*, the community of all Jews, cannot and must not be set aside without the most careful and loving consideration. For this above all is true for us: We are and remain part of this people, and its needs and feelings are cornerstones of our consciousness.

2. *Everything must be weighed on the scale of justice and ethics*. The voices of the prophets, which have played so great a part in the growth of our movement, must not be muted.

3. *The needs of the society in which we live require our attention*. We consider this concern both our responsibility and our right.

These are some examples of what goes into the shaping of limits for Reform Judaism. A generation ago Reform needed to be more dynamic. We took up Fein's challenge, and the period that followed saw an unprecedented expansion of our movement, with Rabbi Alexander Schindler setting much of the agenda.

But our needs have shifted. We need to worry less about reforming what we have and more about making it and keeping it Jewish. While we need to be dynamic, *Reform is and must always be an adjective that modifies Judaism*. In our headlong rush into the future, we must remember that we are part of Jewish history and have unbreakable ties with it.

Judaism is the ground of our religious existence. It belongs to us as well as to the Jewish people. We Reformers are the cutting edge of progress, not for our own sake, but for the sake of Judaism. That has been our goal and that it must always remain.

Two Sample Responsa
Should a Mezuzah Be Affixed to the Synagogue?

Question

Our congregation is renovating and expanding the sanctuary. In the past we did not have a *mezuzah* on the sanctuary door, but the question has been raised whether it is not time to change our practice. An answer from the Responsa Committee will be greatly appreciated. (Rabbi H.N.)

Answer

The Torah says that the divine word should be inscribed "on the doorposts of your house and on your gates." (Deuteronomy 6:9)

The term *house* has traditionally been interpreted as a dwelling place, and the *Shulchan Aruch* expressly states that synagogues do not need *mezuzot* unless they contain an apartment. (*Yoreh Deah* 286:3)

However, custom has gone beyond the minimum requirements of the *halachah*. In Israel, all public buildings and synagogues have *mezuzot*, and this *minhag* is also found in the Diaspora. In Toronto, to my knowledge, all synagogues have *mezuzot*, and I rather think that this custom is not confined to our city. It is my feeling that it will sooner or later spread to most places.

Is there any reason why Reform temples should have a special policy that disagrees with this development? We see no reason for it. On the contrary, the affixing of a *mezuzah* to the entrance(s) of the building will give you the opportunity to stress the importance of this symbol for every Jew. The command to affix *mezuzot* to our private homes and apartments is being increasingly neglected, and it must be made clear that in this respect as in any other, the synagogue serves as a model but not as a surrogate for our obligations. Discuss this issue with your building and worship committees and make the Question an instrument for the teaching of Torah.

Buddhist Jews Wish to Join Temple

Question

A husband and wife who have a Jewish background and are currently practicing Buddhism as well as Judaism want to join the temple and enroll their child in the religious school.

The wife was born Jewish; her husband was converted to Judaism as a teenager. They are presently members of a Conservative synagogue (where their Buddhist practices are apparently unknown) but now want to join a Reform temple because they consider its religious education program superior and also because Reform Judaism seems more compatible to them. The woman is an ordained priest in the Zen tradition. Her husband states that by adding Tibetan Buddhist practices to his life, he has enhanced his Judaism. The two consider their Buddhism basically nontheological, permitting synchronous religious practice. They do not missionize. (N.T., president of the temple)

Answer

The relationship between Judaism and other religions has often been dealt with in halachic literature. Although since the days of Maimonides, Christianity (like Islam) was removed from the category of idolatrous faiths, *teshuvot* have nonetheless consistently taken the view that Judaism and Christianity are mutually exclusive and that Jews—whether born or converted to Judaism—practicing and affirming Christian doctrine are to be considered apostates.[2] If they wish to return to the synagogue, it would be necessary for them to abjure their Christian faith.[3] The question arises: Is Buddhism in this respect comparable to Christianity?

Buddhism originated in the sixth century B.C.E. and has developed into an extraordinarily variegated stream of philosophies and practices. Centered in eastern Asia, it has spread all over the globe, and national subdivisions have created additional complexities.

The most popular form of later Buddhism has been the "Pure Land" or Amitabhist doctrine, which teaches salvation through grace in the Buddha Amitabha. There can be little question that in this form Buddhism is in fact a religion, as we use that term and concept.

While at one end of this religious spectrum one finds theistic and even clearly polytheistic beliefs, other types of Buddhism may, however, be called nontheistic in that they emphasize ethics and contemplative practices. Thus, Zen Buddhism (of which there are also various streams) may generally be assigned to the latter category in that it stresses meditation and self-discipline as the path to individual enlightenment and spiritual growth. Yoga is one of its best-known practices.

Tibetan Buddhism is in some respects quite different from Zen since it has incorporated forms of the pre-Buddhist Bon cult and knows of oracular priests and concepts like divine kingship. However, it, too, stresses spiritual development and has developed distinct practices to achieve it.

Ordinarily, as noted above, when Jews profess another religion, they are considered apostates, especially when they have adopted the Christian or Muslim faith. Is such judgment appropriate also when it comes to Buddhism, and is it appropriate in view of the circumstances of the present case?

If we were to deal solely with the husband, we might be inclined to interpret his statement as meaning that he is engaging in meditative practices that enhance his spiritual awareness. The fact that he learned them from Buddhist teachers would not seem to be in competition with his Jewish identity and practice. Many Jews experiment in this fashion, which would not expose them to the charge of apostasy.

The matter is, however, complicated by the admission of the wife that she is a Zen Buddhist *priest*. Depending on the type of Zen she affirms, being a priest could have various meanings. For the moment, let us assume that, in this case, "priest" (like "rabbi") means primarily a teacher, since Zen—the word means meditation—favors the master-to-pupil or mind-to-mind method of teaching contemplation.

But being a priest demands a special type of identification and commitment, which suggests that the devotee has embraced not only teaching practices like yoga but also the underlying deeper philosophy. Without in any way denying the depth of Buddhist philosophical and ethical doctrines, Judaism sees fundamental differences between these doctrines and the teachings of Jewish tradition.

Judaism clearly affirms this world and does not, as the majority of Buddhist traditions do, denigrate its importance. Reform Judaism especially has downplayed the salvational aspects of our religion and has taught that we have an obligation to perfect *this* world in all its aspects—from the environment to its social structures. Judaism is a deed-oriented rather than a contemplative religion, and while the merits of the latter are great, it reflects a basically different approach to the needs of everyday life. Therefore, Rabbi Leo Baeck took the view that Judaism and Buddhism are complete opposites, "two religious polarities."[4]

To be sure, there is no conflict between Judaism and meditative practices. After all, Jewish tradition itself is familiar with them. But we see a conflict between the world-affirming view we hold and the world-denying view of Buddhism. It is, therefore, inappropriate to consider a Buddhist priest as eligible for membership in the congregation. The husband alone *might* qualify, but as a family the couple does not.

There is also the question of public perception—*mar'it ayin*—to be considered. The Jewish community, and especially the members of your congregation, would be confused by what they would see as an experiment in religious syncretism and a watering down of Jewish identity. The couple must be brought to realize that with all the respect we have for their Buddhist practices and beliefs, the enrichment they think they have brought to their Judaism may fit their own personal needs, but it does not fit the needs of a congregation. Their request to join the congregation should, therefore, not be accommodated.

Yet, there is also a pastoral aspect to their situation. Since they want to be Jewish and do, in fact, practice Judaism on some levels, we must be sure not to push them away. In view of their meandering search for religious meaning—from Christianity (in the husband's case) to Judaism to Buddhism to Conservative and now Reform Judaism—the rabbi should engage them in counseling and help them find their way.

As for the child, halachic tradition would consider him/her Jewish, even if the mother were to be considered an apostate. This view has been affirmed by a CCAR responsum.[5] In view of this, should the child be admitted to religious school?

Assuming that the congregation's bylaws permit enrolling a child of nonmembers, the rabbi's judgment will have to prevail. We would counsel against admitting the child if it appears that he/she is to be brought up in two religious traditions. Rabbi Walter Jacob affirmed, for instance, that a boy could not be a bar mitzvah if he also has had a Christian confirmation.[6] The rabbi will have to consider the possibility that other children in the religious school may be thoroughly perplexed if they learn that a fellow student professes two religious identities. It is difficult enough to teach our children the uniqueness of Judaism and its essentials.

NOTES

1. Leonard Fein, *Reform Is a Verb* (New York: UAHC Press, 1972).
2. Walter Jacob, ed., *American Reform Responsa* (New York: CCAR, 1983), p. 241; idem, *Contemporary American Reform Responsa*, #68 (New York: CCAR, 1987), for references to earlier halachic material.
3. W. Jacob, *American Reform Responsa*, p. 241; also Solomon B. Freehof, "Gentile

Membership in Synagogue," *Reform Responsa for Our Time*, #47 (New York: HUC Press, 1977).

4. Leo Baeck, *The Essence of Judaism*, rev. ed. (New York: Schocken Books, 1948), pp. 60f.

5. W. Jacob, *American Reform Responsa*, p. 241.

6. W. Jacob, *Contemporary American Reform Responsa*, #61.

Our challenge is to root our own lives as Reform Jews in an active and genuine faith in God and, as parents or teachers, to convey to our children a vivid sense of the reality of God. Very simply, I am speaking here about bringing God into our homes and into our classrooms not merely as a character in Bible stories, not merely as an anthropomorphic figure of whom we are skeptical but as the force whom we affirm as the incarnation of our richest feelings, our greatest hopes, our interconnectedness, our ethical sensibility.

When our children feel the budding of compassion, the swelling of love, the sorrow of repentance, it is *then* that we must say to them: "Ah...now you are standing in the presence of God." Then they, too, might be comfortable about making such an affirmation in the presence of *their* children.

Continuity is not dependent upon our making a leap of faith but a leap of consciousness, a willingness to experience our higher spirituality and to name it for what it is: communion with God.

Let us awaken to our full humaneness and in that awakening learn of God's presence. From there our prayers will arise not as a learned skill or memorized liturgy but as a natural response to our awareness of God—as natural as our laughter, our tears, and our breath.

Rabbi Alexander M. Schindler
Keynote Address
National Association of Temple
Educators—Fortieth Anniversary
Albuquerque, New Mexico
December 25, 1994

REFORM: MODERN MOVEMENT IN A POSTMODERN ERA?

EUGENE B. BOROWITZ

For nearly two centuries now almost all Jews who could modernize have done so. They knew that modernity was good for them, that the great gains that democracy, equality, and opportunity afforded them overrode the Jewish problems connected with modernization. The genius of Reform Judaism, as Michael Meyer has shown in his impressive history of our movement, *Response to Modernity*, lay in adapting to and seeking to transform this determining social development. And since this thrust to be part of modernity still drives much of contemporary Jewish life, it continues to energize Reform Judaism.

But if modernity is losing its allure and we are moving toward a postmodern era, then we should be changing certain of our emphases. I propose no more than that, but I consider them course corrections critical to our continuing religious vitality. I regard Alex Schindler's leadership of the UAHC so distinguished by his canny perception of the changes in our historic situation that it seemed a fitting tribute to his accomplishments to venture some thoughts about the agenda facing his successor.

Let me immediately qualify my aims. Since no one can be certain where history and culture are heading, these views are speculative—though they come with considerable evidence behind them and spring from a perspective that uniquely clarifies the many changes we see taking place around us. Then, too, I use the term *postmodern* without stressing the *post*, though some postmoderns want to create a contemporary equivalent to the ghetto. By contrast, I think it important that we carry forward what we believe are modernity's lasting spiritual insights. Nonetheless, *post* must not be slighted for I am also convinced we cannot import modern spirituality into a changed ethos without reshaping its central affirmations.

The cultural shift called postmodernism did not first arise among Jews out of their unique recent experience. Rather, it was evident all over Western civilization as the twentieth century proceeded and doubts about modernity's beneficence became prominent and widespread. Two particular irritants were political malfeasance and the general deterioration of the quality of life, but disappointment increasingly tinged much of life with dejection. The Enlightenment, the intellectual credo of modernity, had promised that replacing tradition with rational skepticism, hierarchy with democracy, and custom with freedom would bring messianic benefits. The conclusion was inescapable: It certainly hasn't.

On a deeper level, the loss of confidence in Enlightenment values came from the collapse of its intellectual foundations. The assumptions about mind, self, and human nature that once powered the bold move into greater freedom now seem questionable. All had a profound influence on modernized Jews, those virtuosi of cultural adaptation. To give three instances: Rereading Abraham Heschel's theoretical works today, one hears his plea for an authoritative, God-centered revelation as a premature response to this change of mood. It also helps explain the evanescence of "modern Orthodoxy" into "centrist Orthodoxy" while the most vital growth on the religious right came among those groups who consciously distanced themselves from the modern. And the utterly unanticipated Jewish turn to mysticism now seems a natural reaction against modernity's rigid rationalism.

A Phenomenon Eluding Definition and Lacking a Center

The demystification of modernity is manifest in many fields, but it has no accepted ideology though some would like to make the French critic and philosopher Jacques Derrida its central theoretician. For many reasons, I think postmodernism is best described as a moving cultural wave continually redirected by people applying its energy to their activity. Architecture offers the most accessible example. There one sees the sleek, spare buildings of the modern master Mies van der Rohe succeeded by the imaginative, decorative ones of his former disciple Philip Johnson. In musical composition the tight clamps of an earlier formalism now often open into looser, more expressive creations. In academic and cultural circles these developments have been closely identified with literary criticism and the effort to refashion philosophy. Here Derrida's influence dominates.

Let me risk the violence of summing up his highly complex, still-evolving thinking in the proposition that cuts to the heart of my concern with his thought: Words are all we have. There is no way, as philosophers long dreamed, of starting our reasoning with notions that are simply "given" or "self-evident" and thus uncontestable foundations for all our subsequent knowledge. For if mood becomes thought only as it is verbalized and is then necessarily shaped by the language in which it is expressed, making sweeping claims for one's thoughts becomes grandiose. Thinking and writing should best be understood, Derrida and many others argue, not as unmasking reality but as elegant wordplay.

This line of reasoning and other convergent ones have as good as destroyed the supreme confidence moderns had in the human mind—that is, as their science and culture exemplified it. But as they have demythologized the Cartesian notion of "clear and distinct ideas," the postmoderns have also deconstructed ethics and turned moral imperatives into just words about words. No Jewish thinker, no sensitive human being could fail to be appalled by this potential nihilism, particularly when we have been witness to one ethical outrage after another. With the memory of the Hitler occupation still alive in France, the Derrideans have not been blind to this problem, and their writing is often touched by a strong moral passion. But none has yet clarified how a deconstructionist could have a commanding ethics, something with the urgency of biblical commands. An American philosopher, Edith Wyschogrod, has made a notable effort in this direction by her study of a number of female moral exemplars, but the distance between good models and compelling norms remains great.

A Theological, Non-Derridean Approach

My own postmodernism has moved in a quite uncommon direction for, against Derrida's confident assertion that it is no longer possible to have any "foundations" for our thought, I know myself to be a

Jew first and an adherent of a philosophical system second. What I believe may be obscure, wavering, and difficult to put into words, but to deny it would be to contradict who I truly am. Despite its hiddenness, my Jewish faith is real, real enough that despite my secularization and skeptical intellect, I try to base my life on it.

Postmodernism supplies me with as adequate a cultural language as I can find to interpret and communicate "my" experienced life of Jewish belief. I hastily add about this "my" (in typical postmodern consciousness of the circularity of all thought) that I do not mean by this "my" individual, interior religious experience—which would be the customary way for a modern religious thinker to proceed. Rather (in typical postmodern particularity), I claim to read ("my"/our) the Jewish people's spiritual experience in recent decades out of my participation and reflection on it. Most of our community is too highly secularized or academicized to scrutinize the religious subtext of what we have been through. But it is just this that grounds the fuller statement of the views in my book *Renewing the Covenant, a Theology for the Postmodern Jew*. I will shortly present its three underlying principles and draw their implications for a postmodern Reform Judaism. But since mine is the first full-scale postmodern theory of Judaism—and a maverick, non-Derridean, theological one at that—let me take a few words to explain why I find the cultural climate created by Derrida's work the least inadequate way today to express my intuition of Jewish truth.

Postmodernism's rejection of foundations ends linear logic's claim to exclusive value and analytic rationality's privileged role as the required style for serious exposition. It thus allows for the kind of "thick" writing in theology that anthropologists have found helpful in describing a foreign culture's many layers. With "objectivity" unattainable—how can the language of any one person claim to be adequate to the truth of everyone, everywhere?—the religious thinker's particularity (gender, race, class, etc.) now has a proper role in thinking, and that speaks to one certainty of "my"/our Jewish religiosity. Lazy, self-indulgent, or anti-intellectual writers can, of course, exploit this postmodern linguistic openness to produce works that seem to me less "thought" than effusion. But I trust the Jewish community to determine in due course which statements of its corporate faith have value.

The Postmodern Difference: My Three Assertions

I can epitomize my understanding of Jewish religious post-modernity as revisions of three modern views: (1) that of people's utter priority to God, (2) that of the individual self's utter priority to community, and, as a result of rethinking these prior two, (3) that of utterly independent personal autonomy.

First, modern religiosity—including the Jewish—is more sure of people than of God. Thus its typical procedure is to identify some certainty about human beings and then move from it toward what people can then reasonably call God. In modern Jewish thought Hermann Cohen's foundation was rationality, Mordecai Kaplan's the experience of growth and development (in a culture), and Buber's the "I-Thou" experience (though his God has some independence). Religion is thus always a personal spiritual search or quest, as secure or as ambivalent as its human base allowed. Making humankind the basis of one's religiosity had the virtue of encouraging people to use their individual and communal power to do the good, a liberation that contributed in countless ways to the betterment of human lives.

This reliance on human knowledge and activism came in conscious rejection of the "premodern" form of religiosity, one dominated by God. Thus, in Judaism, God descends on Mount Sinai, God gives the Torah, and, thereby, God transforms an aggregate of slaves into the people of Israel. So in the Bible and prayer book God speaks, commands, listens, answers, observes, judges, rewards, punishes, forgives, helps, saves/redeems, and much else. Founding Jewish lives, individual and communal, on the one Sovereign of the universe had the great virtue of bringing stability and security into existence and investing it with incomparable holiness. But by the late Middle Ages it also tended to make Jews so dependent on God that, by modern standards, they seemed passive and unduly dependent. This perspective made the freedom granted by the Emancipation a means to fuller humanhood and thus highly attractive. However, we can now see that modernity's self-confident activism tended to let human judgment fully replace God as the ground and guide of human values, a gross overestimation of human goodness and discernment.

For some postmoderns the disillusion with messianic modernism validates a return to classic religiosity with God at its center, and this powers the recent rise of fundamentalism in all the religions of Western civilization. But most postmoderns intuit something different: a relationship between God and people that is less God-dominated than the traditional religion taught but also less people-dominated than the moderns proclaimed. These believers sense the reality of a God who grounds our values yet makes room for human independence and calls human beings into an active partnership.

With the rationalism that was once Reform Judaism's glory now largely discredited, a search for a secure ground of value is underway among us, and its code word is "spirituality." But thus far our leadership has been unable to free itself from the inhibitions that a self-confident modernism made standard among us some decades ago. That is, placing our trust in humankind, we were quite content to put God at the margins of our religious concern. If that did not make Reform Jews agnostics—and a good case can be made for that, characterizing many American Jews of some years ago—we were effectively agnostic. So, rather briefly, we could confidently welcome the "death of God" because we knew that all the real activity in history was in our hands.

Some among us still hold that position, finding it so intolerable that any "God" should relate to a world like ours that they prefer to place their faith in people. But for some time that confidence in human beings has become more problematic than believing in God. Thus it is no longer daring and avant-garde among us to flaunt one's disbelief or revel in one's challenges to God. That change of ethos is a reproach to the institutional lag that still acts as if the old pervasive skepticism still reigned. Speaking boldly about God is not without its problems, but grounding messianic striving and hope in any realistic view of humankind or social institution is illusory.

The Reform movement must find a way to face up to God's real, central role in our faith—and if that spatial metaphor somewhat overstates our non-Orthodox stance, then let me say more precisely that it is God's real, significant, ongoing role in our covenant partnership with God that needs to be made clear. I do not know how long we can go on trying to be religiously relevant to our most sensitive people tying spirituality to study, observance, or liturgical innovation without ever emphasizing the God who stands behind them. Of course, Jewish acts are indispensable. But the spirituality we know we need will not arise without our forthrightly acknowledging the Relating-Other, that Ultimate One who is the ground of the universe and the dynamic source of its values—with God and God's reality understood in any one of the different ways thoughtful Reform Jews affirm. Until that becomes a central, articulated emphasis of the leaders of the Union—and, if it needs saying, of the CCAR and HUC-JIR also—we will have failed the first challenge of the postmodern era.

The Second Concern: How Individualistic, How Universal a Self?

Moderns thought truth to be fundamentally universal, that is, applying to everyone, everywhere even as gravity applied in the furthest reaches of the universe. So defining something meant relating it to the class in which it fit and explaining something meant showing how it operated in terms of a broad-scale natural process. This had the exhilarating effect of indicating how everything could, in theory, be related to everything else, and this pervasive sense of nature's unity brought a new breadth of vision into every field of endeavor. This led Kant to insist that only when moral imperatives applied universally—to everyone, everywhere in the same situation—should they be called "ethical," an idea that still powers efforts to include "outsiders" in our communities. Modernizing Jews have had good reason to love this liberating vision and enshrine it in their intense commitment to ethics as the essence of religion.

Again, this reversed the premodern religious view in which God's revelation came to a particular group and not to anyone else. In classic Judaism only the people of Israel received the Torah, Written and Oral, and by its standards the people of Israel understands itself as chosen, dubbing other peoples "the nations." The people God loves has duties incumbent on it alone and when they are observant they receive God's special favor. This consciousness of God's support made the Jews indifferent to their host culture's sense of spiritual superiority and armored the Jews for their survival over the centuries.

By contrast to the premodern judgment of others by (God-given) in-group criteria, modern Jews first determine what is true universally and then investigate how Judaism exemplifies it. Thus Cohen, Kaplan, and Buber all first determine what is true for everyone—rationality, sociology, or the "I-Thou" experience—and then create a theory of Judaism to conform with it. In the days when the Jewish agenda gave priority to demonstrating Jewish humanhood, this method was invaluable. Its universalistic hermeneutics revealed a dimension of Judaism not previously so evident.

Today, a changed Jewish and human situation has made two flaws in the prioritizing of the universal painfully evident. After the Holocaust, Jewish survival could no longer be a subordinate Jewish concern. And the notion of diminishing our Jewish particularity so as to gain acceptance in a civilization that could conduct or tolerate a Holocaust seemed ludicrous. Many Jews gradually realized that being and staying a Jew was elementally right and that made the old, unbridled universalism wrong.

Moreover, if truth is fundamentally universal, then all particular forms of its expression—including Judaism—are in principle expendable, a view that appears to give sanction to giving up or drifting out of Judaism. In the growing practice of intermarriage, these theoretical musings became a disturbing, practical threat—one recent statistical study indicates a generational abandonment of Judaism. Jews had to face the issue of whether they were content to be a "terminal" generation, one happy to keep Judaism alive for itself and such of its children as wished to carry it on for a while. For that implied acquiescence, if with reluctance, to the ongoing atrophy of Jewishness and the sapping of its vitality. For those whose Jewishness was too elemental for that, it was clear that the supremacy of the universal was a faulty standard.

Many groups in Western civilization had come to a similar conclusion. People of diverse races and cultures began protesting the moral arrogance of an ideal that said, in effect, that they would be more fully human if they became more like the cultured Western, white man. Another blow against the universality of the universal came from feminists who rebelled against the subordination of their gender to male criteria claiming to be correct for everybody, everywhere. Intellectually, these groups had been preceded by Marxism, psychoanalysis, anthropology, and, more recently, by deconstructionism. They denied that anyone, necessarily speaking out of a given class, a given self, a given culture, and a given language, could enunciate something true about everyone, everywhere.

If human beings are quite particular and everything we posit arises from our specific situation, then the particular inevitably precedes the universal. Should one affirm the commanding truth of universalism—as most contemporary Jews are led by their folk experience and faith to do—then it arises out of one's personal/communal/historic situation, in our case, by our being Jews who have learned something from emancipation.

This priority of the particular to the universal is thus the second characteristic of my postmodernity.

In many ways it has been easier for the Reform movement to particularize its modern universalism—more precisely, to balance its universalism with a healthy particularity—than to put aside its old agnosticism. History has forced most Jews to recognize the spuriousness of their old claim simply to be people-in-general who happened to be Jews. And those who have persisted in this (often self-hating) dream of transcending their origins generally drift out of our community. Furthermore, Reform Judaism and the other modernized versions of our faith have made clear how much satisfaction there can be in living as a Jew. So, too, the State of Israel (despite our occasional worries about its soul) has by the impressive quality of its human reconstruction added incomparable pride to that lustrous old title "Jew." The overwhelming majority of Reform Jews has rejoiced in the effort to make Reform freedom a means of deciding what of our tradition and creativity to *add* to our lives. Prior generations, avidly seeking acceptance, only saw Reform freedom as authority to deJudaize. They glorified in departicularization, and their spiritual offspring still decry as "orthodoxy" any effort to reclaim valuable aspects of our tradition.

We have, however, gone nearly as far as one can go in exploiting the human bases of our Jewish loyalty (the Holocaust, the State of Israel, the joys of Jewish living). Earlier generations of Reform Jews knew that the premodern doctrine that God had chosen us was incompatible with a modern, democratic existence. Not being particularistic wimps, they forthrightly asserted the virtue of our particularity as resulting from the "Mission of Israel" to all humankind. Out of a mix of Hermann Cohen's philosophy of Judaism as the religion of reason par excellence and their own sense that it was right to be distinctively Jewish, they said we existed as a people because we were uniquely able to teach ethical monotheism to humankind. Our universal task justified our particular existence.

The "Mission of Israel" has long since faded from Reform Jewish thinking though one occasionally hears it or its like in careless rabbinic or lay rhetoric. The notion that Jews have a unique racial capacity—so Kaufmann Kohler—or a unique intellectual insight into an essentially Kantian universalistic idea simply cannot survive acquaintance with other peoples or realism about how modern Jews live. Furthermore, there is something inherently demeaning about having to justify one's existence in terms of what one does for other people. But no new Reform Jewish surrogate for chosenness has arisen to take its place. As long as a growing turn to ethnic roots among all peoples and a post-Holocaust, pro-Israel consciousness intensified our particularity, the Jewish bent for living rather than thinking about Judaism could mask the problem. But as freedom and acceptance have more fully become the condition of Jewish existence, as religion has retreated from our corporate relationship with God to become only each person's private spirituality, Jewish particularity is in long-term peril.

We Reform Jews are badly divided on what to do about that issue. Large numbers of us affirm the modern notion that a universal humanhood happens in our case to be lived out in the Jewish tradition—a rich and rewarding one. While this view brings some of its adherents to a passionate concern for Jewish particularity, it provides no rationale other than "valuable possibility" for staying Jewish and bearing the sacrifices minority existence entails. Worse, it is a position that makes Jewish existence dispensable or changeable. Allied with this theoretical position are those many people whose families or children have been involved in intermarriages. They do not wish religion to be a barrier between them and those they love. They find the concept of the priority of universal humanhood validating their heart's intuition. And that surely seems a reasonable conclusion from an unreflective Jewish embrace of modernity.

But on what basis can one today confidently assert such a universal truth? It is surely not empirically evident or universally held. Judaism and its daughter faiths can ground it, at least insofar as they have been through the experience of modernization. But they do so because they have their particular faiths in God's unity and God's resulting relationship with all humankind, not because they know this from being people-in-general. And all the biblical faiths consider the historic realization of their universalism a matter for messianic, not historical, time.

There is an experiential basis for this affirmation of particularism, and it comes from the lives of those who have become conscious on a most primal level that there is something true about existence as a Jew, not just for them personally but for their people. Among other illusion-shattering disclosures, the Holocaust made clear that the death of the Jewish people could become a reality; the continuing threats to the existence of the State of Israel confirmed that possibility; and the slow hemorrhaging of Jewish loyalty and dedication through intermarriage has made it a present peril.

As long as the Reform movement does not forthrightly find a way to assert its simultaneous dedication to the equality of all humankind and its unequivocal commitment to the irreplaceable truth of particular Jewish existence, it confirms the disparaging charge that it is essentially a "gateway to assimilation." Continuing silence about our commitment to Jewish particularity makes us unwitting allies of those who find the short-term abandonment of Judaism regrettable but rely on universalism to justify its long-term evolution into ethical living or such. I believe that my restatement of the doctrine of the covenant provides an intellectually solid, humanly sensitive, Jewishly grounded response to that issue. But whether it is my formulation of the universal/particular dialectic or someone else's, only such a forthright affirmation of our particularity will take us beyond the illusions of modernity.

The Third Concern: Retaining but Rethinking Autonomy

With regard to these two matters—greater involvement with God and with Jewish particularity—postmodern Orthodoxy and non-Orthodoxy agree in principle if not in means. They disagree over my third affirmation: the need to keep (but reinterpret) modernity's notion of personal autonomy. Orthodoxy allows individual self-determination only as the Torah, God's revelation, provides for it. Though caricatures of Orthodoxy ignore it, the Torah recognizes substantial areas for personal decision in the observant life. But to stretch these to the point of dissenting from the Law is a sin and, so it is charged in the contemporary polemic, leads to all those human tragedies liberalistic individualism wildly abets. So many Jews, like people of the other great Western faiths, have turned their back on anarchical modernity and its degraded life-styles by choosing to be Orthodox.

Despite the appeal of this reasoning, the masses of the three widespread faiths have rejected orthodoxies. Many do so out of self-indulgence; they want to do whatever gives them pleasure to the extent that they can. But more reflective people, though they agree with some of the criticism of religious liberalism, have not been convinced that it was fundamentally in error. They have found their personal dignity enhanced by the strong sense of responsibility engendered by its teaching about self-determination. Though they seek guidance from their leaders and traditions, they know they are right to then insist on "making up their own minds" about what they have been taught.

In the postmodern context, however, "making up their own minds" cannot mean a return to the self-confident heyday of modernity. Then autonomy assumed that individuals had (or could have) in their minds, in their experience, and in their learning all the resources they needed to determine what they and society should do. In my postmodern understanding, the self is no monad but an individuality intimately structured by its relationship with God and the particular people within which that self functions. So autonomy now has validity only when it is exercised in intimate involvement with God as part of one's community relationship with God, in our case the people of Israel's historic relationship with God, the *berit*, the "covenant."

This theology obviously does not call upon our movement to give up what has been its chief, if occasionally troublesome, glory: its respect for the informed, conscientious individual and its corporate devotion to works of social action. This third principle gives both a solid, postmodern theological foundation. But it also sets autonomy into a new context, and that has certain practical implications for our movement.

Once it seemed that "conscience," a purely human and essentially internal faculty, could give us "God's" truth. Of course, this always carried the overtone of Kantian (more precisely, Cohen's neo-Kantian) autonomy that conscience was utilized in a thoroughly rational manner. That entailed being well informed and testing one's decisions against one's effort to treat others as ends, not as means only, and in terms of their universal applicability. In this process, God stayed very far in the background and the "particular" community considered here was humanity as a whole. Communally, we followed our universal consciences by asking what other liberals were saying and then, generally, joined them by passing resolutions and became involved in political coalitions. (Thus Jewish bioethics has largely become the preserve of the Orthodox and other traditionalists. Serious inquirers find they may have some distinctly "Jewish" wisdom to bring to bear on such issues, whereas Reform Jews will only restate the general liberal positions, perhaps illustrated by some Jewish texts.) The older private and communal styles of Reform Jewish ethical decision making need some reshaping in terms of our emerging postmodern sensibility.

It will be easier to characterize the particularistic component of this shift. On the personal level, it requires us to stop making our decisions without essential reference to our most particular communities, our families, and the Jewish people. We need to say plainly, "Reform Judaism does not teach that religion is simply a private matter between you and God—or simply between you as part of humankind and God." That individualistic universalism may be an irreplaceable aspect of Jewish religiosity, but our faith is violated when those who affirm it do not live it out in community. Thus we need to make plain that Reform Jewish decision making is not just privately consulting one's conscience. Rather, among other critical guides, Reform Jews facing a significant decision should, to begin with, be vitally concerned with what other Jews (our community, in all its pluralism) are saying on this issue and how our decision will affect our community. But our people is not merely contemporary; it has a vast tradition of seeking to serve God in history. Therefore, personally and communally, we need to ground our deliberation in a deep understanding of its prior traditions, specifically, its legal literature, the *halachah*. Since few of us will be able to do this adequately, education, publication, and rabbinics-teaching rabbinates are particularly incumbent upon us. Our institutions, however, have a special responsibility to be informed adequately in their decision making.

There are many social problems that require no profound Jewish study. When the homeless crowd the streets, when people are hungry, one needs no great knowledge of Jewish sources to know what God requires of us as Jews. And while this is more precariously true as one moves into the broad-scale social, i.e., political, arena, there surely are issues where the exigencies of time and of situation as well as of topic allow for the equation of social action with resolution passing and program starting. What is now missing in this largely commendable enterprise are the serious study and careful evaluation of the alternatives in critical areas of continuing social concern. If we have a unique capacity for ethics, it is not evident in the publication of much serious Reform Jewish ethical literature in recent decades. Rather one must look to the American Catholic bishops and some of the Protestant denominations for searching efforts to probe the teaching of their traditions, relate it to the specialized knowledge of our time, and respond to a complex ethical problem faithful to God's perceived demands. We do not have the resources to fund as many such studies as the confusions of our times warrant. Nonetheless, we need to be steadily at work on some key questions, instructing our people with our occasional results, modeling the Reform Jewish conscience sensitized by a thorough study of our tradition as well as contemporary reflection and expertise.

It is far more difficult to state how neo-Kantian autonomy needs to be modified in terms of a living relationship with God. In part that is because attending to God is as much a subtle, inner act as it is actionally and communally expressed/experienced. In part it is because we are unaccustomed to speaking directly about our relationship with God and can become quite uncomfortable when others do. I think that largely comes from our holding on to the modern teaching that human conscience on its own—perhaps vaguely grounded on a "concept of God"—protects us from having to be personally involved with God and God-talk. So we move toward postmodern Jewish autonomy by engaging in the kind of (God)consciousness-raising I am attempting here.

The next thing may well be to change the tone of our public rhetoric from one that radiates self-confidence to one—let me dare it—more piously modest. I do not mean by this to encourage Reform Jewish sanctimoniousness but, as I see it, we generally know a good deal less and are considerably less certain than the current modes of social-political tussling encourage. We generally need God's help a good deal more than we institutionally let on in most matters. And when issues are serious indeed, we should be entering upon them with a certain mix of fear and trembling before God that it is wrong to repress and not acknowledge. In general, we need privately and publicly to be a good deal more prayerful about the stands we know we must take, may God help us. And we need day by day to be building the kind of intimacy with God as part of the people of Israel that will be our chief guide when we come to one of those awesome moments when the little we, our community, or anyone else has done or knows helps us divine what God immediately requires of us.

I think that the ideas I have sketched out here are implicit in my book *Renewing the Covenant* even though I could not have put them so directly there. I am, therefore, doubly delighted to be celebrating Alex Schindler in this fashion for it has again, as over the years, allowed me to learn from my ongoing, if ordinarily more silent, dialogue with him and his work.

While our external success as a nationwide movement is indeed remarkable—we have emerged as the overwhelmingly predominant synagogue movement on the North American Jewish scene—an honest self-appraisal compels us to confess that the quality of our synagogue affiliation is lacking, that in too many instances it is only marginal, mere form without substance.

As liberal Jews, we assert our autonomy; we insist on the right to choose. But all too often we choose nothing at all or, choosing something, we observe it only haphazardly. Moreover, our leadership makes too few demands on its constituency beyond the financial, giving substance to the perception that Reform Judaism is only a religion of convenience, a place where easy answers are given and few if any questions asked.

Somehow we must find a way to reconcile Reform Judaism's exclusive emphasis on spiritual commitment with our movement's need to reach a collective consensus on religious practice in order to remain both authentically Jewish and whole. For when the concept of individual autonomy is allowed to become the central, exclusive concept of liberal Judaism, Judaism is destroyed. When everyone "makes *Shabbes*" for himself, the Jewish community disintegrates.

That is why the choice of the individual should never be fully unfettered. It should always be an informed and responsible choice. That requires collectively establishing criteria against which the individual can measure his way, along with communal discipline strong enough to assure group coherence and integrity. But it should not be so rigid and restrictive that it stifles the vitality that springs from individual freedom.

Our numeric burgeoning can excite our hopes and ambitions, but our efforts will sink into nothingness unless we perceive and embrace Judaism as a serious religious enterprise....We must add meaning to label and substance to form; we must recapture the sense of totality in Judaism, the life built upon the performance of *mitzvot*, without surrendering the notion of personal autonomy that we have made our hallmark.

Rabbi Alexander M. Schindler
State of the Union Message
Houston, Texas
November 1983

RITUAL AND THE RECOVERY OF HOPE MAKING REFORM JUDAISM MATTER AGAIN

LAWRENCE A. HOFFMAN

Ideas matter. The Rabbis knew that, and so, too, did the founders of Reform Judaism, who did not lack for ideas. The synagogue was the place you went to discover the ideas that made life matter.

Not so today. Synagogues no longer impart ideas; they peddle programs—the way synagogue conventions feature workshops, not debates. An illustrative case is a temple that attracts members because "the rabbi uses puppets for the kids." Enlightenment becomes entertainment, and only for children, who are scheduled for puppetry between tennis and shopping.

Cable television has spawned the verb "channel-surfing," meaning the practice of passing time by clicking the control on the channel selector up and down the airwaves to provide diversion with snippets of one program after another. So it goes with human programming, too. As long as programs are what synagogues offer, they become part of the diversion industry, fighting for a spot on the dial of real-life pauses that people make as they surf through a busy day.

When programmers are in charge, people complain of "being programmed." If synagogues do not once again become brokers in ideas, people will turn them off like television sets.

The idea that has mattered most over the last two centuries has been the promise of progress and with it the anticipation of better times, a Messianic Age (we called it) to be realized as part of Israel's mission: Jews allying with non-Jews in pursuit of universal justice, discovering traces of God's holiness along the way. Progress, modernity, autonomy, conscience, holiness, hope itself (for the individual and for history)—these are the very essence of Reform Judaism as we have inherited it. They are under attack, and we need to rescue them as ideas that still matter.

First let us revisit our own story.

From Generation to Generation

By any objective standard, a new generation is dawning. A "generation" is more than a list of babies born by chance in the same year; a mere age-specific swath of the population sample is called a cohort, not a generation. A cohort becomes a generation when it becomes aware of its common history and shared aspirations. Generations, that is, know themselves as such.

They are, for instance, "the Vietnam generation" or "depression children," who share more than a chance coming-into-the-world together. They are touched, sometimes profoundly, by the phenomena of their time, as if fate conspired to drop an event into history while they were swimming there, so that forever after they are carried along by its ripples, awash in the wavelike aftermath of the episode that continues to shape them.[1]

Any new generation calls into question the continuity between itself and the generation that came before—hence, in part, the anxiety over Jewish continuity that the 1990s heralded. The great dividing mark between old and new in our case is the Kennedy-Camelot presidency, which prematurely took to its grave the conviction that all good things are imminently possible. It helps to ask also what each generation means by "the war." The generation now retiring from official leadership positions reached adulthood in the immediate aftermath of World War II, which its members saw as an epic struggle of good against evil and ourselves, the Allies (as the forces of good), triumphant in the end. The new generation came of age in the era called Vietnam, where it was not clear who was good and who was evil, and where it was equally uncertain whether anyone (least of all, ourselves) won at all. Vietnam, Kent State, Watergate, and all the rest were nails in the coffin of untrammelled hope for the victory of good over evil.

As if to make matters worse, heady *Jewish* hope came to fruition in the Six Day War, which coincided with the last years of optimism. The Jewish version of Vietnam was Israel's invasion of Lebanon, after which, even in the Jewish sphere of things, the mythic matchup of good and evil no longer fit the facts on the ground. Young Jewish baby boomers who transferred their secular messianic vision to Israel in the late sixties thus lost their innocence by the eighties.

To be sure, generation-counting is arbitrary; people do not space births for the historian's convenience. So there are generational subdivisions—early and late boomers, for instance, or baby busters (those born to boomer parents), and college students today; generalizations are not fair also to class divisions, racial differences, and the gender divide. Still, for most Reform Jews, it is useful to differentiate generations by the great divide of Kennedy and Vietnam. (That goes for Canadian Jews, too. I lived in Toronto through the Kennedy years but watched American history unfold as if it were my own.) Up to that point Jews were optimistic patriots who called themselves liberals, voted for FDR, established labor unions, helped found the NAACP, and celebrated being modern.

Not that life had been easy for them. Their parents or grandparents had been immigrants. If they had never known the Great Depression personally, their parents had, and a depression mentality was their legacy; they didn't throw things out. Abroad, they watched Stalin ravage Russian Jewish socialism and then saw Hitler murder Russian Jews—or German Jews, or Polish Jews, or any Jews, for that matter. But glasses are either half-full or half-empty, and for the pre-Vietnam Jews, they were always half-full. They said *Lechayim*, and it never occured to them to doubt it.

Reform Jews especially allowed neither the depression nor the Holocaust to destroy their faith in modernity and its chief represen- tative among the nations, the United States—and, on a smaller scale, Canada. Hitler was explained as a European throwback to the Dark Ages; and the depression was a blip on an otherwise rising curve of freedom and prosperity. Like most Americans, Jews resumed their perpetual love affair with the grandeur of tomorrow's "maybe." F. Scott Fitzgerald was not a Jew, but his Great Gatsby was the prototypical American of the twenties, who spoke for all of us in his characteristically modern conviction that "the self seemed unlimited in its possibilities, its pleasures, its sense of itself."[2] Gatsby's Long Island had yet to welcome Jews, but when Jews finally got there, they bought up Gatsby's North Shore home along with his confidence, which merely buoyed the self-assurance they already owned.

Justice Brandeis had boasted that Jews fit right in because "the ideals of America have been the ideals of the Jew for more than twenty centuries,"[3] and historian Solomon Grayzel spoke for us all when he observed, "It is in America that the opportunity of living the Jewish life in freedom has the brightest hopes of realization."[4] Almost exactly a century earlier, Charleston's Rabbi Gustavus Poznanski had anticipated both Brandeis and Grayzel by pronounc- ing "this city our Jerusalem, and this country our Palestine."[5] World War II changed most minds on that score, but mostly for those Jews who could not get in here and needed American Zionists to cham- pion their return to the real Jerusalem over there. Jews who had already sailed past the Statue of Liberty and were using the postwar boom to become Gatsbys of their own held on tenaciously to hope in America and faith in modernity, which meant, above all, faith in the possibilities of what an individual "self" might achieve.

By contrast, the message of the momentary Camelot that died in Dallas, and of the daily pointless Vietnam casualties, was failure, and along with failure, perhaps for the first time ever, came a culture of disillusionment. Americans lost their faith in govern- ment, abandoned party loyalty, and questioned the certainties that their parents knew for sure. Those parents had settled in suburbs, built synagogues, planned for the future; they sent their children to college to make that future happen and then watched in horror as they returned, having gathered somehow on campus that there was no certain future to be won. The bullets that killed John and Robert Kennedy and Martin Luther King, Jr., killed optimism as well. I do not mean economic optimism. That dream died only in the nineties. I mean the old liberal vision of a world made secure from war and want, the dream of humankind united in peaceful coexistence, the kind of liberal aspirations that were the stock in trade of what we now know as classical Reform Judaism.

That dream is now very largely dead. And with its demise has gone what made Reform Judaism unique, the idea-complex that made it matter: its messianic faith in human potential; the reason to remain Jewish (what Reformers had called the "Mission of Israel"); and a life that could touch the sacred because the Torah had instructed, "You shall be holy, as I your God am holy." Almost no one talks like that anymore—not synagogue presidents, not Federation directors, not even rabbis—and as for a better tomorrow, for the world or for us personally, who knows? The failure lies on the right and on the left, where two ideological camps that could not be more different from each other have conspired unknowingly to ravage the life of optimistic religious responsibility.

◆　◆　◆

Ideas matter. Without Jewish ideas, people do not cease being Jews, but they become Jewish drifters, passing ghostlike through their Jewish skin but wanting in Jewish passion. The professional guardians of Jewish continuity, pressed into service like museum custodians to make sure people still visit the artifacts of Jewish culture, understandably stir things up with whatever works: anti-Semitism if it is around; nostalgic memory, maybe; pride in Israel, certainly. When thinking fails, keep busy: raise money; go on marches; program, program, program.

But the mind, like nature, abhors a vacuum. Where old ideas fail, new ones come rushing in like intellectual breath inhaled by oxygen-starved brain cells coming up for air. As near-drowned swimmers breathe whatever air they get, atrophied minds suck up ideas and make of them what they can—for better or for worse. It matters, therefore, what ideas we allow to matter.

If we want continuity, we will have to call into question disillusionment and despair. It is not too late to reaffirm the existence of selves that can make a difference, to raise up unashamedly the

*banner of prophetic religion, and to rediscover the sacred venture
known as life. Reform Jews can resurrect the dead idea of reasonable hope.*

Postmodernism and the Failure of Nerve

Events are not the only pebbles that get thrown into the ocean of
time; ideas, too, radiate eddies of influence. The Kennedy Democrats were advised by economists trained in the liberal tradition
from John Maynard Keynes to Kenneth Galbraith; the Reagan
Republicans were not—that made a difference. Antonin Scalia's and
Thurgood Marshall's respective readings of the Constitution of the
United States are not the same. That also makes a difference. Other
instances come readily to mind. At this writing, it is still not clear,
for example, whether fundamentalist religious ideologues will
manage to reverse the constitutional separation of church and state
in American law or whether tomorrow's jurists will uphold
Madison's historic claim against Patrick Henry to the effect that
since religion is merely "opinion," the Commonwealth of Virginia
may not adopt its Anglican variety as official. Or consider
Menachem Begin who encouraged Jewish settlement on the West
Bank because his mentor, Ze'ev Jabotinsky, taught him a maximal-
ist idea of a Jewish state not simply as a matter of strategy but of
justice and of right as well.

To be sure, the events of human destiny have many causes,
among them self-interest, Machiavellian intrigue, and even
accident and idiocy. But ideas, too, drive history on occasion, and
even when they don't, they may at least get cited to justify what we
want to claim anyway. And no matter how they got there, once
ideas are comfortably set in place, they influence teachers who
influence students, who then make more history happen. Molière's
bourgeois gentleman discovered that he had been speaking prose all
his life but hadn't known it; if we act out the consequences of ideas
all our life, at least we ought to know what they are.

History can thus be sensibly construed as determinative events
allied to ideas. That is why the ripple effect that molds generations,
however obviously prompted by what gets *done*, is traceable in
more subtle ways to what gets *believed* by the people who get things
done. It matters, therefore, whether people will continue to do

things because they still believe, as classical Reform Judaism did, in what we once happily labeled modernity; or whether, by contrast, modernity is altogether a historical distortion of reality, a chimerical fantasy properly laid to rest—in which case, people will not stop doing things, but the things they do will differ from what they would have done had their faith in progress, goodness, and self-competence not been undermined to the point where it ceased motivating them.

Modernity as a motivating vision is in danger of utter abandonment by a twisted version of a new orthodoxy called "postmodernism." Please note: I do not claim that postmodernism properly understood is a bad thing. But I do decry the negative use to which it is put when its advocates denounce the religious visions of progress, ethical certainty, and universal reason. It would not matter if their doctrines were not ideas, but they are, and, as I say, ideas do matter. The Athenians put Socrates to death because they knew that even the most arcane or opaque ideas eventually get translated into actions. Malevolent ideas do insidiously poison minds and scuttle projects, and although we do not on that account still poison those who preach them, we have the obligation, at least, in a democratic society, to erect a rival soapbox from which to preach something else. In synagogues, we call that the pulpit. Good rabbis preach from pulpits because mere programmers do not stand a chance against soapbox orators afire with ideas.

Understood properly, postmodernism is a necessary corrective to the heightened expectations that untrammeled faith in modernity could not fulfill, what Eugene B. Borowitz calls "our generation's disillusionment with the modernists' messianic humanism."[6] The accent is on "humanism," the secular-scientific sense that moral progress is guaranteed, that scientific know-how will itself accomplish everything. Postmodernism correctly calls into question that naive faith in secular technology. But in the wrong hands, the postmodernist critique is used on the left and on the right to support an ideology of despair. If we do not stand firm in our resolve as liberal Jews, this pernicious misreading of what postmodernism entails will spell the death knell of Reform Judaism as we know it.

The most compelling illustration of what is at stake comes from the heated debate generated by the life of a brilliant precursor of postmodernism, Martin Heidegger (1889–1966), who is widely viewed as perhaps the most profoundly influential mind of our entire century. The problem is that this thinker extraordinaire was a Nazi. In 1933, Heidegger accepted the rectorship of the University of Freiburg, after which he traveled around the country lecturing on behalf of Hitler's policies. After the war, he claimed that he had merely hoped to direct the National Socialist agenda in a healthy direction and that when he recognized the impossibility of doing so, he promptly resigned, after (in any case) never siding with the Nazi policy on Jews and (in fact) actively opposing it, as, for instance, in refusing to destroy books by Jewish authors in the university's library.[7] His defense has been largely discredited, however, and in an interview as late as 1966, only six months before he died, he skirted the issue of culpability, holding firm to the racist belief, for example, in a singular *German* capacity to address the malaise of modernity, such that "when the French ...begin to think, they speak German, being sure that they could not make it with their own language."[8]

The point about Heidegger is his extraordinary influence upon postmodernism and the degree to which his own Nazi turn was a consequence of his disillusionment with modernity. He charged modernity with a fixation on science that falsely pictures the universe around us as a static entity and ourselves as mere knowl-edge-gathering machines who keep busy taking readings on reality. The readings give us truths, and the truths add up until, eventually, we know all there is to know. Heidegger blew the whistle on this simplification, holding instead that reality comes into being only as we live out our lives in interaction with our world. The universe is far from static, then; it is not at all divorced from whatever we do with it. Heidegger is called an existentialist because he replaced the illusion of some theoretical body of absolute metaphysical truth with the concept of human existence itself, by which he meant living in the world and shaping both it and us as we do so. He further charged modernity with strangling authentic human existence in the iron grip of scientific technology—an idea that many still find compelling. So far, so good. But he called also for a romantic realization of "the world destiny of the German people" as a corrective against the illusions of modernity.[9]

This was not the first time in history that liberal hope in reason and progress had been challenged by a conservative reaction to modernity's promises. The nineteenth century, too, had witnessed a retreat from universal reason, and it, too, had trumpeted German nationalism, anti-Semitism, and proclamations of the death of Western thought, this time by Nietzsche, who, not coincidentally, was Heidegger's model also.[10] Another philosopher (one who resists the negative portrayal of modernity), Richard Rorty, sides instead with his American hero John Dewey, for whom "progress, the happiness of the greatest number, culture [and] civilization...still have a point."[11] A straight line runs from the rationalism implicit in the French Revolution to Dewey's American pragmatism and its insistence on freedom as an absolute good and progress as an absolute hope. That line is severed by Heidegger's pessimistic conclusion that if God is not dead (à la Nietzsche), it is at least true that "only a god can save us," not we ourselves, "and in the face of a god who is absent, all we can do is founder."[12]

Jewish thinkers like Martin Buber and Emmanuel Levinas, too, had recourse to the idea of an absent God, but that was only *after* the Holocaust, their means of admitting God's apparent inability or unwillingness to save us from the crematoria. By contrast, Heidegger's dismay has nothing to do with the *Shoah*, which, if anything, he helped facilitate by his refusal to hold fast to a reasonable faith in reason. Once again, we see how ideas have consequences. By his own admission, Heidegger's rejection of all that is modern moved him into Hitler's camp. Whereas Heidegger gives us a "tacit and unarguable rejection of the project of the French Revolution... Dewey gives an equally tacit and unarguable acceptance of that project."[13]

It hardly behooves Jews to carp at modernity. The "project of the French Revolution," after all, is precisely what gave Jews their freedom, and for all its problems, modern optimistic democracies like Dewey's America remain far better options for us than those European schools of thought that have sought to retreat behind romantic returns to premodern national greatness—like Heidegger's Germany. I repeat: Postmodernism is not necessarily all wrong.[14] One hopes that Hitler's ovens, Stalin's gulags, and the bombs we dropped on Hiroshima and Nagasaki taught us something about the limits of science, progress, and human nature. But what we should not have learned is to erase modernity from the record as if it were one huge historical blunder. True, we do need a response to the twentieth-century butchery that modernity was not supposed to allow, just as we need to come to terms with the adulation of self that permits all things in the name of selfish hedonism. Maybe, on our own, we human beings cannot so quicky and perfectly adjust the controls that turn off world tyranny; and maybe the vaunted right of the individual self to happiness is not the final arbiter of all things. Maybe, too, we need a little fine tuning for the prophetic hope and human self-confidence that were the essence of classical Reform Judaism as our "modernist" generations were raised to believe in it. But what we do not need, and what is unwarranted, is a rejection of the very modernity without which there would be no Reform, no democracy, no selves with any rights at all—only a *Volk* of the German variety with a right to fulfill its historic mission at any cost whatever. This latter path of reactionary despair is the route we now see all around us—not only in neo-Nazism but in right-wing religious extremism, which knows no absolutes beyond its own parochialisms and invokes God, the New Testament, the Quran, or Deuteronomy to justify actions that fly in the face of universal reason, human rights, the dignity of the individual, and respect for individual differences—all part and parcel of modernity, liberalism, and the kind of Judaism that Reform Jews take as absolutes.

✦   ✦   ✦

Ideas matter, but there are different kinds of ideas. Not all ideas are born of instrumental precision, the piercing laserlike imagery that detects a quality of the world that has been out there forever but that no one knew about before. Some ideas are as funny as they are clever—like a cartoonist's wit that cannot even be translated into the logic of description (you have to see it to get it). Physicists give us "pictured" ideas, like Niels Bohr's celebrated model of the atom, and mathematical ideas, the equations with which they really do their work. Similar to the latter are musical ideas, a sequence of notes and stops that recur in combination with other such ideas to give us a composition that then gets performed in all its symphonic glory.

There are also ritual ideas, the things that we might vaguely have known but that suddenly become crystal clear in the ambience of religious ritual.

Most people do not describe ritual that way. They think of it as mere pomp and circumstance, outer trappings, the fluff of religious life as opposed to the nuts and bolts of belief that give a religion substance.

The return to ritual these days has nothing to do with Orthodoxy, but a great deal to do with the human search for ideas. When old truths come under fire because they are garbed in the form of ideas that no longer convince, they can be translated into a new kind of idea that demonstrates all over again how true they are and how much our very lives depend on them.

Preaching Despair; Seeking Pleasure; Ritualizing Truth

Despite my reservations regarding unwarranted pessimism based on the misapplication of postmodernism, I do not claim that postmodernism is wrong. It is a necessary corrective to the old-fashioned "modernist" notion of how we get ideas. We don't, in fact, just "get" them at all, as if they are packaged birthday presents that passive recipients collect in the mail and then unwrap.

The package metaphor is instructive. To begin with, even with ordinary presents, the package and the thing packaged are not as distinct from each other as the image suggests. Anyone who has wrapped a present knows that packaging affects the thing being packaged no less than the contour of the package strains the paper in which it is wrapped. All the more so, ideas are not raw things that you buy on a stand and then wrap up for delivery. They come prepackaged in carriers—an image of the eyes ("seeing is believing"), perhaps; an echo of sound ("I heard it with my own ears"); or a datum of the scientific laboratory ("a scientific fact"). Magicians and mirages remind us that of the three, eyes or ears alone can be deceiving, so that scientific evidence has widely been taken as the only way of knowing what is for sure "the truth." Science, we think, is "objective."

It is this pure objectivity, even of science, that postmodernism questions, not because science does not work, but because scientists no longer imagine that they are just manipulators of machines that take in data, perform measurements, and spew out objective truths. Certainly even the most sophisticated scientific equipment cannot alone manufacture *ideas*. Ideas are things people come up with as they interact subjectively with their environment. The scientific method lays down rules to make sure that subjective ideas work, in the sense of successfully predicting results and being replicable by others.

It is not just the postmodernists who want to correct our overly optimistic view of science as an objective God's-eye view of the universe that scientists can "get" if they only rise objectively above their humanity. But postmodernism does do that, and it does it well, reminding us in every human enterprise how much we—the observers, the thinkers, the listeners, and the measurers—are very subjectively involved in our projects. We decide on them to start with, and that decision is what makes us measure some things but not others, all of which we then put to use to compose further ideas, which then prompt more advanced experiments (but again, not others), and so forth. In the end ideas matter not only because they are good ideas but because someone finds them sufficiently compelling to push them for all they are worth and thus to make them work as far as is possible. Ideas are like businesses: If no one gets the idea to open them, they never get tried; if the proprietor gets bored even with a good business, it stops being good very quickly. When it comes to ideas, we don't just *get* them, we *plot* them in collusion with a cooperative world around us; and then we *sell* them because we find them utterly compelling. It is their quality of moving us in such a way that makes ideas matter.

I find it exciting to think of the subjective human involvement in idea making at the expense of thinking of ideas as objective, absolute, and distant truths that we merely uncover. Unfortunately, the loss of objective certainty that postmodernism heralds can lead some people to downright skepticism. Since scientific absolutism was the hallmark of nineteenth-century science, they question also modernity itself, along with the attitude of trust we used to have for single autonomous selves outfitted with hope and promise. A recent introduction to postmodern thought summarizes this creeping disease of radical doubt:

> Post-modernists criticize all that modernity has engendered: the accumulated experience of Western civilization, industrialization, urbanization, advanced technology, the nation state, life in "the fast lane."... [They] argue that there is reason to distrust

modernity's moral claims, traditional institutions, and deep interpretations. They argue that modernity is no longer a force for liberation; it is rather a source of subjugation, oppression, and repression.... Post-modernists...avoid judgment, and the most sophisticated among them never advocate or reject.... They never test because testing requires "evidence," a meaningless concept within a post-modern frame of reference.... They offer...diversity rather than unity, difference rather than synthesis, complexity rather than simplification.... Relativism is preferred to objectivity. It is the product of desperation...of disillusioned optimism.... Modern science is myth and Enlightenment heritage is totalitarian and dominating.... Critical theory urges a suspicion of instrumental reason and modern technology...a suspicion about humanism...a skepticism about truth, reason, and moral universals.[15]

From here, it is not far to the conservative retreat into the myth of national historic destiny that so intrigued Heidegger. We in North America have largely been spared that excess, but a comparable failure of nerve has attacked us in its own pervasive fashion, equally on left and right, both of which now share a broad-ranging suspicion of the universalist project of *tikkun olam*, "world repair," that once motivated liberal Judaism. The conservative variety has confused means with ends, arguing from the failure of the liberal economic policies to achieve their hoped-for end that the end is not still to be hoped for. In principle, they despise the postmodernist lesson that there are no universal verities, but they accept its critique of the social-activist program that emerged with the French Revolution and that motivated Reform Judaism. Where they differ from the left is that they have adopted their own set of absolutes: Bible-Belt creationism, among Protestants; for Jews, the most intractable return to faith in a Torah that is literally true, or *halachah* that is not the product of human evolution. These conservative versions of certainty are the magic ring that people grasp when they have lost faith in their own ability to make a difference. When you cannot depend on yourself, depend on God; when human reason has failed to bring a messiah, discount human reason's ability to do anything at all.

Granted, conservative Jewish circles have yet to promote the same degree of reactionary pressure that we find in the churches—we have no Pat Robertsons and Sister Angelicas, whose multi-million-dollar campaigns blanket the networks and punish public servants who dare voice anything remotely equivalent to the social dream that we all took for granted not too long ago. But that is because Jewish conservatives care relatively little about public policy in the Diaspora and so are somewhat less noticeable there. Extremism is alive and well in Israel, however, largely fueled not by native Israelis but by emigrants from Brooklyn, St. Louis, Chicago, and Toronto. Their parents were fed a diet of sour grapes; and the children's teeth are set on edge.

But liberals are as guilty as conservatives for giving up on the idea of human good, the promise of human progress, the conviction that there are universal ethical standards, universal human truths, and a thing called human reason that may not be able to accomplish everything (that much we have learned) but ought not, therefore, to be discounted as promising nothing. Several examples come to mind, many of them from newly popular campus orthodoxies that tend to the left, not the right: postmodernism's ultimate manifestation as deconstructionism, for example, which is anathema to conservatives, but popular among liberals, and may be taken to mean (as my lengthy quotation above illustrates) that everything is mere quicksand; or excessive claims by some to the effect that reason itself is a hierarchic mode of thought that men (but not women) use.[16] The universality of humanity is in danger of being destroyed by people who care so much for individual differences that they see nothing left for everyone to share.

But campus orthodoxies are not the primary manifestation of this cultural despair. There is also new-age religion, despised by conservatives but no friend to social liberals either. The banner of spiritual renewal is in danger of being captured by inner-directed irrationalists who dismiss the biblical conservatism of the ultra-orthodox but adopt their own extremist faith in crystals and snippets from the *Zohar*, often misquoted or misdirected by thirdhand tradents who have no idea what the mystical tradition of Judaism really means but who share with the conservatives the conviction that anything is better than the failed faith in a future that human actors in history can and should pursue.

What, after all, should we make of this recent synagogue bulletin article, drawn at random from one of many such examples that cross every rabbi's desk with regularity?

> In response to spirituality in school, I spent five days at a [UAHC] *kallah* [and was told that] when two people hug they create warmth, the warmth creates sparks, and the sparks become guardian angels. [I was told that] "people are made of stardust" (big bang theory). When I hug the children and adults in my preschool and in my holiday workshop classes, I tell them about being made of stardust and about the guardian angels. I also tell them about the bedtime *Shema* prayer, which talks about [the angels] Michael, Gabriel, Uriel, Raphael, and God watching over us. I get really positive reactions, especially from preschoolers who want to make more guardian angels with me. I feel that I am nurturing their souls and giving them positive images of themselves. Happy hugging!

I have no objection to hugging preschool children. But do we really want to believe that the big bang theory is adequately captured in images of stardust and guardian angels? Are children to be raised with the firm belief in angels watching over their beds? Is the profundity of Jewish mysticism to be defined solely with hugs and a positive image of self?

Are there no ideas left that matter—no challenges beyond an inner-directed quest for a fully satisfied self? No wonder self-help books fill book stores. Sociologist Robert N. Bellah thus charges baby boomers with sacrificing commitment to the public weal in their pursuit of the self, especially what he calls "a life rich in experience, open to all kinds of people, luxuriating in the sensual as well as the intellectual, above all, a life of strong feeling."[17] Other social critics are less charitable. Neil Postman, for instance, satirizes our "Peek-a-Boo-World" where nothing goes deeper than a thirty-second TV sound bite and where the most gruesome images of bestial carnage or starving masses get interrupted by an announcer who summons us to a commercial—"And now, this!"— as if "this" (underarm deodorant? shiny teeth?) ranks equally with "that" (death camps in Bosnia, a child murdered in Brooklyn).[18] Bellah's test case is "Sheila... who describes her faith as Sheilaism [by saying], 'It's just try to love yourself and be gentle with yourself.

You know, I guess, take care of each other.'"[19] Sheila may be an exaggeration—social scientists have had trouble tracking down many more who go as far as she does.[20] And Bellah's call to good old-fashioned commitment à la Alexis de Tocqueville, who saw the dangers of untrammeled individualism when he visited the United States in 1830, may be overly conservative.[21] But poll after poll supports the conclusion that Americans are in search of inner satisfaction but have given up on the vision of a better human destiny and their own personal fulfillment mutually intertwined. Here the new conservatism of the eighties (unlike the classic kind where commitment to the public good had been the priority) and the liberalism that promotes the self above all else meet in perilous opposition to the classical Reform model that we used to label proudly "the Jewish mission." Divorced from the promise that they can make a difference, Reform Jews are thus left with programs for the self: puppets for the kids, youth-group outings, golden-age read-ins, and tot-Shabbats.

We have also seen a return to ritual.

Now ritual, I must stress, is a good thing. Classical Reformers tend to distrust it because it is all too often the new-agers, fed on misapplied postmodernism, who plead ritual's cause. To the extent that they pursue it as a reaction to their disappointment with reason, or as just another outlet for an indulgent self, they miss the point. *Ritual should be viewed as one of the ways in which human beings get at ideas that matter!* Discount the skepticism that postmodernism engenders, and we are still left with the realization that ideas require commitment to their outcome or they will die. And that is where ritual comes in.

Picture again a package, composed of a gift being packaged and some wrapping paper doing the packaging. The gift is somewhat malleable; it changes shape as the paper is stretched taut over its surface. The paper, too, changes shape as it is applied—its old folds are ironed out by the smooth sides of the gift it encompasses, and new folds appear where it is bent around the gift's natural contours. By analogy, we can imagine how ideas get wrapped by ritual.

Look first at ideas. A static view of ideas is that they exist like independent objects waiting for us to "get" or to "latch onto," at which time we announce, "I *have* an idea." From another perspective, however, we can imagine ideas as operating with their own independent force upon us, as when we say that we are "seized by an idea."

Based on these two ways of identifying ideas, we can imagine two different ways of depicting them. As passive objects of thought awaiting our minds to grasp them, ideas are like simple points on a map; our heads are in the center of the page, and the ideas, or points on the page, sit motionless all around us waiting for our cognitive intellect to reach out and "get them." Like hunters circling around their prey, we reach out for the idea in our vicinity and then finally grasp it, announcing proudly, "Got it!" But this simple depiction of ideas as motionless points around our heads is insufficient since our experience with ideas is that they have a life of their own; we say that an idea "came to me in the middle of the night," that it suddenly "dawned on me," or that an idea "presented itself." Ideas thus have momentum. They hunt us as much as we hunt them. Depicting them as simple points fails to identify the force with which they strike us. Borrowing from mathematics, we can more properly depict ideas not as points, therefore, but as vectors, that is, as arrows that vary in length, their force indicated by the length of the arrow. In this new map of reality, our minds are surrounded by ideas of stronger or weaker momentum. Some of these ideas are directed at us with a force sufficient to make them unavoidable. Others are moving in different directions; we will never get these ideas unless someone else mentions them to us, deflecting their course, as it were, into the sector where our own mental capacity operates. When we find that an idea occurs to us, we can thus equally well emphasize our own powers of cognition or the idea's independent momentum moving in our direction, in which case we say, "It suddenly hit me." This dynamic quality of ideas is what makes them matter. They "strike" us with different intensity.

The power of ideas is equivalent to the degree to which they are compelling. But here we get to ritual because packaging matters. Theodor Herzl reports sitting down to compose his initial thoughts on the possibility of a Jewish state after he returned from (of all things) a Wagner concert that moved him because of its romantic nationalism. The final movement of Beethoven's Ninth Symphony is the classic Western musical presentation of the idea of freedom and hope. These are musical ideas that matter; they possess vector force that strikes us profoundly. Pure logic can also work that way. Faced with a seemingly impenetrable intellectual impasse, we may suddenly be excited by a way out; we say, "The logic was inescapable." Not everyone operates with such logical precision, of course. Idea vectors require reception capacity by human beings. What made Einstein great, for instance, was his ability to follow logic to its final necessary conclusion—as when he decided that if the speed of light is constant, everything else must be relative, even what objects weigh, how fast time flies, and how old we are. But logical ideas and musical ideas are alike in that they are ideas: "They come to us" as much as "We grasp them." And grasping is easier when they are powerfully conveyed.

Ritual is such a conveyer: like great music or an unarguable set of equations. All three have an aesthetic quality—a mathematical proof, for instance, is said to be elegant, even beautiful. Ritual is not just self-satisfying fluff: smells and bells and holding hands and eyes glazed over and closed-off minds. It should be the means to a new kind of truth, a multimedia package that shapes ideas even as it delivers them, an emotional and intellectual form of engaging people in their common future. Good ritual follows a script and gives everyone a part. It promotes a play that matters. It is a dramatic unfolding of an alternative construction of reality, a sort of make-believe in which we come in from the cold and dramatize through the ritual script of centuries what our ancestors' fondest visions were, and thus what ours still can be.

Examples are easy to come by. We should rise from our seder feeling more than filled up with food. At least for one fleeting instant we might just shudder at the possibility that we still might be slaves and feel compelled to commit ourselves to freeing others who still suffer subjugation. The final *shofar* blast ought to elicit more than a sigh of contentment that the person who blew it managed to produce a good sound. It might remind us of *shofar* calls at Sinai and their echoes in our own lives, the call to genuine repentance. Every single Shabbat service should gather the lonely, heal the sick at heart, reinvigorate the depressed, and celebrate what genuine community is all about.

True, our rituals don't usually do those things. We don't even require them to. But they should, and they can. And when they do, they present us with *ritual ideas* that defy all doubt. Ritual is our religious means of dramatizing life's grandest possibilities. *In the wake of a postmodern critique of reason, ritual is the way to truths that if only stated baldly may be too good to believe but when presented ritually become too good to ignore.* Ritual uses metaphors ("Next year in Jerusalem"), music (*Kol Nidre* or the *Shema*), community solidarity (our prayers are in the plural), and a host of other dramatic devices to make daring dreams so plausible that they defy easy dismissal. Just how to recapture our ritual so that it speaks the truths we cannot do without is a fine art indeed, but an art that can be learned, for those who know enough to use it.[22]

The problem is that ritual alone is no guarantor of an idea's truthfulness. While rector at Freiburg, Heidegger must have attended many a Nazi ritual that compelled the allegiance of participants. If we do not attend to our own rituals, others will come along with theirs, dramatizing other dreams, some of them nightmares. If we cannot renovate ritual, we will not easily be roused from our stupor of disillusionment. Not that dramatic enactment alone will suffice. If ritual is the inherited drama of the lines our ancestors left us, we might do well to remember that good playwrights are not vacuous thinkers. Our liturgy, as ritual script, needs renewed attention to what it says and how it says it; then every synagogue needs a thorough revision of its ritual competence so that the ritual ideas become credible. Think of Jewish liturgy as the theater of ideas, ideas that we, the Jewish people, have drummed up in happy association with God and history. It opens us to the reality of God and thus to the possibility that we believe anew in freedom, progress, justice, and happiness for all humankind. Without those ideas alive and well again, Reform Judaism will matter less and less and so will Reform Jews who will have lived and died without the world being any better for it. Our time requires a firm recommitment to the ideas of Judaism that matter.

Beyond Busyness

Ideas are the stuff of which human destiny is made. But they presuppose the possibility of order in the universe, the mapping of logical insight onto reality. Otherwise, ideas become delusions. The philosopher René Descartes, a quintessential modernist, began his philosophical quest by searching for true and certain knowledge, something he had to believe because it would be impossible to doubt. He concluded that his root certainty was "I think; therefore, I am." His notion of truth as pure cognition about an objectively given universe that he simply grasped in its static essence is precisely what postmodernism has exploded as an inadequate representation of the way things are.

But Descartes was not all wrong. He wonders whether perhaps some demon has not presented him with his elemental thoughts; perhaps all human hope is delusionary. He thinks; but maybe he, the thinker, does not exist after all. All the more so, no reasonable conclusions need be real, no universal order need exist, no hope need come true, no expectations should be held. If so, it might follow that the human project itself is a sham, and the Jewish version of it is an exercise in futility. Descartes decides that cannot be the case, and so should we.

The generation that knew V-E Day and Camelot has given way to one trained in Vietnam and Watergate. Old ideas no longer move us as they did. But they are not on that account wrong. Jewish truths like the reality of God, *tikkun olam*, and a self allied with other selves in history's flow toward its messianic end remain as true as ever. They need repackaging, perhaps, reshaping for minds that think more suspiciously now than they did when we knew for sure that good was on our side and we would win. They need to be shaped by ritual that does them justice.

We need ideas as much as ever, busyness for its own sake less than ever, if Reform Judaism is to matter once again.

◆   ◆   ◆

For ideas matter. Ideas that are ritually construed empower us to do what we would otherwise never have the courage for. Classical reformers are right to recollect the days when Reform liturgy bespoke dignity of purpose, when rabbis railed against injustice, and when every auditor knew that history is a sacred tale, our lives the latest chapter, inviting us to act as if all good things are possible, as if the Messianic Age is just around the corner, as if tikkun olam *itself lies softly in our hands.*

Things have changed some. Those lines ring with less conviction now; but they are not on that account wrong.

We need ideas that let us hope once again.

NOTES

1. Cf. classic statement by Karl Mannhein, *Essays on the Sociology of Knowledge* (New York: Oxford University Press, 1952); and short summary vis-à-vis baby boomers in Wade Clark Roof, *A Generation of Seekers* (New York: HarperCollins San Francisco, 1993), p. 3.

2. Alfred Kazin, *An American Procession* (New York: Vintage Books, 1985), p. 394.

3. *Menorah Journal*, January 1915.

4. Solomon Grayzel, *History of the Jews* (Philadelphia: JPS, 1947), p. 61.

5. Sermon, March 19, 1841.

6. Eugene B. Borowitz, *Renewing the Covenant* (Philadelphia: JPS, 1991), p. 20.

7. The relevant documents are largely collected in the *Graduate Faculty Philosophical Journal* 14:2–15:1 (1991), Marcus Brainard, ed., subtitled, *Heidegger and the Political*; and Richard Wolin, ed., *The Heidegger Controversy* (Cambridge: MIT Press, 1993).

8. Interview in *Der Spiegel*, trans. in Wolin, *Heidegger Controversy*, p. 113.

9. Martin Heidegger, "Letter to Elisabeth Blochmann," March 30, 1933, *Graduate Faculty Philosophical Journal*, p. 572.

10. Cf. Michael A. Meyer, *The Origins of the Modern Jew* (Detroit: Wayne State University Press, 1967); Wolin, "Introduction," *Graduate Faculty Philosophical Journal*, p. 8.

11. Richard Rorty, *Essays on Heidegger and Others* (Cambridge: Cambridge University Press, 1991), p. 20.

12. *Der Spiegel* interview, in Wolin, *Heidegger Controversy*, p. 107.

13. Rorty, *Essays on Heidegger*, p. 21.

14. See especially Levinas's response to Heidegger, discussed, e.g., in Susan Handelman, *Fragments of Redemption: Jewish Thought and Literary Theory in Benjamin, Scholem, and Levinas* (Bloomington: Indiana University Press, 1991).

15. Pauline Marie Rosenau, *Post-Modernism and the Social Sciences* (Princeton: Princeton University Press, 1992), pp. 5,6,8, 11, 13.

16. See attack on this extreme position by Martha Nussbaum, "Feminists and Philosophy" [a Review of Louise M. Antony and Charlotte Witt, eds., *A Mind of One's Own*], *The New York Review of Books*, October 20, 1994, pp. 59–63.

17. Robert N. Bellah, et al., *Habits of the Heart* (Berkeley: University of California, 1985), pp. 33–34.

18. Neil Postman, *Amusing Ourselves to Death* (New York: Viking, 1985).

19. Bellah, *Habits*, p. 221.

20. See Bruce A. Greer and Wade Clark Roof, "Desperately Seeking Sheila: Locating Religious Privatism in American Society," *JSSR* 31 (1992), pp. 346–352.

21. On Tocqueville's conservatism, see Robert Nisbet, *Conservatism: Dream and Reality* (Minneapolis: University of Minnesota Press, 1985).

22. Cf. Lawrence A. Hoffman, *The Art of Public Prayer: Not for Clergy Only* (Washington, DC: Pastoral Press, 1988); idem, "How to Cure the Synagogue and Satisfy the Soul," *Reform Judaism* (Summer 1994), pp. 32–34; idem, "From Common Cold to Uncommon Healing," *CCAR Journal* (Spring 1994), pp. 1–30.

POSTSCRIPT

The milestone moments of our lives—birthdays, anniversaries, the turning of the years—often evoke a somber mood. Life is fleeting, so we are reminded, and all too often brings us not only the beautiful things that we crave but also those fearsome things in their bewildering variety from which we shrink.

Yet there is a countervailing feeling of hopefulness that such calendar-landmarks evoke with their motif of renewal, of the ever-recurring possibility of life's new beginning. I prefer this feeling by far, willing it to be the dominant pattern of my life. When I look into the mirror, the lines in my face, etched as they were by my life experiences, induce a pessimism; but I quickly resist this lure and remain the inveterate optimist.

This is not just a personal inclination. It is a dimension of my Jewishness for we Jews hope—we remember and we hope. Our memory goes back to the glory of our beginnings; our hope reaches forward to distant days, to a future as bright as any the human mind ever conceived. And so we remember always and always we hope, even at times and in places that defy all hope.

When I was a little boy, my father took me and my sister to Warsaw, where we visited the *shtibl* of the Umaner Chasidim, the devotees of Reb Nachman, the Bratzlaver Rebbe. It was a *shtibl* like all other such *shtibl*s, with one remarkable exception: carved into the wood of the synagogue's ark was not the usual inscription *Da lifne mi atah omed*, "Know before whom you stand," but rather a Yiddish phrase, a sentence in the vernacular, *Yidn, zait sich nisht misyaesh*, "Jews, do not despair!"

Remember, if you will, the setting in which I read this affirmation. This was the Warsaw of the middle-thirties, the days of the gathering storm. The ax was already lifted, its blade well sharpened, the pyres piled high, ready for the burning...still, this summons to hope. I later learned that this had been the *rebbe*'s favorite saying, his constant, lifelong admonition to his followers: "Jews, do not despair...*gevalt*...never despair!"

This experience made its lasting impression. The Bratzlaver's saying is seared into my soul. Words like despair and gloom, hopelessness and doom are not a part of my life's vocabulary. And what if reason dictates otherwise? Then reason must be transcended, for when the philosopher postulates, "I think, therefore, I am," the Jew within me emphatically replies, "I believe, therefore, I live!"

Rabbi Alexander M. Schindler
President's Installation Address
New York, New York
November 1973

ABOUT THE CONTRIBUTORS

DR. S. ZALMAN ABRAMOV, a former member of the Israeli Knesset and chairman of the Board of Overseers, HUC-JIR in Jerusalem, among other prestigious positions, is a recipient of the Mount Scopus Award of Hebrew University and author of *Perpetual Dilemma: Jewish Religion in the Jewish State*.

DR. RACHEL ADLER teaches courses in Talmud, liturgy, and feminist biblical hermeneutics for the American Jewish Congress Feminist Center of Los Angeles. She serves on the editorial board of *Tikkun* magazine, on the board of the Western Region of the Association for Jewish Studies, and as a part-time faculty member of the Los Angeles school of Hebrew Union College-Jewish Institute of Religion.

YEHUDA BAUER is Jona M. Machover Professor of Holocaust Studies at the Institute of Contemporary Jewry, Hebrew University, and chair of the Vidal Sassoon International Center for the Study of Antisemitism, as well as the editor of the *Journal of Holocaust and Genocide Studies*.

ALAN D. BENNETT, the former executive vice president of the Cleveland Bureau of Jewish Education, is a founder and past president of the National Association of Temple Educators. He has published over 200 articles and is author of *Journey through Judaism: The Best of Keeping Posted* (UAHC Press, 1991).

RABBI EUGENE B. BOROWITZ is the Sigmund L. Falk Distinguished Professor of Education and Jewish Religious Thought at the New York school of Hebrew Union College-Jewish Institute of Religion. His most recent books are *Renewing the Covenant, a Theology for the Postmodern Jew* and, with his students, *Reform Jewish Ethics and the Halakhah, an Experiment in Decision Making*.

REVEREND JOAN BROWN CAMPBELL is the general secretary of the National Council of the Churches of Christ in the U.S.A., a position she has held since March 1991. Ordained in 1980, she is a minister in both the Christian Church (Disciples of Christ) and the American

Baptist Churches in the U.S.A. and is the first woman minister to serve as NCC general secretary.

RABBI NORMAN J. COHEN is the dean of the New York school of Hebrew Union College-Jewish Institute of Religion and professor of Midrash. He has written both scholarly and popular works in the field of Midrash, and he lectures widely in the Reform movement and in the general Jewish community.

RABBI JEROME K. DAVIDSON, senior rabbi of Temple Beth-El of Great Neck, New York, serves on the faculty of the Hebrew Union College-Jewish Institute of Religion. He is past president of the Synagogue Council of America and in his youth was national president of NFTY. He was chosen as 1995 "Rabbi of the Year" by the New York Board of Rabbis.

DR. JANE EVANS, the former executive director (1933–1976) of the National Federation of Temple Sisterhoods, now Women of Reform Judaism, is honorary president of the Jewish Braille Institute, a member of the Governing Body of the World Union for Progressive Judaism, a representative of the Non-Governmental Organizations of the United Nations, a life member of the Commission on Social Action, and a founding delegate and continuing member of the World Conference on Religion and Peace. She currently serves as a consultant to the Union of American Hebrew Congregations.

DR. LEONARD FEIN is a writer and teacher. He has been connected with the Reform movement since 1970, when he edited *Reform Is a Verb*, a study of Reform congregational life. Since 1987, he has been Senior Visiting Scholar at the Religious Action Center, the public affairs arm of the Reform movement.

DR. ALBERT H. FRIEDLANDER is the dean of the Leo Baeck College in London and rabbi of the Westminster Synagogue. He is the author of a dozen books on theology and history and has been a visiting professor of theology at major European and American universities.

RABBI ROLAND B. GITTELSOHN is rabbi emeritus of Temple Israel in Boston and a past president of the Central Conference of American Rabbis. He has also served as a vice chairman of the UAHC Board and as founding president of the Association of Reform Zionists of America.

RABBI ARTHUR HERTZBERG is professor emeritus of Religion, Dartmouth College; Bronfman Visiting Professor of the Humanities, New York University; and the author of *The Zionist Idea* among many other books.

ARON HIRT-MANHEIMER is the editor of *Reform Judaism* magazine, co-author of *Jagendorf's Foundry: A Memoir of the Romanian Holocaust, 1941–1944*, and the editor of more than fifty books.

RABBI LAWRENCE A. HOFFMAN, professor of Liturgy at the Hebrew Union College-Jewish Institute of Religion in New York, is a past president of the North American Academy of Liturgy. His many books and articles on the history of Jewish prayer and the role of worship and ritual in general have appeared on four continents and in eight languages. Dr. Hoffman is currently engaged in reconceptualizing Jewish spirituality and directing an extended research project designed to reshape synagogues into spiritual places.

HIS EMINENCE, WILLIAM CARDINAL KEELER is Archbishop of Baltimore. As president of the National Conference of Catholic Bishops, Cardinal Keeler is the church's chief spokesman in the United States. He is a member of the Holy See's Council for Promoting Christian Unity, working to improve relations between Catholics and Jews.

DR. HENRY A. KISSINGER served as United States Secretary of State in the Nixon administration. He received the Nobel Peace Prize in 1973, the Presidential Medal of Freedom in 1977, and the Medal of Liberty in 1986. At present he is chairman of Kissinger Associates, Inc., an international consulting firm. He is the author of ten books.

PROFESSOR JULIUS LESTER is the author of twenty-five books of fiction and nonfiction for children and adults. He teaches in the departments of Judaic Studies, English, and History at the University of Massachusetts-Amherst. He also serves as lay religious leader at Beth El Synagogue in St. Johnsbury, Vermont.

BERNARD LOWN, M.D., is emeritus professor of Cardiology, Harvard School of Public Health; Senior Physician, Brigham and Women's Hospital; recipient of the 1985 Nobel Peace Prize with Dr. Eugene Chazov on behalf of the International Physicians for the Prevention of Nuclear War (IPPNW), which they co-founded. He is chairman and founder of SatelLife, a partnership in satellite communications for health in the developing world.

DR. EGON MAYER is a professor of Sociology at Brooklyn College and the director of the Center for Jewish Studies of the Graduate School of the City University of New York. He also heads the Jewish Outreach Institute and is the author of major studies on Jewish intermarriage.

DR. MICHAEL A. MEYER is Adolph S. Ochs Professor of Jewish History at HUC-JIR in Cincinnati and international president of the Leo Baeck Institute. His books include *Response to Modernity: A History of the Reform Movement in Judaism* and *Jewish Identity in the Modern World*. He is currently editing a four-volume history of the German Jews in modern times.

RABBI EUGENE MIHALY, during almost five decades at HUC-JIR, has taught generations of rabbinic and graduate students as professor of Rabbinic Literature and Homiletics and as the Deutsch Professor of Jewish Jurisprudence. He also served for a number of years as executive dean and vice president for Academic Affairs.

SHIMON PERES, foreign minister of the State of Israel, received the 1994 Nobel Peace Prize. He is the author of *The New Middle East*.

RABBI W. GUNTHER PLAUT, a past president of the Central Conference of American Rabbis and currently chair of its Responsa Committee, is the author of twenty books on history, Bible, theology, and sociopolitical issues. His latest book is *Asylum—A Moral Dilemma*. His magnum opus, *The Torah: A Modern Commentary*, of which he is the editor and principal author, was published by the Union of American Hebrew Congregations.

DR. JAY T. ROCK, an ordained Presbyterian minister, is the co-director of Interfaith Relations and the director for Christian-Jewish Concerns of the National Council of the Churches of Christ in the U.S.A. He holds a doctorate in the History and Phenomenology of Religions and has taught courses in Jewish mysticism, chasidic literature, the Holocaust, and Christian-Jewish relations.

DR. CARL SAGAN is the David Duncan Professor of Astronomy and

Space Sciences and director of the Laboratory for Planetary Studies at Cornell University. Co-founder and co-chairman of the Joint Appeal by Religion and Science for the Environment, he is a recipient of the Pulitzer Prize, the Public Welfare Medal of the National Academy of Sciences, and the Nahum Goldmann Medal of the World Jewish Congress.

RABBI HAROLD M. SCHULWEIS is spiritual leader of Valley Beth Shalom in Encino, California. He is founding chairman of the Jewish Foundation for Christian Rescuers/ADL and the author of *For Those Who Can't Believe*.

RABBI JACK STERN is rabbi emeritus of Westchester Reform Temple in Scarsdale, New York, where he served for twenty-nine years. He is chairman of the UAHC Ethics Committee and a past president of the Central Conference of American Rabbis. He and his wife, Priscilla, reside in Great Barrington, Massachusetts, where they are affiliated with Hevreh of Southern Berkshires.

ALBERT VORSPAN is senior vice president emeritus of the UAHC. He served as senior vice president under Rabbi Schindler's presidency. He was director of the Commission on Social Action of Reform Judaism and is the co-author with Rabbi David Saperstein of *Tough Choices: Jewish Perspectives on Social Justice*.

RABBI MARGARET MOERS WENIG serves as spiritual leader of Beth Am, The People's Temple in New York City and as instructor of Homiletics and Liturgy at the New York school of Hebrew Union College-Jewish Institute of Religion. She lives with her partner, Rabbi Sharon Kleinbaum, and two daughters in Brooklyn, New York.

RABBI BERNARD M. ZLOTOWITZ received his doctorate from Hebrew Union College-Jewish Institute of Religion. Rabbi Zlotowitz is the senior scholar for the UAHC. He is the author of numerous books and co-author of *Abraham's Great Discovery* (NightinGale Resources), *Drugs, Sex, and Integrity: What Does Judaism Say?* (UAHC Press), and *Our Sacred Texts: Discovering the Jewish Classics* (UAHC Press).